5

The promise
of happiness

for Jessica and Abigail

The promise of happiness

Value and meaning in children's fiction

FRED INGLIS

CAMBRIDGE UNIVERSITY PRESS

CAMBRIDGE

LONDON   NEW YORK   NEW ROCHELLE
MELBOURNE   SYDNEY

Published by the Press Syndicate of the University of Cambridge
The Pitt Building, Trumpington Street, Cambridge CB2 1RP
32 East 57th Street, New York, NY 10022, USA
296 Beaconsfield Parade, Middle Park, Melbourne 3206, Australia

First published 1981

Photoset, printed and bound in Great Britain by
REDWOOD BURN LIMITED
Trowbridge & Esher

British Library Cataloguing in Publication Data
Inglis, Fred
The promise of happiness.
1. Children's stories – History and criticism
2. Literature and society
I. Title
823'.9'1209   PN1009.A1   80–49986
ISBN 0 521 23142 6

My mind, because the minds that I have loved,
The sort of beauty that I have approved,
Prosper but little, has dried up of late,
Yet knows that to be choked with hate
May well be of all evil chances chief.
If there's no hatred in a mind
Assault and battery of the wind
Can never tear the linnet from the leaf.

An intellectual hatred is the worst,
So let her think opinions are accursed.
Have I not seen the loveliest woman born
Out of the mouth of Plenty's horn,
Because of her opinionated mind
Barter that horn and every good
By quiet natures understood
For an old bellows full of angry wind?

Considering that, all hatred driven hence,
The soul recovers radical innocence
And learns at last that it is self-delighting,
Self-appeasing, self-affrighting,
And that its own sweet will is Heaven's will;
She can, though every face should scowl
And every windy quarter howl
Or every bellows burst, be happy still.

And may her bridegroom bring her to a house
Where all's accustomed, ceremonious;
For arrogance and hatred are the wares
Peddled in the thoroughfares.
How but in custom and in ceremony
Are innocence and beauty born?
Ceremony's a name for the rich horn,
And custom for the spreading laurel tree.

From W. B. Yeats, 'A Prayer for my Daughter'

'The wisest thing – so the fairy tale taught mankind in olden times, and teaches children to this day – is to meet the forces of the mythical world with cunning and with high spirits . . . The liberating magic which the fairy tale has at its disposal does not bring nature into play in a mythical way, but points to its complicity with liberated man. A mature man feels this complicity only occasionally, that is, when he is happy; but the child first meets it in fairy tales, and it makes him happy.'

From 'The Storyteller', in Walter Benjamin, *Illuminations: Essays and Reflections* (Harcourt, Brace & World 1968, Jonathan Cape 1970).

Contents

novelists alike in view of Victorian society – private life and the progress of consumer society.

Preface

It is worth emphasizing once more that an introduction is just
that: the author inviting a possible reader to meet his book, or
rather, those of his own ideas which are set down in a book.
And, like anyone else making an ordinary sort of introduction,
I am anxious that those waiting to meet and greet the book –
eagerly, suspiciously, with reserve or openly, in all the
different frames of mind with which we all of us do await
introductions – should not completely mistake the sort of thing
it is. While it is true that the first part of the book intends to set
out something of my approach to my subject-matter and to
suggest the ways of seeing and the contexts of reading and
interpretation which I recommend to readers, it may be worth
trying to prevent misunderstanding as soon as possible by way
of these few introductory sentences.

My subject, certainly, is children's fiction. But this is neither
an inventory of the available titles, nor even a critical guide to
the best of them. I have used such guides, naturally, and it is
right to pay the most generous tributes that I can to the best of
them: John Rowe Townsend's really excellent *Written for
Children*, a compendious list of the best texts which is also a
lively read and, so I found, a stock book of brief, sympathetic,
and accurate judgements. Nor could I have worked so rapidly
and readily without the help of Aidan Chambers's boundlessly
prompt and energetic, occasionally pugilistic writings on the
subject. But in taking children's fiction as my ostensible
subject, I have also been intent upon a wider and more
impalpable subject: the nature of popular culture, and the way
these particular forms of the social imagination try to fix
admired social values in a story, give them place and name and
continuity.

I am not, as is plain from a glance at my primary sources in the bibliography, trying to cover everything. Rather, I try to take the novels some very intelligent men and women have written for children, and to use them in order to understand what picture of virtue and happiness, what forms of experience, we believe may be given to our children so that they can live well in the world. I am therefore trying to write not so much literary criticism or, heaven help us, Education with a capital E, as social theory, and if that rather dismal phrase is any help, it means, I take it, a combination of theories about how the world goes *and* how it *ought* to go.

It is in this very general push of inquiry that I want to make this book take its place beside my previous books. Like any others who count themselves intellectuals, I am struggling on in the intolerable wrestle with language and experience, trying to make them lie still and shapely. I therefore want to remark upon the continuity of this book with its predecessors, not because they happen to be mine, but because they study very different materials with the intention of finding in the everyday lives and practices of men and women the values and meanings to which we give our lives, and which return to our lives the human worth that they embody. My last book, *The Name of the Game*, was about sport. The stuff of that book had been and remains some of the happiest experiences of my life, and one of its passions. At the same time, sport is also such a passion for a great many other men and women, and therefore a proper study for the human scientist who hopes not only to understand the world, but to make it a better place.

The emphasis of these inquiries falls, I hope clearly, on the human values carried, lived, renewed and replaced in the lives, the customary and educated lives, of men and women. In the case of the book on sport, for example, I tried to follow a recent and congenial admonition in social theory to treat social action as a 'text', to be interpreted for value and meaning, and to be judged accordingly, just as you would a novel or a film. This time, I seek to reverse the procedure, and treat the texts of these novels as social actions; treat them, that is, as the active processes of production, readership, membership, education, and leisure consumption which they are.

In these ways, perhaps, the lines may declare themselves between experience and theory; or to put the same thing another way, between culture and politics.

For by these tokens, the energy behind this book comes not only from my own experience of reading as a child, but from the delight brought by my daughters' reading. Their active collaboration in the thought that has gone into the book is its real foundation. At the same time, their reading shades out into the broad constituency for whom I would most like to speak: their friends, their teachers, their favourite novelists, the reading public of children's fiction.

Within that large and loose agglomeration, its not unkindly indifference, there are of course particular listeners whose attention to this book has already been critical and essential. I am especially grateful to John Adams who gave me my first Puffin reading list when I first began to keep pace with my children's reading of novels a few years ago. I am more recently and deeply in the debt of Dennis Butts for his always kindly and forceful unseating of ready-made notions, and for his rapid and pointed reading and criticism of a first draft. I learned much from Frank Whitehead and Alan Wellings when I knew little about children's literature and was working with them in the early stages of the Schools Council research survey of children's reading habits. I owe much to Lesley Aers and her direct, brisk and affectionate treatment of my ideas. As always, and more than he will know, I have argued the form and substance of the book through in my mind with and against the ideas of Quentin Skinner. Although this conversation was largely sustained in his absence in Princeton, the sense of his generous, sympathetic, searching intelligence was with me whatever I wrote. I am grateful to David Mallick for his instigation of an invitation to speak to the Australian Association for the Teaching of English, during which visit I sorted out many of the ideas in the closing chapters, and I am grateful also to a long conversation with Hugo McCann at the same time, which gave me just the lead I was looking for. Lastly, I must thank my very dear Cressida for all her help: as a warm listener, as a critic of great stamina and good humour, as a source of books and suggestions of books. She also provided Joan Roberts as typist, who dealt calmly and elegantly with an impossibly double-crossed holograph. So also did my own long-suffering, equable and excellent secretary, Maureen Harvey.

The quotation from W. B. Yeats's 'A Prayer for my Daughter' is included by kind permission of Michael Yeats and

Macmillan & Co. Ltd. The stanzas from J. V. Cunningham's *Collected Poems* and from Philip Larkin's *The Whitsun Weddings* and *High Windows* are included by kind permission of Messrs Faber & Faber.

Part I

Theory and Experience

I

The terms of reference

The great children's novelists are Lewis Carroll, Rudyard Kipling, Frances Hodgson Burnett, Arthur Ransome, William Mayne, and Philippa Pearce – to stop for the moment at that comparatively safe point on an uncertain list. But nothing is safe in the discussion about bringing up children, in and out of school, and the mildest first response to that opening is likely to be, 'Says who?' And if the proper answer is that a lot of serious, grown-up people say so, what sense does it make to call them writers for children at all? Even if we find, as we do, that plenty of children admire these authors' books, the crudest gangster–Philistine can point out that a lot more children admire the novels of Enid Blyton, admire them in millions and in 128 languages.

These are the most immediate tangles anybody gets into who starts to talk about children's fiction. In no time at all, as temperatures climb, the teacher, the parent, the critic and the child are caught up in the savage wars of playground and library, wars of class, sex, race, status and intelligence. The old categories are down; democracy is just an Augustan name for a riot of opinion.

And yet there is a plain, blunt way through cant, just as there is through any well-intentioned, jargon-laden, heavily schematic theory of education. It is to ask who would not want his or her child to read the best books. We begin there. We try to say what some of the best books are like, so that we can hand them to our sons and daughters. It is this expression of the gift relationship which most gives spine and structure to this study. It is an attempt to answer the question, 'Which are among the best books?', so that people like ourselves, who are teachers, parents, novelists, librarians, kindly uncles and aunts, nice neighbours, may give them away.

3

The intention of this chapter is three-fold: it is to give an elementary version of the argument that true judgements as to value *are* possible; secondly, to try to show that the best prose is itself evidence of human goodness and a way of learning how to be virtuous; thirdly, to suggest how the intrinsically human habit of fiction-making is essential to the making and maintenance of identity.

Only a monster would not want to give a child books she will delight in, which will teach her to be good. It is the ancient, proper justification of reading and teaching literature that it helps you to live well. No one can be sure it will do this; no one can be sure his or her child will grow up to be an excellent and happy person. But they want it, more or less passionately, and they do what they can to make it possible. The report of the five hundred years or so of good and great men writing about post-Renaissance literature is that good books help to make happiness and virtue possible. Childhood is the time, and imagination the faculty, which we have spared from Kant's awful separation of the two; our hope is that the joys of strong imagining conduce to virtue. Shelley's conviction in 'The Defence of Poetry' has become our rather more watery, pale hopefulness:

A man, to be greatly good, must imagine intensely and comprehensively; he must put himself in the place of another and of many others: the pains and pleasures of his species must become his own. The great instrument of moral good is the imagination; and poetry administers to the effect by acting upon the cause... Poetry strengthens the faculty which is the organ of the moral nature of man, in the same manner as exercise strengthens a limb.[1]

We have too many examples to hand in recent history of extremely imaginative beastliness to suppose that the imagination leads only to good. But it is surely a fact in morality that the imaginative capacity to put oneself 'in the place of another and of many others' is a necessary condition for the understanding of other people's actions, and that such understanding is in turn a necessary condition of the quality of attention to others we know as compassion and forgiveness. For morality on the one hand must square the facts of life with a

[1] P. B. Shelley, 'The Defence of Poetry', in T. L. Peacock, *Four Ages of Poetry* (1921), p. 107.

radical recurrence of absolutes in the way that so many alien cultures arrange their attitudes to death and killing, to sex, to property and shelter; on the other hand, those same cultures ungainsayably insist on the truth in relativism.

'Relativism' we may define roughly as the doctrine not merely that there are different moral views (which is just a fact) but that these views cannot be compared for their truth or superiority one to another; truth is relative and 'true for them'.[2] Given these conflicting demands on morality, free imaginative play must surely be 'a great instrument of moral good'. What is more, like any and all of the faculties of mind, the imagination must be strengthened, in Shelley's words, by exercise, just as a limb must be. Nobody could make too much of the analogy of physical exercise; the imagination is far too tricky a thing for us to speak easily of its growth and development. We cannot, to speak flatly, educate girls and boys to become women and men of syncretic imagination, in the sense in which we can make exercises and build programmes for the development of powers of criticism or to educate people to think logically and clearly and recognize nonsense when they see it. Stuart Hampshire says: 'In so far as we could plan the work of the imagination, we should not think of it as the imagination; we should have no further use for the concept. It is a power which we do not expect to understand, and, we may even say, we do not want to understand it.'[3] The imagination is desirable not only because the giant extension of world communication means that we have to understand what it is like to be someone else in another country, but also because the same extension and the technology which went with it bring unprecedented strangenesses which only a quick leap out of the received frames of mind into a quite different cognition of the world may oppose and control. One consequence of the truisms about the rates of change has been that men have to think faster. Whether they will keep up with themselves is the biggest question to ask of the world as it picks up speed towards 2001.

The celebration of imagination was a measure of its novel place in the map of the mind from 1800 onwards. The poets put

<hr />

[2] See Bernard Williams's paper, 'The Truth in Relativism', in *Proceedings of the Aristotelian Society*, XIV, 1976.
[3] In 'The Future of Knowledge', *New York Review*, March 1975.

imagination at the centre of human creativity, and, in Yeats's great phrase, the 'radical innocence' of children as capable of its most uncontaminated play; the theoreticians of childhood followed them. Today, the dullest and most dead-eyed of primary teachers pins up smudged finger-paintings and empty doggerel in the name of developing the children's imagination. Such tinsel tribute-money is worth more, one supposes, than the tawse, and dictation in copperplate. But it is no less likely to kill off the life of the imagination. Contrariwise, the greatest poets of English literature flowered inside what sounds at this distance like the inexorable treadmill of the dark Elizabethan grammar-school curriculum. The best *we* can do by way of a creative environment is to fill the shelves with the best books and persuade children to read them.

Which brings us back to the questions, 'Who chooses the best?' 'Are they best for children or adults?' Now it is clearly true that we all of us may improve in our powers of imagination; we may intelligibly speak of that faculty as growing and developing. We may also speak of its decline and demise; plenty of staffrooms have dead souls in them, plenty of fiction shelves have dead books on them, too. The cause of either growth or decline will be personal and it will be social. Heaven knows where it lies in the chemistry of the cortex, or, come to that, in the solar plexus: it is self-evidently true that some individuals, with every opportunity in the world, just are without any imagination at all. On the other hand, we may with rather more confidence point at details of our social life and say not only, 'Look, there, that's dead as a doornail', but also, 'That's deadly, that'll *cause* death in the imagination.' And whoever asks, 'Who's to say what kills and what gives life in the imagination?', the only reply is that good and intelligent parents and teachers and custodians of children try to say, as they always have said (as, moreover, they *ought* to say), what is good for their children. The shocking ugliness and cruelty of image and action in the latest horror comics and movies can only be horrible and harmful, and any sane teacher will want to keep his children out of such harm's way. It is a peculiarly nasty symptom of the relativizing of values that any such careful adult may be accused of an arbitrary and bullying authoritarianism simply for stopping children from reading what is not only unimaginative – the routine stereotypes of horror comic images[4] are as garish and inexpressive as Korky the Cat at the *formal* level – but also inhuman. In their content, the pictures say loathsome things.

Isn't there a contradiction in saying so? If we say something is unimaginative, surely it can't do our imaginations any harm? The first answer is a blunt one; it implies much about the assumptions from which this book works. It is this. Never mind if it does you no harm: to be unimaginative is to be in the wrong, is to be enfeebled and less than adequate, is to be partly dead or crippled. By the same token, for pornography to be described as such not by a lawyer but by a teacher or a critic, it is only necessary to show that it *is* obscene and depraved, not that it causes these conditions in others.[5] It is therefore of the first importance that the adult concerned (*sic*) knows what he thinks about children's books or television or films, just as he would naturally want to know what he thought of his children's schooling, his children's treatment of other children and of other adults, friends, enemies and strangers – in short, their manners and their morality. He would want to judge these things on the basis of a sufficient knowledge, compatible with not being nosey or officious or oppressive. The point stands, however. Irrespective of what the child makes of an experience, the adult wants to judge it for himself, and so doing means judging it for *it*self. This judgement comes first, and it is at least logically separable from doing the reckoning for children. *Tom's Midnight Garden* and *Puck of Pook's Hill* are wonderful books whoever you are, and that judgement stands whether or not your child can make head or tail of them. The joy they bring revives in us the childlike qualities of freshness and innocence and delight which, for instance, traditional Christianity has always required grown-ups to keep alive if they are to be at all redeemable. They are the same qualities which the secular conscience of the West has sought, ever since the Romantics drew attention firmly back to children, so that it may counterpose such innocence to the advance of industrialism and its grimly utilitarian and computational machinery. So a beautiful novel

---

[4] Is it 'arrogant' or 'sweeping' to condemn them all? A measure of relativism's influence is that I have to ask such a question. The interested may care to look up a copy of any Marvel comic, and then turn to P. M. Pickard, *I Could a Tale Unfold: Violence, Horror and Sensationalism in Stories for Children* (1961).

[5] A point I take from an editorial on 'Pornography', in *The Human World*, 7 (1971), pp. 1–18.

for children touches that quality of mind and spirit in us which issues as a cadence of attention – the attention (and responsiveness) we call innocence. The best children's books reawaken our innocence. That is the pleasure they give. The richness of a grown-up world is partly paid for by a loss of that quality. Tolstoy and Shakespeare are giants whose human capability remains so astonishingly large and inclusive that they can express innocence in an Imogen or a Perdita or a Levin when everything around these characters is heavy with experience, knowingness, and the chance of corruption. But even their works are, as we say, mature; innocence lives in an enclave of the author's. The music of their work *is* so full and grand because there is so much experience in it.

There is another kind of writing, as there is of everyday discourse, which renders innocence in the pure, radical way of William Blake's great songs. It is there in men and women of a peculiar gentleness and naïvety; it is there in some writers: T. F. Powys, at his rare best, Tolstoy in his stories for children,[6] Hans Andersen, Wordsworth in some of the *Lyrical Ballads*, Oscar Wilde in *The Happy Prince*, James Thurber in *The 13 Clocks*. There are plenty of examples. These few must do to suggest the quality of attention to the world, and of rendering the reality of that world in language, which characterizes the best writing for children. I do not mean that these writers are naïfs or primitives, nor that the men and women who exhibit this strength are unworldly or simple in anything but an admirable way. These names suggest the moral and intellectual quality which must occur somewhere in the sensibility and intelligence of a good writer for children. It is perhaps included in what Hazlitt called, to Keats's applause, the 'gusto in the voice',[7] and it issues finally in stories which meet Tolstoy's impressively simple criterion for any novel: that 'he alone can write a drama who has something to say to men – something mighty important to them – about men's relation to God, to the universe, to all that is infinite and unending'. It is this combination of seriousness and simplicity which is quite unlike the forced earnestness of the bibliotherapeuticians[8] ('Here's a book

[6] Ian MacKillop put these back on the reading list in his essay in *Children's Literature in Education*, 11 (1973).
[7] William Hazlitt, 'On Gusto', *Works*, XVIII (1855).
[8] A notion borrowed from Dennis Butts in his introduction to *Good Writers for Young Readers* (1977).

which I think will help you with your problem') and their favoured authors, who would serve up the diet of the devout *New Society*-and-*Guardian*-reading PTA, and make children's stories from a recipe of divorce, urban poverty, young sex, car thefts, all roundly beaten up with a couple of muggings.

The simplicity I speak of is at first glance a question of style, and the question of style is now approached very variously: by linguists of their various persuasions, by critics, by men and women. This, for instance, is an example of style in a story which was once staple for children:

In this combat no man can imagine, unless he had seen and heard as I did what yelling, and hideous roaring *Apollyon* made all the time of the fight, he spake like a Dragon: and on the other side, what sighs and groans brast from *Christian's* heart. I never saw him all the while give so much as one pleasant look, till he perceived he had wounded *Apollyon* with his two edged Sword, then indeed he did smile, and look upward: but 'twas the dreadfullest sight that ever I saw.

Now there are those who believe that this style is one which, if children are to know their culture at all, and are to be able to speak its poetry and know that for the serious thing it is, they must meet in *Pilgrim's Progress* and the Authorized Version, and elsewhere. There are also those who reckon that the unfamiliar archaism of this prose makes it incomprehensible to children, and further, in this instance at least, that the style is as it is because it carries a view of life which is bigoted, narrow, primitive and joyless.

This division works not so much between groups of educators as within individual ones. Upright and excellent men and women believe that children should read the Bible and feel its strength, but do not believe that what it says is true. At the same time, they want their children to make their own decisions about what they read, and to understand this reading for themselves in such a way as to make it tell in their experience of the daily world. To put the opposition briskly, they want to say, 'Here are good books; read them, they'll do *you* good', at the same time as they say, 'My books aren't necessarily your books: you must (within limits) read what you want to read, and choose it for yourself.' In other words, there is, as always, a necessary high tension between teaching and learning, between morality and identity. For anyone to be said to be teaching, it must follow that others are learning, but it is a much harder business to say what they are learning, and how wide the gap between teacher's (or parent's, or novelist's) intention and child's behaviour has to be before anyone can say teaching and learning are not happening (though both parties may still be very busy).

The argument is harder yet with imaginative experiences. Can the novelists of whom this book treats be said to be teaching anything? Is Bunyan teaching in the passage I quote? He certainly intended to teach that your adversary the devil walketh abroad as a roaring lion, and his story was a vivid and memorable way to present this truth to the Baptists of Bedford. But what could a modern child make of the story, especially one brought up in the rinsed-out doctrines and thin prose of the Series III Prayer Book?

Our secularized answer is that such a child must know Bunyan's style for what it is. That, however, is too readily priggish an answer of the type forever put in its place by Michael Frayn's hero at the funeral of an elderly colleague:

'For this corruptible must put on incorruption, and this mortal must put on immortality. So when this corruptible shall have put on incorruption, and this mortal shall have put on immortality, then shall be brought to pass the saying that is written, Death is swallowed up in victory.' Yes, thought Dyson, at that I can feel a pricking behind the lids of my eyes! And yet . . . do I in any sense believe that poor old Eddy shall put on immortality? Isn't it rather terrible that what brings the pricking behind my eyelids is not old Eddy's death, or even the thought of human mortality in general, but certain strokes of rhetoric – certain alliterations, repetitions, and verbal sonorities which don't hold any literal meaning for me? I'm more moved by literature than by what it describes![9]

Is this what the admonition to write in a proper style turns out to mean: that children will be moved by biblical resonances, and perhaps be able to write in some of them for themselves?

Not quite. For you can only write in such a style if you are capable of the quality of mind and spirit which it betokens. Prose isn't an infallible test of anyone's virtue, but it is as good as we have. Bunyan's simplicity of seeing is perfectly unselfish;

[9] *Towards the End of the Morning* (1967), p. 174.

the words seem to withdraw, and become transparent, so that we see with Bunyan's eyes, and Bunyan matters, not for himself, but because his writing makes the scene visible with a proper dread. To write such prose – and hence to read it – *is* to see the world in such a way; it is to fix the world in such a light, not that it is held forever in the colours of this man's temperament, but that his prose, drawing on the forms of language which his genius found in his culture and his historical models – the Bible, the Elstow tinkers, the Civil War, the new Baptists and Quakers, Bedford prison – catches hold of the truth that is truthfulness.

This is more than a flourish. I take the view in this book that formal Christianity will never recover a unified and social form in this country; if it were to, Bunyan's version, for all its undoubted strength and the meaning it gave to life, death, salvation and hellfire, would be one of its grisliest and most foreshortened versions. When, therefore, I quote Tolstoy to demand of writers that they deal seriously with the infinite and unending, this is not to require of a novelist that he recommend religion to his audience. It is to ask that he or she be capable of writing with the seriousness and simplicity which can suggest what Tolstoy wanted, which is capable also of moving into central areas of experience and saying what it has to say, plainly and intelligibly. Ah, if only more novels and poems could speak with such directness, then if literature is what we take it to be, the world would be a better place! But literature, as Wallace Stevens surprisingly noted, will only be the better part of life, if life is the better part of literature. And so the seriousness of the good novelist is of a piece with his gift to create life; his delight in the energy of the world issues in a creative energy of its own, whatever it makes.

As to the poetical character itself . . . it is not itself – it has no self – it is everything and nothing – it has no character – it enjoys light and shade; it lives in gusto, be it foul or fair, high or low, rich or poor, mean or elevated – it has as much delight in conceiving an Iago as an Imogen . . . [10]

Well, yes; the supreme fiction-maker gives malignity and evil a heartiness and good appetite they all too obviously have. That

[10] John Keats, letter to Woodhouse, 27 October 1815, from *Selected Letters*, ed. F. Page (1954), p. 172.

energy of creativeness is what gives life to Apollyon, and gives it to the barest, simplest little cameo from a children's tale. At the calm end of *No More School*, William Mayne brings back the teacher in whose absence through illness the hamlet's primary-schoolchildren have gone steadily on running their own classes, forgotten in the tiny schoolhouse:

Everybody stood up. Miss Oldroyd stepped into the room, and looked about. Ruth wished the school had been perfectly tidy, without any dust, and with the board clean. Shirley came away from the teacher's desk and closed the book she had been reading from. 'What are you doing here?' said Miss Oldroyd. 'I thought you had all gone to Burton school.'

No one said anything. Shirley looked at Ruth. Ruth looked at the rest of the class, and then at Miss Oldroyd.

'Haven't you been to Burton school at all?' said Miss Oldroyd.

'No,' said Fletcher. 'It's a spot and all.'

'Did Mrs. Tunstall come down here, then?' said Miss Oldroyd. 'Where is she now?'

Ruth put her fingers in the belt of her dress and twisted it. 'We did it ourselves,' she said. 'I taught some days.' She was not going to let Shirley be blamed.

'And I taught the other days,' said Shirley. 'I was teaching now.'

'They were so quiet,' said Miss Oldroyd. 'I thought the school was empty. I was taken aback you know, when I saw you all here. I only came to get some books and see about Monday's lessons. But I don't think you really need me, do you? Can I go away for another month?'

'We thought it would be all right,' said Ruth. 'It was my fault, I thought of it, and I made them come.' She was not sure yet whether they were going to get into trouble for what she had led them to do. Miss Oldroyd had only been talking, without saying so far what she felt. Ruth felt something like crying beginning to make a lump in her throat and prickle behind her eyes. She twisted her fingers very tight in her belt.

'I think you've done very well,' said Miss Oldroyd. 'I see you've even got some new pupils, too.'

The lump in Ruth's throat grew very big indeed, and her eyes suddenly grew very hot. It was because hot tears were filling them. The hot tears began to run down her face, and the lump in her throat melted into a sob. She tried to keep her face straight, but it wrinkled up; and then she was crying properly. (p. 107)

Coming after the graceful curve of the story – out of the safe frame of everyday protectedness to the open space of their brief, glorious, frightening independence and back to normality – this calmness, this cool sweetness of expression is fine and moving.

But it isn't enough (is it?) for a story to be moving; where shall we be moved to and why? What William Mayne does here is make an ending, with grace and breeding. He shows *how* to end well, as the tears become too much, in so vivid and affecting a way, for Ruth; they become too much because Ruth and Shirley had taken on more than they could manage for more than a short time, and the fullness of that short intensity brims over at its limit, both of time (Miss Oldroyd has come back) and of their dauntless little hearts. So Miss Oldroyd, and adult readers too, if they have a heart, join the children in a few tears. And then it's clear that Keats, absolutely right in emphasizing the poet's gusto, his delight in creation, isn't right when he implies that the story is simply left to itself, to get on with what it means.

William Mayne serves here as a touchstone of the seriousness and creativeness we expect to find in great literature. The passage stands oddly – but not *so* oddly – beside Bunyan. He, too, writes plainly of the natural order of things, and the place of children within it. And when we say of fine prose that it is vivid, we mean just that: it recreates the life of the event at the same time as it gives us a way of accommodating its meaning. That's why, as I put it earlier, reading the best prose properly *is* to see the world by, so to speak, 'becoming' the prose – that's what it is to be 'absorbed'. So, in this small scene, the prose creates in us both the physical and sympathetic responses we would feel if we were really there, listening and watching. Ruth's fingers twisted in her belt, the blockage in her throat, are each melted in the tender warmth of hot tears, and the break-up into sobs. The stiff tension of the month's independence, with all its joy and anxiety, 'wrinkles up' and dissolves in a good cry.

Now the point is not that, as some solemn prater of the curriculum might have it, children should encounter such prose in the interests of style and its cognates: skills, techniques, received usages, and whatnot. Nor, in the subtler versions of liberalism, do we want children to be moved by rhetoric and to write down prose in order that, whatever the content of their experience and its utterances, its form be open, personal, sincere, transparent. No, teachers and parents must also be committed in some way to the content of their children's lives, both in and out of the imagination. They want them to be good, to live well, to know and tell the truth. Truth and goodness, on this argument, are both form and content, at once what you do and how you do it.

Notoriously, however, at a time when we live with the inheritance of so many and conflicting moral systems, it is exceedingly difficult to find agreement on where truth and goodness may be found, and what it is to live well. Our moral axioms inhabit a rather thin, scorching, upper air. It is very hard to find ways of turning them into things we can do, which all will agree are pure, lovely, and of good report. Consequently, we have to return virtue to the individual conscience, and hope to validate all its actions by individual criteria made into universals: sincerity, dignity, integrity, honesty, authenticity. These are the master-symbols of an individualized morality. They have led to nobility and self-sacrifice in the name of the individual's rights and the freedom which guarantees those rights. For two centuries the novel has been in Europe, and now in Africa, the Caribbean, the USA, the English-speaking cultures, the main laboratory for inquiry and experiment in this moral world-picture.

Hence the importance in our picture of the right and proper growing up of children in both style and form. Right style ensures the qualities of sincerity and authenticity[11] which guarantee seriousness; the novel is the form best suited to the individual's testing out and exploration of these qualities in the particular, incomparable situations which give them their unique, irrecoverable meaning. It is worth adding that insofar as television plays have replaced novels as the most popular makers of moral myths, their interaction of technology and cultural form[12] issues in the privacy of the screen in the front room, with the same laboratory drama of individuals struggling against the intractability of an outside and hostile world.

I suppose Matthew Arnold saw this giant tendency first – in

---

[11] ·I quote the title of Lionel Trilling's book, *Sincerity and Authenticity* (1972), but revise his argument to suit a rather different case.
[12] The title of Raymond Williams's book on TV, from which I take this point. See *Television: Technology and Cultural Form* (1974), especially pp. 19ff.

English, at any rate (de Tocqueville anticipated him, with *Democracy in America*). But he was vastly optimistic; after the decline of religion, he prophesied that

the future of poetry is immense ... more and more mankind will discover that we have to turn to poetry to interpret life for us, to console us, to sustain us.[13]

Nowadays, for all our proper conviction, we hand over the novels to our children with a far more doubtful air. 'Here, literature won't exactly *save* you, but it will show you how to go about things.' Necessarily, it seems, we concede the victory of individualism. Each child must be left to choose his own values. The best we can hope for is to give him a style in which to do it.

The word 'style' returns me to the passage from *No More School*. I have tried to give 'style' an ampler, more rich and penetrative meaning than is implied in the cant term 'lifestyle'. 'Lifestyle' is, symptomatically enough, substituted for 'life'. The change in ordinary talk illuminates the changes in values. Life has become the adoption of lifestyles; you may choose your new style from the superculturemarket, and the style will remain yours until you want to choose a new one; life is choice, and choice is the constant which confirms you in your selfhood through the many fashions of your assorted identities. It is a necessary consequence of an emphasis on individuality and authenticity that membership of institutions becomes more provisional and the institutions themselves become more porous. In a conflict between the two, integrity requires you to renounce loyalty. If honour crosses with conscience, with the honesty and sincerity of conscience, conscience will win. Either commitment – to honour and loyalty or to integrity and conscience – is serious; each commands respect. Sorting the claims of either requires of us unusual truthfulness and courage. Either way it should be clear how the way in which William Mayne writes is as incompatible with lying and cowardice as John Bunyan's way. Mayne's simplicity and modesty *embody* – and because they embody, they *are* – a way of living well. And it is a psychological fact, as well as one of importance to moral philosophy, that any person may find

[13] Matthew Arnold, 'The Study of Poetry', in *Essays in Criticism* (1938), p. 2.

moral help by attending closely to admirable objects: the lives of good people, works of great art, religious or political doctrines.

It sounds circular, as though I am saying – as indeed I am – that to study what is excellent helps towards excellence, but quite without my being able at any point to interrupt the circle with a definition of excellence. If we are to acknowledge the force of relativism, however, and the diffusion and clouding of our moral structures wrought for both good and ill by 400 years of individualism, then excellence – or to choose a more sacred word, perfection – can only gain meaning for action from particular embodiments, of both form and content. Consequently, the language in which morality finds form and content composes one version of the social actions which are morality and politics themselves. It is the action – the action in thought or speech or art – which makes morality, and by this token form and content are mutually embedded.

I have to take this rather tricky route through the chartless overcrowdings of modern morality for two reasons. The first is that this offers a way to join the parallel tracks of literature and ethics. Secondly, we can say that the seriousness and disinterest of attention shown by good writers transforms itself from a state of grace to a mode of action by discovering a narrative. This state of being cannot remain detached and objective; of its nature, it must both create and respond as it contemplates and engages with an action.

These two reasons serve to explain the place of honour literature has been given in moral and educational discussion in the past half century. It is in these times the readiest vehicle for talking about moral seriousness. By example, it provides a body of what theologians used to call 'middle axioms', that is, mediators between abstract principle and moral action. The interplay of culture and technology which produces the contents pages of the *Radio Times* naturally lends itself to the same agenda. Television sets are nearly as controllable as novels. You can switch them off when you like; you watch them, just as you read novels, at home with your family. Although the disparity between the word and the image may be measured on a different scale from the one in hand, for our immediate purposes, novels and television plays are fundamentally alike. They provide room for moral speculation in the spaces of stories about a world whose rules and conventions are historically negotiable.

In this way, moreover, novels are contiguous with everyday life. They are extensions of our conversation about the world with our friends and neighbours. And this is the moment at which to insert a theme to be developed later. For the discussion of children's novels makes it easy to see something which is true of all imaginative experience. It is the circularity of forces within which the conversation with a book goes forward. There is the writer; there is the novel. No doubt it embodies what the writer has to say, but it has its own rules, as well as being apt to take on its own queer life, so that even if a novelist wants to hammer his novel down with a big nail of an idea, it may yet, in Lawrence's phrase, get up and walk away with the nail. There is the reader to consider also, and whether child or adult, the reader must take the novel from someone's hands – the bookseller, the librarian (before them, maybe, the TV producer and his boss, the programme planner), the teacher in school or university or extra-mural class, the friend in the next house or in the playground. Each of these people is gathered within the vast field of force known as a culture, the electricity of which is the source of energy behind all these actions and transactions. Normally we look only at the exchange between reader and author, or more occasionally, among educationists, the bond (to use Denys Harding's term) between parent or teacher and child or pupil.[14] But that bond is tied with an enormously wider circle of people, and it is at least a beginning to think of this circle – perhaps better imagined as an endless social and historical spiral than as a closed ring – as the membership of a conversation.

It is not a metaphor which can be transfigured as one of those curvilinear diagrams favoured by some scientists of social interaction. The trouble with those is that the physical limit of two dimensions on a page causes them to picture social life as a map without a history, a geography whose notation has no compass and can only draw roads.

Think, with Michael Oakeshott, of the conversation of culture; in conversation, we are – as we say – most at home in one language, and one idiolect within that language; which is not to say that we cannot learn other languages and join other

[14] D. W. Harding, 'The Bond with the Author', *Use of English*, 22, 4 (1971).

conversations, even when we must get by on gesture. Oakeshott says:

> in conversation, 'facts' appear to be resolved once more into the possi-
> bilities from which they were made ... And the final measure of
> intellectual achievement is in terms of its contribution to the conver-
> sation in which all universes of discourse meet.[15]

It is a conversation of such a kind in which novelists and their
readers take part. To say so enables us, in more homely part, to
make a modest admonition of practice in the human sciences.
We shall often understand and value human life in a particular
aspect rather better if, so to speak, we suspend our identifying
categories – novels in this case – above a larger, more
problematic range of human activities – for our purposes, the
discursive practices of storytelling and fiction-making.
Novels, in short, are only the specific forms of the discursive
practice of myth- and fiction-making. In the allusive, prodigal
notation of Wallace Stevens, as *he* tussled with his *Notes towards
a Supreme Fiction*, he similarly declared:

> There is a project for the sun. The sun
> Bear no name, gold flourisher, but be
> In the difficulty of what is to be.

The nameless sun is an old 'gold flourisher'; our project is to
make it anonymous and thus return it to the 'difficulty of what
is to be', the constant, inane motion of things which can only be
named as they become facts.

By the same token, we return children's novels to the restless
flow of possibility. In this new setting for discrimination, the
rather arbitrary uniformity of the category 'novel' or even that
of 'book' can be seen for the multiform thing it is. Thus, to call
Lewis Carroll's *Alice*, Alan Garner's *The Stone Book*, and *The
Hobyahs* all novels, and to devise a way of criticizing these
works, is less to our purposes than to return them all to the
'discursive practice' of imagining-fictions-for-children. And
that, in turn, only makes sense in a much larger context, a more
complex field of discourse.

So, children's fiction is part of the larger practice of adult
fiction, and this is in its turn part of the practice of informal
fictioning which is an essential human activity, a cast of the

---

[15] *Rationalism in Politics* (1962), p. 235.

mind such that it sees the world as endlessly possible, and unmanageably infinite. These fictions declare themselves at every point of our working and our dreaming lives. They arise from culture; in age, they speak in the imperfect tense:

I gleaned all my boyhood. I ran away from it once but came to grief, and since the results have been with me all my life, I will tell you about it. When I was six I got fed up with being in the gleaning-field with all the women, so I ran off to help the boy who worked the cattle-cake machine. In no time my hand was caught and my fingers were squashed. The farmer was just coming up by the granary on his horse when he heard me screaming. 'What have you been up to, you young scamp?' he shouted. 'My fingers – they're in the cake-breaker!' And he said – I shall never forget it – 'Get you off home then!' But when he saw my hand he changed his tune and said, 'Get up to the house.' The farmer's wife tied some rag round my hand and took me home and my mother wheeled me miles to the doctor's in a pram. My sister was home from service, so she came with us and held me while the doctor scraped grease out of my wounds with a knife, stitched up one finger, cut another, pared it like a stick and tied what was left to the bone, and then moved on to the next finger. I lifted the roof, I can tell you. There was no anaesthetic, nothing. My sister began to faint and the doctor got on to her something terrific. 'Damn silly girl – clear off outside if you can't stand it! Fetch my groom in.' So the groom came and held me until it was finished. All the time the doctor worked he shouted. 'What did you do it for? Why? Damn little nuisance! Stupid little fool!'[16]

And in youth, they speak tenselessly:

A book about my life
Once my life was running all over the place in the house and on the road. The road was very narrow and wide and long in that thing that my life did that day with my energy is allway used up my life is a little life. My little life was a good one. like this good life. My life is a big misery in my life there are some things in my life there are dogs in the peg shop, there are good dogs.
    Once my life was a running life I did not like it at all It was at my hous. I shude not my life is a misery in the olden days. In the olden day the were snakes in the jungle. My life, saw a bharner in the dish were it gos. my life was a good bit of life. there was my life all grown in the feled with a cow. mowing in the feled. The pigs were with my life. My life was a baby life just then I gor big.

[16] From Ronald Blythe, *Akenfield* (1969), pp. 37–8.

One day my life was running all over the place. My birds wer in my life. My life is a big life in the sumer [17]

Either way, the fiction-making powers of individuals are bent to make forms and images (we may call them) sent out to join the conversation of mankind. The old man is telling the facts as he remembers them, and in the telling the present and the past grate upon one another, take each other's measure, and the past emerges in a different shape, a different aesthetic and moral shape, to work its strength in the present and change its meaning.

The old farmworker's memories are part of that same discursive field – imagining-fictions-for-children; his history is the children's mythology, with some versions of which they sort and interpret the present.

I emphasize the line running from his selection from his memories to the stories other people write down for their children (of whatever age). As soon as the first details of his tale strike home, we begin to sympathize with the old farmworker. He tells his tale so plainly and with such dignity – just the bare facts, as we say, but what facts! Whose anger doesn't rise at the rough butcher of a doctor, his callousness of class, the awful lack of compassion, just as at the same time we respond admiringly to the old man's calm lack of resentment *now*, mingled with his sharp sense of the bitterness due to the way poor children were treated in those days. In no time, we begin to be part of the story; with a shock we remember that Ronald Blythe is telling it to us for Leonard Thompson, and that he is only one of the intermediaries between us and the original. But that shock is also a comfort. For our response is that of any member of a human community. We start to listen to the stories the community tells itself. We enjoy listening. How on earth can we say we enjoy listening to this painful little anecdote? But we do, even as we wince at the grisly detail – 'pared it like a stick'. The pleasure is that of any member of a group listening to a well-told tale. (If it was badly told, we'd be bored.) It comes alive because of the vividness and terseness of the language.

Thus far, any listener quite naturally applies the technique of literary criticism. He tests the words in his ear for their reality

[17] Jenny, aged 10, quoted in Connie and Harold Rosen, *The Language of Primary School Children* (1973), p. 247.

and purpose, for their moral resonance and the relation of that to the character of the storyteller. 'A grand old man', you might say. 'What a store of memories. My word, but it was a hard life then, especially for children. But something to it, wasn't there, that we've lost now? I mean, things haven't only got better since then . . . haven't we lost his robustness, his acceptance of things. . . ?', and so on. You'd connect the story (wouldn't you?) directly to the storyteller, and then consider his intentions and motives in telling it just that way. All this time, as you talked of what he said, as *I've* talked of what Leonard Thompson said to Ronald Blythe, we would each of us watch the story, wish the farmer or the doctor to damnation for their unfeeling, imagine what happened next, imagine involuntarily, because of the vividness of the telling, what the bit of surgery felt like, and then recoil from it with wrinkled faces not because it hurt us (how could it?) but because the effort at sympathetic imagination became too much for our bodies, and some nervous ganglion squirmed in revulsion. So, bit by bit, we seek out of this busy moral and psychological traffic an attitude towards the story. We 'come to terms with' or 'place' it, a pair of clichés which, if they mean anything, mean just this: that the story offers itself on certain terms – those that I have proposed one version of – and we move forward with our own, *our* sense of what such a past means in our present, and then, settling for some balance between it and ourselves, find a place to put it down in that hall of the human mind which may be lit by the different lamps of memory and imagination, and by both at once.

This is a first picture of the spiral of interpretative understanding necessary in reading, decoding, interrogating and misreading the tales men tell, whether informally or in novels. *No More School* and the farmworker's reminiscences are alike in many of their structures, and in the structures of our response. One way of making that clear is to sketch the commonplace psychology I have described, and appeal for recognition. Don't you, and I, do these things *whenever* we listen to a story?

We surely do. We tie our bond with the author. He talks to us, and we listen to him. In this, as in any other human encounter, we look out for what we can trust in the narrator. We get to know the attitudes and qualities which his voice carries; we learn, as we do with our garrulous or our taciturn neighbour, what he is like, when he exaggerates, where his judgement may be counted on and where not. As with the neighbour, so with the novelist: the more the writer is a good man, the more we take the stories as truthful and the judgements as excellent. This is not to say that good novelists are all good men, although, with Iris Murdoch, I would want to say that, insofar as they are good novelists, they at least know more about the direction of goodness than a bad one does:

> The great artists reveal the detail of the world. At the same time their greatness is not something peculiar and personal like a proper name. They are great in ways which are to some extent similar, and increased understanding of an art reveals its unity through its excellence. All serious criticism assumes this . . .[18]

Now we may trust some authors, and we may enjoy many others while mistrusting them. But what Iris Murdoch says here about the identity of great writers connects with the remark of Tolstoy's quoted earlier: a serious writer has something of importance to say about all that is infinite and unending. The remark may have a touch of tautology about it, but never mind: we know what he means, as we know what Iris Murdoch means. We trust good writers and good men with ourselves: we expect them to tell the truth, to act well, to be courteous towards us (if we are courteous towards them), at times perhaps to advise us, certainly to give us examples.

Talking in this way emphasizes the sociability of reading, even if the author is long dead. Reading novels is part of the conversation to which education seeks to introduce children. And so the experience of trust, in a person or a book, especially in a world which so much threatens children, returns us to seeing how ethics are social and not personal, and to rejoining ethics with aesthetics. Think of the daily prohibitions and protections which face children: 'Don't go out in the lane', 'Hold my hand', 'Cross the road only at the zebra', 'Never take sweets from a stranger', 'Don't play with those rough boys.' Country or city is full of terrors, real and artificial, and those of us who, in so many different roles, have the care of children need a sure and rapid screening to distinguish wolves from guide- and guard-dogs.

[18] *The Sovereignty of Good* (1970), pp. 88ff.: the quotation is from p. 96.

Perhaps it is in this way that I can make sense of saying that ethics is a branch of psychology, and not intend some reduction of its importance in doing so. In a remarkable passage, Simone Weil simply affirms a psychological frame of mind as an ethical truth. The corroboration rests in everyone's experience:

At the bottom of the heart of every human being, from earliest infancy until the tomb, there is something that goes on indomitably expecting, in the teeth of all experience of crimes committed, suffered, and witnessed, that good and not evil will be done to him. It is this above all that is sacred in every human being.

The good is the only source of the sacred. There is nothing sacred except the good and what pertains to it.[19]

Faced with this corroboration, there is no need to become knotted up in very much moral or political philosophy. Nor does the matter rest in its being asserted by Simone Weil that we expect, in some passive way, good to be done *to* us, and that therefore this sacredness is another version of self-interest. Insofar as we expect good to be done to us, we know we shall recognize it for what it is (and will recognize the justice of harm done to us if it is just). By the same token, if we do harm to others we shall know it and, somewhere in ourselves, be deeply ashamed. This doesn't make ethics simply into the business of identifying motivation, and approving or condemning it accordingly. It is a peculiarity of the times that we are more interested in admired states of feeling than in both good and effective action. But Simone Weil is not commending a state of feeling; she is saying, nakedly, that we know what the good is when we see it, and are outraged when it is not done to us.

This is, for her and for this book, a fixed point of experience. Indeed, it marks the point at which morality and identity cross, first and last. It is what Iris Murdoch, following Simone Weil, intends when she speaks of the necessary mysteriousness of the good. Freed of class and history and culture, the notion of goodness represents at once 'a magnetic centre'[20] towards which human nature must tend if, in a secular universe, it is to find meaning in its short life. At the same time it is the deep, lived gauge of the actions of others within ourselves. This intuition of goodness represents a measure not of the effect of

[19] Simone Weil, 'La Personne et le Sacré', *Ecrits de Londres* (1951).
[20] *Sovereignty of Good*, pp. 92ff.

others upon us (which would remain an uninteresting clot of self-regard and self-interest – frequent enough, of course, but not at all what is meant) but of any human action at all. No doubt there will always be characters like Iago and Nero and Richard III who calmly and without any need of justification do not recognize these measures. But our horror at such people is a witness of the normal expectation not just of better things, but of goodness itself, of which Simone Weil is writing.

A human being's sense of who he or she really is grows from this ethical-psychological fact. That is the point from which morality and identity start in human consciousness, and as all the psychiatrists who have criticized Freud agree,[21] the one is the guarantee of the other. The point, however, is neither psychoanalytic nor even in conflict with Freud's theories. It is not even directly developmental. The argument to hand is that there are reasons for action which are specifically moral; it is precisely because they represent moral requirements that they *can* prompt any motives at all, not the other way round. Substantially, the position is that of Kant, who also sought to hold together ethics and psychology: he is the ancestor of our popular morality, for all the horrors wrought upon his ideas in the name of freedom in the seventies, and his is the tradition it is timely to invoke. For I have not in the least taken my eye off children and their literature in this short excursus. It is when we look at what we want children to be and do and become that we are made aware of the inescapability of a moral psychology. The quotation from Weil shows that, like Kant in his greatest essay, she too places at the centre of things the individual's metaphysical conception of his ethical self. Whereas nowadays people have taken too much to heart the lesson of Kant's *Principles of the Metaphysic of Ethics* and sought to fight for their merely personal freedom against the dark oppressions of baby, the pram and the kitchen, Weil and others place the energetic centre of morality in the reality of oneself as simply an individual among other individuals. The facts of these matters set men and women beneath a moral government which may be disobeyed wilfully or by free choice (whichever way you want to put it), but whose rules are not the consequence of our desires; they are expressions of the practical necessity of good.

'The words of Mercury are harsh after the songs of Apollo' is

[21] An early example being Ian Suttie, *The Origins of Love and Hate* (1935).

the last line of *Love's Labour's Lost*. But it is the overpowering strength of literature that it both speaks the words *and* sings the songs. The voice of Apollo is the voice of freedom, the free self able to do what the hell or the heaven it likes. The voice of Mercury tells the self which is which. Both fly in the great empyrean blue to which the imagination is the window:

And immediately

Rather than words comes the thought of high windows
The sun-comprehending glass,
And beyond it the deep blue air, that shows
Nothing, and is nowhere, and is endless.[22]

Freedom, in other words, may occupy frighteningly open spaces; it only has meaning when the free self *does* something. That self is given – given to you and to me. The tiniest baby, Simone Weil would rightly say, would be outraged by wrong done to it; the self it is, or better, the human being it is, is human because this is so. And this continues to be so whoever you are, and however differently you might have turned out. You might have lived in another country, or even at another time, you might even have been a different person – it is not too much strain on the imagination to think so – but this givenness of an inalterable principle of ethical life which is, in some irreducible way, *you*, would remain.

It would, however, be a you of a rather ghostly and attenuated kind. If I am right to start from an ethics which is squarely identical with metaphysics, there is still a lot of psychology to come. Similarly, that phantom principle of life which, in my version of essentialism, is a human being, expects good and fears the worst. It is free and therefore it can imagine alternatives. Violated by evil, it also knows that it may choose evil itself. In either case, for better or worse, the limits of its imagination are the limits of its action. A dismal autobiography may kill off an individual's imagination. A brutal culture may kill off a society's imagination. Just as the definition of goodness can only take place within the life of a culture, and can only come to mean something in terms of what you can do in that culture, so the self and its imaginings can only find identity within those same terms. You cannot be a Kalahari Bushman in

[22] Philip Larkin, *High Windows* (1974); from the title poem.

North Yorkshire. Not only would your neighbour be right to think you off your head, the material world would not support what could only be an idea.

It follows from these truths that the imagination and the ethical self follow some line of development. We know this from our own experience. We watch it in our children. It is natural to look for help from those who profess to understand the sequence if not the principle of this regulation. But for all the weight of books on the library shelves which tell us of the stages of children's development,[23] I don't think they can ever be more than corroborations of common sense – and common sense may itself lay a killing hand on both ethics and imagination.

This is not to fall into a drastic version of individualism: 'Every child is unique.' It is to say that the development of both ethics and imagination is peculiar, erratic, and reversible. Jean Piaget, the great architect of the scheme of children's development, had to invent the category of 'uncoupling' to account for strange breaks in some children's development, and it is a notorious truth of such inquirers as Kohlberg that the stages of child development towards moral maturity tend to reflect progress towards an ideal version of the good White Man, an ideal which is constantly being adjusted by a changing moral and political history. All the same, the universal cultural experience is that each individual makes certain passages in his or her life, and however much a person may sometimes want to go back, the social definitions of the stage crossed into provide new standards of judgement and new obstacles to regression. Thus, when a child goes to secondary school, enters the sixth form, becomes a student, a husband or wife, a parent, each passage has its rites and each role its standards. The most commonplace remarks make this clear: 'Don't be a crybaby', 'You're a big girl now', 'She's thoroughly irresponsible', 'He's too young to get married', 'She's been a wonderful mother to those kids.'

Moral and imaginative development is partly a matter of luck, as I said. Or at least it is a matter of taking the oppor-

---

[23] See, for example, L. Kohlberg, 'The Development of Children's Orientation towards a Moral Order', *Vita Humana*, 6 (1963), pp. 11–33, and his 'Continuities and Discontinuities in Childhood and Adult Moral Development', *Human Development*, 12 (1969), pp. 93–120. David Satterly is sceptical about most such work in 'Stages of Development: Help or Hindrance in Educating Young Children', *New Universities Quarterly*, 29, 4 (1975).

tunities as they come along. But inasmuch as we may speak of and work for development at all, it is not enough to fall back on the horticultural metaphors (and that's all they were) of the post-Romantic psychologists such as Pestalozzi, Froebel, and Preyer, about children's growth and flowering, about nature and its nurture, about the cultivation of morality and identity. There is of course force in these, as in any metaphors; they resisted, as Chapter 3 suggests, the combined grimness of the utilitarian and evangelical Victorian nursery. But while their 'naturalness' and its cultivation has some non-cultural limits and determinations (there surely is a human root, a radical human nature beneath cultural differences), the natural, flower-like growth of children is only and richly a consequence of the social and historical structures and practices which shape, colour, feed and permit the growth.

'Structure' is a tricky word to use of something as uncertain and impalpable as everyday social life. For all its popularity as a useful term in the human sciences, it implies a fixity and a solidity which deceive as they reassure. At the very least, we might speak sensibly of culture as a system of practices, conventions, habits, routines, and rituals, all of which are no doubt made intelligible by their structural regularity but which cannot possibly be understood by way of schematizing their deep or atomic foundation. Their intelligibility for members of society reposes, as I say, in their being held in regular place by rules and conventions, but saying so does not give us permission to think of society and its history as merely a 'process without a subject'.[24] Social experience only *is* experience for its actors insofar as they can make some sense out of it. The homely phrase, 'it doesn't make sense', tells us in its innumerable contexts much of what we want to know about social identity. Everybody tries to make sense both to themselves and to others, and they can do so only as they acquire the systems of 'durable, transposable dispositions'[25] which enable them to operate the principles of improvisation which constitute 'sense' in social action.

'Making sense' therefore has a strongly aesthetic overtone to

[24] The phrase is Louis Althusser's in the volume *Lenin and Philosophy* (1971) where he professes the most disdainfully subjectless view of social action.
[25] I take this phrase from Pierre Bourdieu, in his *Outline of a Theory of Practice* (1977). He coins the agreeable term 'habitus' for this system. See pp. 78–83.

it, which comes out clearly when we consider the way in which a loving parent seeks to instil the order of things in his or her child. Feeling that her two- or three-year-old child has had a distressingly neglected or untidy day, one in which she has hauled the child from place to meaningless place, broken the rhythms and routines of the day by late meals, long phone calls, standing in the cold and wet, a mother will try to put the day to rights at its close by insisting on a calm and calming sequence of known, loved customs. She bathes her child and dries him in a warm, enveloping towel before the fire; gives him a warm drink, tucks him thoroughly and enclosingly in, reads a story with careful attention to the pictures, kisses him goodnight and makes sure the regiments of soft animals are arranged in their due place.

These are the customs which both instil and confirm the order of things. We would do well in considering the many forms through which culture works to reproduce and transform itself, not to cut back our vocabulary to the reductive 'structure'. The many terms which designate the regularity of social action – convention, custom, habit, ritual, value, and so forth – all denote *differences*, of meaning, of reason, of cause. Each has its rules, no doubt, and in that sense embodies a structure; but each is endlessly regenerative. Intelligible action by an individual secures a 'conditioned and conditional freedom . . . as remote from a creation of unpredictable novelty as it is from a simple mechanical reproduction of the initial conditionings'.[26]

It is in a development of such notions that we can best keep hold of the tension between culture and the self, and the movement of both in the lives of children. A child is itself, and being so, may act with its own idiosyncrasies and freedom. But a child may only live and express these as a culture gives life and expression a social form and sense. This is the twistpoint of personality and cultural influence. The most potent of these influences is, in the industrialized nations, class.[27] The penetrations of class into the whole being of men and women is much mentioned, if less understood, in our culture on both sides of the Atlantic. Now it is clear that there is no direct equation

[26] Bourdieu, *Outline*, p. 95.
[27] See, from a vast literature, the following studies which may be used to footnote these few remarks (I go back to the topic in Chapter 4): Richard Sennett and Jonathan Cobb, *The Hidden Injuries of Class* (1972); J. Westergaard and H. Resler, *Class in a Capitalist Society: A Study of Contemporary Britain* (1975).

between poverty and underdevelopment. The simple socio-logical determinism of the culture of poverty is as untrue as the simply psychodynamic determinism which would say that loss of a loved figure is bound to cause taciturnity and with-drawal. It is at least plausible that the special forms of life created by the poor and oppressed have a resistance and vitality lost by the more emollient styles of the well-off. But the common experience of teachers and of the poor themselves is that poverty in modern life makes culture brutish, strips down morality to a first-aid box, and extinguishes the power of the imagination to present other worlds, because other worlds are unimaginable. This is the most brutal experience of class, and it points the moral. It is the city life-in-death of which Marx and Engels and Dickens and Mayhew wrote; it is, in Liverpool, Chicago, Naples, Barcelona, New York, and London, with us yet. And the converse is true. The rich don't live like the poor. Insofar as the poor have a distinctive and energetic form and content in their culture, such as Dickens found in some corners of London, they will be entirely unlike the rich.

The brief, familiar example illustrates the general common-place: you and your culture make one another out of a ceaseless but *ordered* process of reciprocity. This process has, so to speak, a double helix of forces from which each person changes an identity. Down the one spiral run the given essences, that is, the absolute necessities of a person's life. Let us say that these include time, causality, freedom,[28] sex, teleology (or, more homely, meaning), geography.

These terms are not offered in any very final sense. Let them serve as essential units whose relations to one another, mean-ingless by themselves, are capable of transfiguration into an in-finite number of identities. What distinguishes this list is that these are absolute terms which any identity *must* (just because they are essential) decode and recode in its own life.

The second spiral carries, by contrast, the substances which express and give meaning to the brute, contingent facts of life. Let us say that these substances include home, friendship, nation, history, intelligence, love, independence. This is another, rather arbitrary list; but it allows me to take a selection of these terms, and to suggest how an identity makes itself out

[28] The first three taken from John Harvey's discussion of 'the syntax of experience', which prompts my own notions. See his *Character and the Novel* (1963).

of necessity and freedom, fact and accident, essence and substance.

You might replace several of the terms with similar but not identical ones: 'nation' simply with 'membership', with either of these being counterposed to 'independence' and moral autonomy. For 'history' you might read 'culture', except that identity is itself a radically reflexive construct, and can hardly reflect back from anything but the past. Each term implies relationships of an ever-widening constituency: with oneself (including what we mean when we speak of our own relationship to ourselves – 'I'm not happy with myself'), with one's family, with one's friends, one's people, with human beings and their history. Each field of relationship implies a family of cognate values – independence is related to integrity, self-respect, individual dignity, self-reliance and so forth; nation to patriotism (and hatred of foreigners), mutual help, honour, pride, loyalty. Of course, a number of such values belong as much to, say, home, or friendship, as to the larger dimensions of a nation, but I offer the list with all its abbreviation and arbitrariness simply to suggest a theory of personal and moral life which parents and teachers may recognize. Each child as it grows up needs to find a way of accommodating itself to these dimensions. The process of accommodation is regulated according to the child's intelligence, and the strength of its love of and for life – life in itself and others. Because intelligence varies drastically according to age and to attributes, as well as to mood, encouragement, context, it is hard to say exactly how to nourish its growth.

This is my rough and ready picture of the shape of moral identity. That identity has an essential structure and must make itself, at least in modern, Western cultures, out of the substances and essences I have listed. I have not gone into the political implications of the list; this simple diagram is for the moment a picture both of the self *and* of the novel. I would have to produce a different map in order to talk about poetry and its possible contribution to development. But the argument of this book pretends a broad likeness between novels and people. I know that this is crudely put, but it simplifies the argument to speak of both novelists and parents and, indeed, children as seeking to make sense of their lives by giving them the forms of fiction.[29] Each life, by this token, is a work of art; and each work of art is a life.

For our purposes, then, the structure of a novel and the structure of a person are the same, and both are moral. In both cases, also, the author is after something. As the philosophers say, art is teleological: it has a point and purpose and an end. It will vary, this purpose, from person to person, and this variety is a function of the freedom which is part of the fact of existence. So who we become is, in part, what we make of ourselves, and it is in this sense that we are all poets, and seeking to construct a version of ourselves both feasible and right. Fictions, both in and out of books, are nets in which to catch the facts of the matter, the truth which is accessible only to an always increasing vision of a fuller, more aware and freer life.[30]

The quest is timeless. The quests of innumerable children's and folk tales bear witness to its transhistorical power as an image of men's searching for a holy treasure. But living in time and its misprision, history, means that our quest has to imagine an actual end. The bird we seek to catch in the net of our imagination, the sacred chalice at the end of the rainbow, remain as blindingly beautiful treasures in the tale. But what they mean in our lives is real and historical. They measure the gap between the good life and the real life, and real life has to find a way of using the chalice. The glowing, mysterious image has to mean something. Thus, fictions stand to life as metaphors to reality. They are an image of alternatives and possibility. So if we speak of the best children's books, in a famous formulation, as bringing to an intense focus 'an unusually developed interest in life', 'a vital capacity for experience', 'a marked moral intensity', then these noble phrases in no way suggest closure or rigidity, or, worst of all, portentousness. The generalities take their force, as these days they must, from the moral effort to make experience *mean* something at a time when, as I argued, 'zero-structures' and

[29] I repeat this point in quoting Richard Gregory on pp. 309ff. Liam Hudson argues in the same direction in 'Life as Art', *New Society*, 12 February 1976.

[30] The image of a net with which to catch meaning is, first, C. S. Lewis's, in 'On Stories' (1947), reprinted in *The Cool Web*, ed. Margaret Meek *et al.* (1977), picked up by Mary Warnock in 'The Need for Fiction', *TLS*, 25 March 1977. I take these three critical criteria from conversations with and an unpublished paper by Charles Taylor, to whom I am most grateful.

'radical personalization' (Basil Bernstein's phrase) leave the individual with everything to do for himself.

It has, however, been the great strength of English literature – of which children's fiction is a part – since Blake, Wordsworth, the Brontës and Dickens, that its sense of responsibility goes far beyond the individual and his personal relationships. The test to have in mind is that children's novels be characterized by their responsibility to the demands of immediate life, and that life as irremediably historical. The point of my insistence on the historicality of values and meanings is that this book is written on behalf of children and their literature. The stories we tell them are intended to make life in the future. This doesn't mean that, in some ghastly extension of Mrs Doasyouwouldbedoneby, stories are there to dictate, nor that they are just training for grown-up life. (If, for instance, we saw a child we knew to be fatally ill, reading a novel with pleasure or, come to that, with distress, we shouldn't be so mean as to think that he was wasting his time.) With John Keats, let us speak of the world not as a vale of tears, but as 'a vale of soul-making'. The difficulty is then dialectical: how shall you make a soul which is faithful to a lost yesterday and strong enough to meet a discontinuous tomorrow?

For key human values are on the move. In Bernstein's phrase, 'radical personalization', the attempt to free oneself from all social bonds and structures in the name of individuality, is emerging as the beautiful, elegant, ageless and carefree child of consumer capitalism at just the point in world history when she must change utterly to survive. Faced by the facts of over-population and famine, the deep, illiberal entrenchments of world bureaucracies, the limits of food and water, of energy and capital, the threats of world instability balanced on the point of an off-the-peg nuclear missile, the children of the rich West have reacted by breaking all but thin lines of contact with their parents and their parents' traditions. A preferable set of values might usefully turn away from exploiting the globe for their own comfort, and rebuild a rather more careful moral economy, which reverences the nonhuman life of the world. They might sort out what matters to them so that work and its aura of master-symbols – ambition, success, competition, busyness, production – fill a less central place in life. The new authenticity could do with yielding at a pinch to the old selflessness.[31]

The only certainty about forecasts, however, is that they will be wrong. Telling our children stories about how to grow up, how to live well, is bound to be for parents and teachers and novelists an endlessly provisional business. The great test is our common humanity. Seriousness, certainly; but unless the reading we create and recommend is delightful and wonderful, then the truth cannot be in it. The seriousness rests in the importance our children have for us – not only as the representatives of an unknowable future, but as *our* moral measures of the present. Any morality which does not test itself in the scale of your children's lives is likely to be rather abstract.

Understanding children's stories is a matter of breaking into the field of force which the social circle of writers, parents, teachers, children, publishers, TV producers, and so on, all generate. Understanding the story is a matter of grasping at that totality, and reconstructing some, at least, of its many electric currents. Such understanding entails judgement. We have to judge in order to understand; the understanding enlarges the judgement. That is to say, we can only interpret, redescribe to ourselves, and understand by testing a fiction against our frame of judgement. According to the strength of that frame, we accommodate the fiction. It changes us, and we change it. We proceed with an altered frame of judgement. Faced with a rival interpretation and judgement, the best man wins; best, that is, in terms of wisdom, enlightenment, capaciousness, and conviction.

This argument applies also to the best writer. William Mayne's *No More School*, from which I quoted, is so good because it perfectly adjusts its moral frame to what a particular child – aged seven, a good reader and sensitive, or aged eleven, backward and easily scared – *can* comprehend. The adult finds the book easy to understand and can make sense of it for these two children. 'Making sense' *is* making the judgement.

The heart of the matter is language. The purity and simplicity of which I began by speaking are the marks of what we

---

[31] I condense here parts of three important arguments: Robert Heilbroner, *An Inquiry into the Human Prospect* (1974), Barrington Moore, *Reflections on the Causes of Human Misery* (1970), and Charles Taylor, 'The Politics of the Steady State', reprinted in *New Universities Quarterly*, 32, 2 (1978).

might call sacred texts. Sacred texts include *Pilgrim's Progress*, most fairy stories and a few novels and tales, most obviously for the very young: *Peter Rabbit, King of the Golden River, The Children of Green Knowe, We Didn't Mean to Go to Sea, Treasure Island, The Stone Book* are all examples. A sacred text has a special kind of autonomy: you cannot ask of it, 'Is it sincere?' 'Is it mistaken?' It exemplifies Yeats's 'radical innocence' in its most naked form.

As experience stains the gaze of innocence, the prose becomes more complex, more inclusive and allusive. It is so in growing up. And yet the prose in which we speak to children speaks to all readers of what is precious to us. The odd thing these days is that sometimes it is *only* to children that we say these things. As an example of some of the best prose in English, I shall quote a few lines from *Little Dorrit* in order to suggest how interpretation and judgement as I have spoken of them move together in dialectic. It is very much to the point that Dickens in these passages displays both a moral authority and a boyishness which is at once the mark of a great writer and a great and trustworthy man. Such a writer can speak directly to children even if they misunderstand him. It is an odd sign of the times that the writers now capable of anything like such a mixture of ardour and wisdom are only likely to be found writing for children. We only risk speaking of love, joy, peace, longsuffering, gentleness, truth, when we talk to the children. Insofar as this wasn't true for Dickens, is he now an archaism or an emblem?

His chivalrous feeling towards all that belonged to her made him so very respectable, in spite of his small stature and his rather weak legs, and his very weak hair, and his poetical temperament, that a Goliath might have sat in his place demanding less consideration at Arthur's hands.

'You speak, John,' he said, with cordial admiration, 'like a Man.'

'Well, sir,' returned John, brushing his hand across his eyes, 'then I wish you'd do the same.'

He was quick with this unexpected retort, and it again made Arthur regard him with a wondering expression of face. (pp. 795–6)

Dickens is able, within the morally far wider vocabulary of Victorian society which it was his genius to have deepened and enriched, to speak with confidence of chivalry and respectability, and to give a force to the idea of manliness invoked at first with a trace of condescension by Clennam (who didn't altogether expect such dignity in John Chivery), and then redoubled by the startling swiftness and justice of John's reply.

The whole point of the scene is that it is Arthur Clennam, the hero, who is convicted of blindness and self-deluding self-pity, and John who has to show him so, 'scouring', in Dickens's phrase, 'a very prairie of wild words'.

'I mistaken, sir!' said Young John. '*I* completely mistaken on that subject! No, Mr. Clennam, don't tell me so. On any other, if you like, for I don't set up to be a penetrating character, and am well aware of my own deficiencies. But *I* mistaken on a point that has caused me more smart in my breast than a flight of savages' arrows could have done! *I* mistaken on a point that almost sent me into my grave, as I sometimes wished it would, if the grave could only have been made compatible with the tobacco-business and father and mother's feelings! *I* mistaken on a point that, even at the present moment, makes me take out my pocket-handkercher like a great girl, as people say: though I am sure I don't know why a great girl should be a term of reproach, for every rightly constituted male mind loves 'em great and small. Don't tell me so, don't tell me so!'

Still highly respectable at bottom, though absurd enough upon the surface, Young John took out his pocket-handkerchief with a genuine absence both of display and concealment, which is only to be seen in a man with a great deal of good in him, when he takes out his pocket-handkerchief for the purpose of wiping his eyes. Having dried them, and indulged in the harmless luxury of a sob and a sniff, he put it up again. (p. 798)

Great love expresses itself naturally in great feeling, but it takes a large capacity for feeling to contain and order it. Young John, who has great goodness but no great capacity for feeling, is so swept up by the potency of Little Dorrit's excellence that he is overcome by a feeling which only can brim over into tears. Being the soft, gentle, but common fellow he is, tears and acts of incoherent magnanimity are the only expressions he has.

Dickens's command here is absolute. He puts his prose through no tortuous gymnastics in order both to understand and to judge his characters. There is a precise fit between prose and subject-matter, and because this is so he is able to use his direct moral terms – 'respectable', 'absurd', 'a great deal of good in him' – alongside the tender and tempestuous decency of Young John's mode of speech in order to make the connection between imagination and sympathy. The movement of John's speech from the grave to the tobacco-business, and the excellent candour of Dickens's judgement together verify and make real their liberal meaning. Insofar as Dickens can write and his readers can feel, the novelist and the reader are one.

Such prose can only come from a man gifted with a large and unironic generosity of spirit allied to an astonishing sense of the vitality of things. Dickens was, of course, a genius; but he took his chances from Victorian society, and *its* broad liberal temper, its largeness and lucidity, its courageous hatred of the horrors it had made. Dickens could, in other words, bring together in his prose the best of his society – the finest life it made possible – with his own vision of the good.

I shall argue that, in our own time, it is writing for children which gives the authors, lesser men and women no doubt than Dickens, the chance to bring culture and the individual spirit into one focus. It also gives them the chance to express a range of the imagination which adult writers, in response to the confusion and evasions of the times, have squeezed out of reference.

Dickens, therefore, offers the constant scale of judgement and comparison: not in stature, but in the nature of a writer's gifts and purposes. His is the writing of the fullest and most mature experience. But the special quality of his genius includes the innocence and boyishness now confined to the children's shelves. The argument of this chapter is that if such a man can shape the prose of his times to express all that is in him, he will be of Dickens's type; that on a smaller scale the best writers for children moving into adolescence do this; that the effort of matching your prose to your wisdom is the very heart of understanding human action, and its proper and justified epistemology.

2

Looking back into the
blank of my infancy

Dickens is the greatest poet of childhood who has ever written
in English. That this is so is surely due to his having retained the
faculty of which he writes so movingly in *David Copperfield*:

I believe the power of observation in numbers of very young children
to be quite wonderful for its closeness and accuracy. Indeed, I think
that most grown men who are remarkable in this respect, may with
greater propriety be said not to have lost the faculty, than to have
acquired it; the rather, as I generally observe such men to retain a
certain freshness, and gentleness, and capacity of being pleased,
which are also an inheritance they have preserved from their childhood. (p. 61)

David Copperfield may be made to stand as one of those great
classics which is great because, among other reasons, it speaks
with such eloquence and generosity of love and misery and life
and death in ways which capture the hearts and imaginations of
readers of many different ages. That short quotation catches
and places a quality to be found in good writers for children and
in adults who remember their childhood well and gladly. It is a
grace which may touch the greyest and most extinguished of
men or women, as they turn to remember their favourite
stories.

Perhaps to talk of any such re-creative absorption – not
obsessions but the healthy, the wholesome, the glad and life-
giving activities which join us together and in the sensible and
excellent cliché 'take us out of ourselves' – is to rediscover that
Dickensian strength. Many arts and crafts and maybe a few
forms of work offer an occasion for self-forgetful joy and
peace: gardening, playing music, cooking, mending odd bits
of domestic machinery, painting, playing with a calculator,
birdwatching. Many kinds of work, even in the teeth of

37

destroying noise, dirt, cold, boredom, and, no doubt, the alienations of capitalism, may be made to yield up richer satisfactions than are dreamt of in much social philosophy. Work may
be a simpler pleasure than the conscientious stereotypes allow
us to think. The divisions of labour are never more deadly than
when they separate all forms of work from play. And yet work
may be playful, and play – for the purposes of this book – is the
purposive and endless exploration of other possibilities. 'Free
play' takes place in the space won between working for a living
and the customs, rituals and routines of family life, of (in
Sweeney's words to which we shall return in Chapter 12) 'birth
and copulation and death'. Play is free both in the important
sense that you don't have to pay for it and in that it has few
limits, its rules and conventions encourage variety and
novelty, the ease and joyfulness of creating new possibilities
out of the form and its laws. Any human activity *may* break out
into an Eden where play is possible; some great heroes and
saints even manage to do so in prison. But by normal standards,
we have to keep special spaces of the culture free for 'recreation'
and what we call our leisure, by which we generally mean the
repair-time in which we can reanimate the naturally creative,
making, and speculative energies and impulses of the human
spirit.

The simplest, most perennial version of this image- and
metaphor-making faculty of every human being is storytelling. Stories fill innumerable crevices of social life brimfull:

> Now therein of all Sciences (I speak still of humane, and according to
> the humane conceits) is our Poet the Monarch. For he doth not only
> shew the way, but giveth so sweet a prospect into the way, as will
> intice any man to enter into it . . . with a tale forsooth he cometh unto
> you, with a tale which holdeth children from play, and old men from
> the chimney corner; and, pretending no more, doth intend the
> winning of the mind from wickedness to virtue.[1]

Well, there is an unbroken line of descent from Philip Sidney's
famous vignette to the pantomime Dame and female imper-
sonator of the television music hall: 'So I says to her, "Mrs
Cummins," I says. . .' What is particularly gratifying about
Sidney's remarks is that he can so unselfconsciously speak of
poetry as queen of the sciences, which seems much more satis-

---

[1] Philip Sidney, *An Apologie for Poetrie* (1595).

factory than to speak so rhetorically with Shelley of the 'unacknowledged legislators of mankind'. By 'poetry', I take him for my purposes simply to mean storytelling; and by 'science', he meant only what the sixteenth century could mean – the disciplined, inevitable effort of the Renaissance intelligence to turn systematic inquiry into reliable knowledge, to organize thought into symbols capable of holding and telling the truth about the world whether of men or of matter. What Sidney also sees, and within English literature was the first to see, is the connection between the practice of such a science and the everyday lives of ordinary old people and young children. In all societies the good storyteller is honoured; his mode of thought is a *familiar* mode of thought: it belongs indeed to the family. 'Once upon a time there was a beautiful princess. . .' The great popular texts of criticism from Sidney to Wordsworth to Leavis speak of this community of storying, the 'man speaking to men' in Wordsworth's moving phrase, the 'inevitable creativeness of ordinary everyday life', in Leavis's.

Stories are the natural way we all have for speculating about the world, or for *not* so speculating. That is to say, they may represent theories, which can be checked; or they may be acts of magic, intended to hold what is real and uncontrollable at bay. Either way, playing with stories is something we start naturally to do as children, and are encouraged in by the special forms of our culture and its shared imagination. This is the process of criticism and creation by which the mind works and the person lives. Thus, in the poet's anecdote, he sees a pretty girl, and asks:

> How can I, that girl standing there,
> My attention fix
> On Roman or on Russian
> Or on Spanish politics?
> Yet here's a travelled man that knows
> What he talks about
> And there's a politician
> That has read and thought,
> And maybe what they say is true
> Of war and war's alarms,
> But O that I were young again
> And held her in my arms.[2]

[2] W. B. Yeats, 'Politics', *Collected Poems* (1961), p. 392.

In the space between lines four and five the girl will turn her adorable face to look at me, and smile deliciously, and we shall fall at once into brilliant conversation, and ... but the newspaper or some person from Porlock admonishes me that life is real and life is earnest and I must (I truly must) turn back to the great business of the world, to the balancing of its many payments-on-both-sides, its full-and-frank-discussions and its rumours-of-wars. But O that I were young again.

In Yeats's poem, the girl wins the day. But so does the real world because he knows he isn't young again, and won't ever hold her in his arms. In the same way, in our fantasies we improve on the real world by rewarding ourselves for its not coming up to our hopes; and then we rebuke ourselves by telling ourselves off for having such impossible aspirations. Only we don't really aspire because we know we can't reach that high or far. And so on. This onward spiral of reward and rebuke[3] is the creative–critical movement of the intelligence, and its process is such that at any point of intervention it would be morally difficult to say which movement of the story was reward and which was rebuke. The girl is superseded by the much-travelled man and war's alarms; they in turn are dissolved by the girl, and Yeats is left longing, and knowing that his longing is just that. The poem stops but not the process of fiction. And who knows, one day things may be different, and the girl *will* turn ... etc. etc.

It is in these ways that we think at all about our lives. The process of fiction is insistently and necessarily reciprocal and dialectic. Faced with choices by experience, we go back over the road which brought us to these alternatives, and forward to imagine how they may look in the future. We interrogate the past in order to win from it believable pictures of the future.[4]

There are no guarantees in this process that our fictions are sure inoculations against foolishness. The stories we have stored up in the culture may turn out to be drastically misleading or irrelevant or plain false. Falsehood itself is, by definition, a difficult thing to spot. Charles Tomlinson writes, 'the artist lies/ For the improvement of truth. Believe him',[5] and this

[3] Terms I take from an unpublished paper and a conversation with Dan Jacobson, to whom I am most grateful.
[4] I paraphrase an argument taken from Andrew Harrison in *Making and Thinking* (1979), especially chaps. 6 and 8.
[5] In 'A Meditation on John Constable', *A Peopled Landscape* (1960).

paradox merely emphasizes that *War and Peace*, which is a
fiction, tells us more about the real history, the life-in-earnest
which history once was, than any history of Napoleon's
expedition to Russia. Conversely, some purportedly true
stories may be drafted in the service of sentimental lies miles
away from all usefulness or truthtelling. There is a deep tension
in our culture between the old nursery injunction, 'Don't tell
tales' and the famous vignette of Philip Sidney's. Alongside
Sidney, however, not only do the old eighteenth-century
gentilities still strike an echo – that 'What are you reading?'
'Oh, just a novel'– but so does an even earlier Puritanism which
in Hawthorne's New England proscribed fiction because it
was a lie. And even now, which of us is not brought up sharp by
the information that the story before us is true, that it has the
compelling absoluteness of accomplished fact?

There is, I suppose, no getting away from the fact that we
respond differently to a story which we know to be true. But
when we tell each other a true story, we intend – as we say in
another vivid, domestic phrase – 'that it lose nothing in the
telling'. Telling the tale involves us in trying to recreate the life
that the events really had as they happened. And to do that we
inevitably compress, reshape, select, and exclude from the
impossibly rich mess of actual events in order to rip out the
essential structure of the event and to make out what it really
means. 'What it really means' is itself a tricky phrase, and it is
my contention – without launching into the abstractions of the
philosophy of social science – that we count ourselves as
understanding a piece of social action (a story, that is) insofar as
we can make sense of it; and that making sense is a matter of
testing the action against our criteria of judgement, both
rational and aesthetic. That is by no means all there is to be said
about understanding social actions and the way people describe
them to us – it doesn't, for instance, leave a large enough place
for our tolerance of the unintelligible as justifiable to the author
himself – but it will do by way of emphasizing the identities
within our various responses to what people tell us of other
people's lives.

In other words, there is no break between our response to the
social actions we watch *and* take part in, those which are
described to us by others – gossip, if you like – and the stories
which we and others make up, the fictions. The truism is that

from babyhood onwards, we join a community of stories
which we each of us adjust to suit our place in the world and
make it intelligible. The blank truism is only broken into
enlightenment when we look at the stories themselves. Such
looking is, in that useful phrase, practical criticism.

The stories may, as I noted, be true or false, good or bad,
useful or useless. Just as all philosophy is a footnote to Plato, so
all developmental psychology might take *The Prelude* as its
essential dictionary. Wordsworth, first and greatest of the
theorists of childhood launched by the Romantic movement,
takes us into the mystery of the fact that culture and being act on
each other to make both the individual and his world.

> Emphatically such a Being lives,
> Frail creature as he is, helpless as frail,
> An inmate of this active universe:
> For feeling has to him imparted power
> That through the growing faculties of sense
> Doth like an agent of the one great Mind
> Create, creator and receiver both,
> Working but in alliance with the works
> Which it beholds. – Such, verily, is the first
> Poetic spirit of our human life,
> By uniform control of after years,
> In most, abated or suppressed; in some,
> Through every change of growth and of decay,
> Pre-eminent till death.[6]

As Wordsworth notes, the shaping or fiction-making spirit
may be thoroughly suppressed as well as cultivated by
circumstances. Indeed, suppression, abatement, what Ted
Hughes calls 'the lobotomy of the national imagination',
seemed to him then as to us now just a more likely consequence
of the child's assimilation of the culture than that the spirit
should be kept 'pre-eminent till death'. Wordsworth's great
poem, however, was written in the effort to show how the pre-
eminence might be sustained in the teeth of the recurrent
tendency of the social world to regulate and distinguish and
straighten out, against which he affirmed the blessedness of
uncertainty, richness, over- and undergrowth, the incorrigible
beauty of unplanned and untheoretic life. In Book v of *The
Prelude*, entitled simply, 'Books', he summons a great roll-call

6 William Wordsworth, *The Prelude*, Book II, ll. 252–65.

of childish heroes and heroines to stand for all that unrepentant, formless energy out of which, in the teeth of the curriculum planners, children weave the essential form of themselves, and draw a template for their children's children.

> Oh! give us once again the wishing-cap
> Of Fortunatus, and the invisible coat
> Of Jack the Giant-killer, Robin Hood,
> And Sabra in the forest with St. George!
> The child, whose love is here at least, doth reap
> One precious gain, that he forgets himself.
> These mighty workmen of our later age,
> Who, with a broad highway, have overbridged
> The froward chaos of futurity,
> Tamed to their bidding; they who have the skill
> To manage books, and things, and make them act
> On infant minds as surely as the sun
> Deals with a flower; the keepers of our time,
> The guides and wardens of our faculties,
> Sages who in their prescience would control
> All accidents, and to the very road
> Which they have fashioned would confine us down,
> Like engines; when will their presumption learn,
> That in the unreasoning progress of the world
> A wiser spirit is at work for us,
> A better eye than theirs, most prodigal
> Of blessings, and most studious of our good,
> Even in what seem our most unfruitful hours?[7]

Wordsworth knew the vast insurgency of these heroes. Fortunatus, Jack the Giant-killer, and the rest are the names of the imagination for the lawlessness and resistance, the excellent stubbornness of the human heart.[8] They are ways of asserting a different order against the way things are and have to be. Robin Hood is a robber, but utterly uncommon in his selflessness and courage, his generosity and indestructible gaiety; like England, his men were merry. Jack the Giant-killer, strongly disapproved of by the teachers of the early nineteenth century who were Wordsworth's contemporaries, was an admirable version of the diminutive cunning which can overthrow the brute power of giants, both domestic and political.

In all such tales Wordsworth recognized one ancient,

---

[7] *Prelude*, Book v, ll. 341–63.
[8] They have a recent historian in Gillian Avery, *Childhood's Pattern* (1975).

subversive strength of literature: that it always acts as a critic and a creator of the world in which it lives. To say so is not to fall into a cosy denim radicalism – the sort which dismisses Jane Austen as a snob and commends Zola because he writes about coal-miners. A conservative order may well be preferable to the best-intentioned chaos and old night; spontaneity and sincerity may be sadistic and horrible; honesty may be a lousy moral policy; parents may know lots better than children. But insofar as the best contribution of English life, literature, and thought to the advancement of learning and the state of nations has been poetry and fiction, it is because these latter have sought out a powerfully contextual moralism, whose situation is the actuality of particular poems and works. Its characteristic national idiom is protestant, dissident, nonconformist, and if the strength of its churches is now to be found cherished in its fiction, there are worse places for it to be. Its liturgy elevates doubts, qualifications, ambiguities, a fertility of multiple meaning, as its host. Its heretics are quickly become its saints. At the same time, one adds that such an idiom and tradition can all too quickly fill a frame of mind-killing philistinism and spirit-killing scepticism.

For better and worse, the English idiom found a national home in the house of fiction. Its peculiarly individualist temper, its firm demarcation of private from public, its opposition of the individual to society, both as its hero and as its victim, all found ample accommodation in the novel, as created and exported by the liberal imagination. On this account, the novel is a formal, technical version of the science everyone practises. Its idiom seeks, of necessity, to find its morality in discrete contexts. It has to. The inheritance of the protestant and empirical moral spirit is such that it must work not from general precepts but from particular situations. The novel is the best way to think through each strenuous moral struggle in the explicit detail which it demands. That has been the vast strength of the form as it developed through the achievements of the Victorians, and the novelists of today seek to accommodate the moral changes of which they are, among others, the custodians, within that loose, baggy, capacious structure. In novels for children, we find, as we would expect, the explicitness made even more direct – to the point of simplification. The lesson I want to labour is that novels for children are adult messages, bidding the children farewell into the future. So those fictions above all are offered to children to take with them and adjust to what they find for themselves.

In that case, as I said in the first chapter, it isn't enough to study the children's novels *tout court*. We need to keep a decently and tactfully pedagogical eye on what the children are likely to make of them. And because in this part of the book I have sought to light up the manifold relations of theory and experience as, in and out of the academies, we seek to hold them together, it may give the argument the concrete life it seeks to turn briefly to a biographical fragment of one individual reader, a man born just before Hitler's war, always an abandoned and lavish reader, surrounded throughout childhood and schooling by books and left to read them as he liked; going on from this generous, always happy sense of the plenty and possibility of literature to its formal study under, among others, the greatest teacher of English the English universities have ever known.

The point in turning to my own experience is, as before, more than personal. For those who are lucky, remembering the stories they read as children is a delighted, gleeful sharing: 'One precious gain, that he forgets himself'. In remembering the stories loved and lost in childhood, the stories in which the now grown men and women were once lost, the utter extemporal absorption at the top of the stairs, in bed under the bedclothes with a torch, behind the sofa, perched on a swing, lying on damp, warm cut grass, on the hot sand, in the brimming bath, in these keen remembrances they are joined again in a vivid life which their culture occasionally makes it possible to share. This is what we mean by recreation.

In his *Autobiography* Edwin Muir writes of the 'fable' which stands largely overshadowing the conscious life we lead. As one speaks of the fable, it seems to prefigure in its vast outline the life of every man, and every man checks his own actual life against the enormous potentiality of this other story, of the person he is not and can never be. This aura of potential life moves and dispenses in our dreams as well as in our reflections, and I think it is what we strive to catch in the net of our reading.

It is clear that no autobiography can begin with a man's birth, that we extend far beyond any boundary line which we can set for ourselves in the past or the future, and that the life of every man is an endless repeated performance of the life of man. It is clear for the same reason that no autobiography can confine itself to conscious life, and that sleep, in which we pass a third of our existence, is a mode of experience, and our dreams a part of reality. In themselves our conscious lives may not be particularly interesting. But what we are not and can never be, our fable, seems to me inconceivably interesting. I should like to write that fable, but I cannot even live it; and all I could do if I related the outward course of my life would be to show how I have deviated from it; though even that is impossible, since I do not know the fable or anybody who knows it. One or two stages in it I can recognize; the age of innocence and the Fall and all the dramatic consequences which issue from the Fall. But these lie behind experience, not on its surface; they are not historical events; they are stages in the fable.[9]

To go back to the reading you did as a child is to try to see how you made yourself out of the fable, and all that you inevitably missed, denied, abated, and put down. For the premise of this book is that the fables you read as a child are the brightest and the best you ever encounter.

Begin with comics. When we turn back to those immortal figures, Korky the Cat, Desperate Dan, Lord Snooty, we are returning to moments of irrecoverable vividness and joyfulness, against which the present can only seem banal. Lord Snooty and his pals belong to the age of radical innocence, which moves in and out of the fabulous at will and without its even being clear which of two worlds is more real. There never were such teachers in mortar-boards carrying such thick canes, there never was a paradise in which Lord Snooty was at one with the working class: Scrapper Smith, Happy Huggins, Skinny Lizzie, the two weird baby twins Snitchy and Snatchy and, even more brilliantly improbable, Gertie the Goat. There could never be such cow-pies as Desperate Dan ate, pudding-basin and all, nor such a bristly jaw as could ignite whole forests, nor such a fist as struck down walls and houses (but never other men). Dilly Dreeme, the lovable duffer, Lettice Leefe, Hungry Horace, Dennis the Menace, Weary Willie and Tired Tim join the throngs of these shades in a busy, insubstantial and immortal limbo, where souls wait for ever. Their ancestors walk the tall tales of a millennium, making a

[9] Edwin Muir, *An Autobiography* (1968), pp. 48–9.

brief bow in Shakespeare and Dickens at a time when the opportunity was there for an imagination of genius to seize upon everything in popular culture, and then going back to haunt comics, and music halls, and animated cartoons.

These characters offered an extraordinary pleasure. It was one of many striking insights in that remarkable film *Kes* to note that a comic was and is taken in by children in complete gravity. Billy Caspar reads the *Dandy* with utter absorption and an expressionless face.

I remember the flatness of Mondays and Fridays when no comic was delivered for my sisters and me. We were a comfortably off family, and my parents strikingly tolerant as well as generous: they encouraged us to read as much as we could and while, as parents should, they screened what came into the house, they were admirably and lightheartedly liberal in what they gave us to read. *Dandy* and *Beano* came out on alternate Tuesdays, as they still do, and were delivered with the morning paper. On Wednesday, so were *Knockout* and *School Friend*; on Thursday, *Girl* and the *Rover* or the *Adventure*, depending which football or cricket serial I was following – I changed loyalties to the Thursday comic as often as I did from cornflakes to Weetabix; but all the others were fixed points in the changeless landscape in which my mother and father were such solid, fixed, and living proof that the world was uniform, harmonious, and untouched by time. That is why my sisters and I went on reading comics when an outsider might have thought they were too childish for us. The experience of living within the solidities of my family made us unconscious, as children naturally are, of change and the marks of time. More mature reading came along with the comics, and happily co-existed with them. I read *Dandy* and *Knockout* beside *Kidnapped* with no sense of incongruity. We fell upon the comics and squabbled over precedence because they were the margins of an organized day which remained magic and separate. We knew what was in them, and yet anything might be in them. Not only that. We could master their strangeness and surprises immediately. In a world subject to the arbitrary proscriptions of adult legislation, we read the comics fast, and they magically debarred the incomprehensibility of boredom.

Perhaps television has done the same for children born, let us say, since the IBA charter was granted in 1954, and a TV

became part of the accepted furniture of every household.[10] I
don't know. I do know that I came down to read the comics at
breakfast time (the only meal at which we could read at table)
with a sense of delicious expectation. My sisters wrangled
about who should read which on the bus to school. I kept the
boys' comics, and when I turned to the long prose stories, I
took off into a world which captured and held me, staring-eyed
and focussed only upon the unbroken columns of tight print
until I came out at the end.[11] Reading Nick Smith, the
Incredible Wilson, Rockfist Rogan, and the rest was hardly *like*
reading Korky the Kat or Big Eggo (the ostrich, for heaven's
sake). We read the comic-strip stories in a different spirit. It's
hard to catch now, but I think that the crazy banality of those
serials, their endless release of the forces of misrule, marked out
a secret garden to which the comics guaranteed entrance and in
which a trivial riotous pointlessness eternally obtained. There
is nothing intended here about the provision of 'security'
which some of the gentler, goofier spirits amongst primary
teachers sometimes claim for comics. Korky is not so much a
security against the inanity of the world as he is both
circumscribed and unpredictable, like an early Disney
character or a quantum particle. You never know what he will
do, but he will do it according to his own laws of motion,
which are held in by the frames of the pictures.

It was quite different with Wilson, Alf Tupper, Nick Smith,
and Baldy Hogan. I wanted so much to believe in the reality of
the football stories that I quarrelled quite passionately on the
top deck of a bus with a sceptical friend who insisted there was
no such person as Nick Smith. Like the other heroes, Nick
Smith, who was captain of one of those blankly named, non-
existent Midland towns which have disfigured the map of
literary England since Barchester (Ambridge is with us yet),
was, rightly and unironically, a footballer and sportsman of
complete probity and honour. The core of the week's episode
was always announced in the single illustration, itself (like the
stories) rather in the style of Socialist Realism, with broad-
shouldered, heavy-muscled, expressionlessly handsome

---

[10] 40% in 1956; 91% in 1977 – 53% of them in colour (*Social Trends*, HMSO 1979).
[11] It is a measure of the victory of the image over the word – a victory, at least in part, for
unreason – that these prose stories have now been replaced by pictures. See J. J. Taylor,
'The Reading of Comics by Secondary Schoolchildren', *Use of English*, 24, 1 (1972).

giants scoring impossible goals with whizz-marks behind the ball.

One week Nick Smith was being sent off in the illustration! It transpired that, partly concussed in a collision, he subsequently couldn't see an opponent whom he unintentionally fouled. His good name was only cleared when the referee saw him walk heavily into the edge of a dressing-room door which was straight in his line of vision, and realized that the hero's excuse was entirely truthful. The point is that his good name had to be cleared, for as in all these stories, the hero remains consistently and unselfquestioningly admirable. Like Roy Rogers on Trigger and the Lone Ranger on Silver, the sportsmen are excellent by virtue of their actions, not their motives. The essential structure is assertive – the hero tensed against the events. In himself he is finite and circumscribed – unconscious, so to speak, but all-powerful. He stands in the line of the chivalrous and knightly men who have embodied the central virtues of the West in its stories since the Provençal troubadours first took to the road. Nick Smith and the Lone Ranger have no need to be gentlemen any more than they are knights: their honour is synonymous with their manhood.

It is a tricky point. But a structural strength of these simple tales is that role and identity are one. There is no strain or gap between how a footballer (or cowboy or fighter pilot) ought to be and how this man behaves. Individual integrity is perfectly satisfied by the definition of the role and its duties. A main shift in the values we live by has, in real life, made this definition often a breaking strain for many people. Their sense of themselves insists upon its own claims as paramount – 'I have a duty to myself.' While the fact of this struggle, and the battles won or lost in the name either of individual integrity or of loyalty and duty to an institution, is present in so much adult experience and its fictions, it is fitting that the simple, single structure of what we tell children should hold out the chance of beatitude. A fortunate man may be able to hold together his pictures of himself and his responsibility to the world. The heroes of popular culture have no difficulty in doing so.

Alf Tupper, the tough of the track, was an interesting example of this effortless unity of desire and actuality. For he was an exaggeratedly working-class hero, who lived in dreadful squalor in a derelict home with smashed windows beside a railway bridge, and ran through the wet nights across broken tarmac, under the black shadow of the dockside hulls, along the canal behind the gasworks. He was a prophetic figure. Many real working-class runners have followed him on the same harsh and lumpy cinders. Alf Tupper could only run well on fish and chips, that evocative class emblem, although the sporting accuracy demanded by the reader of *Rover*, *Wizard*, *Adventure*, *Hotspur* also required that he train properly and do believable times on the track. He was constantly put down by the snobberies of those who ran athletics (much truth there!) and unfailingly put them down in his turn by winning. All his readers, in and out of private schools, were on his side because the snobs were obviously awful and in the wrong, and his toughness simply confirmed his integrity by its lack of fancy frills. It was never in question, to himself or anyone else; he was as innocent and independent as Tom Jones.

The cowboy movies – with heroes such as Roy Rogers, Gene Autry, the Lone Ranger – and in the same genre, Johnny Weissmuller as Tarzan, together with the comics, like so much popular culture, inhabit a classless prehistory. They represent the democratic dream which surfaces ingenuously in so much of the fiction provided for children (all those parentless holidays), and in which society imagines its own best aspirations fulfilled without a struggle. The timeless view of life characterizes childhood, and it makes the dream of immortality unquestionable. A child's world is or ought to be folded in a vast and boundless calm; when it is not, then surely a timeless and placeless justice has been violated. In Edwin Muir's words, 'That world was a perfectly solid world, for the days did not undermine it but merely rounded it, or rather repeated it, as if there were only one day endlessly rising and setting.'

Class is at once too obvious and too irrelevant a term to apply to children's fiction. Its undoubted presence (whatever it is) has to be faced and grasped. But I think that children's reading, whatever class messages may be carried to the necessarily class-conscious adult, is always and endlessly capable of being relocated in the classless paradise. Indeed, this is surely true of all morality. The most vacuous abuse is levelled by raucous tongues at so-called middle-class values in and out of school, and regularly in the columns of those well-known proletarian organs *New Society* and the *Guardian*.[12] But to speak of classless values is another way of appealing to trans-historical values; and although values take their special content and cadence from a particular local history, it makes sense to speak of courage, candour, trustworthiness, and truth as meaning something in all historical circumstances – in the Trojan ditch, outside Harfleur, at Bloemfontein, or on the picket lines. Teaching a proper recognition of the provisionality of values has led us – and contemporary children's novelists in the van – to put so much stress on the relativism and personal nature of values that it becomes extremely difficult to use the words 'truth' and 'goodness' without being dismissed (and derided) as an absolutist or, worse still, 'theological'.

But what, after all, *is* a value? It is, I take it, a way of gathering within a single field of moral force a diverse range of behaviours, qualities, and actions which are generally approved of. It is of the nature of things that items in such a range may be included or excluded according to historical location. To stick to examples of military honour, it would be chivalrous in an Elizabethan aristocrat to allow an opponent to pick up the weapon he dropped, and foolish in an Ulster policeman. But it is true that what the word courage means remains more or less the same, even across hundreds of years and thousands of miles.

It is part of the timeless quality in a child's view of the world that he or she learns and reverences values quite innocent of any relative qualifications. *Huckleberry Finn* is the best fictional example of that truth, for there Huck names as lies or cruelty or beastliness all the behaviour which is so, quite without fogging the judgements in adult clouds of subjunctives. Huck tells the truth, and he does so in order to get at what we – and all children – most seek from life, which is justice, or fairness.[13] He has to

---

[12] Cf. a *New Society* example of a particularly plonking and humourless kind. I am grateful to Peter Hollindale for showing it to me:

'There are two major attitudes in [Beatrix Potter's] books that have made them important as nursery literature, as opposed to children's books. These are the twin upper-class (and bourgeois by short-range assimilation) attitudes to animals – that one loves them but that they are also killed – and towards the concept of a hierarchical system in society – that there are gardeners and washerwomen in the natural order of things. The latter was clearly true in Miss Potter's day when it would have been unexceptionable, but now it can only implant or reinforce an unachronistic [*sic*] view of society at an early age.'

[13] Terms first put together by John Rawls in a preliminary essay, 'Justice as Fairness', for his book *A Theory of Justice* (1972).

struggle with himself to act fairly towards Jim, no doubt; but he *knows* what is the right thing to do, as opposed to the comfortable betraying of the runaway slave which would earn him his society's approval. He shows a moral purity which is not innocent of relative judging, but confutes it.

It is this quality which we admire in children and fear to lose. Blake's poems *Songs of Innocence and of Experience* express in their antinomy this essential notion in human life. Lose your innocence, he tells us with his own version of Christ at his back, and you shall hardly escape damnation; but experience will come to us and bring a wisdom which only the continued life of our childish innocence can prevent from being tainted by the maturity which tilts with cynicism and apathy, tolerance of the intolerable, and finally despair.

It is in this way that we may speak of classlessness in children's reading. To a contemporary liberal parent's muscle-bound self-consciousness, the main message of those intermittently awful books in which from eight or nine onwards I saturated my imagination would be what is undoubtedly there: their relentless snobbery, their incipient Fascism, their arrogance and brutality. But the fierce delight I found in *Bulldog Drummond* was not in releasing God knows what adolescent anti-semitism; it sprang from pure admiration for the reckless, athletic courage of the hero, the simplicity and vividness of his moral and pugnacious reflexes, and, within the terms of the novel, his sense of fairness, his taste for schoolboy humour and lightheartedness which, since I was a schoolboy, was my taste as well. Fairness may look a queer word to use of the man who, faced with the hunchback Jew of amazing physical strength, 'could not find it in himself to fight him as he would an ordinary man, and therefore flogged him with a rhinoceros hide whip until his arm ached, and then flung him down the stairs, where he lay cursing'. The deep satisfaction with which I relished that (I'm quoting from memory) was not, I like to think, due to my suppressed racialism neatly conjoined to my respectable distaste for the deformed, but to a sense of due order and an eager admiration for its direct and manly restoration. A murderous crook had been rightly punished. By this same token, the shifty and shiftless provocateurs of the unemployed in the same novel (*The Black Gang*) are whisked away to a remote island, in what is, given their underhand and self-seeking cowardice, a perfectly just way. The political message did not bother me. On that world-view, Drummond acted as squarely as Biggles always did. And I drank deeply from both Sapper and his smaller edition in the boys' league, W. E. Johns.

Now it is no doubt impossible to be drunk on such writing, and not to absorb some at least of the heavy moral fumes given off by such authors. I knew the four rounds of Bulldog Drummond with Carl Peterson, and the books of W. E. Johns, Percy F. Westerman, Taffrail, and half a dozen others intimately. In all these writers, as in their betters of the same kidney, Buchan and Kipling, there is a range of moral attitudes which have hardly been made obsolete by the march of history since they were always clearly repellent. But there are no less deathless and finer attitudes there as well. It is a tricky piece of introspection to decide what it was that proved so pleasurable to a twelve-year-old in such a passage as this:

Then I learned a truth I have never forgotten. If you are fighting a man who means to kill you, he will be apt to down you unless you mean to kill him too. Stumm did not know any rules to this game, and I forgot to allow for that. Suddenly, when I was watching his eyes, he launched a mighty kick at my stomach. If he had got me, this yarn would have had an abrupt ending. But by the mercy of God I was moving sideways when he let out, and his heavy boot just grazed my left thigh.

It was the place where most of the shrapnel had lodged, and for a second I was sick with pain and stumbled. Then I was on my feet again but with a new feeling in my blood. I had to smash Stumm or never sleep in my bed again.

I got a wonderful power from this new cold rage of mine. I felt I couldn't tire, and I danced round and dotted his face till it was streaming with blood. His bulky padded chest was no good to me, so I couldn't try for the mark.

He began to snort now and his breath came heavily. 'You infernal cad,' I said in good round English, 'I'm going to knock the stuffing out of you,' but he didn't know what I was saying.

Then at last he gave me my chance. He half tripped over a little table and his face stuck forward. I got him on the point of the chin, and put every ounce of weight I possessed behind the blow. He crumpled up in a heap and rolled over, upsetting a lamp and knocking a big china jar in two. His head, I remember, lay under the escritoire from which he had taken my passport. (John Buchan, *Greenmantle*, p. 129)

The enemy is beastly and bullying; physically he is hard as granite and gigantic also, but it is a grotesque, brutish strength. There is no beauty in it. The German will kill Richard Hannay if he can, and concentrated in the traditional image of the single sweet knockout punch is the manliness, the just retribution, the bravery, the athletic sureness, which can only command admiration. The pleasure is a consequence of the admiration and the satisfying roundedness of the event. To that extent a child's enjoyment is aesthetic: the event is well shaped and highly compressed.

But of course the response can't be simply aesthetic or simply moral. It is also social. And so, as a child, I undoubtedly took in the strong social and political loadings of John Buchan, and took them in not so much through the local stereotypes which have their hilarious side – the Prussian Colonel has a bullneck, duelling scars and a close-cropped square head; the beautiful spy is lithe, exquisite, terrifying, and haughty – but through, as we say, the atmosphere of the book. I fairly breathed in the intense moral idealism of the adventure novels about men shaped by the public schools. The intensity of this idealism is present only in the negative in most of the best-known biographies to come out of the English public schools, and those were written forty or fifty years ago – I am thinking of Cyril Connolly's *Enemies of Promise*, Stephen Spender's autobiography, Robert Graves's *Goodbye to All That*, much of George Orwell, and a dozen lesser books. These writers were all dissident; they were intent on identifying the hypocrisies of ruling-class idealism, and never saw its power and its deep, tense, contradictions. To borrow a phrase,[14] until quite recently – say, the early 1960s – all leading boys at public school were trained up to sing the most passionate tenor arias of selfless aspiration and devotion, but to a non-existent heroine. It was an objectless and utter yearning.

Most boys came through it in one piece, no doubt. But not without loss. When they encountered the blocks and blankness of an adult life with no room to express the ideals, many retreated from the awful gap between their desires and the humdrum actuality by hiding in cynicism, or adultery, or daydreams. Buchan's values rested on the war economy of a liberal

[14] From Jim Hunter, *The Flame* (1966), itself a study of the same idealism without an end.

ruling class. That is why they throve so strongly in postwar public schools and propaganda movies. But the gap between Buchan and the present takes the measure of a drastic break in continuity. The revived economies and the reconstruction of Europe after 1945 created – in a slogan – the ethics of the consumer and his higher self, the free, distinctive individual. By the middle of the 1960s the drive towards this much more individualist ethic, which recent children's writers, like any artists, have tried to absorb, understand, resist, and nurture, had swept aside the old-style idealism which found such crude, powerful expression in Buchan, Kipling, Jack London, Baroness Orczy, Rider Haggard, and as you grew out of them, Conrad and Dorothy Sayers. But when I went to Oundle in 1950, bold and shy, eager to win all the trophies the place held and tearfully homesick at the same time, I hid, in the short solitudes the place permitted the free spirit – Sundays, odd halfhours here or there – in the solid worlds of complete, cased editions of Kipling and Buchan and company until my whole small soul had disappeared into their operatic world, its heraldic drama, its foreshortened but sweeping historical movement, its moral battlecries.

The special savour of this heady, heavy mixture comes out in the plangent notes with which Buchan ends *Mr Standfast*. The references to *Pilgrim's Progress* are a test of cultivation in our times. I first read Bunyan at the age of eleven, and was swept up by the music of the Authorized Version and its epic scale into the same empyrean blue as John Buchan. Unless a child feels right through him the movement of those cadences, he simply will not be able to hear the music of most of seventeenth-century literature, or a good deal thereafter. To that extent, as I have said, he won't be able to understand his history. But those cadences may be fatally misleading. Their echoes, here transposed to the portly complacencies of Edwardian Anglicanism, moved this reader then, as now, to tears:

But I did not need him to tell me the name, for I had divined it when I first saw the new plane drop from the clouds. I had that queer sense that comes sometimes to a man that a friend is present when he cannot see him.

Somewhere up in the void two heroes were fighting their last battle – and one of them had a crippled leg.

I had never any doubt about the result, though Archie told me later that he went crazy with suspense. Lensch was not aware of his opponent till he was almost upon him, and I wonder if by any freak of instinct he recognised his greatest antagonist. He never fired a shot, nor did Peter . . . I saw the German twist and side-slip as if to baffle the fate descending upon him. I saw Peter veer over vertically and I knew that the end had come. He was there to make certain of victory and he took the only way . . . The machines closed, there was a crash which I felt though I could not hear it, and next second both were hurtling down, over and over, to the earth.

They fell in the river just short of the enemy lines, but I did not see them, for my eyes were blinded and I was on my knees.

After that it was all a dream. I found myself being embraced by a French General of Division, and saw the first companies of the cheerful bluecoats whom I had longed for. With them came the rain, and it was under a weeping April sky that early in the night I marched what was left of my division away from the battle-field. The enemy guns were starting to speak behind us, but I did not heed them. I knew that now there were warders at the gate, and I believed that by the grace of God that gate was barred for ever. (*The Four Adventures of Richard Hannay*, III, *Mr Standfast*, p. 371)

Kipling was the supreme master of these effects. I return to him in Chapter 6, and here it must do to say that children, as things are, *listen* to stories far more than adults. Reading is a skill not so easily or so long ago acquired that they have silenced it and made words on a page only visual. Children can hear a story, if only they will; an oral and a print culture are not so separate in their world. Kipling's greatness is one which, as we know, is not proof against corruption, over-ripeness, decadence, a sentimentality of the nursery and a prurience of the torture-chamber. The special eloquence of his full, brassy prose may be, as Buchan's may be – together with the cheaper effects of cheaper writers – betraying. Betrayed to what? I think I would claim that a boy or girl of twelve or thirteen grows up by surrendering to the irresistible swell of such cadences as these; but in doing so, they each are captivated by feelings their best selves will one day want to control: at times to put them down, at times to be carried away by them:

The man uncovered his face. 'I thought they would stone me,' he said. 'I did not know I spoke before a King.' He came to his full towering height – no mean man, but frail beyond belief.

The King turned to the tables, and held him out his own cup of wine. The old man drank, and beckoned behind him, and, before all the Normans, my Hugh bore away the empty cup, Saxon-fashion, upon the knee.

'It is Harold!' said De Aquila. 'His own stiff-necked blood kneels to service him.'

'Be it so,' said Henry. 'Sit, then, thou that hast been Harold of England.'

The madman sat, and hard, dark Henry looked at him between half-shut eyes. We others stared like oxen, all but De Aquila who watched Rahere as I have seen him watch a far sail on the sea.

The wine and the warmth cast the old man into a dream. His white head bowed; his hands hung. His eye indeed was opened, but the mind was shut. When he stretched his feet, they were scurfed and road-cut like a slave's.

'Ah, Rahere,' cried Hugh, 'why hast thou shown him thus? Better have let him die than shame him – and me!'

'Shame thee?' said the King. 'Would any baron of mine kneel to me if I were witless, discrowned, and alone, and Harold had my throne?'
(*Rewards and Fairies*, p. 267)

If a child never learns to feel the power, elementary and thrilling as it is, of such music, there is a stop, a blankness in its sensibility *and* its intelligence. It is a tricky thing to say, but the living-through of such self-surrender, of such captivation, is a way of both learning the feeling and being capable of knowing and acting by the moral quality.

I used to read those lines time and again, and each time the queer, crisp ripple of excitement tingled along my spine; the brimming tears which never quite fell, the chokey lump in the throat, were the result of having too much response to the passage and that response not knowing what to do with itself. You see the same in children in the right mood listening to a well-read story in the classroom; when it ends, their eyes are brimming, they don't say anything, and they yawn hugely and stretch. To be able to feel the proper wonder and admiration at the death of King Harold, the forty years' loyalty of Hugh (Kipling has *King Lear* audibly on his mind) is necessary in order to be capable of patriotism. This is not to say that a feeling *causes* a moral, in this case, patriotic quality to exist in a person, or causes someone to act patriotically. Feelings are not the sole basis of ethics any more than motives are. But in order to act intentionally as a patriot (or indeed, as in the case of Hugh, as a gentle knight), it must be possible for someone to 'know the feeling', as we say, and understand what the word means.

When I used to read and re-read Kipling and company, the institution in which I was reading was itself still strongly patriotic. In the 1950s, the appeal to patriotism could still confidently be made, with greater strength no doubt to the propertied classes, but still in a trans-class and intelligibly national way. I grew up in a moral climate in which patriotism was a necessary value not only for the maintenance of self-respect – it justified the killing of men and women, vengefully and in huge numbers – but needful also to bind up social divisions and deep wounds, to give meaning to the killing overwork and dreadful drudgery in factories, air-raid shelters, and the *Blitzkrieg*, to clear an ethical space where other virtues like heroism, selflessness, courage, without which the war could not be won and lost, could flourish.

These precepts thrived in the idealizing, rather abstract, thin air of an English public school. As with so much moral education, especially in a relativizing age, they lacked 'middle axioms' when it came to living in a polity; that is, it was hard to know how to translate precepts of heroism, leadership, courage, and selflessness into action. (Hence the cynicism of so many old-school-tied businessmen.) But Kipling's kind of writing resounded off the high, clear marble of such an Aegean morality in rolling echoes. The schoolboy who responded to this prose used it to give experience and context to the rather spectral virtues such schools then embodied.

Such writing fairly glowed in so much of the poetry I loved. And why shouldn't it? For the virtues of heroism and candour, and so forth, which any man may think of as classless, must be felt to be known. For all that we have in the past 50 years and more seen the name of patriotism used to cover so much ghastliness and cruelty, it remains a strong potential for good. What a child *does* with Kipling, as with any other writer, may lead to good or evil. The sentimentalizing of childhood is an Anglo-American vice, and we should never warm to the insistence of occasionally priggish librarians and school teachers and books like this one if they press for the young to read wholesome literature, or not at all. Minds, like bodies, grow strong only with some strain and risk. Not only that: children, like adults, may take from books what their authors or the approving parents never intended them to take, or dreamed they could find. I constantly sought out that plangency of cadence which stirred my yearning for high ideals, and which slithered so thrillingly along my back. I found it in the grand, round movement of the poems I had to learn by heart, and those which simply stole it away.

Long before I knew their names, I was caught up and made dizzy by the joy and rich satisfaction of the internal assonance, the swiftness and onward movement of these rhymes, their juicy mystery:

> Ay; though we hunted high and low
> And hunted everywhere,
> Of the three men's fate we found no trace
> Of any kind in any place,
> But a door ajar and an untouched meal
> And an overtoppled chair. ('Flannan Isle')

Anything ringing or haunting, anything grand, with great names in it, anything ghostly enchanted me. A strange, palsied, portly old bluestocking taught us when I was eleven. I learned by heart and loved from my heart 'Drake's Drum', spoken in a clear, cut-glass treble, Newbolt's 'He Fell Among Thieves', Chesterton's 'The Donkey' (and giggled myself sick in the back row transposing all the initial letters of the last verse) and 'The Secret People', Masefield's 'The Rider at the Gate', Kipling's 'Mine-sweepers', with its glorious rollcall of incongruous ships' names, the 'Ode to a Nightingale', the 'Wife of Usher's Well', 'Helen of Kirkonell', and most piercingly remembered of all, de la Mare's 'The Listeners'. As Keats wrote in one of his letters, 'How can I help bringing to your mind the Line', so I cannot help quoting Walter de la Mare:

> 'Tell them I came, and no one answered,
>   That I kept my word,' he said.
> Never the least stir made the listeners,
>   Though every word he spake
> Fell echoing through the shadowiness of the still house
>   From the one man left awake:
> Ay, they heard his foot upon the stirrup,
>   And the sound of iron on stone,
> And how the silence surged softly backward,

> When the plunging hoofs were gone.
> ('The Listeners', in *Collected Poems*)

It was the fullest combination of ingredients I was looking for: the ghostly listeners in an empty house, the vividly presented scene in the forest, the echoes of knightliness sounded by any horsemen, the easy, plain pace of the verse, the appeal to a manly uprightness – "I kept my word," he said.' And even now, I know it by heart. I speak its splendid words without looking down, and, in the words of a greater poem,

> The house was quiet and the world was calm.
> The reader became the book; and summer night
> Was like the conscious being of the book.
> The house was quiet and the world was calm.
> The words were spoken as if there was no book
> Except that the reader leaned above the page...
> (Wallace Stevens, 'The House was Quiet', in *Collected Poems*)

'The reader became the book'... and yet it is myself who am thrilled to the bones by these glowing cadences. D. H. Lawrence had written most evocatively of his experience:[15]

Nothing is more difficult than to determine what a child takes in, and does not take in, of its environment and its teaching. This fact is brought home to me by the hymns which I learnt as a child, and never forgot. They mean to me almost more than the finest poetry, and they have for me a more permanent value, somehow or other.

It is almost shameful to confess that the poems which have meant most to me, like Wordsworth's *Ode to Immortality* and Keats' *Odes*, and pieces of *Macbeth* or *As You Like It* or *Midsummer Night's Dream* and Goethe's lyrics such as *Über allen Gipfeln ist Ruh*, and Verlaine's *Ayant poussé la porte qui chancelle* – all these lovely poems which after all give the ultimate shape to one's life; all these lovely poems woven deep into a man's consciousness, are still not woven so deep in me as the rather banal Noncomformist hymns that penetrated through and through my childhood.

> Each gentle dove
> And sighing bough
> That makes the eve
> So fair to me
> Has something far

---

[15] I have quoted him when writing of literature and children before now in my *Ideology and the Imagination* (1975).

> Diviner now
> To draw me back
> To Galilee.
> O Galilee, sweet Galilee,
> Where Jesus loved so much to be,
> O Galilee, sweet Galilee,
> Come sing thy songs again to me!

To me the word Galilee has a wonderful sound. The Lake of Galilee! I don't want to know where it is. I never want to go to Palestine. Galilee is one of those lovely, glamorous words, not places, that exist in the golden haze of a child's half-formed imagination. And in my man's imagination it is just the same. It has been left untouched. With regard to the hymns which had such a profound influence on my childish consciousness, there has been no crystallising out, no dwindling into actuality, no hardening into the commonplace. They are the same to my man's experience as they were to me nearly forty years ago . . .

Now we come back to the hymns. They live and glisten in the depths of the man's consciousness in undimmed wonder, so that the miracle of the loaves and fishes is just as good to me now as when I was a child. I don't care whether it is historically a fact or not. What does it matter? It is part of the genuine wonder. The same with all the religious teaching I had as a child, *apart* from the didacticism and sentimentalism. I am eternally grateful for the wonder with which it filled my childhood.

> Sun of my soul, thou Saviour dear,
> It is not night if Thou be near –

That was the last hymn at the board school. It did not mean to me any Christian dogma or any salvation. Just the words 'Sun of my soul, thou Saviour dear', penetrated me with wonder and the mystery of twilight.[16]

What is that wonderful haze that lies about the earliest poetry I know? Why should I want, and want so much, my own children, children I teach (adults I teach, for that matter), to experience it as I do – to share it? Whatever the reason, the wish is strongly and generally shared by parents and educators – the children's literature constituency. The re-enchantment of the universe is the point of a great deal of what is written for and read to children. Does it need any justification? Isn't it enough

[16] D. H. Lawrence, 'Hymns in a Man's Life', in *Selected Literary Criticism*, ed. A. R. Beal (1955).

to point at a child's eyes shining when she hears of magic case-
ments opening on the foam of perilous seas in faery lands
forlorn?

If we want a justification, perhaps the authority of the
Ancients will do to provide it. When Aristotle and Horace and
Donatus, and following them, Boileau and Dryden, sought to
explain what poetry did for you, they said, first, that it caused
an intensity of wonder and woe, and second, that to experience
wonder at the world and its doings was a necessary part of being
human and rational. We might, after the Romantic poets and
aestheticians, put a different stress on the same point and say
that the renaissance of wonder resisted the killing abstractions
of an over-scientific view of the world, and kept active the feelings that make us distinctively human. Either way, wonder is
in part the feeling, in part the quality of attention given to the
world, which provides an exit from the dreadful prison of a
tight, enclosed, hard self.

It is, therefore, essentially connected to the imagination as I
spoke of it in the first chapter. The power of language to mobil-
ize that imagination is everyone's faculty (which is not to say it
will or can never be lost). Words are magical, at least when they
are used in certain ways. The magic power of particular lines
and images was a treasure I discovered early. I cannot say I
learned it. But I had the chance to find it. I piled up a rich involuntary hoard from the poems I met. I have, like Russell Hoban,
treasured them ever since, and I couldn't forget them now if I
wanted to. They lie at the very brim of consciousness, ready at
the right touch – which may be made by some quite accidental
event – to be released into the rapid, electric currents of my
present thought at any time.

I bought Roger Lancelyn Green's Puffin *Robin Hood*. On the title page
was a stanza from the Alfred Noyes poem, *Sherwood*, and it gave me
gooseflesh when I read it:

> Robin Hood is here again: all his merry thieves
> Hear a ghostly bugle-note shivering through the leaves . . .
> The dead are coming back again, the years are rolled away
> In Sherwood, in Sherwood, about the break of day.

I wanted it to be Sherwood again, about the break of day. . .
   . . . The beginning of my book came back to me then, just like
Proust's Combray – all at once and clear and vivid. 'Saxon hind' was

what my book called the serf, and I could see the scene again as it first came to me through the words in the cherry tree. I could see that sunlight through the passing leaves, the prisoner trussed up on the sledge like meat, helpless, rolling his eyes in terror as the Sheriff's foresters drag him to his death. Robert Fitzooth, not yet Robin Hood the outlaw, encounters the group and questions the Sheriff's men. The Chief Forester taunts him about the power of the bow he carries, doubts that such a stripling can wield such a weapon. Fitzooth shows his strength and skill with a long shot that brings down one of the King's deer. And with that he has fallen into the forester's trap – like the prisoner, he has forfeited his life with that shot. The Sheriff's men attempt to take him, but he kills some of them and frees the 'Saxon hind'. They escape into the greenwood, and the outlaw life of Robin Hood begins.

The light and the air of that first encounter have never left my mind, and the sounds of the forest, the hissing of the sledge runners over the grass, the rattle of weapons, the shouts, the whizzing arrows. It is the metaphorical value of that action that has made it so memorable for me: the free and active wild self of the forest, armed and strong, freed the bound and helpless captive self and so became the outlaw self I recognized within me – the self indwelling always, sometimes kept faith with, sometimes betrayed.[17]

Alfred Noyes's poem rouses my blood as it does Hoban's. Those lines and the others I've quoted are piled in my memory in huge, ambiguous harvests – along with *Songs of Praise* and the magnificence of:

> With gold of obedience, and incense of lowliness,
> Kneel and adore him, the Lord is his name,

the gentleness of:

> It streams from the hills, it descends to the plain,
> And sweetly distils in the dew and the rain,

the delicious sombre plainness of Tallis's canon:

> Teach me to live that so I may
> Rise glorious at the awful day,
>   the awful day.

Something in all these verses sorted with the slightly hollow chivalry, the clean-limbed manliness, the simplicity and un-

---

[17] Russell Hoban in his contribution, 'Thoughts on a Shirtless Cyclist, Robin Hood and One or Two Other Things', to *Writers, Critics and Children*, ed. G. Fox, G. Hammond *et al.* (1976), pp. 95–103.

equivocal conviction of being in the right, the soaring, innocently egotistical idealization of intention and action which I
found in my adventure stories. The class into which I was born
and the public school which carried its symbols could still, in
the 1950s, see nothing incongruous in the maintenance and celebration of these values. The sexual revolution hadn't gathered
the headlong momentum of more recent years, sixth-formers
nearly all became National Service officers before going to
Cambridge, the school remained proud of the undoubted fact
that it fielded the best schoolboy rugby xvs in the world.

I gave myself wholeheartedly to the value system of these
institutions; the novels which filled so much of my imaginative
life were perfectly of a fit. It is in such circumstances that we can
fairly speak of what we read directly affecting how we live. But
the exalted ritual performances of school – sports, worship, as-
sembly, prizes and parades – were not my only life. They were
the structural complement of the adventure novels. On the
other hand, I came from a bourgeois family whose bonds were
close and deeply affectionate, whose rootedness in a north-
country town gave the lives of all its members confidence and
independence, and in which an unusually strong mother –
strong in mind and spirit – gave an order, a beauty, and a tranquil domestic happiness which was always the true base of my
life; only there was I, in the good phrase, truly at home.

The adventure-story reading fitted a part of this atmosphere,
certainly. But its strong, demonstratively affectionate quality
opened up dimensions of feeling for me which could only ever
be occupied by longing when I was away at school – hence a
more or less permanent homesickness. The reading which
endorsed and impelled this range of more 'feminine' virtues
reflected the deep cultural division which, in turn, runs parallel
to (*not* 'is caused by') the labour divisions of economic life. The
advent of a hugely accelerated success in the creation of capital
surplus as industrialization took off in the early nineteenth
century meant that the dominant members of the new successful classes – in England, that unique mixture of aristocratic
landowner and bourgeois industrialist concentrated at its best
in the dash and brilliance of Disraeli – put certain virtues and
values into storage with their womenfolk until they needed
them again. In the public arena, what the new men wanted was
sobriety, ruthlessness, precise computation, just anonymity,

probity, resolution. They displaced to the private world the values which we now think of as womanly: gentleness, tenderness, sensitivity, pliability, demonstrativeness, a personal response. It is significant that these also have since 1900 or so been offered as the benefits of a training in literature.

This is the skeleton of a history given more flesh and blood in the next chapter. The point here is that the unusual strength of my family's ties and bonds always pulled me to a literature which gave the bonds context and expression. I read my sisters' books, partly because I read everything on the shelves, partly because those values sounded as deep in me as the manly ones. I read *Little Women*, *Jo's Boys*, *The Secret Garden*, *The Railway Children*, and I read Angela Brazil and Madcap Mollie with the same delight as I read of Teddy Lester's 100 against the Australians, made clandestinely at a country house weekend while he was still a schoolboy. I read Angela Brazil away at school, ashamedly covering the outside with brown paper and writing *Billiards for Beginners* as a suitably boylike phoney title. It wasn't until I met at Oundle that excellent schoolmaster and hilarious but loving mimic of all such stories, Arthur Marshall, that I began to feel that perhaps these tastes were not *only* regressive and infantile.

I have no doubt that they were these bad things, but they were not *only* these things. With them, I read Frank Richards, Malcolm Saville, and the many dozen of the Enid Blyton school stories – the Malory Towers stories, the Sea, Valley, Island of Adventure, the endless Five series. I certainly took in from these books their overpowering snobbery, the meanness and vengefulness of so much of the morality, the herd victimization of silliness and vanity. But I couldn't have read them *for* these undoubtedly strong ingredients. Partly I read them for their utter unreality. The adventures were such as to hurt no one, and I wanted to be sure of painlessness. Partly I read them for the untaxing safety of their stereotypes – the facility with which the children won the day to the amazed acclamation of parents and police, the unrufflable, wholly impossible calm of big boys, the clinging unreliability of little girls. Indeed, I was hardly troubled by the notion of 'character' at all. I wanted the placid, predictable turn and return of events, and Enid Blyton, who, as George Orwell said of Frank Richards, could only be a syndicate of writers packed into one body, served up the looked-for safety of stories essential to the regular repair-time which we all of us take out of our dealings with the difficult world. Reading Enid Blyton is much like reading comics. Awful, and indeed worse than comics, because so lacking in their lurid high spirits and loud vulgarity. Awful, but unimportant.

Reading P. G. Wodehouse was, and remains, another matter altogether. And yet I am sure that when I first found an old orange-cased Herbert Jenkins edition of *Summer Lightning* on my father's shelves, my pleasure in reading it was rather like that which I took in Enid Blyton: the same safety, the same lack of character, the same delightful absorption in events. But Wodehouse, supremely, made me laugh – happy, joyous, ringing laughter, laughter at the unbelievably comic situations, laughter at the glittering inventiveness of the language:

It is curious how you can be intimate with a fellow from early boyhood and yet remain unacquainted with one side of him. Mixing constantly with Gussie through the years, I had come to know him as a newt-fancier, a lover, and a fathead, but I had never suspected him of possessing outstanding qualities as a sprinter on the flat, and I was amazed at the high order of ability he was exhibiting in this very specialized form of activity. He was coming along like a jack-rabbit of the western prairie, his head back and his green beard floating in the breeze. I liked his ankle work.

Dobbs, on the other hand, was more laboured in his movements and to an eye like mine, trained in the watching of point-to-point races, had all the look of an also-ran. One noted symptoms of roaring, and I am convinced that had Gussie had the intelligence to stick to his job and make a straight race of it, he would soon have out-distanced the field and come home on a tight rein. Police constables are not built for speed. Where you catch them at their best is standing on street corners saying 'Pass along there.' (*The Mating Season*, p. 213)

I shall come back to Wodehouse, as I shall to the last of the heroes in this brief Pantheon built to commemorate the uses of literacy in a well-off, well-loved, sunlit childhood. I put Arthur Ransome in this group because, along with Blyton, Wodehouse, Malcolm Saville, he wrote of the absolute safety of a Lake District (and Norfolk Broads) bounded by the absolute justice of the parental writ. Ransome mattered fundamentally because I saw him also as a celebrant of the great world of home. The splendour and detail of his stories, taking place as they did in an unending and paradisal holiday, were woven from a love of the landscape of which he wrote movingly in a late preface to the Puffin edition of *Swallows and Amazons*:

I have been often asked how I came to write *Swallows and Amazons*. The answer is that it had its beginning long, long ago when, as children, my brother, my sister and I spent most of our holidays on a farm at the south end of Coniston. We played in or on the lake or on the hills above it, finding friends in the farmers and shepherds and charcoal-burners whose smoke rose from the coppice woods along the shore. We adored the place. Coming to it we used to run down to the lake, dip our hands in and wish, as if we had just seen the new moon. Going away from it we were half drowned in tears. While away from it, as children and as grown-ups, we dreamt about it. No matter where I was, wandering about the world, I used at night to look for the North Star and, in my mind's eye, could see the beloved skyline of great hills beneath it. *Swallows and Amazons* grew out of those old memories. I could not help writing it. It almost wrote itself.

I associated Ransome with the other writers as spokesmen for and custodian of my domestic, atavistic and, in a loose sense, 'feminine' self. But the strength of his love for his landscape struck chords which were also sounded in Malcolm Saville's far slighter books about Shropshire. I felt, and feel, about the Cleveland hills and dales, the magical lilt of its villages along the old railway line – Kildale, Commondale, Castleton, Danby – as Ransome did about the Lake District. He gave voice for children to that extraordinary loyalty to place which the Romantics put into circulation (and found in Shakespeare), and did so quite without sentimentality or overblown patriotism.

I began with Ransome's sense of place. But as the quotations show in Chapter 4, he has immeasurably more to give. He and Kipling, in their different worlds,[18] took me past the cardboard figures who performed the events of the Biggles books, into the depths and meanings of character which are the subjects and objects of the English novel, and the foundation of the morality we call liberalism. Ransome was a far lesser artist, but a far plainer, less affected, more honest man, and his prose speaks out for these qualities. But both men set their books firmly in a believable reality, both loved their home landscape fiercely (think of how beautifully Kipling presents Sussex), both gave

[18] Although, as Ransome's excellent *Autobiography* makes clear, he was quite at home in Kipling's world.

their characters a racy, quick, idiosyncratic and attractive speech. In my world, Ransome spoke through the cooking and camping and sailing to my solid domesticity set in a timeless holiday, and Kipling to the ardour I had learned from my class and my history for some desperate glory: *dulce et decorum est pro patria mori*.

There was no tidy progression in my experience of literature, any more than there is in anybody else's. I moved backwards and forwards through levels of difficulty and maturity, first meeting *Pilgrim's Progress* and *David Copperfield* at eleven, and being uncomprehendingly transfixed by them, while at the same time reading the *Rover* and Elinor Brent-Dyer without the least sense of incongruity. My favourite books were those I could use for any purpose. That is, I could use Ransome's *Swallowdale*, or Learie Constantine's *Cricketers' Carnival*, or Ian Hay's *Pip*, or Kipling's *Rewards and Fairies*, or Malcolm Saville's *Seven White Gates*, in any way I liked. I was at home with those books as with my friends; they were reassuringly the same, the arc of their narratives turned comfortably around me and returned to a safe place. Hunched behind the sofa where it was warm and dark and close, I could re-enter their worlds for ten minutes or two hours, for a repair-time or for company, for solace or for excitement. I could read, skipping large portions because I knew the story so well, and picking out the pieces I liked best ('the ball came down and found Pip waiting for it with hands which at that moment would have gripped a red-hot cannonball'), treating the book as well-known equal. Or I could listen to them gravely, for the story as told by a parent, with all of a parent's infallible wisdom and experience heavy in its sentences, the sense, so awful and fascinating to a child, of the adult's having done and seen unmentionable things:

Next second the strands had parted, and I fell back with a sound in my ears which I pray God I may never hear again – the sound of a body rebounding dully from crag to crag, and then a long soft rumbling of screes like a snowslip. (John Buchan, *The Three Hostages*, p. 446)

I absorbed those books, and dozens like them, all through. Even now, whole paragraphs unroll before my mind's eye – like Lawrence, I know them more deeply than I shall ever know the wonderful novels which gave shape and meaning to my existence: *Persuasion*, *Anna Karenina*, *Middlemarch*, *Great Expectations*, *The Rainbow*, *The Ambassadors*. They fitted both my dreams and my reality, and I was comfortable with them. It is not easy to over-value this frame of mind. The books alter the frame, and we alter the books. Such a 'fit' may be found between callow spirits and dreadful books, between this hoodlum and that William Burroughs, and then we may justly fear for the consequences. But learning, in a spirit of confidence and humility, to meet with books as both masters and friends is a condition of listening to great writers. I learned that greeting and its gift with a fortunate readiness. Through the mixed bag of stories I have mentioned I found clear ways to put my imagination at rest between the imperious demands of the self and the moral demands of the impersonal world.[19]

In a preface to his own poem, *Endymion*, John Keats wrote:

The imagination of a boy is healthy, and the mature imagination of a man is healthy; but there is a space of life between, in which the soul is in a ferment, the character undecided, the way of life uncertain, the ambition thicksighted: thence proceeds mawkishness, and all the thousand bitters which those men I speak of must necessarily taste in going over the following pages.[20]

Keats is robustly optimistic about boy and man. Many people – more than he allows for – never come out of the ferment. It seethed in me when I brought my boy's books up against a man's world and found that they didn't fit. They fitted the rugby pitch and they fitted the Parachute Regiment – they were meant to. They fitted my home, which was stronger than either. But they didn't fit a wider, messier world. My enormous luck was to find a teacher and a shelf of books who between them provided a way of understanding the world and living honourably in it. Well, you need luck to discover that strait way and narrow gate; my argument has been that as things are, the best guides to it for children are the best novelists for children.

---

[19] A distinction I take from Michael Black, *The Literature of Fidelity* (1975).
[20] *The Poems of John Keats*, ed. H. W. Garrod (1956), p. 54.

3

The history of children –
little innocents and limbs of Satan

The last chapter described the reading career I know best: my own. This is not to say that we each of us know what is best for us ourselves, nor even – what is made to sound like common sense – that we each know best what happened to us in the past. Wiser men may tell us more about ourselves than we could ever have seen alone. Similarly, good historians may well know better what was going on in the past, and most importantly, what it *meant*, than the actors who were actually living the life-in-earnest which the past once was.

This is the point of introduction for this chapter. A potted history may serve to give that individual career, that 'text', its longer, wider context. A foreshortened history gives biography its meaning. It shows what values are possible at a given time, and explains something of the particular versions which individuals have and make of values. The first emphasis in such a history is that the idea of childhood itself has a history. The cheerful picture of a genteel meliorism which is the most popular account of the past probably works best for children. If, in our popular valuations of the past and its meanings, we present it (*sic*) as surpassed but mythologized, the necessary lower ground from which the efforts of heroes and heroines have brought us to the sunlit heights of today, such a story works best for children.

It makes tentative sense to speak of the modern idea of childhood as emerging from the great shift of values at the end of the eighteenth century. But it makes such sense only if we see that idea not as a natural evolution but as a contingent arrival in the consciousness of a smallish number of symbol-makers, especially poets, and the more or less cultivated audience who read them. On the other hand, one finds the great new batteries of human rights first applied to children at the same time as the vast dislocations which expressed themselves in the French and American Revolutions, in the abrupt acceleration of technological innovation of which Priestley, Murdoch, Watt, Matthew Boulton, Brindley are the great names in England, in the paintings of Blake and in John Wesley's sermons. For the sake of brevity, therefore, we shall date the origins of the modern idea of childhood in the poetry of Blake and Wordsworth.[1]

Blake and Wordsworth were the first geniuses of English Romantic literature to place the meaning and experience of childhood at the centre of their picture of morality and of the growth of the imagination. Indeed, it partly defines a Romantic that he take such a view of children: the expansion of the sensibility into areas of experience which had been forgotten since Shakespeare, the new attention bent upon subjects long excluded from the discourse of normality – upon children, outcasts, idiots, foreigners – these are among the changes which we call Romantic, and our world is their consequence. But the same historical conjuncture which prompted Blake to publish the *Songs of Innocence* in 1789 created the industrial energy which drove flocks of wretched children ever deeper into misery.

The lives of most children were grim enough before industrialization and worse, as always, for the poor. As the new historians of childhood widely note, it is the extraordinary silence about children which, when we look for the history of children, we most note in the records. When Ben Jonson wrote his beautiful little epitaph to his first daughter, the poem which commends her soul to the Virgin whose name she bore in life, and, with a heartbreaking gracefulness, bids farewell to the corpse in its grave:

> Which cover lightly, gentle earth

it seems likely that *our* hearts are more touched by this echo of a Latin epigram than at the least Jonson's contemporary readers were. For his poem is strikingly rare in a poetic age in being about a child. Peter Laslett notes that 'probably the most conspicuous feature of traditional society to be gathered from its

[1] I follow Peter Coveney in *The Image of Childhood. The Individual and Society: A Study of the Theme in English Literature* (1967).

vital statistics is its overwhelming youthfulness';[2] he goes on elegantly to list the ranges of our ignorance about the lives of children:

In the pre-industrial world there were children everywhere; playing in the village street and fields when they were very small, hanging round the farmyards and getting in the way, until they had grown enough to be given child-sized jobs to do; thronging the churches; for ever clinging to the skirts of women in the house and wherever they went and above all crowding round the cottage fires.

The perpetual distraction of childish noise and talk must have affected everyone almost all the time, except of course the gentleman in his study or the lady in her boudoir; incessant interruptions to answer questions, quieten fears, rescue from danger or make peace between the quarrelling. These crowds and crowds of little children are strangely absent from the written record, even if they are conspicuous enough in the pictures painted at the time, particularly the outside scenes. There is something mysterious about the silence of all these multitudes of babes in arms, toddlers and adolescents in the statements men made at the time about their own experience. Children appear of course, but so seldom and in such an indefinite way that we know very little indeed about child nurture in pre-industrial times, and no confident promise can be made of knowledge yet to come.

We cannot say whether fathers helped in the tending of infants or whether women and girls, sisters and aunts as well as mothers, did it all as women's peculiar business. We do not know how the instruction of children was divided between the parents, though it is natural to suppose that boys at least would learn how men behaved and how they worked the lathe, the plane, the plough, the loom, from watching their fathers all and every day. Such letters as they learnt, and the stories of the past, traditionally came to them at their mothers' knees, and their religious training too. But there is nothing as yet to confirm that this tradition is wholly correct. We are even more ignorant of what happened when the children left the house and went out to play; whether it was in family groups, or whether it was neighbourhood gangs, even village gangs, embracing rich and poor, the privileged along with the rest. We do not know very much about what they played, or even about what they were encouraged to play or to do.

We know a little about what they were taught when they went to school, which was almost all Christianity and a little classics, and about the rigour of their treatment there. But very few of them went

---

[2] Peter Laslett, *The World We Have Lost* (1965) p. 105ff. This book was the first to come from the hand of a founder-member of the Cambridge Group for the History of Population and Social Structure. See also *Household and Family in Past Time*, ed. Peter Laslett and Richard Wall (1972).

to school, and we can only suppose that when they were at home they were as peremptorily treated as they would have been in the class-room. The most important material object in the world of the child may well have been the rod, but these myriads of children have left almost nothing material behind them. A cradle or two in most old houses, a hobby horse, a whipping top and one or two other tra-ditional toys, that is all, and most of these once belonged to little gentlemen and gentlewomen, not to the ordinary children, our own ancestors.

The Stuart gentry seem to have dressed their children like them-selves, at least for the purpose of having their pictures painted. The peasants and craftsmen appear to have done the same. But we cannot say how far children were universally thought of as little adults, though the notion of a world of the child distinct from the world of the grown-up seems to be no older than the early Victorians. Nothing can as yet be said on what is called by the psychologists toilet training, and reckoned by them to be of great importance in the formation of personality; there seems no likelihood of our discovering whether indeed it varied from Puritan to Anglican, from gentry to peasantry, from town to country. We do not even know for certain how babies were carried about. It is, in fact, an effort of the mind to remember all the time that children were always present in such numbers in the tra-ditional world, nearly half the whole community living in a condition of semi-obliteration, many of them never destined to become persons at all.

Laslett mentions the seventeenth-century commentator Gregory King who guessed – and from the archives it seems a reasonable guess – that 45 per cent of the population were chil-dren, and the table of mortality rates which Laslett quotes serves to explain both a certain necessary unfeelingness on the part of seventeenth-century writers and parents towards chil-dren who only looked set for a relatively long life if they got as far as 20, and the far greater consciousness of individual poten-tiality on the part of modern parents who have every confi-dence that they will see their children well into middle age and their own demise. According to King, the average expectation of life for a baby in 1690 was 32 years; in Breslau at the same date it was 27.5; in India and Bangladesh in 1975 it was 35. In the UK in 1978 the average age of death for men was 68.7 and for women 72.5.[3]

[3] Laslett, *The World We Have Lost*, p. 93, quoting Gregory King, Public Record Office. The last statistic is taken from *Social Trends*, HMSO 1979; the figures for the Indian sub-continent from *UN Yearbook 1977*.

But the change marked, for my purposes, by Blake and Wordsworth was and is far more than statistical. Indeed, the relevance of this short historical incursion is structural and qualitative. It seems clear from the demographers that what we have learned to call the 'nuclear family' – the two-generation family with only two or three children[4] – is neither a consequence of industrialization nor the instrument of its divisive technology. On the contrary, historians variously draw a fluctuating pattern of family sizes in relation to the connections between kinship systems and forms of social order and control. David Herlihy describes a movement from nucleation towards extension (instead of the conventionally reversed movement in most social histories from about 1400 to the present day) in early medieval families, and there have been other punishing criticisms[5] of the model of family development which in correlating progressive nucleation with the development of modern society has been a help to both Marxist and individualist, to say nothing of contraceptive, accounts of history. The proper account looks more like short-run common sense than history; it is that family size varies, as it has done these past few years, in time to the giant pulses of economic and political conditions; its expansions and contractions beat in time to those irregular movements; terror, starvation, slump, warfare are timelessly unpropitious circumstances either for seeing much of your folks, or for planning and bringing up a large family.

If family size is neither invariable nor related to particular social change, and if its reduction absolutely cannot be tied to the industrialization of society (nor the latter-day version of the same history, 'modernization'), we still have to remark on, even if we cannot account for, the change in family attitudes which, from towards the end of the eighteenth century, the outbreak of the two great revolutions, the advent of Romanticism, and so forth, fundamentally altered the system of family values and gave a new definition of childhood.

[4] Compare also the notoriously steep decline in numbers of children in the nuclear family over the past 120 years. Average number of children (taken from *Britain in Statistics*, Harmondsworth: Penguin 1975) 1871: 6.1; 1891: 4.75; 1901: 4.0; 1911: 3.2; 1931: 2.75; 1951: 2.2; 1961: 2.3; 1971: 2.0.
[5] David Herlihy, 'Family Solidarity in Medieval History', in *Economy, Society and Government in Medieval Italy* (1969), pp. 173–9; Georges Duby, *La Société aux XI'et XII' Siècles dans la Région Maconnaise* (1953) – both quoted in Christopher Lasch, *Haven in a Heartless World: The Family Besieged* (1978).

Before the childhood years which Wordsworth describes in *The Prelude* and which lay between his birth in 1770 and his going to Cambridge in 1787, the majority of reports we have of childhood constantly impress a modern reader with atrocious and punitive horror. There is no need to reach back into the fanciful and polemical byways of psychohistory to document with Lloyd De Mause a shattering chronicle of two millennia of rape, brutality, violent and bloody punishment, coprophagia, deliberate terrorism, neglect, and utter callousness. De Mause's history is so packed with horrors that one can only wonder that anyone ever survived the experience of childhood, and that if they did, how anything approaching a decent and rational social order ever arose. But whatever your view of his laxly post-Freudian theories about the projection by adults of their own self-loathing on to (in a seventeenth-century description) 'the new borne babe . . . full of the stains and pollutions of sin which it inherits . . . through our loins',[6] children *were* often horribly treated by adults, probably in most countries and certainly in urban England up to the end of the last century. J. H. Plumb, summarizing a large corpus of work, mentions the boy punished for bed-wetting by being forced to drink 'a pint of piss', Pepys as sexually abusing and beating with a broomstick his child-servants, and the practice of heavy flogging as pretty well universal, and here as elsewhere[7] concludes that 'towards the end of the seventeenth century . . . Parents, or rather some parents, ceased to beat their children as regularly and as savagely as their own parents had done them; swaddling clothes were given up, allowing the baby to be active; breast-feeding replaced wet-nursing so that motherly love was now directed to the child; more marriages were made on grounds of affection; a new world of family warmth was slowly being born . . .' Lawrence Stone, in whose support Plumb writes, speaks of the growth of 'affective individualism' through the eighteenth century – a growth he affirms is perfectly independent in its origins of technological and economic change, though it may have been helped along by these.[8] Both writers

---

[6] Richard Allestree, *The Whole Duty of Man* (London 1658), quoted by J. H. Plumb, 'The New World of Children in 18th Century England', *Past and Present*, 67, May 1975.
[7] J. H. Plumb, review-article, 'The Rise of Love', *New York Review*, 24 November 1977.
[8] Lawrence Stone, *The Family, Sex and Marriage in England, 1500–1800* (1977).

join Laslett and the pioneer of child history, Philippe Ariès,[9] in seeing the tendency of European social life very gradually concentrate on the family and the virtues of domesticity, and in placing the source of energy for this redirection in the middle class. But retrieving any evidence for the earlier stages of this change is an exiguous and chancy business, as they all acknowledge. Ariès, studying, in his words, 'iconographic documents in the hope of discovering the tremor of life which he can feel in his own existence', pushes the origins of modern family life so far back into the sixteenth century it hardly makes sense to speak of family structure as 'modern' at all. But he stresses that the retreat from sociability, the advent of private lives, is the real mark of modernity, as it is of comparative wealth. Very poor families crammed into two or three rooms have obviously less privacy today than the rich, and at every stage the life of the urban poor retained the crowdedness, a heavy interdependence combined with the roughness and callousness enforced by suffering, cold, and hunger, which bring the worst of medieval Paris alive in much of contemporary Naples.

The history of childhood is, necessarily, an intercalation in the history of the family. There have always been families and, indeed, the *idea* of families: the medieval historians, working effortfully from local records in Austrian, Languedoc and Suffolk villages, have turned back the claim Ariès seeks to document from paintings painted for church and nobility that the concept of the family is post-Revolutionary, and have confuted the notion of the tidy development of family life in parallel with the rise of the bourgeoisie, the advent of capitalism, new technology, and possessive property-holding. What happened was, as always, much messier.

The colloquial view of most of European life before the eighteenth century is that it was unlike the present in being entirely characterized by terrible pillage and slaughter and nonchalant cruelty. It is a view which you can only hold without heroic feats of psychological repression if you are somebody lucky enough to be born after 1945 in an English-speaking country, and even there you will have to keep yourself carefully ignorant of your parents' experiences. Similarly, the same poster picture outlines forms of family life which were for practically everybody brutally dominated by the facts of serfdom,

[9] Philippe Ariès, *Centuries of Childhood* (1973), p. 392.

an utter absence of property or rights or decent shelter, by biting cold and omnipresent dirt. What we find, for instance, in so much of the Mediterranean life of the sixteenth century reconstructed by Fernand Braudel in his 'total history' supports the poster picture. But we also find in Braudel pockets of civilized life which were then, as now, free for a season of famine, plague and brigands; we find records of such life as containing within its terms all that we would now think of as the best of family life.[10] Simply to list the nations of the Mediterranean littorals is to remember that Greece, Turkey, Lebanon, Israel, Algeria and so on have hardly been without bloodshed these past thirty-five years. By the same token, looking up Alan Macfarlane's history of individualism,[11] we also find the claim convincingly supported that in England, at least, even medieval families recognized rights and freedoms which their self-congratulatory descendants of Victorian and modern times supposed to have been conferred by the delights of industrialism.

What is being argued, therefore, is once more the difficulty of fit between the story of history as progress and the contrary facts which insist that in real life some things get better as others get worse, and that to see any purposive improvement in all this bedlam takes a beady eye and a good deal of faith. Much is made, among the new students created by the expansion of teacher training in the West, of the history of childhood and family. What is offered here is a modest revisionism provided for these contexts in order to emphasize three things: first, that the images of childhood and happy family life did not spring straight from the heads of the Romantic poets; second, that childish happiness and misery are pretty evenly distributed through world history and that cruelty to children can only be said to have shown some modest diminution in the richest countries during the past four or five generations; thirdly, and most pointedly for our purposes in this chapter, that the critical innovation of industrial society has been the mass institutions and the advent of their bureaucracies: factory, prison, asylum, hospital, school. These separate edifices, and the labour relations they generated, threw an enormous weight of signifi-

[10] F. Braudel, *The Mediterranean and the Mediterranean World in the Age of Philip II*, 2 vols., vol. II(1973), chaps. 5 and 6, 'Societies', 'Civilizations'.
[11] *The Origins of English Individualism* (1979).

cance upon family life. As I am about to argue, it was naturally the fluent and the powerful amongst the social classes who sought to name and understand this new weight of significance. For the past century or so, some very intelligent men and women have conducted that inquiry through the novel and on behalf of their listening children.

This special concentration of emotional energy in the family and the imagination from which it was created is the subject of this book. But the family itself has been going for centuries, even though it is immensely hard, in reconstructing (from the records) the meaning of a concept like 'family', to say to what extent the word was used in the past as we use it now. The history of a social institution is necessarily (if only partially) the history of the language used to talk about and within it. Nonetheless, however variously and inclusively men have used the word when speaking of their family these past 800 years, they at least meant *some* of the things we still mean by it. There are too many new Wellsians[12] among historians on both political wings who seem only capable of cheering the late twentieth century on its triumphant progress, who are quite innocently incapable of interpreting the written records of the past with a sensitive eye and a critical ear, and who consign all family life before the advent of the washing machine and *Playschool* to the cesspit of history. Well, one can only retort that privation and suffering are every bit as liable to create closeness and mutual devotion as the comfort of the Habitat lifestyle, that the absence of written record is in itself evidence of nothing except (sometimes) the inability to write, and lastly that parental love is too complex and multiform, but also too profound and mysterious, to be the sole product of the West European mortgagee–ratepayer. Family life has many historical forms; it is not a shrine, nor is it a term of solitary confinement.[13] It may be either heavenly or hellish, but it is certain that it is neither simply modern nor simply private. The warm, plentiful, and universal associations which coil richly about 'family', 'home', 'kitchen', 'safety' are beautifully brought out by Janet Lewis as she recreates the life of a wealthy farmer's family, and his

[12] A point strongly made in a review of Stone (1977) by E. P. Thompson, 'Happy Families', *New Society*, 8 September 1977.

[13] As you might suppose both from the Ken Loach movie of that name, and from much of R. D. Laing's and Aaron Esterson's casework. See David Cooper, *Death of the Family* (1972) for the most strident attack.

dependants, high and lonely in the hills of the Languedoc, early in the sixteenth century:

Here, in the more even glow of the fire, the face of her new father held nothing terrifying. Seamed, coarsened by exposure to rough weather, the darkened skin caught the gold reflections squarely, without compromise or evasion, admitting all the engravures of time. The beard was short, rough and grizzled, parted to show a cleft in the long chin. The mouth, not smiling, but just, had a heavy lower lip which could admit of anger. The nose was short and flattened, the cheek bones were high, the forehead was high and wide, the eyes, now gray, now black, as the light changed, were calmly interested, calm in the assurance of authority. He sat at ease in the stiff-backed rush-bottomed chair, his dark jerkin laced to the throat, his right hand resting on the edge of the table, vigilantly surveying his household, like some Homeric king, some ruler of an island commonwealth who could both plow and fight, and the hand which rested on the table was scarred as from some defensive struggle in years long gone by. Without bearing any outward symbol of his power, he was in his own person both authority and security. He ruled, as the contemporary records say, using the verb which belongs to royalty, and the young girl seated beside him, in feeling this, felt also the great peace which his authority created for his household. It was the first of many evenings in which his presence should testify for her that the beasts were safe, that the grain was safe, that neither the wolves, whose voices could be heard on winter nights, nor marauding bands of mercenaries such as the current hearsay from the larger valleys sometimes reported, could do anything to harm the hearth beside which this man was seated. Because of him the farm was safe, and therefore Artigues, and therefore Languedoc, and therefore France, and therefore the whole world was safe and as it should be.[14]

The novelist's reconstruction of a scene placed solidly in the records from which she is working is also unusually evocative of an ideal image of family life and the childhood it includes. Story-writers for children continuously return to the creation of an ideal kitchen – Beatrix Potter's Mrs Tittlemouse and Jemima Puddleduck have one, so has the Badger in *The Wind in the Willows*, so have Little Grey Rabbit, Bilbo Baggins, the Railway Children, the Swallows and Amazons. The image may not be precisely transhistorical, although all that is meant

[14] Janet Lewis, *The Wife of Martin Guerre* (1977), pp. 22–3. This remarkable novel is distinguished for its fidelity to the historical records and the genius with which these are brought to life. See Donald Davie, 'The Historical Novels of Janet Lewis', *Southern Review*, II, 3 (1966).

by hearth and hospitality, by the essential human capacity to make our own space out of the deserts of spacelessness all around us, will bear a good deal of movement across time and geography, but it lives for the length of European history.

By the same token, it sounds wilful to talk of the emergence of such general ideas as parental love as being of recent origin. The cruelties dealt out to children in the past were surely of a piece with the more naked and casual brutalities of times in which executions were public, bears were torn to pieces in the baiting pits, and mutilated lazars left to die in the streets. These are the evils of a past which a lively social conscience is bound to acknowledge by reflex. The same conscience is properly ready to wince at the reminder of present more bureaucratized depredations wrought both in general and upon children, in and out of total war, genocidal policy, and the homelier paragraphs about baby-battering in yesterday's newspaper. The change is one of visibility; cruelty and punishment in the past were inflicted as public signs; in the present, they disappear into the anonymity of home and bureaucracy. Either way, it takes a crazily selective optimism to write, as Lloyd De Mause does[15], of the development of child-rearing practice from 'the Infanticidal Mode (Antiquity to fourth century AD)' to 'Abandonment Mode (fourth century to thirteenth century), Ambivalent Mode (fourteenth century to seventeenth century), Intrusive Mode (eighteenth century), Socialization Mode (nineteenth century to mid-twentieth century)', triumphantly concluding with 'Helping Mode (begins mid-twentieth century)'. From this latter 'mode' – so the four books tell us in their reports on its successes – 'it is evident that it results in a child who is gentle, sincere, never depressed, never imitative or group-oriented, strong-willed and unintimidated by authority' (p. 54). Well, it is a relief to know that human difficulties are at last to be solved by bringing children up properly. But perhaps the warnings implied in a number of object-lessons, James Mill's and Thomas Gradgrind's among them, should have been enough to forestall such an extravagant version of the popular belief that history simply provides us with the materials of self-congratulation.

Guardedly, however, and when all the qualifications have

---

[15] In his contribution 'The Evolution of Childhood' to his own volume, *The History of Childhood* (1974), pp. 1–74.

been written into the more lurid theories of the development of the family and its children, then within a shortish timespan (say, post-Renaissance) and a limited geography (Europe north-west of the Mediterranean and west of the Volga) it is believable to speak of a new image of childhood as emerging from the upheavals of the Romantic movement, international revolution, and the new industrial technology. The secondary histories I have quoted are in unison on the view that the value and meaning of childhood began to change noticeably through the eighteenth century. Without wanting to make this change simple-mindedly a consequence of new ideas coming into circulation – the Idealist fallacy in history – the familiar names of Locke,[16] Rousseau,[17] and then, as I have said, Blake and Wordsworth serve as landmarks of the new direction of key social meanings. These writers seek out the definitions in prose and poetry which fix and respond to the vast and anonymous movements of historical change. And this is presumably the task which every theorist (let the term include artist, moralist, and scientist) sets himself. It is to create images (figures of speech of all and any kinds – metaphor or metonymy) capable of grasping the order and motion of things. On these terms, Blake and Wordsworth captured a new and confident sense that the men and women who had grown up from the children they had all once been were limitlessly capable of embodying an entirely new social order, one moreover not based on the powerful and rationalist pessimism of secular puritanism – the vanity of human wishes – but created by a richly spontaneous and individual insistence upon the uniqueness of experience and ethics. Two moral traditions have followed from these two pictures of human nature and how it ought to act.

In the first, or 'low' view, children and adults alike are 'the limbs of Satan'; salvation is sudden and capricious, and children 'are not too little to die, nor too little to go to hell'.[18] In such a morality, human beings are too corrupt for human nature and its psychology to be any ground of duty. It follows that obedience to God is necessary but is perfectly separate from what we

[16] John Locke, 'Some Thoughts concerning Education' (1693) in *Educational Writings*, ed. J. L. Axtell (1968).

[17] J.-J. Rousseau, *Emile ou L'Education* was first published in English in the *London Chronicle*, September 1762.

[18] Janeway, *A Token for Children*, London 1671–2, quoted in Coveney, *The Image of Childhood*, p. 44.

want or need. Virtue can never marry herself to happiness. In the second moral picture – the 'high' picture most vividly painted by the Romantics – morality begins in the human heart and that heart is the moral motor of 'the little innocent', the intuitively virtuous little creature who will always act well if the environment so allows, and who will only be corrupted by the depravities of a society too long sunk in its unnatural and hypocritical ways. In Romantic morality, in its many forms from Kierkegaard to latter-day existentialism, virtue is grounded in the subjectivity. It follows that, although this ethic gives pride of place to the individual's desires, it provides no way at all of deciding what to do if those desires turn out to be monstrous, nor which to prefer in the case of a bitter and belligerent disagreement. The low view of human nature acknowledges the darkness of men's hearts, but has no way of persuading them to act well; the high view gives a justification of men's actions, but only if they happen to act well.

From the mid-nineteenth century on, bringing up children veered balefully between the child as limb of Satan and the child as little innocent.

I have spoken as though bringing up children were just a matter of telling them the moral facts. Indeed, plenty of parents and teachers continue to act as though this were so, both on the progressive and on the authoritarian wings; there is a case for saying they can do nothing else. But moral behaviour takes both form and content from social structures, it *expresses* social structures, and it is at the same time one of those structures itself.

There is no mystification in this use of the word 'structure'. All I mean is that we build values and the behaviour which embodies values into a system. As we say, we seek 'to make sense' of things, of what we do and what happens to us. It is this frame of interpretation and decision that I mean by 'structure' – a systematic way of deciding, even in trivial circumstances, which moral value shall be dominant, consistent with our superordinate frame of reference.[19] To take our subject in hand, our value system (or our ideology) comes into play when we find our slow, timid, not very bright child reading a difficult

---

[19] I take these three criteria – consistency, dominance, supremacy – from Stefan Körner in *Experience and Conduct* (1976), pp. 27–38.

book of which we strongly disapprove. According to the consistency and the relative dominance of our values, we will either let the child carry on, or take the book away from her, or coax her out of it, or distract her, or secretly take it back to the library.

That decision is not to be taken in a moral laboratory. It is the product of our moral structures, which are in turn shaped by the individual, by society in its many institutions, by the material facts of life. Each of these is in play with the others; each expresses ideology. Whatever efforts people make to free themselves, they live within the structural expressions of value and meaning, sometimes holding them apart, sometimes letting them collide, sometimes, if they're lucky, finding them harmonious. The point of my excursus into the history of the family and of childhood is that although *size* by itself will tell you little about family life, and although many mistakes may be made about that size, size and scale together will tell you much about the meaning of family life.

It cannot be doubted that the scale of children's significance in the family increased enormously from the late eighteenth century onwards. At the same time, the family and its larger social meanings altered in response to the pace of the economy. Within these changes, the two moral traditions of childhood – 'limbs of Satan' and 'little innocents' – realigned themselves according to the personalities involved, the dominance of the new bourgeoisie, and the defensive redoubt into which family life itself retreated. From that redoubt, that strong, deep, but shrinking stockade, came the great tradition of children's novels.

The children's novels spring from the impulse to change the scale of childhood: the powerful sense on the part of the writers that even as the new age gave name and hope and energy to all those wretches who had been discounted from history for centuries – to idiot boys, chimney-sweeps, illegitimate children, harlots, orphans, nursemaids, pickpockets, and crossing-sweepers – so at the same time, other, monstrous forces of the times drove these same wretches into new and deadlier miseries, in the coal mines, the factories, the building sites, the slums:

I'm a trapper in the Gamber pit. I have to trap without a light, and I'm scared. I never go to sleep. Sometimes I sing when I've a light, but not in the dark; I dare not sing then. (girl, aged 8)

Chained, belted, harnessed like dogs in a go-cart, black, saturated with wet, and more than half-naked – crawling upon their hands and feet, and dragging their heavy loads behind them – they present an appearance undescribably disgusting and unnatural. (commissioner)[20]

For children, the centre of social meaning is the family. This is true, perhaps even truer, for those children the Victorians called the waifs and strays. Being without a family, like being without a state, only underlines that absence of being and identity. Name, family, state: without these things you are nobody. For children, their 'name-within-a-family' is the strongest definition of who they are.

That being so, the name-within-a-family is the origin and centre of identity. It is the first ground of value. But as this chapter has emphasized, that ground is much fought over, not only within the family, but by the forces that press from outside. From the mid-nineteenth century onwards, the imagery used to describe the family included terms like 'haven', 'refuge', 'harbour', 'arbour', 'garden of Eden', 'secure little plot', 'tiny domestic principality' and so forth.[21] I am asserting here that the conditions of nineteenth-century political and economic life forced the *haute bourgeoisie* who were the prime makers of the symbolic and expressive culture – the values and meanings their members really sought to live by – to build a new moral system to express, contain, and resist the unprecedented experience of the new political order.

It is necessarily true that the advent of this value system had a particular class genesis, in this case the now dominant *haute bourgeoisie*, the progeny of the successful marriages between the old landowners and the new entrepreneurs. Those marriages provided the plots of innumerable novels, just as – to repeat the tenor of Chapters 1 and 2 – they were and remain the substance of so much gossip. The alliances of Elliotts and Wentworths in *Persuasion*, of Prices and Bertrams in *Mansfield*

---

[20] Quoted from *Report of the Commission on the Employment of Young Persons & Children* (1842) in Coveney, *The Image of Childhood*, p. 94.

[21] This is not an effort to continue Raymond Williams's kind of research in *Keywords* (1976), though there is help there, especially under 'Family' (p. 108). These terms I found in a quick search, in *Our Mutual Friend, Little Dorrit, Jane Eyre, Clara Hopgood, East Lynne, The Trumpet-Major, The Manxman*.

Park, of Bennets and Darcys in *Pride and Prejudice*, of Eyres and Rochesters in *Jane Eyre*, of Brookes and Chettams and then, very differently, Brookes and Ladislaws in *Middlemarch*, all these solid marriages put the new class squarely on the highway. But their great novelists, and the children's novelists who followed them, were in a position – had, that is, the historical opportunity and the individual intelligence – to see what values would do most for human worth in this place and time. And at their best, they went on to criticize, as great writers will, the values most cherished in the name of an imagined but ideal social order, placed this side of paradise, either past or future.

The nineteenth-century novelists were the symbol-makers for a new order. They were leaders of the new order, and they spoke for its strongest purposes, and against its worst tendencies. They placed marriage and its cognates – romantic love, parental love, family life, privacy, home, the essential terms of the politics of the garden – at one pole of the electric current whose opposite pole was the public life of capital and production. Family structure became the ground of personal values.

So, no doubt, it always has been, as my potted history makes clear. But I am placing the family[22] as the central missing link in the interconnections of values, identity and politics which are the elusive particles of the human sciences. The stories told and read in the family, and those read in the primary schools whose ideal moral order is the family, throw into sharp relief the submarine movements of culture and personal being or as it may be put, of ideology and the imagination.[23] In these novels, their authors battled with the new social experience in such a way as to make intelligible and to reproduce the different images of family life emerging from the solidity and anguish, the greatness and the repression, of the big gabled houses with their dim, green gardens and massive doors, then being built in Altrincham, Ranmoor, Headingley, Clifton, Edgbaston, Wimbledon, Hoylake, and stations on every suburban line. For the scientist of Western man, this version of the family stands at the twistpoint of power and spontaneity, of class and spirit, of order and chaos.

[22] And following Christopher Lasch, *Haven in a Heartless World* (1978) in doing so.
[23] I develop a simple axis for the application of these constructs in my *Ideology and the Imagination* (1975).

It always makes sense to speak of the family, at least in post-tribal societies, as the social-structural institution entrusted with making sure the next generation more or less fits the patterns provided by culture and society. As I said, not only does it teach the moral and social rules, it does so within a system which ties these rules to an identity-shape, to the meaning and rigidities of roles, to modalities of thought and feeling. In the family, the child builds speech and self, and the two in tandem. It is the most obvious commonplace, hugely enforced by the social scientific discoveries of a century, that the family shapes identity and personality for ever. It prints a template in the very grain of a child's being which ever afterwards he or she seeks to fit over all experience – the experiences of love and authority, of dominance and freedom, of time and cause.

In the march of 'modernization', whatever we may think of the joys and miseries it brought, the emergence of the child coincides with, and is caused by, the broad theories of the Enlightenment and the Romantic movement about the importance of individual sensibility and moral autonomy. These changes brought about a drastic intensification of emotional life in the bourgeois family. The spokesmen for that family were the myth-makers of the high Victorian suburbs. How were they to place children in the forms of the new world outside the front door?

In the first place, the concentration of capital and production which provided the energy of the nineteenth century also required the creation of the giant institutions and edifices of industrial England which I have listed: factories, schools, hospitals, prisons, district dormitories. If, with Marx, we are to speak of *Verfremdung*, estrangement or alienation, as the most destructive and wounding experience of labour under capitalism, it may best be done in terms of the domination of these giant institutions which the enormous labour of bureaucratization since 1900 or so has only served to render more looming, incomprehensible, and labyrinthine.

The buildings which housed these 'divided' activities – work, punishment, instruction, illness, relief, sleep – were also emblems of a social life in which nothing overlapped and everything was tidied away into its neat categories. The new word 'rationalization' nicely catches the anodyne processes which are now seen written into the tidy bye-laws of freeways, playspaces, shopping precincts, and industrial estates, of three dozen new towns. According to these sensible-sounding divisions, father went out to work and mother minded the children. In itself, this departure was merely traditional – women always had looked after the children along with doing all the housework. That was how children started to learn, sooner or later, about labour and its divisions.[24] In the Victorian bourgeoisie, what was new to the child about father's invisibility during the day was the set of values confirmed and signified by his absence. 'Father' has always expressed power, authority, and discipline, in the family and in society; the peculiar concentrations of English nineteenth-century history darkened the shade of his rule. That he ruled largely in his absence, and therefore in the abstract, served to give these notions greater dread. At the same time, he was warden of other key virtues which kept the private family held in its tension with the public market. These other virtues included practicality, hardheadedness, industriousness, courage, endurance, heroism if need be, resourcefulness, self-control, leadership, magnetism, all these gathered under the very general heading of manliness. In turn, manliness connoted the embodiments of command, mastery, power, conviction. At the same time, at least in the noblest versions held out by poets and rhetoricians of what it was to be a man, a father expected of himself and his children a high moral idealism and earnestness.[25] It is this idealism which so powerfully shaped the moral structure of the public schools until very recently, and declared itself in the young subaltern's reading-list – in John Buchan, Dorothy Sayers, Geoffrey Household. What happened, even as idealism was itself declared a virtue (which because of circularity it is logically pointless to do), was that morally earnest Victorian leaders could find no actual object on which to agree as characterizing ideal success. They therefore recommended an objectless aspiration, a pure moral ardour in which aspiration is identified simply as passionate yearning for Will Ladislaw's 'indeterminate loftiest thing'. Idealism was transmuted into a keen emotion, blindly searching for a vague, glorious target.

In men, the target or object was action, and women were

---

[24] See David Hunt, *Parents and Children in History: The Psychology of Family Life in Early Modern History* (1972).
[25] See Walter Houghton, *The Victorian Frame of Mind* (1957), pp. 218–304.

both the prize and the audience. In women, the object of their aspiration was first a man, and subsequently his children. But this idealism is more specific, and therefore more easily held within the frames of everyday life. The most powerful ideal of Victorian women was to be passionately in love; it remains the most powerful imagined state of popular fiction. When, in the nature of things, this passionate state became either inappropriate or inaccessible (as they became older, or as marriage replaced betrothal), the passionate aspiration was displaced onto the children who, because they sought endlessly to renounce the power of maternal dependence while longing to remain dependent, experienced in the high emotional tension of the mother–child relationship a vivid struggle to achieve autonomy by transcending self-love and becoming capable of the love of others.

It was Freud, supremely, who battled to codify these electric forces, and he sought to do so out of the human experience which was to hand, in his case the wealthy Viennese Jewish families of the late nineteenth and early twentieth century. Those families, as has been widely noted, were in many ways unlike contemporary European families (let alone North American or other families outside European cultures). The typical Judaist father was indeed an absent patriarch, severe, punitive, and both passionate and unbending. English-speaking Victorian families were sufficiently the same, as the shelves full of Victorian novels and autobiographies[26] bear testimony. These structures, in which father and mother divided power and love in the way I have described, compressing a range of values into one or the other parent, gave rise to Freud's key concepts. Like any theorist of fields of force, he hypostasized certain main lines of energy as forming decisive figures which were each reprinted in the structure of each personality (or self, and the self's identity). These figures trace themselves in the triad *superego – ego – id*, and the triad itself vibrates in relation to the oedipal struggle to supplant the father and love the mother, to bring into equilibrium the consequent lines of love and hate, and to bend daemonic energies within manageable limits as they flow irresistibly on towards Thanatos (death wish) or Eros (pleasure principle).

[26] Best seen, perhaps, in the character of Mr Murdstone in *David Copperfield*; the patriarch is more sympathetically dealt with by Edmund Gosse in *Father and Son* (1907).

The power of Freud's scheme is that it is dynamic; it places personality squarely in the family; it recognizes the desperation of inner conflict, its profundity and endurance through life; it gives a name to the facts of repression and a source for the importance we give to sexuality and the fear of death. Freud offers a theory about the causes and the meanings of virtue and wickedness which well suits the post-Romantic emphasis on the passions and on individuality.

Now this book is not a tract in post-Freudian analysis. Freud's work was in any case drastically modified and reconstructed by those who followed his initial lead. Some of what he wrote is in parallel with the theories of Jung. But the point of this brief synopsis of his theories is to press upon the complex, delicate, and irresistible intersection of personality (psyche), social structure (the stratification of power, particularly as the family reflects and reproduces it), and social values (ideology). Freud may be charged with neglecting social structure,[27] and with supposing that the conflicts he revealed were timeless. But he connected personality in its essential shape to the forces of family life.

The great theoretician whose account of the causal and shaping force of social structure dominates the nineteenth century is Marx. Marx, in his turn, neglects the psyche; he shows no awareness of the presence of the subconscious. For our purposes, however, his strength is that he insists on the penetrative and pervasive omnipotence of the systems of production – the irresistible torque of capital on plant, on labour, on profit, and back again, the spiral curving upwards for ever. He saw that this energy coursed through the veins of individual families, inasmuch as it penetrated classes and history.

The mystery of the commodity form, therefore, is simply that it takes the social characteristics of men's own labour and reflects them back to men as the objective characteristics of the products of labour themselves, as the natural properties of these things. It thus also reflects the social relation of the producers to the totality of labour as a social relation of objects, one that exists independently of the producers.[28]

Mine is not a Freudian thesis, nor is it Marxist. But the power of Marx's model, unclear as it is as to how determinist these

27 Except, perhaps, in his late and brilliant essay, *Civilization and Its Discontents* (1930).
28 Karl Marx, *Capital*, vol. I, p. 77.

processes are, is that it describes and explains how economic systems become part of our way of seeing and judging the world in all its aspects. It's hard to say exactly what the sometimes canting phrase 'the systems of production' really means, but it surely makes sense to speak of these as critically shaping all our social relations, and as penetrating even our profoundest centres of value and sacredness. The process hinted at in the short quotation from *Capital* is busily at work in all our dealings, as are the battles italicized by Freud. If we are to speak, as we must, to our children of love and goodness and duty, we must do so in a morality capable of including the theories of Marx and Freud, and capable also of precepts which will advise us how to act not as single, isolated selves, but as social beings, in a living history.

The names of Marx and Freud serve to suggest the entirely new analysis required by the conditions emerging during the second half of the nineteenth century. It was out of the same conditions that the first novels which had any more to them than nursery homiletics were written for children. I pass over such claims as can be made for the books which came from Newbery bookshops from 1780 onward.[29] They are noteworthy simply because they date the arrival of pulp fiction written for children; significantly enough, they follow a few decades after the arrival of such fiction for middle-class women.[30] Similarly, the celebrated *History of Sandford and Merton* by Thomas Day which came out between 1783 and 1789, and his successors in the first 40 years of the nineteenth century – Mrs Trimmer, Hannah More, Mrs Sherwood and *The Fairchild Family*, and later Mrs Ewing, Mrs Molesworth, and the early providers for boys of spirit like Captain Marryat and R. M. Ballantyne – are all more morally earnest products of the same industry. But these latter names, along with the advent of a novel like *Tom Brown's Schooldays* (1869), mark a new stage in novels for children. The writers who follow them make up a first, essential tradition. They are explicitly seeking for metaphors with which to understand this new world, and for a morality by which to live well within it.

[29] See J. H. Plumb's article already cited, also Gillian Avery, *Childhood's Pattern* (1975), pp. 13–120, and S. Roscoe, *John Newbery and His Successors 1740–1814: A Bibliography* (1973).
[30] See R. Mayo, *The English Novel in the Magazines, 1740–1815* (1962).

The new social structure isolated and intensified the life of the family. The genesis of novels for children lies there. The Romantic movement gave new flame and brilliance to the individual spirit; capitalism isolated that spirit within the individual family (of whatever size); Victorian Christianity provided a patriarchal theodicy to fit the reasonably well-off.

This elementary diagram of forces gives us a way of understanding the interplay of families and their fiction. The vigorous individual tensed himself against the patriarchy; both forces wrestled with the contradictions of a political economy which on the one hand drove them back to dress their wounds in the sanctuaries of private life, and on the other called them out to assert their enterprise in the dangerous competition for economic reward and destruction. The great nineteenth-century novels give rich, vivid life to the struggles of freedom with authority, love with power, parent with child, passion with duty, sincerity with convention, individual with society. These books, wonderful books, are not great *because* they speak up for these slogans; they are great because they work their way through to a resolution of what it means to live them fully. But they begin with the rousing music of these calls to moral and political action.

The emotional life of the Victorian family was intense, irresistible, and intolerable. Its pressure was not caused by its size, nor by its alleged 'nucleation'. It was caused by its becoming, in the value system of the ruling bourgeoisie, a mixed metaphor of harbour, flower garden, cloister, and dugout. Its shrine and its magazine was and remains the family home. Such metaphors have led naturally to their embodiments in terms of social roles. Over the years, that is, certain occupations define the dominant meanings of those values: thus women as nurses, primary-schoolteachers, playmates; men as soldiers, engine drivers, sportsmen.

The clear boundary line between public and private life corresponded to the line between 'outer' and 'inner' life. Inner life was placed in the care of the loving and sympathetic mother and centred upon the feelings; outer or public life was abstractly embodied by the absent father, and carried in the austere authority of social institutions. The modality of inner life was passionate but passive, of the outer life, reasonable, repressed, and effectual. Because, however, the liberal spirit has always been so strong in the class which shaped this family structure out of the history available to it, the best intelligences of its membership have always sought to criticize the splits, wounds, and cruelties wrought by their own value systems and their institutions. Such criticisms are the stuff of the best children's and adults' novels.

The best writers seek to create an ideal social order out of the values there are to hand. Or, in case it seems again that I am saying that novelists (for adults or children) should deal only with the wholesome things of life, and never treat of material which might bring a blush to a young person's cheek, let me put the same point like this: a novelist ought to create fictions which criticize the life he finds about him from the standpoint of the finest life he can imagine. His work enables his readers to find the best and fullest, the freest and most admirably self-aware versions of life which it is possible to lead in the circumstances of the time.

I take these three criteria of value[31] as the necessary points in a trigonometry of human life. But it is a tricky argument to establish briefly, and I am anxious not to be misunderstood. Terms like 'best' and 'fullest', 'freest' and 'most admirably self-aware' commit my argument about novels not so much to certain fixed judgements, as to the inescapability of judgement itself. Once upon a time, students of literature were warned not to look for social messages in a novel; trusting the tale and not the teller was a way of putting it, never very satisfactory. But the claims that novels rendered up their meaning from within looked, with the passage of time, merely time-serving. Novelist and reader alike come to novels with a purpose; they have questions of their own to answer, and the novels they read and write, if they are serious, are at least ways of asking them. In which case, having asked for the freest and most fulfilled versions of life in particular historical circumstances, although that inquiry cannot exonerate you and them from living the life relative to the time, the judgement to be lived through and made on the result is passed in the name of the best you can convincingly imagine. Thus the imagination may hold

---

[31] Proposed by Charles Taylor in unpublished paper, already referred to in Chapter 1, n. 30. I am immensely in his debt for his help, and grateful for his permission to use his ideas here. See also his paper, 'Force et sens: les deux dimensions irréductibles d'une science de l'homme', in *Sens et Existence* (1975).

together desire and plausibility. The old mistake was to suppose that the cultivated reader's response to the novel was chastened by his taste and sensibility, without seeing that those qualities are remorselessly social and historical. The new mistake is to suppose that, this being so, judgements are *merely* social and historical, and that there is no way of knowing truth, goodness, beauty and wisdom for what they are; indeed, that these incorrigibly moralizing terms are ones to do without, both in literature and in life.

Both mistakes drive the reading and writing of fiction deeper into the relativist's world-picture with which I want to do so much battle as will show it to be well-intentioned, deeply obtuse, and self-contradictory. Relativism insists that all human action is relative to its situation and can only be understood in terms of that situation. So far, so good. However, the validity of human meaning in that situation turns out to be quite special to it, and someone who comes across it 'has no right to interfere' – or even to judge it, since the people in the situation are doing what they must, and what they must is none of our business. Typical examples include the beliefs and practices of primitive peoples, and the beliefs and practices of children. The same position is implied in a whole vocabulary of everyday moral terms which include such staff-room platitudes as 'I've no right to impose my views on them', 'It's just my opinion; you must choose for yourself', 'Who's to say that this is a good book – it's up to the individual', 'Isn't it rather arrogant to claim you know best?' The most notorious elision of moral arguments transpires in the complacent phrases, 'true for me' or 'true for them'.

The phrase exemplifies the extreme attenuation to which recent history has brought our moral language. Truth is no doubt a complicated property, and truthfulness a rare quality not only by virtue of its inconvenient consequences, but because it's hard to know how to give it body and language. (Though these self-doubting agonies can be overdone. We most of us *know* when we are lying. My wayside pulpit-point is that we no longer care very much.) Nonetheless, what is true, is true, however hard to find. The truth can't just be my truth and his falsehood. The existence of God or ghosts isn't just a matter of personal preference.

The argument about relativism can hardly be dealt with fully here. Its good intentions stem from the conviction that you shouldn't just bulldoze over people's lives and ways of life. Its obtuseness resides in not seeing that on many occasions its precepts are intolerable and lethal: Nazism is not exempt from judgement, however true it was for Eichmann; similarly you would hardly agree to offer yourself up to a cannibal as his 'juicy little, right little, missionary stew', for fear that a disobliging refusal would otherwise non-relatively interfere with his world-picture. Lastly and more technically, relativists contradict themselves in non-relatively setting up an absolute principle which their other principles cannot justify.

It seems a fair guess, however, that only idiots or saints could really live the relativism of its advocates. What is so important for my purpose is that the forms of relativism and those of individualism are now bonded in an impregnable self-satisfaction within so much of the present-day social and moral structures.

This chapter has insisted that the imagining of the good life and the criticism of the bad from which the novelist and his reader start is both a literary and an everyday human activity; its practice opposes itself to relativism. The terms of judgement change; their 'irreducible dimensions' do not. This is true even in the short span covered by the novels in this book. We live at a time when by and large individuals are valued above institutions, when your choice is more precious than your duty, when personal sincerity surpasses fidelity. These are the terms of moral judgement; they provide the context of everyday ethics. The novels in this book seek, as they and their fellows must, to criticize these present values on the grander scale of freedom, fulfilment, and self-critical awareness. These are in Taylor's phrase the 'irreducible dimensions', the rounder form of human morality. They are the necessary sources of energy and of the direction of human purposes which are the ground of being.

This is to assert the position of a classical humanism. That is, human beings seek out of a natural, ungainsayable motion to live in such a way that they are free and fulfilled and aware of themselves as realizing these states or not. Success or failure can only be a matter of definition – the definitions a particular history and society make possible. The stand Lewis Carroll makes for Alice is not the same as that which Mark Twain makes for Jim and Huck Finn, but both novelists stand up for children's and for human fulfilment. And if fulfilment and freedom sound as though they may be too easily revamped by the tunesmiths of the advertisements, they are checked by that no less human motion of altruistic self-criticism of which I spoke in the first chapter, and from which we may devise an argument to explain the sense in which a concern for the interests of others depends on a full recognition of their reality; that recognition is of course possible only if one can view oneself impersonally.

On such an argument, novels are criticisms of life, just as this book is. Each mode of thought ponders the values and meanings of the day, and seeks out the images of life, past, present and in the looked-for future, which help rediscover the right tension between the individual and the social institutions without which he is nothing. They set the critical balance of scepticism and belief, the right relation between the world and the self, which make a good life.

The strong line which starts from the bourgeois family of the nineteenth century in all its intensity, passionate unhappiness and rapture, its close bonds and inescapable embraces, wears steadily more threadbare as this century goes forward. In the contracting scales of human understanding from geology to archaeology to history, a single life is hardly more visible than a millimetre. The reach of this book is hardly longer than that of a single life. The first great novel for children is *Alice's Adventures in Wonderland*; it was published in 1865. Its genesis lay in the force-field of the Victorian family, with its energy lines surging inwards from the Romantics, the market, and the voice of God the Father.

That energy moved irregularly along two axes. On the one, Victorian family life, with all its repressive and creative power; on the other, the individual spirit. Either term of the co-ordinates could work for good or evil. Family life can exert a killing obliteration of the self or it can give that self the loyalty, the home, the love which it cherishes. The free spirit can find its own singleness of creative life, or it can become downright egotistical. *Alice's Adventures in Wonderland* speak up for Alice's unquenchable spirit against the arbitrary conditions, the vanity and cruelty of so many adults, their feebleness masked by their tart and punitive rituals for the scrutiny of children, their craziness and hypocrisy. In the name of the comedy of things, Lewis Carroll told children how childish adults were, how accurate a picture of the world children could make by imagining their elders in a bestiary.

Very few people, 115 years later, speak to children as the Queen spoke to Alice. By now, the free-spirited child does not know what to join or where to place his or her loyalty. The structures of domination have receded to the unintelligible distances of government and bureaucracy. Insofar as the family is a problem (in the language of the bureaucracy itself, the 'problem-family') it threatens children because it cannot hold together, or because it is itself oppressed and sickened. What has happened? What are the structures of personality which modern family life makes possible, again for good and ill, in the present? Any schematic answer of mine can only be rough and ready: the careful and precise answers are there in the novels, insofar as they are any good. But as a way of emphasizing the push of this inquiry, perhaps it will do to say that first of all values were divided into public and private, into the competition of capital and the collaboration of domesticity. Subsequently, capital and the creation of investment surplus moved into an unholy combination with the symbolism of the romantic individual. It is too inclusive and simple a heuristic to offer as any more than a handhold into present-day imaginative life, but let us say that since 1945 the demands of capitalism for well-trained consumers have deeply penetrated the terms of private life. The new technology fitted itself to the old class system; the doctrines of individualism drove the huge engine of production, waste, investment and innovation. As consumption came to subtend production, so the organization of leisure came to dominate family life. To maintain and increase levels of consumption, first wives went out to work, and then the teenagers. By the same token, and in order to maintain spending power, overmanning became essential, and unemployable teenagers were paid enough to keep them buying and window-shopping. The essential material unit became the individual spender; his and her ideal type the golden-tanned, brilliantly smiling and carefree beauties of advertisement and scented soap opera. The boundary of the Victorians between public and private became infinitely porous beneath the soft, penetrative bombardments of consumer culture. Resistance to these is become a moral imperative at a time when it is clear that the dream of the consumer culture is fairly and squarely over. The heroes and heroines of as mixed a bag of modern adolescent novels as K. M. Peyton's *The Beethoven Medal*, Alan Garner's *Red Shift*, Jill Paton Walsh's *Goldengrove*, William Mayne's *The Jersey Shore*, Rosemary Sutcliff's *Dawn Wind* are all unmistakably children of their time. They have been granted its ambiguous freedoms and, give or take a bit, have no trouble with their parents. What they need to find are new certainties to be made out of old confusions. The history of the best families has taught them that they have no absolute entitlement to agreeable experiences, or not at least without a schedule of duties attached. Their distance from their Victorian and Edwardian counterparts is taken by the extent of their independence. The children of the new novels count Alice as their sister, and Ratty and Mole as their playmates, but they have to do a great deal more for themselves these days.

Part II

Texts and Contexts

The Old Books

4

The lesser great tradition

I mentioned *Alice* as the first masterpiece of literature written if not only for children, at least so that children may understand it. To say so raises at once questions of definition in the genre of children's fiction. Too much genre-chopping is a tedious side-industry of literary theory: dead for a docket. Let us rather count as children's fiction whatever children read. Obviously, a great many novelists address themselves directly to children; equally obviously a great many adults read those novels with pleasure and as adults.

On one hand, it is simply ignorant not to admit that children's novelists have developed a set of conventions for their work. Such development is a natural extension of the elaborate and implicit system of rules, orthodoxies, improvisations, customs, forms and adjustments which characterize the way any adult tells stories or simply talks at length to children. The conventions are less formal than habitual.[1] They include, for obvious reasons, making children the protagonists – the subjects of the book – but not so much characters to 'identify with', in the loose phrase, as characters who are intelligible and recognizable; not so much people like oneself, as people whose like one knows. The conventions also permit less concern about probability, both in plot and in circumstances; since, for reasons we shall look at later, children in novels need to be freed from too much parental tyranny, the opening circumstances often work to clear parents away. But the cavalier treatment of probability extends a good deal wider than such simple ground-clearing. It displays a readiness to dispense with time and space, to wheel on gothic engines, revenants, ghouls, monsters, to permit wild coincidence and hair's-breadth escape,

[1] I take most of these characteristics from Dennis Butts in his introduction to *Good Writers for Young Readers* (1977).

each detail of which has its particular justification, but all of which are more roundly commended to children's novelists as encouraging the freest possible *play* of the imagination, as is proper for children. The ideal-type children's novel is often shorter than most adult novels, to suit the stamina of its readers, and its conscious limitation on formal intricacy (the author usually takes for granted her or his own omniscience, for example), and on difficulty of syntax, its greater simplification (though not superficiality) of moral issues, together with pain-staking and explicit commentary, are all self-explanatory tokens of a proper earnestness and instructiveness on the part of the novelist.

On the other hand, these reach-me-down taxonomies are no help when you pick up *Pilgrim's Progress, Pickwick Papers, The Prisoner of Zenda, The Plague Dogs* or *The Jersey Shore*. It is more help to think of an overlap of readership and author's inten-tions, heavily shaded where the main lists of Puffins and Armada Lions fall, paler as the circle of readership overlaps less with the author's intentions, as it does with the class of 'sunken best-sellers' like Rider Haggard's and Daphne du Maurier's which I discuss in Chapter 6, and paler too where the author is taken up by a very different readership from that which he first set out to address, as perhaps happened to Richard Adams with *Watership Down* or to the author of *The House with the Green Shutters*.

Alice's Adventures in Wonderland, then, is a case in point. It really doesn't matter whether you classify it as a children's or an adults' novel. Much more use is C. S. Lewis's much-quoted and attractively warm-hearted remark: 'No book is really worth reading at the age of ten which is not equally (and often far more) worth reading at the age of 50.' *Alice* is a great work; I read it with greater pleasure and understanding now than ever I did as a child, but I press it into my child's hands.

We may argue as to whether it really initiates the main line of children's fiction. There is nothing else in literature like it, and yet it is profoundly influential. It stands obliquely to all the others of this first group which I name as the beginning of a great tradition of children's fiction in England. Those that follow – *The Secret Garden, The Railway Children, The Wind in the Willows* and, in a later chapter, *Puck of Pook's Hill* – are settled much more clearly and comfortably in the landscape of the Victorian novel. Their authors can call on the structures of feelings and the cadences of the Brontës, Dickens, and the early George Eliot. They are all of them well read in the mistier poetry of Tennyson and the Rossettis; they see the lovely countryside of late Victorian England through the prints and paintings of the Pre-Raphaelites.

Lewis Carroll is another master altogether. And yet, as my short history was intended to make clear, he transpires from the Victorian culture and the family life which was made by the bourgeoisie from the materials to hand – their Christianity, their capital, their nursery. As I insisted, he doesn't simply *reflect* that life; he criticizes it in the name of the greater freedom he saw as being due to children, and visible within their best representatives. He brought to life, as great writers will, the best tendencies of the children of the age, their dauntlessness, their confident selfhood, their sharp, bright vision of the cowardliness and bullying of their elders. Inasmuch as Alice is Victorian, and intent on seeing and judging quite artlessly the overdone respectabilities and deadly formulae of the times, she speaks for values and victories which are distinct from the present. To that extent, we read her historically, to enlarge and deepen our present by seeing it in that longer perspective. Inasmuch as Alice is timeless, it is because the vast energy of human pretentiousness is also timeless, and the deceits and small cruelties practised by adults on children, and by men on men, vary only in degree and not in kind. To see, with Lewis Carroll, that this energy is both perverse and overwhelmingly funny is to give children a great moral truth: that if you find the world comic you will not fear it. And although fear in itself is not vicious, you may as well reserve it for what is fearful.

In a famous and indispensable essay on *Alice*,[2] William Empson set a standard for the criticism of children's fiction. I shall not treat the novel at the same length, but use Empson only to endorse W. H. Auden's claim that 'Alice is an adequate symbol for what every human being should try to be like.'[3] That's rather a bald way to put it, of course, but Alice's combination of gravity and pertness, radical innocence and virtuous intelligence, courage and courtesy, makes her, as

[2] In *Some Versions of Pastoral* (1935).
[3] 'Today's Wonder-World Needs Alice', in *Aspects of Alice*, ed. Robert Phillips (1974), pp. 29–40.

indeed she was, the best child of the Dean of Christ Church, both Queen of Oxford high society, and its subversive judge, especially at the end of *The Looking-Glass*:

There was not a moment to be lost. Already several of the guests were lying down in the dishes, and the soup-ladle was walking up the table towards Alice's chair, beckoning to her impatiently to get out of its way.

'I ca'n't stand this any longer!' she cried, as she jumped up and seized the table-cloth with both hands: one good pull, and plates, dishes, guests, and candles came crashing down together in a heap on the floor. (p. 337)

This is the final, satisfying resolution of anger and frustration, and who hasn't thought of doing it? The child's deepest rebellion finds its ideal image; the call to a larger freedom expresses itself by piling into one enormous rubbish heap all the machinery of greed, snobbery, waste, pride, voluptuousness, which may be found on and around the High Table at Christ Church.

Alice herself is changeless. Her maturity, at seven years six months, is that of the perfectly achieved little girl – perfect not in the governess's book, but in Lewis Carroll's. Thus, in the extremely subtle scene with the Gnat in *The Looking-Glass*, what comes out most strongly is her fear of inadvertently hurting so dreadfully sensitive and tender a creature. At the same time, she *will* speak the truth quite candidly and without trouble, because not hurting people's feelings is a negative virtue, and judging rightfully is a human duty. So the Gnat says 'That's a joke. I wish *you* had made it.' The Gnat jokes piteously but unstoppably. Remorselessly anxious to please by being found comical, he also hopes to please by handing his best jokes over as the most generous gift he can think of. But 'Why do you wish *I* had made it?' Alice asked. 'It's a very bad one.' And she goes on, with a combination of great good sense (there's nothing anyone can do for the Gnat) and the unfeelingness which is a necessary part of great good sense, simply to leave the Gnat to stew in his own juice of self-pity and self-loathing.

In *Alice*, and perhaps in life, well-bred little girls are perfect and complete. The shift from latency to puberty is, on this view, so drastic as to constitute the advent of a new self. Certainly, it is easy for the adult to see the sexual symbolisms in those extraordinary and powerful dreams told, as they are, with a glassy calm which keeps terror at bay just as long as you stay within Carroll's tone of voice, and don't imagine too keenly what the language says. So the frightful images of tumescence in Alice's swelling to a monstrous size and as quickly diminishing, especially when we see her neck grossly extended in Tenniel's drawing, or see her crammed into the shrinking room, don't need any sexual interpretation for us to remember the horrible nightmares which are common to us all. We can manage them, as children can, because they are so calmly told. But they appear so abruptly and in such an *uncaused* way as to make it impossible to forget more elemental and life-shaking possibilities in the most social and conventional of encounters in this dense, Oxonian world.

The pity of things is part of their comedy. In Jonathan Miller's television adaptation of *Wonderland* for the BBC in 1968, he made an anthropomorphic reversion of Carroll's ideas: he put back the people for whom the mythical creatures were the tropes. Thus, Ralph Richardson for the caterpillar, John Gielgud for the Gryphon, Peter Sellers for the King of Hearts. For the benefit of adults revisiting the story in all its bitter nostalgia, he restored the child's-eye view of their elders and betters (can anyone forget the hacking anonymous cough during the trial, placed as it was in a *church*, and therefore quoting to every lapsed Anglican his own experience of meaningless matins, broken only by Aunt Edie's hacking cough). As a critical comment on Carroll's masterpiece, it couldn't be bettered. Alice, in all her brisk, pert, sympathetic independence, faces out the impossible adults and their crazy rituals with her own moral strength and the absolute class confidence which is the support of her virtue. Nobody touches her, for all their threats, and although she shows a decorous timidity, she is never really disconcerted, she laughs easily, and she treats everyone not only according to their station, but according to their deserts:

The table was a large one, but the three were all crowded together at one corner of it. 'No room! No room!' they cried out when they saw Alice coming. 'There's *plenty* of room!' said Alice indignantly, and she sat down in a large arm-chair at one end of the table.

'Have some wine,' the March Hare said in an encouraging tone.

Alice looked all round the table, but there was nothing on it but tea. 'I don't see any wine,' she remarked.

'There isn't any,' said the March Hare.

'Then it wasn't very civil of you to offer it,' said Alice angrily.

'It wasn't very civil of you to sit down without being invited,' said the March Hare.

'I didn't know it was *your* table,' said Alice; 'it's laid for a great many more than three.'

'Your hair wants cutting,' said the Hatter. He had been looking at Alice for some time with great curiosity, and this was his first speech.

'You shouldn't make personal remarks,' Alice said with some severity; 'it's very rude.' (pp. 92–3)

It's hard to keep up solemnity, prating on about a scene so familiar in our folklore, so intrinsically funny. Alice keeps steadily on, holding together the essential human link between manners and morality, glowing in all her prim sanity in the midst of this richly insane world. But child and grown-up alike can only delight in the boisterous anarchy, the image of a cast of mind which pushes the semantic sport of early linguistic analysis into the madness which is just the other side of its genteelly pointless antics:

'Why, what are *your* shoes done with?' said the Gryphon. 'I mean, what makes them so shiny?'

Alice looked down at them, and considered a little before she gave her answer. 'They're done with blacking, I believe.'

'Boots and shoes under the sea,' the Gryphon went on in a deep voice, 'are done with whiting. Now you know.'

'And what are they made of?' Alice asked in a tone of great curiosity.

'Soles and eels, of course,' the Gryphon replied rather impatiently: 'any shrimp could have told you that.'

'If I'd been the whiting,' said Alice, whose thoughts were still running on the song, 'I'd have said to the porpoise, "Keep back, please: we don't want *you* with us!"'

'They were obliged to have him with them,' the Mock Turtle said: 'no wise fish would go anywhere without a porpoise.'

'Wouldn't it really?' said Alice in a tone of great surprise.

'Of course not,' said the Mock Turtle: 'why, if a fish came to *me* and told me he was going a journey, I should say, "With what porpoise?"'

'Don't you mean "purpose"?' said Alice.

'I mean what I say,' the Mock Turtle replied in an offended tone. And the Gryphon added, 'Come, let's hear some of *your* adventures.'

'I could tell you my adventures – beginning from this morning,' said Alice a little timidly: 'but it's no use going back to yesterday, because I was a different person then.'

'Explain all that,' said the Mock Turtle.

'No, no! The adventures first,' said the Gryphon in an impatient tone: 'explanations take such a dreadful time.' (pp. 134-5)

It is an amazingly packed novel. Whichever page you turn to is rich in its implication, familiar and fresh. Both *Alice* books are rich enough to merit the extensive commentary they have received – I can hardly forbear to praise, where it has not been so very widely pointed out, the delight and facility of Lewis Carroll's verse. The verse parodies which punctuate the books could only be the work of a man not only accomplished as a minor poet, but deeply soaked in the rhythms and inflections of the verses and masters (most obviously Wordsworth) which he seeks to parody. There can hardly be a better introduction to poetry, as Auden noted. But of the many strengths of Carroll's masterpieces, it is enough for my purposes to note three. Each finds its likeness in other novels of this sketch of a great tradition.

The first is that, for all their brevity, the two *Alice* books are packed with *characters*. The busy world of the Victorian novel and the Victorian market place fills the rooms and gardens with social meeting. Whatever the peculiarities and crippled places of the White Knight, the Red Queen, the Gryphon, Gnat, Mouse, Duchess, and Hatter, they are unmistakably *there* (perhaps even most memorably there when, like the Cheshire Cat, they keep disappearing). The novels, like bourgeois social life at the time, occupy a peopled landscape, and it is supremely Carroll's intention, as it is Dickens's, to present 'the arrogant and the froward and the vain' as they 'fretted, and chafed, and made their usual uproar' (the last line of *Little Dorrit*). Christ Church and Oxford were Carroll's subject-matter, and in 1865, these places were sufficiently near the centre of things for them to prefigure the essence of Victorian bourgeois life.

Against this teeming and always located social life, Carroll's second strength is to counterpose this ideal little girl. The peculiar vantage point of this eccentric, original mathematician–logician, placed by his gifts and his bachelor solitude in that wide margin of history, gave him the ideal instrument with which to praise and blame his society. As I said, Alice is the best daughter imaginable – best, that is, not to a governess, not even to a Dean of an Oxford college, but to her author, able to see what Victorian manners and morality could do if they really set themselves to bring up a morally excellent daughter, a calm and pure centre of consciousness. If you celebrate courtesy *and* courage, calm good sense *and* dauntlessness, grace *and* candour, you can hardly do better than Alice. The theory of education and childhood development which the Romantics put into circulation has Alice as its first, best triumph. To say so is not to slur over her priggishness nor her wholesome self-centredness, for it is part of the greatness of what Carroll has done to make these qualities essential to her charm.

The third strength is implied both by the busyness of the world of *Alice* and by the solid presence of the heroine. It is that Carroll criticizes the society he pictures in the name of that society's best self. Like Huck Finn, Alice is innocent and right. The world is experienced (though it doesn't learn from experience, but dodges its lessons as hard as it can) and wrong, either confidently (the Duchess) or timorously (the White Knight). Either way, Carroll will leave none of the conventions undisturbed. He upturns pictures of the self (the Duchess says: 'Never imagine yourself not to be otherwise than what it might appear to others that what you were or might have been was not otherwise than what you had been would have appeared to them to be otherwise'), of sex (the Knave of Hearts, the rosebushes and Tiger-lily), of language and reality (the woods of namelessness where the pretty doe comes, the nastier riddling of Humpty-Dumpty), of death, everywhere:

'There's one other flower in the garden that can move about like you,' said the Rose. 'I wonder how you do it –' ('You're always wondering,' said the Tiger-lily), 'but she's more bushy than you are.'

'Is she like me?' Alice asked eagerly, for the thought crossed her mind, 'There's another little girl in the garden, somewhere!'

'Well, she has the same awkward shape as you,' the Rose said: 'but she's redder – and her petals are shorter, I think.'

'They're done up close, like a dahlia,' said the Tiger-lily: 'not tumbled about, like yours.'

'But that's not *your* fault,' the Rose added kindly. 'You're beginning to fade, you know – and then one ca'n't help one's petals getting a little untidy.'

Alice didn't like this idea at all: so, to change the subject, she asked, 'Does she ever come out here?'

'I daresay you'll see her soon,' said the Rose. 'She's one of the kind that has nine spikes, you know.'

'Where does she wear them?' Alice asked with some curiosity.

'Why, all round her head, of course,' the Rose replied. 'I was wondering *you* hadn't got some too. I thought it was the regular rule.'

'She's coming!' cried the Larkspur. 'I hear her footstep, thump, thump, along the gravel-walk!' (pp. 209–10)

Carroll has his plangent note – he strikes it most moistly in the dedicatory verses. But the image of a hot July afternoon in a spacious English garden is largely free of that note. The garden and its larger landscape is the setting of both books. This metonymy for a whole frame of feeling about childhood and its stories, and about the England in which they are cast, embraces also these first novels I take, and recurs as motif in a great many more. The power of that metonymy – the secret garden of childhood and of England – shapes a whole way of thinking and feeling. It is most simply and boldly detailed in Frances Hodgson Burnett's great novel, *The Secret Garden*.

It is also set out most systematically in the world of Beatrix Potter; she may serve as a brief, preliminary example of what I mean. In an ideal reading course for the very earliest years onwards, Beatrix Potter offers herself as the best first fiction for so many of the reasons for which I have commended Lewis Carroll, and she exemplifies here the grammar of literature for Victorian children at its most elementary. She perfects the conventions for the very young in the scale of her books, the delicate adjustment of water-colours to narrative, the grave tone, the careful examination of vocabulary. The imagery of Beatrix Potter's world balances a colonized, accomplished horticulture and agriculture, and the stable but mysterious Nature which lies untamed beyond the garden wall. Everybody's daydream of a perfect holiday for children occurs in such a scene. For the grown-up such a holiday, a pastoral idyll beside the sea or up the dale, lies always glowing at the horizon of memory, twenty, thirty, forty years back. For a nation or for a class, it lies just over the rim of its oldest members' memories – Edwardian summers, the old Queen's last Jubilee, the *fin de siècle*.

The world of Beatrix Potter lives in that geography: Lewis Carroll sent Alice paddling down the Cherwell in the south of the same limitless blue afternoons. But like Carroll, Beatrix Potter peopled her county in a very dry-eyed and dry-toned style. The awful antics of the fubsy little animals in the pages of her latter-day imitators cannot be made her responsibility. On the contrary, the stern and dangerous world in which Jemima Puddleduck is almost eaten by Mr Fox, and Squirrel Nutkin loses his tail as a punishment for cheeking Old Brown the owl, is marked by what we might now think of as a distinctly Victorian moral realism, its sanctions and severities. At the same time, Beatrix Potter, in her tiny compass, has quite enough strength to give her characters life and idiosyncrasy such that it is clear that these creatures are part of Lewis Carroll's or Dickens's society too. In *The Tale of Mrs Tittlemouse* alone, we have the heroine's neurotic over-cleanliness, Mr Jackson's sodden, genial, and repulsive bulk – 'tiddley widdley widdley, pouff, pouff, pouff' – and the mad, importunate assortment of unwanted guests. A critical child's-eye view is given plenty to dislike from an early age. And the same eye and imagination can feed delightedly on every little girl's favourite game of a hole-home, wonderfully safe *underground*, with 'her own little box bed'.

Beatrix Potter sets down, in the thoroughly settled farmlands, gardens, and villages of Westmorland, the colour and variety of Victorian society, its firm structures, its strong base in home and family, its disobedient heroes, its polite little girls, its rich patterns of gentility and roguery. Young readers can best begin there: she includes so much of the great abstractions – history, morality, class, work – and gives them her special vividness, in both words and water-colour.

I have made this short digression into Beatrix Potter in order is to stress her affinity with Lewis Carroll. Both are Victorians, and great ones in their way. There is much more to Carroll, of course, but my immediate point is to stress what a powerful image of the world they hold out to children, and how much there is for children to *recognize* there. Both writers have that peculiar strength of those who are intensely, if variously, attuned to a child's-eye view (Beatrix Potter could be a tough old egg): they can invent a world in which children can immediately pick up their bearings, find experiences and characters presented on their own, the children's terms ('You are *not* to go into Mr Macgregor's garden . . . but Peter, who was very naughty . . .'), and go on to find the world of the book deepening, shaping and altering the world outside the book. A child who begins with the secure social structure, the settled place, the regular patterning of bravery and retribution in Beatrix Potter is doing far more than meet the conventional fixities of Victorian England. The bold imagery and striking, simple narratives carry with them a staid, strong version of what to do and how to act. By the time the child gets to *Alice*, he or she finds the house of fiction a much more ambiguous and subversive and wildly comic place. It is one in which action is harder and purposes go abruptly astray, in which you are more likely to be put upon in grotesquely cunning ways, and in which you can do what is rational and right only by seeing how ridiculous the world is, and keeping the facts to yourself. To that extent, *Alice*, like the greatest fairy stories, is perennially truer to children's lives than those novels which show them turning their world upside down.

The Secret Garden stands at another corner of the forces contained by this assortment of novels. As I said, it catches and intensifies in its central image all the energy which the Victorians directed at the home. The garden cherishes those strong, glad, positive qualities which were driven from the man's business world and left to the tender but passive care of the mother. But Frances Hodgson Burnett has a greater ambition for her book. She seeks not only to cherish the values of the garden, but to imagine them restored to the new public life of an ideal social order. 'An ideal social order' is just a slogan, of course, and yet my earlier assertion stands: implicit in every good story we tell to our children (setting aside the storytellers who are rancid with cynicism) is the moral: 'Look, this is how the world ought to be. Try to make it like that when you're grown up. We haven't managed it, we older ones; perhaps you will.' Whatever has happened to the idea of beauty and happiness in adult art, our children must keep faith with their radical innocence. That is our own, and the novelist's, act of faith for the future. It expresses our faith that our children will *have* a future.

But *The Secret Garden*, like the other novels I praise in this book, seeks to imagine the finest life possible and to use it to criticize and improve the life being lived around it at the time. Frances Hodgson Burnett wrote straight from the well-springs of Romanticism; the influence of the Brontës is felt on every page of the novel. She takes the great convictions of the Romantics that the 'nature', not, so to speak, of Edmund but of Edgar and Cordelia,[4] needs only to be given a breathing-space to express itself in pure and excellent lives. But she turns certain expectations back to front in order to celebrate this commonplace. First, sensing (in 1911) the oppression and etiolation of family life, she removes her hero and heroine from their parents' care by making one an orphan, and the other, Colin, abandoned by his widower father in despair. She gives the children an ideal mother in Mrs Sowerby, instinctively sagacious, upright, compassionate; and in a brilliant insight makes Colin into a hypochondriac hysteric, thus providing a real consequence and a metaphor for the distortions wrought by Victorian family life. Frances Hodgson Burnett reinvents a pagan Garden of Eden for the children where culture is detached from labour and returned to creativeness, and which Dickon, the Pan-boy, tends and understands in the name of the mystery which Romanticism sought to keep intact from science. In this Eden, nature dissolves class – gardener and Pan-boy share the broadly human vocation of nursing the invalid boy to straight health, and helping the queer, difficult, yellow-faced little girl back into her natural fresh-cheeked shape.

I have spoken as though the book were a dull diagram from an old myth-kitty. In fact, it is alive and quick, full of warm, sympathetic strength of feeling. The Sowerby family are at times too close to picture-postcard peasants for comfort, but the great joy which anybody must feel as spring swings round again is marvellously recreated for the little girl who has never seen it and has known only the arid limitlessness of the Indian plains:

Mary was at his bedside again.

'Things are crowding up out of the earth,' she ran on in a hurry. 'And there are flowers uncurling and buds on everything and the green veil has covered nearly all the grey and the birds are in such a

---

[4] A distinction taken from John Danby, *Shakespeare's Doctrine of Nature* (1956).

hurry about their nests for fear they may be too late, that some of them are even fighting for places in the secret garden. And the rosebushes look as wick as wick can be, and there are primroses in the lanes and woods, and the seeds we planted are up, and Dickon has brought the fox and the crow and the squirrels and a new-born lamb.'

And then she paused for breath. The new-born lamb Dickon had found three days before lying by its dead mother among the gorse bushes on the moor. It was not the first motherless lamb he had found and he knew what to do with it. He had taken it to the cottage wrapped in his jacket and he had let it lie near the fire and had fed it with warm milk. It was a soft thing, with a darling silly baby face and legs rather long for its body. Dickon had carried it over the moor in his arms, and its feeding-bottle was in his pocket with a squirrel, and when Mary had sat under a tree with its limp warmness huddled on her lap, she had felt as if she were too full of strange joy to speak. A lamb – a lamb! a living lamb who lay on your lap like a baby! (*The Secret Garden*, p. 169).

The great strength of this book is the life it gives to these moving commonplaces. Mrs Burnett starts from the positives of Romanticism and goes on to turn these positives into solid details – the garden itself combines the ideal remembered holiday in a golden age, potent to children and adults alike, with a classless, reasonable, and joyous Utopia of the future. Only forty years later, Philippa Pearce wrote her great threnody, *Tom's Midnight Garden*, over that same vision. But Mrs Pearce, as we shall see, is not only a writer of genius, she has the benefit of knowing what happened to some of the Edwardian visions, and how they died. Mrs Burnett's fine book speaks with an optimism which it is notoriously difficult to recover.

She fits easily in this ground plan of the earliest novels in the children's tradition, beside Edith Nesbit. I take *The Railway Children* because it is so well known and well filmed, and because along with *The Secret Garden*, *Alice*, *The Wind in the Willows*, much of Walter de la Mare, Kipling's 'English' stories (like *Puck*), Little Grey Rabbit and Christopher Robin, it lives in that breathing-space forced by men's imaginations and by their struggles and sacrifices, between the family home and the world of work, production, money-making, or the creation of surplus value. These children's writers, in the wake of both poets and politicians, saw the freedom of the countryside as both fact and metaphor for the restoration of a humanness in danger of killing divisions from home and work. It is no accident that so many of these writers were women (or self-consciously separate and 'impractical' men like Dodgson, de la Mare, Kipling). The women saw the separation of manly and feminine virtues as deadly, and attempted to free children from the results of this split. The children (in *The Wind in the Willows*, the animals) have to work out their lives away from parents and placed in the space between home and work. The railway children, for instance, have lost caste when their father is (wrongfully) imprisoned. Their mother must work at her writing to make ends meet. Freed from the moral divisions of labour in the family, with mother ruling at a distance but perfectly combining justice with mercy, the three children set out to make their own moral and political economy.

Once again, they construct that moral economy in a landscape memorably uniting culture and nature. As nowhere else, the railway is at home in the Yorkshire dales where the cuttings follow the natural line of the dale, and the stations are tucked so neatly into the lip of the bank, their fluttering ribbons of bargeboarding setting off so prettily gritstone building and steep beds of wallflowers. The children's first productive move is to steal coal. They are caught by the station master and put to rights about *that*. In a rather touching scene a little later, Peter ensures that the kindly, authoritative station master really knows that it is the erstwhile coal-miner whom he greets so benignly on his way down to work:

It was the Station Master who said 'Good morning' as he passed by. And Peter answered, 'Good morning.' Then he thought:
     'Perhaps he doesn't know who I am by daylight, or he wouldn't be so polite.'
     And he did not like the feeling which thinking this gave him. And then before he knew what he was going to do he ran after the Station Master, who stopped when he heard Peter's hasty boots crunching the road, and coming up with him very breathless and with his ears now quite magenta-coloured, he said:
     'I don't want you to be polite to me if you don't know me when you see me.'
     'Eh?' said the Station Master.
     'I thought perhaps you didn't know it was me that took the coals,' Peter went on, 'when you said "Good morning". But it was, and I'm sorry. There.'

'Why,' said the Station Master, 'I wasn't thinking anything at all about the precious coals. Let bygones be bygones. And where were you off to in such a hurry?'

'I'm going to buy buns for tea,' said Peter.

'I thought you were all so poor,' said the Station Master.

'So we are,' said Peter, confidentially, 'but we always have three-pennyworth of halfpennies for tea whenever Mother sells a story or a poem or anything.'

'Oh,' said the Station Master, 'so your Mother writes stories, does she?'

'The beautifulest you ever read,' said Peter.

'You ought to be very proud to have such a clever Mother.'

'Yes,' said Peter, 'but she used to play with us more before she had to be so clever.'

'Well,' said the Station Master, 'I must be getting along. You give us a look in at the Station whenever you feel so inclined. And as to coals, it's a word that – well – oh, no, we never mention it, ah?'

'Thank you,' said Peter. 'I'm very glad it's all straightened out between us.' And he went on across the canal bridge to the village to get the buns, feeling more comfortable in his mind than he had felt since the hand of the Station Master had fastened on his collar that night among the coals. (*The Railway Children*, p. 51)

It is well done. Edith Nesbit restores Peter to the company of honourable men; the station master has the dignity and the office to be unselfconsciously generous and courteous in all encounters. Like Mr Perks, he has to be highminded to do this, and it is the strenuous highmindedness of the book which, as with the others of the Victorian and Edwardian era, may some-times become irksome. But the highmindedness coincides with great humour and finesse. The second stage of their economy-building is to go to the kindly old gentleman for aid.

The kindly old gentleman has beamed his rubicund way through many a novel since Mr Brownlow rescued Oliver in *Oliver Twist*. In the case of *The Railway Children* I don't think there is any need to say, in a beady-eyed way, that a philanthro-pic railway director could only have the money to be so philan-thropic if he snatched the bread from the bleeding lips of the starving proletarians. In *The Railway Children*, the old gentle-man represents the possibility of a prompt and rational altruism, the possibility, even the likelihood, of which we would always seek to urge upon children. Odd though it now sounds to say so, it is the dream hidden in the idea of a welfare state; the institutions of health and shelter were intended to carry those qualities of care, magnanimity, and understanding which the old gentleman has the power to display.

It is important in the simple moral patterning of the novel that the children, upheld by the altruism of so many people – old gentleman, railwaymen, doctor – which their own earnest commitment to goodness may be said to have called out, themselves go on to act philanthropically. In the third stage of their economy, they make a collection of birthday presents from the villagers to give to their honoured friend Mr Perks the porter at the station. But Mr Perks, in his self-reliance and self-respect, is deeply affronted by the implication of a condescending charity and by the view he understandably imputes to the villagers that he cannot meet his proper domestic responsibilities:

'Then the shovel,' said Bobbie. 'Mr James made it for you himself. And he said – where is it? Oh, yes, here! He said, "You tell Mr Perks it's a pleasure to make a little trifle for a man as is so much respected," and then he said he wished he could shoe your children and his own children, like they do the horses, because, well, he knew what shoe leather was.'

'James is a good enough chap,' said Perks.

'Then the honey,' said Bobbie, in haste, 'and the bootlaces. *He* said he respected a man that paid his way – and the butcher said the same. And the old turnpike woman said many was the time you'd lent her a hand with her garden when you were a lad – and things like that came home to roost – I don't know what she meant. And everybody who gave anything said they liked you, and it was a very good idea of ours; and nobody said anything about charity or anything horrid like that. And the old gentleman gave Peter a gold pound for you, and said you were a man who knew your work. And I thought you'd *love* to know how fond people are of you, and I never was so unhappy in my life. Good-bye. I hope you'll forgive us some day –'

She could say no more, and she turned to go.

'Stop,' said Perks, still with his back to them; 'I take back every word I've said contrary to what you'd wish. Nell, set on the kettle.'

'We'll take the things away if you're unhappy about them,' said Peter; 'but I think everybody'll be most awfully disappointed as well as us.'

'I'm not unhappy about them,' said Perks; 'I don't know,' he added, suddenly wheeling the chair round and showing a very odd-looking screwed-up face, 'I don't know as ever I was better pleased. Not so much with the presents – though they're an A1 collection – but the kind respect of our neighbours. That's worth having, eh, Nell?'

'I think it's all worth having,' said Mrs Perks, 'and you've made a most ridiculous fuss about nothing, Bert, if you ask me.'

'No, I ain't,' said Perks, firmly; 'if a man didn't respect hisself, no one wouldn't do it for him.'

'But everyone respects you,' said Bobbie; 'they all said so.' (pp. 160–2)

The best of liberal values lies in that touching passage. The children, in their innocence, have come up against the lines of class in Edwardian England which they hardly knew to be there, but because their innocence is such that they have themselves created a different structure of moral intention in all the villagers, the new economy may fit the best terms of the old morality. Perks's self-respect matches the children's goodness. Mrs Nesbit sums the lesson up with great tact at the end of the chapter:

When the clergyman called on Mrs Perks, she told him all about it. 'It *was* friendliness, wasn't it, Sir?' said she.

'I think,' said the clergyman, 'it was what is sometimes called loving-kindness.'

So you see it was all right in the end. But if one does that sort of thing, one has to be careful to do it in the right way. For, as Mr Perks said, when he had time to think it over, it's not so much what you do, as what you mean. (p. 162)

Speaking in this way of this fine novel makes it too much into an Edwardian moral homily. In the reading Edith Nesbit's tone is light and blithe and brisk; she very rarely lapses into the gushingness to which her combination of motherly earnestness and uplift inevitably tend. My brief analysis perhaps serves to show how these novels commend to children the best versions of the values made possible by Victorian society, and how the novelists brace those values against both the family and the big world in the creative effort of all writers to transcend division and find a new unity of culture and being.

The last book I want to take in this chapter by way of laying the foundations of the children's novel tradition is *The Wind in the Willows*. (I attach *Puck of Pook's Hill* later.) It would be hard to imagine a parent who loved it not wanting his child to love it. It extends my simple polygon of novels. For while it strongly echoes, as it must, the structures of morality and belief which characterize Frances Hodgson Burnett, Lewis Carroll, Edith Nesbit, and all, it radiates its own geniality and comedy, boisterous high spirits and an unimproving eventfulness which stand squarely with books like *Three Men in a Boat* and *Stalky and Co.*, with the best school stories (*Billy Bunter*, and the early P. G. Wodehouse) and the most graceful elegies on the English landscape of the home counties. A provenance which mixes successfully Frank Richards, Kipling, and Richard Jefferies is bound to be complex, and the delight of this novel rests partly in its rich embodiment of the great fact of friendship and its no less strong representation of the still amazing beauty of the Thames above Pangbourne.

It is a version of pastoral, and none the worse for that. I cannot resist quoting the moment early in the novel, when Mole has first befriended the Water Rat and accepted the invitation to a picnic:

'Shove that under your feet,' he observed to the Mole, as he passed it down into the boat. Then he untied the painter and took the sculls again.

'What's inside it?' asked the Mole, wriggling with curiosity.

'There's cold chicken inside it,' replied the Rat briefly; 'cold-tonguecoldhamcoldbeefpickledgherkinssaladfrenchrollscresssand-widgespottedmeatgingerbeerlemonadesodawater –'

'O stop, stop,' cried the Mole in ecstasies: 'This is too much!'

'Do you really think so?' inquired the Rat seriously. 'It's only what I always take on these little excursions . . .' (p. 13)

Friendship confirmed by the gift of food: that basic anthropology speaks straight to the heart and empty stomach of any right-minded reader:

> Think where man's glory most begins and ends,
> And say my glory was I had such friends.[5]

Friendship is the central theme of the novel, and because its heroes are a mixture of young men-about-town combined with bachelor clubmen up at Oxford and down in the country with all the blitheness of English ruling-class prepositions, the novel has rather less of the historical body of the contemporaries whom I have put beside it.

It emerges no less straightforwardly, however, from their fertile ground. In this case, the heroes are the model men of

[5] W. B. Yeats, 'The Municipal Gallery Revisited', in *Collected Poems* (1961), p. 370.

private means whom its readers once hoped to become. They are
made manageable according to Beatrix Potter's formula by
being turned into hedgerow and riverside animals (and not
routine cuddly ones, either) – toad, rat, mole and badger. The
four figures reproduce faithfully enough the cartoon types:
Toad as public schoolboy–playboy–country-house owner;
Rat as soldier–poet; Mole, middle-aged recluse emerging as
practical administrator–soldier; Badger, older, larger, wiser,
more shaggy and authoritative, as Senior Clubman–commanding officer–judge–ideal father. Badger is untidy and
shabby and crustily careless of manners and correctness; his
morality is that of good form and a decent gentlemanliness.
The four friends translate readily into the heroes of John
Buchan and Sapper, as well as into those of P. G. Wodehouse.
They do no work, but they rule the river quite naturally. They
live in Kenneth Grahame's projection of an ideal early-to-
middle manhood, reinvented for children, and therefore as
sexless, carefree, sun-drenched and mischievous as the heroes
of so many more official period pieces. Their jollity and harmlessness free them from the lethal self-righteousness of, say, the
Dornford Yates thrillers; the gaily overdrawn braggartry and
childishness of Mr Toad himself give children the satisfaction
of doing all these awful and illicit things while at the same time
disapproving of them with Rat, Mole, and Badger. It is the
drawing of Toad, and of the others also, which gives such
colour and charm to the book – it is hard to think of it without
smiling – and Toad's precipitous veering from impossible
swank and snobbery back to cringing self-abnegation is so
much like the extravagant changeability of early puberty that
children can hardly fail to recognize it, to love Toad (because he
is like them) and to turn very censorious towards him (because
they are like him).

I do not mean to suggest that children, in the cant phrase,
'identify with' the characters. It is a point to which I return in
detail in Chapter 8. What they do, and we adults do, is see how
like and unlike ourselves and our friends these characters are.
The four main figures of *The Wind in the Willows* are far more
than potential militia subalterns in pre-1914 vintage summers
before the dark of Passchendaele. Their life is still our life, it
seems; or perhaps Kenneth Grahame holds out in intense,
remembering wistfulness an image of happiness perfectly

combined with innocence, and all of us would wish our children to feel the strength of such an image. It has its forced and plangent moments, no doubt; the golden dappled sunshine of green glades is nowadays switched on to fill advertisements for country-fresh plastiwrapped pies, or girls and the latest Audi. Grahame's effects have occasionally that same sentimental blur. We may put it by saying that his novel, for all its vigour and warm beauty, is redolent of a nostalgia which is strongest when grown-ups remember their childhood at its best. That nostalgia deeply and necessarily stains a great many books for children and is a source of strength as much as weakness: it is a cadence in which to judge the present against its own ideal antecedents. The passage in which Rat and Mole, cold and lost one wintry evening in the snow, are finally delivered out of the storm into the warmth and safety of old Badger's kitchen is one whose power takes the measure of a deep longing for an ideal country cottage and its farmhouse kitchen. The advances of consumerism chronicled in Chapter 3 mean that, in reading this passage today, we can envisage all too well the rich tints of a hundred commercials:

The floor was well-worn red brick, and on the wide hearth burnt a fire of logs, between two attractive chimney-corners tucked away in the wall, well out of any suspicion of draught. A couple of high-backed settles, facing each other on either side of the fire, gave further sitting accommodation for the sociably disposed. In the middle of the room stood a long table of plain boards placed on trestles, with benches down each side. At one end of it, where an arm-chair stood pushed back, were spread the remains of the Badger's plain but ample supper. Rows of spotless plates winked from the shelves of the dresser at the far end of the room, and from the rafters overhead hung hams, bundles of dried herbs, nets of onions, and baskets of eggs. It seemed a place where heroes could fitly feast after victory, where weary harvesters could line up in scores along the table and keep their Harvest Home with mirth and song, or where two or three friends of simple tastes could sit about as they pleased and eat and smoke and talk in comfort and contentment. The ruddy brick floor smiled up at the smoky ceiling; the oaken settles, shiny with long wear, exchanged cheerful glances with each other; plates on the dresser grinned at pots on the shelf, and the merry firelight flickered and played over everything without distinction.

The kindly Badger thrust them down on a settle to toast themselves at the fire, and bade them remove their wet coats and boots. Then he fetched them dressing-gowns and slippers, and himself bathed the Mole's shin with warm water and mended the cut with sticking-plaster till the whole thing was just as good as new, if not better. In the embracing light and warmth, warm and dry at last, with weary legs propped up in front of them, and a suggestive clink of plates being arranged on the table behind it, it seemed to the storm-driven animals, now in safe anchorage, that the cold and trackless Wild Wood just left outside was miles and miles away, and all that they had suffered in it a half-forgotten dream.

When at last they were thoroughly toasted, the Badger summoned them to the table, where he had been busy laying a repast. They had felt pretty hungry before, but when they actually saw at last the supper that was spread for them, really it seemed only a question of what they should attack first where all was so attractive, and whether the other things would obligingly wait for them till they had time to give them attention. (p. 68)

It is however the real power of such images that lies behind the colossal success in commercializing a nostalgia for the past. Nostalgia is presumably an index of the longing for a more complete membership of society, for a closer fit between people's deepest feelings and the permitted forms of expressing and shaping those feelings. There is little doubt that the imagery of consumer living, whose most vivid and popular versions are found in the advertisements, offers an accessible and satisfying picture of an ideal life. The accessibility is always partial – partial in the numbers of people wealthy enough to win the access, but partial also in that the terms of the consumer life and the productive systems which live on and off that life require always that the image be infinitely unrealizable. The farmhouse kitchen of the colour supplement remains forever just out of reach; its ideal version always includes the last detail, the last copper pan or varnished pine dresser which is absent from the real world.

The strength of Grahame's description is that, although a touch sentimentalized, he has made the Badger's kitchen out of the real world about him. The Selfridge's window-dresser cannot recreate the deep familiarity of old furniture:

> I see the hands of the generations
> That owned each shiny familiar thing
> In play on its knobs and indentations,

And with its ancient fashioning
Still dallying . . .[6]

Badger's kitchen unselfconsciously embodies continuity: the
magic reverberance of the word 'home' and all its rich cognates
tingles in the plenitude of the ceiling hung with 'bundles of
dried herbs' and 'nets of onions', the 'long wear' of settles still
fifty years short of antique fayres and the long container lorries
shipping the past away to become the new profits of California
and eastern Australia. All that home means in Kenneth
Grahame has since undergone a sharp attenuation under the
minute, relentless bombardment of the doctrines of mobility,
obsolescence, and acquisitiveness.

It is hardly the strength of Grahame's book that it shows up
what is phoney in the antique reproduction cult. My point is
twofold. First, that Grahame drew for Edwardian children an
ideal playground for their adolescence. He took them out of the
steamier corners of family life and showed them the joys of a
parentless and carefree summer, in which home and well-fed
warmth and friendship and security were freely available; their
own 'home' in *The Wind in the Willows* is every child's dream
hidey-hole, which he effected out of a blend of an Oxford
college staircase and bachelor rooms in the Albany, untroubled
by money or guilt or girls.

Secondly, Grahame strikes a chord in his prose which has
vibrated in European literature since *The Cherry Orchard*. He
sings an elegy to the vision of a perfect adolescence passed in a
Garden of England whose sweet Thames ran softly until 1914.
His own yearning for his fantasy is audible right through the
book, and innumerable fantasies since have strengthened its
hold on our popular culture, in magazines, novels, television
series and their glimmering trailers. It is not a trivial point that
they are insurgent working-class weasels and stoats who are
thrown out of Toad Hall at the end but the point does not touch
the heart of Grahame's matter; the recovery of home is as important there as it is when Mole finds Mole End again one
snow-threatening Christmas Eve. By the same token, Toad's
vanity, braggartry, cowardice and irresponsibility are class-
lessly offensive and endearing. Quite simply, Grahame creates
a Utopia – it is referred to by all the other writers I have looked

[6] Thomas Hardy, 'Old Furniture', in *Complete Poems*, ed. James Gibson (1976), p. 485.

at in this chapter – and its outline is visible today. He is Victorian (or Edwardian) in the life and body he gives *his* version of pastoral – the lovely untroubled countryside, the friendship, the mammoth meals, the scrapes and escapades, the solid sense of place and of home. His moral world is, one would say, coterminous with that of J. R. R. Tolkien, were it not for Grahame's greater fondness and gaiety of spirit.

The Wind in the Willows sits with its fellows in this first group as one of the shaping spirits of all that was to be written for children thereafter. If you want your child to have the tradition of literature in her bones, then she (and he) should read these writers. Their books grow in the late and fertile flowering of cultivated property-owners in Victorian England. Their strengths and their weaknesses are those of that mighty class.

5
Class and classic –
the greatness of Arthur Ransome

These days, class is our cliché. We use the idea not only to identify attitudes but also to explain behaviour and, having done both, to disapprove. Thus: 'That's a very middle-class judgement', 'This novel has a down on working-class values.' Especially within educational and cultural conversation, class is universally accepted as the dominant cultural category, and used often in obtuse or careless ways, as though it were always clear what the term meant and how one may apply it.

Now the claim may in any case be contested that class really *is* the 'dominant cultural category'. My argument in the last chapter was certainly that the ruling class, the Victorian bourgeoisie, established the main tradition of intelligent children's literature in England – I said nothing at that stage about its importantly different origins in the USA. But the novels I picked out stand alongside the greater tradition of adult fiction of which Dickens is the summit, in their buoyant and positive creation of a life whose liveliness criticizes by example the special deathliness of Victorian class society. Nor is class everything, as Dickens above all makes clear. The family was and is a no less paramount cultural category, and it is the argument of this book that we can only understand and judge this corner of life – literature and children – if we see it as, so to speak, a field of force or of energy, whose wave functions start from class, from family (and family size), from productive power (in terms of work), from capacity for satisfaction and fulfilment (in terms of education, both formal and informal), and from beliefs and values. In a rough metaphor, we could speak of lines of radiation coming from the innumerable atoms which compose social institutions such as 'class', 'family', 'work', 'education', 'ideology'. Such a metaphor at least seems more adequate to the facts of life than to speak of class in the way a conservative might, as a necessary but intermittently tottering structure, or as a left-wing revolutionary might, as the source of the conflict essential to the onward march of history.

To insist on the elusiveness and insubstantiality of class as a social fact is not to fly in the face of political theory, especially that of the nineteenth century's greatest theorists, Marx, Weber, and Durkheim. These names will suggest the weight of a tradition which has rightly identified class as the central concept with which to analyse the European world. The trouble is not only that the term is used so broadly as merely to serve as a signpost towards the facts of power or authority, it has also become intensely fashionable in some corners of educational discussion to diagnose class influences as decisive, not so much as a help towards critical thought as a sign to the congregation of the speaker's purity of doctrine. Thus, this representatively crass passage does nothing to help us understand either class or the novels in question:

> The strength of class division is particularly apparent in *The Railway Children*, where the workers are known by their surnames and speak a different language from the main characters in the story. Charity and doing good are seen as the answer to social problems.
>
> *Swallows and Amazons*, a 'classic' of later vintage (1932), is another typical example of this group of books in which the children are exclusively middle-class and in which, if members of the lower classes appear at all, it's decidedly on the fringe. Here, two sets of children with boats play a pirate game. One group, the 'Swallows', camp on an island but mother, from the mainland, along with other adults, is always on hand to help and advise about the practicalities. Thus, the children can combine adventure with security which probably mainly accounts for the book's popularity.[1]

There is no great call to beat to death such off-the-peg inanities, beyond saying that 'charity and doing good' aren't exactly bad answers to social problems. The quotation illustrates the same stock fixity of stare in the passage quoted earlier on p. 51 which kills off Beatrix Potter for mentioning washerwomen. It is the intention of this chapter, however, to show that the category of classic is as necessary for children's as for adults' literature, and in no need of Dixon's inverted commas. His use of them presumably implies that any judgement as to

[1] Bob Dixon, *Catching Them Young: Sex, Race and Class in Children's Fiction* (1977), p. 58.

classic status is as crudely class-bound as the personnel of the novels themselves, and that the authority taken upon themselves by those who confer the title 'classic' is a spurious concealment of the realities of wealth and property.

It won't do. What I intend in this chapter is to oppose the reach-me-down usage of staffroom gossip and its deployment of the concept 'class', by seeking to show that a gifted novelist, though starting inevitably from his or her class, criticizes the narrow limits of its horizon by showing in the creation of a narrative what it would be like truly to live up to the terms of its best values. Each of the novels offered for admiration in this book fulfils this purpose; Arthur Ransome is my immediate witness, called to show the exceeding silliness, widespread in the contemporary discussion of literature, of generalizing with such largeness. The way in which this passage foreshortens two hundred years of thought and of the struggle to make sense of life in stories takes one's breath away:

Naturally, since literature specifically written for children begins with the Puritans, and therefore with the final consolidation of capitalism, we're mostly concerned with the conflict between the bourgeoisie and the working class, which continues into our own times. Most children's literature, therefore, in spite of the different forms it takes – some of which we have just been examining in detail – has the overall effect, whether conscious or not, either on the part of the writer or on that of the reader, of indoctrinating children with a capitalist ideology. [2]

Set aside the blithe conviction that fiction simply indoctrinates; it has at least the merit of taking the power of literature, though not the resistance of readers, seriously. The mistakes here are to *identify* 'bourgeois society' with 'capitalist ideology', and to confuse 'class values' with *values*. No doubt members of social classes choose to cherish certain values and exclude others, but the values themselves are not therefore peculiar to the class. Think of the great values which I listed in Chapter 1 as the main dimension of personal meaning – home, friendship, love, intelligence, independence. Each of us then lives a particular version of these as rooted in our corner of society. How could it be otherwise? But it makes little sense except as a battlecry to the dim and faithful to call, for instance, all that Macbeth has

[2] Dixon, *Catching Them Young*, p. 70.

lost by his perfidy – 'Honour, love, obedience, troops of friends' – to call these 'class values'. It is not even sense to claim that a narrower range of qualities are exclusive to the middle class – say, ambition, self-discipline, individualism, competitiveness. Such qualities have all been visible, if only in local versions, as long as historical evidence has been available.

What is more, it is clear that as this century has advanced, the selection of values which the classes made at an earlier stage of industrialism has drastically altered. The value-structures of liberal individualism (in a phrase) now bind together, for better and worse, most of that three-quarters of British and American society with access to consumer living. Only the poor and the immigrants might not now respond to the calls of such master-symbols as integrity and fulfilment, individual rights, sexual freedoms, personal sincerity, the free acquisition of material comforts. And the poor man who so ignored these irresistible prizes would do so either because they were unattainable or because he was a man of amazing independence.

To match the changes of this century, we must have a different theory of class. It would be one capable of understanding that the greatness of Arthur Ransome's best novels has very little to do with the children in them being at private school and possessing the spare cash to buy little boats. Such a revision would not seek to do away with the power of Marx's analysis, which is for my purposes the identification of the real facts of exploitation and alienation, and the unjust asymmetry with which men and women experience these things. With some plausibility in nineteenth-century England, Marx explained that these injustices rest upon the existence of classes, and classes he identified by their possession of or exclusion from effective private capital. In a famous criticism,[3] he is then charged with predicting the condition of Utopia by mixing hypothesis, arbitrary redefinition, and hopefulness:

> For if private property disappears (empiral hypothesis) then there are no longer classes (trick of definition)! If there are no longer classes, there is no alienation (speculative postulate). The realm of liberty is realised on earth (philosophical idea).

However reasonable Marx sounded in *Capital* in 1880, the wide space which has opened between the provider of capital and the

---

[3] Ralf Dahrendorf, in *Class and Class Conflict in Industrial Society* (1959), p. 95.

managers of production on the one hand, and between a highly skilled and elite workforce and an underemployed, unskilled labour tribe on the other means that Marx's model no longer grips on the facts. While it is undoubtedly still true that class may work as poisonously as ever in people's lives,[4] understanding how and why this is so is not helped by describing an action or an attitude as either middle- or working-class.

The broad point stands: a class society is one in which 'class relationships are of primary significance to the explanatory interpretation of large areas of social conduct'.[5] That social conduct naturally includes novels. At the same time, there remain in the thick and multicoloured stuff of our cultures wide areas of social life which are not dominated by class relationships, areas in which the individual as producer and user retains a satisfying range of control, power, and authority over what he produces and uses. The comfortable area of social life – weekends occupied by hobbies, pastimes, do-it-yourself, gardening, societies, and, supremely, sport – is one in which it is hardly useful to interpret and value what is going on in terms of class relations.

The way to break out of the close trap which fixes our sight only on class relations is to concentrate instead on the nature and structure of exploitation and the meaninglessness brought upon people's lives either by the oppression of others or by the less specific failure of a society to provide anything to live by. Such a shift of attention returns us to the grim facts of pain, want, cruelty, misery, and to the moral effort to recover the will and the compassion to see these facts and to know how much they may be altered and how much they may have to be borne. This is the effort to find the freedom which is the ground of truth; and truth, however local and partial, is, in turn, a necessary condition not only of reasonable discourse, but therefore of beauty and goodness.

This vision of a re-established trinity of beauty, truth, and goodness is a non-Marxist's way of commending a classless society. Marx's vision of classlessness offered in an unspecific way a structure which would dissolve alienation and enable the unity of culture with being, the coincidence of a society's

---

[4] See Richard Sennett and Jonathan Cobb, *The Hidden Injuries of Class* (1972).
[5] Anthony Giddens, *The Class Structure of the Advanced Societies* (1973), p. 132.

deepest feelings with their natural expressions. He provided a way of thinking towards unenvisageable ends, and although it is entirely foolish to suppose that classlessness is a guarantee of a stop to exploitation, it acts as a necessary idea with which to criticize the present in the name of the future.

The name of the future is the name of our children. So when the Victorian novelists of both *grande* and *petite bourgeoisie* criticized and celebrated the present through the lives of Alice, the railway children, Colin and Mary, Ratty and Mole, they were doing so in the name of freedom, truth, and goodness. That peculiar combination of intelligence, social position, opportunity, and grace transpired in their books. They needed their social position to write as they did; insofar as they were not merely writing to justify their own advantages, they wrote for the future; children's novels provided them with the means to unite virtue with happiness.

Arthur Ransome completes this first list of children's classics. It could be longer, of course; it will be extended with Kipling's name. As it stands, it suggests both the range and the structure of a remakable new tradition. Its first golden age went up to the First World War, as it did for the adult novel; its second golden age, or at the very least the second period of intense creativeness and some really original achievements, began, let us say, with the publication in 1958 of *Marianne Dreams* and *Tom's Midnight Garden* and is still going strong. In the years between, the level of both production and achievement fell away somewhat. Ransome's work may well be used to mark the terminus of the Edwardian age. Nonetheless his steady rate of production over so many years together with the fact that he began late, at the age of 46, and that *Swallows and Amazons*, published in 1932, was the twenty-first book he had written, means that he straddles the years between the wars, and is the dominating writer for children during that period.[6]

---

[6] It is agreeably relevant to note in anticipation of Chapter 13 that Ransome's great years are also those of P. G. Wodehouse, and to remark that A. A. Milne published the two volumes of Christopher Robin tales in 1926 and 1928. They may be used to round out the early stages of the tradition, and to clinch my arguments about class. The Christopher Robin tales remain unilluminated by mention of class. They are tales of a Garden of Eden, certainly, and as in most such Gardens, nobody has to produce anything. But the network of friendships, the excellent comedy, the simplicity and tellingness of characterization – remember Eeyore, Rabbit, Owl, Tigger – while they speak the

In temper, style, and ethics Ransome belongs entirely to the best Edwardians. His biography is entirely apt, indeed pat, to the history of the Victorian bourgeoisie as I told it. He was brought up near Coniston of poor but vigorously cultivated and intellectual parents, and in their frugal, active lives learned the practice of sailing and fishing, together with the theory of the arts, and particularly of writing. His lifelong friend was the great English Hegelian, R. G. Collingwood; his head of house at Rugby was the Labour Party intellectual R. H. Tawney. Ransome lived precariously but adequately in Grub Street and among the *belles-lettristes* of pre-1914 England, but his energy and the range of his interests and his friends took him well outside the world of his contemporaries in the little magazines such as Edward Garnett[7] and Lascelles Abercrombie. He was a particular kind of Englishman, a sort of cross between George Mallory and the young Joseph Conrad. He lived on his wits and practically no money for years in what sounds like perfect equability; when he became a foreign correspondent of the *Manchester Guardian*, he comfortably fitted its nonconformist and Asquithian manner. It is no surprise to find him in Russia right through the Revolution and it is also comfortably consistent with his life and personality, though also amazing, that he married Trotsky's secretary! There *is* after all something in Ransome which is stolid and unimaginative; it comes out in the *Autobiography* as well as in the children's novels. But this something is also equable, serene, brave, and all-competent.

No individual can be made into a predetermined product of his history. The evidence is all around us that systematic upbringings may go awry; there is just no knowing what life will do to children, nor how they will turn out as a result of being done over. But I take Ransome's biography in this brief space to indicate how completely his strength and warmth, his broad-shouldered, bluff stride across life, are of a piece with his family life, his social contexts, and the beliefs which subtended these relations and led him to the work he did. He is as unlike the present writers for children as he could be. Like them, he looks to the creation of free, autonomous spirits amongst the

---

language of a Kensington nursery, are entirely free, human, and equal. Rabbit makes it plentifully clear however that these classless conditions leave plenty of room for the assertion of power well called bossiness, and Eeyore at the least *feels* exploited.

[7] See Ransome's *Autobiography* (1976), p. 140.

children about and for whom he writes. But the Swallows and Amazons have little of the polymorphous independence admired by the new class which writes for children. That is why Ransome, for all that he sustains continuity so easily, marks the end of a line of values. As a novelist, he too is an agent of the symbol-making industry. But shaped by the history which produced Kipling and Conrad, as well as Wilfred Owen and Lord Asquith, Ransome envisions a way of life, a human order, and a set of values, which for all their beauty and vividness, can only find a rather ghostly harbour today.

But come! A novelist, even when writing for children, does not have to show the future exactly how to live. He can, he does, show what is excellent and delightful, whether others can imitate it or not. He wants to recreate what is joyful in order to communicate joy (doesn't he?). In Stendhal's great phrase, all art holds out 'the promise of happiness'. How shall the promise be kept?

At first sight, it could only be kept by our sending children to live in that blissful never-never land (what a brilliant name Barrie coined there!) of so many television serials. For all the devout injection of socially conscientious detail about the 1914–18 war or the hunger marches, the magnitude of popular response to innumerable television programmes cast in a reminiscent haze of antique furniture and ripening corn stems from the nostalgia so pervasive in the structure of contemporary feeling. Its presence is to be expected in novels for children, not only because these will reflect the climate of feeling which everyone breathes but also because storytellers seek to recreate the perfect happiness of their own childhood, so that the children may enjoy it for themselves. The necessary myth of a golden age, as I put it earlier, just over the rim of the oldest parent's memory, is a way of berating the present for not having lived up to the intense purity of longing and the unrealizable aspirations which childhood set as a standard for the adult world. So the glowing image of a golden age helps men and women, as they say, to grow old gracefully.

> . . . the pubs
> Wide open all day:
> And the countryside not caring:
> The place-names all hazed over
> With flowering grasses, and fields

Shadowing Domesday lines
Under wheat's restless silence;
The differently-dressed servants
With tiny rooms in huge houses,
The dust behind limousines;
Never such innocence,
Never before or since,
As changed itself to past
Without a word – the men
Leaving the gardens tidy,
The thousands of marriages
Lasting a little while longer:
Never such innocence again.[8]

The predominance of such feeling these days has complicated origins. The television serials point at the gap between a fluid, uncertain and intimidating present and what are made to look, at this distance, like the settled solidities of the past. The rich, glamorous patina of colour photography and television transmission is cast over the settles, the nets of onions, the polished brick floor of Badger's kitchen and, glowing in a memory faithfully rebuilt in the studio, declares to a people that the world we have lost was a better world. And with their deadly accuracy of timing, the symbol-traders of the big bazaar turn the past into an industry, and compress that great gust of popular feeling into the sights the tourists will pay to see. Hence the dizzy success of stately-home serials and all the antiques-and-décolletage epics since the *Forsyte Saga*. Hence also the movie of *Swallows and Amazons*, the lovely solitude of the lake they had to go to the tip of Scotland to find, the tin advertisements, the haze, the voice of the hidden waterfall and the children under the apple trees, and the swelling sound of music as the brown sail broke and filled for the first time on the wide water.

The real history,[9] as Ransome wrote it, is very different, and what the reader, both child and adult, will find in him is quite without these plangent chords. Even where Ransome is clearly recollecting his own best childhood memories, of the drought summer in *Pigeon Post* or the long, hard frost of *Winter Holiday*,

[8] Philip Larkin, 'MCMXIV', in *The Whitsun Weddings* (1964), p. 28.
[9] I take the phrase, with its anti-sentimental and propagandizing implication, from Raymond Williams, in *The Country and the City* (1973). I take much from his argument, too, although I doubt that he would agree with me.

and transposing them from the 1890s to the 1930s, he writes the plain, straight, rather practical, unreflective prose we would expect of the man he was.

It is his subject-matter which counts. So it is with any author, of course, and the difficulty which many contemporary children's writers have in finding a proper subject-matter is a symptom we shall have to turn to. Ransome was lucky. He had his subject-matter in the activity which made him happiest, sailing. Consequently it doesn't really matter that the Swallows and the Amazons and the D's are only ever to be seen on holiday. In other novels, there is an immediate and comic implausibility that the date set for the end of the world from which the child-heroes must rescue it falls conveniently in April or August – I am thinking not only of Enid Blyton, but also of writers with more serious pretensions like Susan Cooper or Judy Allen (see Chapter 10). But the holidays for Ransome's children do not simply provide the leisure time in which to solve some detective problem. They are sailing-time, and since sailing is so many things at once – pastime, means of commerce, transport, means of warfare, the occasion of worship and of burial, the frail collusion of culture with the barely harnessable powers of Nature, or just a pleasant Sunday afternoon – since sailing is these many things, it can stand for much in adult life which could otherwise only feature in a children's novel in a rather unreal way.

In literature, if you think of sea-going, you think of Joseph Conrad. Now Conrad not only was aware of, but made into the subject of his writings the relation of irony to membership, of belief to scepticism. His proud membership of the Mercantile Marine was the occasion for his turning upon his pride the oblique force of a mind which grew up in Poland, spoke French first, and chose English for its written artistry. By comparison, Ransome is a simple man. But these solid novels convey his commitment to the mysteries of sailing in terms which Conrad would have approved. The simplicity is a function both of those to whom Ransome speaks – the children who would not understand the angles of the Polish mariner's obliquity – and of the situation of the children in the fiction. They do not need to question what they are doing: it is its own reward.

That point is made in his adult way by Conrad's spokesman in the magnificent short novel, *The Shadow-Line*, which describes the Conrad-figure's accession to his first, thrillingly unlooked-for command:

I knew that, like some rare women, she was one of those creatures whose mere existence is enough to awaken an unselfish delight. One feels that it is good to be in the world in which she has her being. (p. 245)

And subsequently:

Half-an-hour later, putting my foot on her deck for the first time, I received the feeling of deep physical satisfaction. Nothing could equal the fullness of that moment . . .

So when *Swallow* is shipwrecked in the second novel of the series, Captain John's utter dismay shares all of Conrad's deep loyalty not only to an individual ship, but to a tradition of work honourably done and skills cherished and observed:

Captain John knew all the bitterness of a captain who has lost his ship. Now that it was too late he was telling himself that he ought to have guessed that the wind would be so much stronger. Yes, it was clear that he ought to have reefed. If he had reefed, the jibe would not have mattered so much. Besides, it was not as if they had been racing. He could quite well have sailed some distance down the lake with the sail out to starboard and then jibed carefully or even come up to the wind and gone about so as to reach the entrance to Horseshoe Cove with the sail out to port just as he wanted it for running in. It was all his fault. And now *Swallow* was gone and it was only the third day of the holiday. What was it his father had said about duffers? Better drowned. John thought so too. And then a new flock of black, wretched thoughts came crowding in like cormorants coming to roost. *Swallow* belonged to the Jacksons at Holly Howe. What would they say? It was all very well for Peggy and Roger to chatter about shipwrecks. He knew what Titty was thinking as she stood dripping, looking at the waves breaking on that hateful rock. For Titty and himself, *Swallow* was something alive. And now, with *Swallow* gone, how could they live on Wild Cat Island? How could anything lovely ever happen any more? (*Swallowdale*, p. 76)

It is comparatively rare for Ransome to introspect into his character's feelings even this far. But the mystery of sailing-boats gives his plain, technical writing its resonance. After Conrad's captain has walked quietly aboard, up to the poop, past the gleaming brass fittings and finely polished rails which are themselves part of an orderly, compacted culture, the power and experience in rightly handling technique which is technology, he goes down to the captain's cabin:

Deep within the tarnished ormolu frame, in the hot half-light sifted through the awning, I saw my own face propped between my hands. And I stared back at myself with the perfect detachment of distance, rather with curiosity than with any other feeling, except of some sympathy for this latest representative of what for all intents and purposes was a dynasty; continuous not in blood, indeed, but in its experience, in its training, in its conception of duty, and in the blessed simplicity of its traditional point of view on life. (*The Shadow-Line*, p. 247)

For the Conrad-figure, simplicity is a blessed relief. For the Swallows and the Amazons it is beyond question; questioning sailing could have no point. That is no doubt their excellent innocence, and a child's birthright. The fact that a later generation has sold the birthright for a mess of indecision is hardly the children's fault. Anyway, the moral stands: Ransome's novels most exemplify beautiful absorption in activity for its own worthy sake. Sailing is such an excellent subject because it enables such absorption without seeming silly, as so many of the sports which attract a similar absorption can appear to be to an outsider.

Not sailing. It has a long history; it is a way of rejoining your history. Especially in Britain, also in New England, the ghosts of sailors are buccaneers, explorers, traders, naval officers. The games played by the children in *Swallows and Amazons* quote Queen Elizabeth and Francis Drake as well as Cortez and *Treasure Island*. They quote Nansen of the *Fram* and Scott of the Antarctic in *Winter Holiday*, Natty Bumppo and Mallory and Irving in *Swallowdale*, Klondyke gold-miners in *Pigeon Post*. The romantic wildness and solitude of the Lake District in the thirties gave Ransome a context in which children might re-invent that heroism. He removes parents to the limits of the geography of which he writes, so that their writ runs safely along its perimeter, and the children are left the large space in the middle in which they may become themselves.

Such a liberal freedom, however, is defined in tension with the precise conception of duty of which Conrad speaks. Sailing is nothing if it is only trade. Trade in its popular-cultural forms

does appear in these tales, as I mentioned: it is a disappointment
to the conservation-conscious present when the triumph of the
children in *Pigeon Post* is to have discovered copper on the fells.
The contemporary imagination all too easily puts the jugger-
nauts and yellow hardhats of RTZ above Coniston Water. To
Conrad and to the Swallows, Amazons, and D's alike, '. . .
faithful service was all right. One would naturally give that for
one's own sake, for the sake of the ship, for the love of the life of
one's choice; not for the sake of the reward. There is something
distasteful in the notion of a reward . . .' (*Shadow-Line*, p.
235). Well, yes, there is, and there is a faintly sour taste on the
grown-up tongue in Ransome's hard good sense (after all,
there *is* copper but no gold in Westmorland) at coming up with
this reward at the end of the book. The far more memorable
and, to child or adult, satisfying finale comes with the firestorm
and the heroic but credible saving of the fells for the farmers and
the little hedgehog. The conservationist is much happier with
that curtain. Freedom does not, after all, find perfect expression in conjunction with markets or enterprises, and it is
Ransome's strength to hold freedom in balance against its
moral counterweight, duty.

Yet he is a novelist, and a good novel is neither a moral
diagram nor a homily. I mean that Ransome takes life
seriously, unselfconsciously so; and that therefore the actions
of his characters are important, not just for themselves, but
because they are principled. Inasmuch as the novel is, in
Lawrence's words, 'the one bright book of life', it is the best
way we have of mapping the moral and metaphysical explora-
tions of our lives. So these children are free moral agents, and
they live within a secure framework of a role and its duties. In
this way they are unlike present-day children, these short thirty
or forty years later. The Swallows' father is in the Royal Navy;
the children each assign to themselves a naval rank: John is
Captain, Susan First Mate, Titty Able-seaman, Roger Ship's
Boy and, in perhaps the best of the novels, *We Didn't Mean to Go
to Sea*, Engineer.

It is hard to pick one novel out for special attention amongst
so many contenders. Ransome's writing is unusually full and
expansive in the world of children's novels. Most contemporary novelists now write, no doubt rightly, for very much more
short-winded readers. Other novels – *Great Northern?* or *Coot*

Club for instance – embody much more richly Ransome's passion for natural life, and they communicate this, not in some spirit of dreadful brightness in order to tell children about birds, but as a full response to the experience of natural beauty, of sailing and walking amongst that beauty (in the Scottish Highlands), and of keeping alive a non-exploitative moral attitude towards the natural life which belongs there. Those novels I have already mentioned, which include the endearing and sometimes tiresome Nancy and Peggy as well as Dick and Dorothea, take in a wider range of experience and, though always carefully plotted with a studied regard for relevance and form, allow themselves a more discursive pattern of episodes: the visit to the charcoal-burners in *Winter Holiday*, the moment of discovery in *Secret Water*.

It is interesting also to note the divisions of labour as the author parcels them out. John and Roger are the full-time naval officers; Dick Callum represents the intellectual in the disinterested pursuit of knowledge. Even when building the furnace in which to smelt gold, he is concerned only about experimental success, not about the rewards. Work is the thing: Susan and Peggy do all the cooking and the domestic organization, and Titty and Dorothea act as the poets loyally following the precepts of their masters, but always standing a little way away from practice, and imagining other, ideal versions of it. Nancy throws into relief the difficulty of knowing how to live in terms of the life and values commended on and around the lake. She is the source of the creative energy which goes into the fantasies of arctic exploration, gold-mining, night warfare, and so on; when ill, she still dominates *Winter Holiday* by semaphore. Ordinary life is not enough for her, and so she animates and directs the remorseless cartoon life which the others willingly adopt. Each of the others, however, puts into that life what can recognizably emerge in a rational, everyday form: for John, the sequence of naval duties; for Susan, the parallel sequence of domestic duties; for Dick, the project of pure inquiry. But what *would* it be like to be married to a grown-up Nancy – with a forlorn Peggy in tow?

We can afford to be indulgent in reply. Plenty of tomboys become staid and personable matrons. In any case, it is an important historical aspect of these children's times that the rituals of passage between adolescence and adulthood were far more clearly marked. The innocence of childhood was formally required of children for far longer – until, indeed, the awkward age. These children responded to these expectations as any child did – until, that is, the strange and inexplicable changes towards a new ethics of adolescence forced themselves through the frames of social conventions. So Nancy, the leader of the six children,[10] who stands farthest away from everyday life and relationships, is in the limiting sense entirely childish, and for all Uncle Jim–Captain Flint's believable benevolence, he connives far too much at her childishness. She is a convincing character who focusses Ransome's own over-indulgence; he never breathes a word of criticism towards her.

Nancy's absence from *We Didn't Mean to Go to Sea* points us to the nature of its success, in terms of both form and content. For in this novel the adventure is real and not fantasy, and it is entirely credible. Furthermore, the title catches the exact point of anguish in the book: the children unintentionally break their solemn promise not to leave the safety of the estuary above Harwich, but then in the name of duty both to the boat (and its owner) and to the traditions of sailing, as well as to their own safety, have to sail the boat before a gale-force wind, at night, and in immense seas, across to Flushing. A series of minor accidents and misdemeanours leads up to their slipping their cable in a fog when the owner of the boat is caught ashore in an accident (*his* wrongdoing, according to seafaring duties, is ever to have left his boat at all). From then on they compound their wrongs helplessly by doing the only thing which is right – making for open water.

The form of the story is spare. The children make the outward journey in extreme danger, improvising and learning desperately all the way. On the journey out, everything is confused, everybody misinformed. The journey home restores the due order of things under the splendid calm and omniscience of the children's father. Throughout the journey, but especially on the nightmare trip to Flushing, the four children are held to the duties of their roles – Captain–older brother, Cook–First Mate–older sister, Able-seaman–younger sister,

---

[10] I realize there are other excellent Ransome novels which introduce other children, but the Swallows, Amazons and D's are surely the best known; in any case my general argument stands for the other books too, especially if I am right to take *We Didn't Mean to Go to Sea* as the best.

Engineer–younger brother. Or rather, they live through the experience which is the occasion for growing into those roles.

'Role' has become a much-misused word. Here, let it denote a particular set of social functions, themselves held in place by certain social meanings. To fulfil the role is then to discharge those functions; in so doing, one meets the expectations of others. This is to meet the duties of a role. But duties specify themselves broadly. Hence the power of sea-stories. They suspend at very high tension the pull between duty and personal responsibility, and they inevitably relate to both the education and training from which the realities of duty and responsibility grow. The four children feel that pull fairly and squarely in the middle of their beings:

It was worse for Susan than for any of the others. John was having a tricky time steering with the wind dead aft, afraid every moment that there would be a jibe, and that the boom would come swinging across. Titty and Roger were peering into the fog keeping a look out for another of those huge iron buoys that were as dangerous as rocks. But Susan was thinking of Jim Brading desperately rowing to and fro over the place where he had left the *Goblin*. What would he do when he found that the *Goblin* had gone? Telephone to Mother at Pin Mill? . . . The thought of Mother answering the telephone and hearing that Jim Brading, in whose charge they were, did not know what had become of them, came at her like a blow. They had been allowed to sail with Jim Brading only because everybody had promised that they would not go outside the harbour. And here they were sailing blindly a bigger boat than they had ever sailed before. Mother would never have trusted them alone in a boat like the *Goblin*, even inside the harbour on a calm day of sunshine and clear weather. And here they were outside the harbour, sailing faster every minute, in a thick, choking fog and rising wind. They could not have broken that promise into smaller bits. (*We Didn't Mean to Go to Sea*, p. 126)

After all, the children are not in the Navy, and Susan is perfectly well in a position to argue with John. Her sense of family obligation matches his obligation to sailing; he is responsible for the little cutter *Goblin* and therefore to all the rich network of expectations which sailors must have of other sailors in the name of mutual understanding and order, and in the name, too, of life itself. Susan speaks for the imperative of keeping their promise to their mother at all costs, a promise no less in pieces for having been broken unintentionally; she speaks also for avoiding the anxieties which their disappearance will cause. The strain and stiffness of these contrary pulls veer between utter dismay and quarrelling as John decides to put to sea.

Right through these pages, indeed right through the book, Ransome's touch and pacing are faultless. We are a third of the way into the book before the awful moment at which they realize the *Goblin* is dragging her anchor. The calm and leisurely movement of the narrative has not been for a moment redundant, although a child would hardly be likely to notice the relevance and interconnectedness of all the detail. Heaven knows how those lessons are learned, and indeed we do not need to know.

I suppose that a novel becomes too complicated for children at the point at which they cannot understand a good teacher (parent or not) who explains to them the way the novel works. The implication is something like that for anthropologists who claim intelligibility for their explanations about the lives of primitive peoples, insofar as a member of such a people could understand the explanation, though he could never have thought it out for himself. The novelists work at the same difficult business of telling people what they do not know but can recognize.[11]

Ransome is as workmanlike with his art of novel-writing as he would have been with the art of sailing; and so, naturally and easily, he allowed the strapping, handsome undergraduate who has taken the children under his wing to tell them enough about his boat to make it possible for them to sail it, but never too much to bore the reader and make the novel into a sailing manual, nor to take the terror out of their ignorance when the catastrophe comes.

The tranquillity and pleasure of the first part of the novel are sharpened by the tension with which we wait for the adventure. The writing is plain and wholesome and firm; it is undecorated and its cadences fix only the scene and no special attitude towards it. In Charles Tomlinson's phrase, 'fact has its proper plentitude':

It had been still dusk when they went into the inn, but those few minutes had made a difference. Lights had sprung up everywhere. There was a string of blazing lamps over the Parkeston quays at the other side of the river. There were lights in Harwich town, and lights

---

[11] Cf. Peter Winch, *The Idea of a Social Science* (1967).

far away across the harbour in Felixstowe. The flashes from the buoys that had been hardly visible by day kept sparkling out, now here, now there, the white flash of Shotley Spit buoy, the red one of the Guard buoy, and others of which they did not know the names. There were riding lights on all the anchored barges and on the ships in the harbour. The wind had dropped to nothing, and long glittering lanes led from every light across the smooth water. And there, a little way above the pier, lay the *Goblin*, she too with a light on her forestay, and the glimmer of the cabin lamp showing through her portholes. (p. 67)

Ransome's matter-of-factness and his careful enumeration of technical detail have their limiting aspect, no doubt. There are plenty of people who are simply bored stiff at once by his subject-matter. There are those who are bored immediately by Conrad. There are certainly some aversions which you can do nothing about, however open you remain to a change of heart, and however well taught you are. His matter-of-factness may seem flat to those with a taste for a rounder rhetoric, and some of his novels have their heavinesses and their long troughs. In this one, however, the length is never *longueur*. For all its 300 pages, it is economical. And his digressions are courteously adjusted to his audience:

They were being as quick as they could. It was no good going to help them till he had the anchor itself ready for use. Now anchors are made in two parts. There is the crown with the two flukes and the long shank. All that is in one piece. Then there is the stock. This is a bar which goes through a hole in the shank, and has a short bend at one end of it, so that when it is not in use it can lie flat along the shank. (p. 105)

Ransome pauses in the tale while he makes sure that his audience knows what he is talking about. He looks up, so to speak, explains what he means, and then goes on.

This attention to technical detail is the heart of the book. Not only is Ransome writing about what he knows and loves best in all the world, it is the subject-matter which brings together practice and morality in an absolute fusion. Ransome was not a reflective writer, nor even one, it seems, who busied himself with the expression of emotion at all (he resists the notion that literature is there for the expression of personal feeling). The circumstances of *We Didn't Mean to Go to Sea* allow personal feeling to transpire straight from action and not reflection. Events from outside force right conduct on those with the knowledge to perform it. Right conduct brings right feeling – fulfilment and happiness. Right conduct for novices in extreme danger at sea in very high winds, fog, and the dark is a matter of correct technique and the following of necessary and rational rules. Less immediate consequences will have to wait their turn; when this kind of work is to be done, it must be done right:

> He leaned on the tiller and tried to see both chart and compass at once. Yes, it must be all right. Clear water all the way till you came to the Sunk lightship right on the edge of the chart. Out there they would be all right. Jim had waited out there himself. This was what Jim would do. This was what Daddy would do. John, in spite of being able to see nothing but fog, in spite of the broken promise, in spite of the awful mess they were in, was surprised to find that a lot of his worry had left him. The decision had been made. He was dead sure it was the right decision. Sooner or later the fog would clear and he would have to think about getting back. Now the only thing to do was to steer a straight course, not to hit anything, to go on and on till he was clear of those awful shoals that were waiting to catch his blindfold little ship. John, in spite of his troubles, was for the moment almost happy. (pp. 132–3)

But Ransome is much too good a story-teller to leave John in his relief. Susan is torn by distress and by panic before utterly unlooked-for events – not because she's a girl but because her terror is entirely justified. The terror comes home to us with sudden force when the children all realize that the buoy is not swinging loose, but that they are sweeping down with the tide towards it:

> 'Oh John,' gasped Susan, 'That was the Beach End buoy. We're out at sea . . .'

and the chapter ends. Her distress breaks up the calm competence with which she faces the world and is her real self. The mark of this collapse is her abandoned, violent seasickness; she knows and feels how bad things are, and so do we. Roger, however:

> drove in the handle of the foghorn, once, twice, and again. If John said it was all right, it must be. He patted Susan's cold hand. (p. 135)

It's rare for Arthur Ransome to write of introspection at all, and the brief, tense notation fits his modesty as it does the limited range of John's feelings (limited, but as we see, capable of considerable, if taciturn, depths). But John, though surely close to one version of Ransome's ideal early self, is not a novelist, and in himself he is smaller than the book's wide range of reference.

One admires the sheer vividness of the description, for one thing. It would be insidious to anthologize pieces that describe the storm, as one might with some of Conrad's effects in *Typhoon* or *The Nigger of the 'Narcissus'*. In any case Ransome's best effects are often his briefest:

They looked astern, and could see grey water, white tops of waves, and a strip of pale sky under grey clouds. Of the land there was nothing to be seen at all. The *Goblin* was utterly alone, racing along, up and down, up and down. Fast as she was sailing, the seas moved faster still. Wave after wave swept up on her quarter, lifted her, and passed on. Wave after wave came rolling up, broke with the loud noise of churning water, and left a long mane of foam. (p. 144)

Such prose is not in any way external to the action. This comes out in the touching pages which describe the rescue of the almost drowned kitten. The incident is attractively done in itself, as well as suggesting (as John and Susan think on our behalf) how the children might themselves have been struggling feebly on a spar in the empty sea. The kitten's rescue serves as emblem of return to warm, normal living.

That return to society is initiated by the excellent Flemish pilot. Ever since hearing from Jim Brading, the young owner of the *Goblin*, of a man legally defrauded of his boat by salvagers, the children have among all their fears of the forces of nature also feared other, more human, predators. In the event, their solemn, comic efforts to keep the truth from the Flemish pilot dissolve under the quickness of his uptake and his warm, instantaneous, generous admiration. As happens in *The Railway Children*, as happens in life, children's unselfregarding and courageous efforts to live up to the best ideals of adult life simply melt away the defensive conventions of that life. The adults are melted not only by the touchingness of young people seeking to fulfil such a daunting conception of what they owe before they have the grown-up strength or experience; it is not only a matter of poignancy. The children also take the measure of all that the adults have left undone by not, in the loss of innocence, living right up to ideals. In acting so well, the children remind the adults of all that they had once hoped the world could be made to be like, if only they themselves did their best. And this recreates new world possibilities, the chance of which the pilot takes here.

The rest of the novel is largely a long, though stirring, coda. Indeed, the pleasure it gives is due to the excitement's being over, and our resting in the calmness of a beautiful safety. The children come home in the care of their father whom they find, quite plausibly, in Flushing on his way to Harwich. This was the reason for their being on the estuary at all. In a memorable paragraph, he gathers them into the calm domains of his authority, its justice and its love; to see these qualities, Ransome looks through the eyes of Titty, the poet:

Daddy was certainly very unlike anybody else. Captain Flint could be counted on in the same sort of way, but even Captain Flint, if he had met them all in some place where he had least expected them, would have called them all by name, Captain John, Mate Susan, Able-seaman Titty, and would have asked at once about the parrot and Gibber, and whether the ship's boy was hungry, and then he would have been in a hurry to know all about it, how it had all happened, and so on. But Daddy, in the presence of the pilot, was asking no questions at all. He had come aboard just as if he had left them only for a few minutes instead of being away in the China Seas for ages and ages. Titty could hardly believe he had ever been gone, as she saw him hauling aft a bunt of sail and waiting, saying nothing, while John, equally silent, put a tyer round the part that was already rolled up. Silent they both were, John and Daddy, but she knew by the way they looked at each other across the sail they were stowing how glad they were to be together. (p. 263)

They are restored to the harmony of a perfect social order. But they are restored while having added to it. They come home changed, and home to the new expectations of their parents, who love them and deal justly with them. It is no doubt a necessary corrective to a baseless hero-worship that our latter-day children's novels show so many parents to be the weak and cowardly bullies and crybabies many of them are. But one of Ransome's many strengths is to suggest the continued need for such ideal parents as Commander Ted and Mrs Mary Walker, so un-Victorian but also so excellently authoritative. They are part of the ideal social order prefigured by this marvellous book. The children live out a brief version of the good life, one in which the natural, abrupt dangers of life require exceptional courage, skill in understanding and handling an antique culture, warmth, natural sympathy, independence. They join culture and nature together again – the sailing-boat and the sea – and therefore quicken work into creative life. And having succeeded temporarily in doing these things for themselves, and finding both the intensity of existence and a form within which to contain and express it, they go back to the huge happiness of home. The novel shows its readers how to keep 'the promise of happiness'.

6

Girl or boy: home and away

Ransome's name links the two peaks of fiction for children. It also completes the first list I propose for a bookshelf of best novels for children. I have used the books named so far to suggest how these writers tested and explored a diversity of values which children could really be asked to live by. I want to turn now to a matter raised in Chapter 3 which has, in the present uncertainty of social values and shared ideals, come into peculiar prominence. It is the connection of personality – self and identity – to socially preferred images of manliness and womanliness. Having spoken briskly of how not to use the word 'class' in the last chapter, however, I don't want to launch into an analogous attack on the concept of sexism.[1]

This chapter is not an exercise in the study of, as they say, sex-role stereotyping. It is an effort to take up the divisions into masculine and feminine virtues that characterize Victorian and Edwardian culture, and to look at these in relation to the personal identities that were made out of these terms by the novelists, especially as those identities lived and worked at home, or out in the world. Insofar as the divisions of virtue and value followed the divisions of labour, we should find that the feminine virtues are the private ones, those that belong at home; the masculine ones will be those with public purchase, with open power, and they will flourish on the open market. If these divisions operate, which novelists mediate and moderate them? Is there any who will speak out against them and for a completed, more manly man, and womanly woman both capable of living these differences in both worlds? And in either case, what shall Walter Mitty do, poor thing, if we deny him the fantasy which is his only real life?

---

[1] But see Ann Dummett, 'Racism and Sexism: A False Analogy', in *New Blackfriars* (November 1975), pp. 484–92. See also Margrit Eichler, *The Double Standard: A Feminist Critique of the Social Sciences* (London: Croom Helm 1979).

They went out through the revolving doors that made a faintly deris-
ive whistling sound when you pushed them. It was two blocks to the
parking lot. At the drugstore on the corner she said 'Wait here for me,
I forgot something. I won't be a minute.' She was more than a minute.
Walter Mitty lighted a cigarette. It began to rain, rain with sleet in it.
He stood up against the wall of the drugstore, smoking . . . He put
his shoulders back and his heels together. 'To hell with the handker-
chief,' said Walter Mitty scornfully. He took one last drag at his cigarette and snapped it away. Then with that faint fleeting smile playing
about his lips, he faced the firing squad; erect and motionless, proud
and disdainful, Walter Mitty the Undefeated, inscrutable to the last.
(James Thurber, 'The Secret Life of Walter Mitty', in *The Thurber
Carnival*, p. 79)

The manly man of Victorian adventure stories has had an
increasingly sardonic press of late. George Orwell noted of the
change from E. W. Hornung's *Raffles* to James Hadley Chase's
No Orchids for Miss Blandish that Chase manifests a new tendency to an amoral power-worship, irrespective of motive,
law or humanity:

Several people, after reading *No Orchids*, have remarked to me 'It's
pure fascism.' This is a correct description, although the book has no
connection with politics and very little with social or economic problems. It has the same relation to Fascism as Trollope's novels have to
nineteenth century capitalism. It is a daydream appropriate to a totali-
tarian age. In his imagined world of gangsters Chase is presenting, as
it were, a distilled version of the modern political scene, in which such
things as the mass bombing of civilians, the use of hostages, torture to
obtain confessions, secret prisons, execution without trial, floggings
with rubber truncheons, drownings in cesspools, systematic falsifi-
cation of records and statistics, treachery, bribery and quislingism are
normal and morally neutral, even admirable when they are done in a
large and bold way. The average man is not directly interested in politics, and when he reads, he wants the current struggles of the world to
be translated into a simple story about individuals. He can take an interest in Slim and Fenner as he could not in the G.P.U. and the
Gestapo. People worship power in the form in which they are able to
understand it.[2]

We have come a long way down the road to the cesspool since

---

[2] George Orwell, 'Raffles and Miss Blandish', in *Collected Essays* (1961), p. 247. See
also Richard Hoggart, *The Uses of Literacy* (1958), pp. 256–72, for his treatment of the
sex-and-violence novel.

1939, when *Miss Blandish* was published. The power-worship of films like *The French Connection* and *A Clockwork Orange* is quite candid, and revenge in such circumstances is made easy and instinctive; there is no moral problem about it. There is a contrast even in films as cheaply glamorizing and tawdry as the James Bond movies, especially when Sean Connery played the hero. They evidence a perfectly unselfconscious technology-worship, but they are full of small ironies, parodies and jokes at the expense of the hero. Since the hero of such films and novels has always been a large, characterless blank space into which reader or cinema-goer can pour all his fantasies, such self-consciousness becomes not so much a comment at James Bond's expense as a scepticism about the notion of heroism itself.

If we make this point political, then this is hardly surprising. Fascism at its outset offered to satisfy genuine human needs. Noting this, John Fraser turns to a definition of Fascism as 'the political movement which leads most frankly, most radically towards the restoration of the body – health, dignity, fullness, heroism – towards the defence of man against the large town and the machine', and goes on to comment on its more insidious and less prominent justification of brutality, the delights of wanton hurting and destructiveness, and its power-worship.[3] Fascism has so hideously disgraced itself this century that any serious person will be suspicious of slogans about mas-culine power unless restricted to spaghetti Westerns and the humourlessly successful, lean-hipped, tight-lipped posturings of Clint Eastwood. So too with other versions of a new picture of manhood: there have been dreadful savageries done in the name of the proletarian hero, and it is hard to take seriously his guerrilla image. The Anglo-American style of understated, self-mocking, wry-smiling heroism defined itself in wartime, and was handed on in a much less important setting to James Bond.

In a state of unbelief, in which no system of values is shared and in which the aids of technology have so enlarged the range of physical action while making it so much easier and less sig-nificant, it is hard to know what heroism can look like. What does this mean? It means it is hard to know what to admire,

[3] John Fraser, *Violence in the Arts* (1974), p. 104.

whether in fact to be physically courageous is admirable at all. And such courage having been a main definition of the very heart of manliness since the *Iliad*, the idea of manliness itself is abruptly amputated. John Fraser describes a couple of photographs taken in 1914, one of French, the other of German troops marching to the front:

Where the First World War is concerned two anonymous photographs from 1914 do as much as volumes of contemporary patriotic rhetoric to bring home to one how solid was the structure of martial feelings created by two or three decades of militarism. One is a superb shot of soldiers in a French regiment swinging along jauntily under full packs through a city street and bantering with a couple of happy, admiring girls who have darted out to them from the watching crowd. The other is an uncannily similar one of German troops leaving likewise for the front – cheerful, good natured, similarly informed with that enviable kind of untroubled, casual masculine energy and certainty that appears to have been so marked a pre-1914 phenomenon. Regardless of whether they were in error about what they expected to find, it is inescapable that in both pictures one is observing *warriors* going off to something exciting, something wished for, something eminently proper.[4]

That untroubled certainty and energy have gone. The Vietnamese war, in which so much dreadful killing was done from B52 bombers six or seven miles up in the air, was partly such a beastly affair because it was fought by computers rather than by men. One of the attractions of war to men of all political persuasions is that in the right circumstances it simplifies and compresses the moral intensities of life, and makes astonishingly brave and selfless acts into everyday occurrences. The technologizing of warfare has reduced that moral arena.

And yet, as I write, small boys in a playground outside my window are ear-piercingly spraying each other with those universal vocal bullets that go in a sort of quick, staccato wail – 'ah-ha-ah-ah-ha-ha' – and dying glorious and knee-skinning deaths two or three times every playtime. Their gleeful games quote to one another every day the ideal of heroism. Just how long they will be able to translate heroic ideal into practice as they get older remains unclear. It is likely that certain sports,

[4] John Fraser, *Violence in the Arts*, p. 106.

particularly mountaineering and deep-sea sailing, will offer leisure versions of heroism, and indeed this is the longstanding appeal of many sports like rugby and boxing which formalize collision and violence.[5] But sport can hardly provide for a nation's heroes, and heroism is the main value in the ideal of manhood which a nation holds out to its young boyhood.

The origins of little boys' playtime lie at least as far back as the three decades of militarism which Fraser mentioned. Little boys have played soldiers for centuries, of course, but those three decades – 1880–1914 – not only coincide with the rise of children's novels, they also coincide with the tremendous advent and flourishing of a new kind of bestseller, one which combined the manipulation and expression of cheap feeling and rootless action in the right proportions for a mass market. It is one definition of a bestseller as opposed to the more usual definition by sales, that it tends to repeat and express the commonplaces of popular culture, and never to criticize or transcend them. That general point may be fixed more exactly by saying that its characters are, in John Berger's distinction, more idols than heroes:

The idol is self-sufficient: the hero never is. The idol is so superficially desirable, spectacular, witty, happy, that he or she merely supplies a context for fantasy and therefore instead of inspiring, lulls. The idol is based on the appearance of perfection; but never on the striving towards it . . .[6]

There is more to be said for fantasy, as I shall try to show, and there is perhaps less to admire than Berger supposes in the strenuous moral earnestness implied in a 'striving' towards perfection. But here is one distinction between bestselling entertainment and art, even though entertainment versus art, or the idol versus the hero, are not exclusive categories, or merely different names for the class warfare between high and popular culture, but rather ways of beginning to organize criticism and understanding of what is really there on the page *for the reader* (and many different kinds of reader). When the criticism of the story is faithful and correct, the new account of the story does not stand in place of the old (criticism is not a paraphrase of the original novel), but persuades us to see the book in a certain

[5] See my *The Name of the Game* (1977) for a development of this argument.
[6] John Berger, *Permanent Red* (1960), p. 212.

way which wasn't ours at the outset. Thus a small boy starts with playground gunfights and goes on to adventure yarns as part of his natural development. As he grows, he comes to find that action of little importance, though never indifferent.

This process in the criticism of novels can vary in the complex exchange of writer's intentions, reader's expectations, and critic's or teacher's educationally meant advice on how to read a particular novel. I spoke in Chapter 2 of the way I experienced for myself the rather contentless ideals of a novelist like John Buchan. I might have brought out more strongly the difficulty he obviously felt in giving content to the forms of heroic endeavour with which he and his class were left after the First War. This feeling comes out in his novel *John Macnab*, in which the three heroes, prominent members of the power elite, and suffering from acute accidie, devise for themselves the jape of masquerading as Highland poachers. Their only way to recover happiness is by playing at the simplicities of the thriller, like Nancy the Amazon in Arthur Ransome's books. The lesson cuts both ways, of course, because Buchan does notice what to children is always painfully clear – the desperate boringness of so much of life, even for the rich and powerful. Buchan's heroes are bored stiff, and are still boyish enough to be able to do something about it.

Children hate boredom in a peculiarly intense way – so intense that hatred sometimes replaces the boredom. Then we may look to find outbursts of inexplicable violence and destructiveness, if only in attacking a younger sister. It is as though no child can bear the meaninglessness which presses upon him to the point of boredom. At such moments, there is no way of organizing life into natural and self-explanatory activity. The future has suddenly stopped emerging from the past. It has withdrawn to the circumscribing walls of the past and, for the moment, even waiting is pointless. The *ego* is trapped in a present which is apparently timeless. It contains no promise of an end; and it is the guarantee of loss which so heightens the times which are full of pleasure.

Locked into boredom, the only escape is into fantasy. 'Escape' and 'fantasy' are not simply disapproving words of a stern, critical, and teacherly supreme unction. If you break out of the prison of boredom into the freedoms of fantasy, the escape can hardly be held against you, as though it were somehow morally superior to *stay* bored, and thereby 'come to terms with' the boringness of old life itself. What is morally important in this is what you do with your fantasy when you make free with it, and how it stands towards the life you have temporarily and imaginatively escaped from.

Tangled in the same moral thicket is the judgement required of us about the quality of that life itself. It makes sense to live in a fantasy world, if your real life is poor and beastly, and you are powerless to do anything about its conditions. It is understandable, if not excusable, that Walter Mitty, pecked to tatters by his carnivorous hen of a wife, lives in a fantasy of personal and victorious heroism instead of facing his real victimized misery. It is on the other hand weirdly illuminating to learn that US Presidents, in a job which requires striking gifts of intelligence and magnanimity and resolution, can be avid readers of trash like the James Bond novels.

In each pupil's case, the morally anxious teacher-critic has some indefinite notion of a suitable fit between novel and reader. What adventure story *should* a boy read? When they were written, the romantic–militarist adventure stories of the end of the nineteenth century could only have been absurd and sometimes revolting to the men who wrote *Treasure Island* and *Huckleberry Finn*. Anthony Hope's *The Prisoner of Zenda* is a really savoury old-fashioned melodrama. No man of principle could be expected to catch himself reading it without the most cutting condescension. In its time it sold prodigally; one may guess that many of its readers were indeed merely escaping, in the reprehensible sense, into a world of garish light-operatic effects and sentimental moral choices, in which they could pretend to an authority and mastery over events that real life would never provide. And yet the thing lives. An intelligent reader either in Hope's day (*The Prisoner of Zenda* and *Rupert of Hentzau* were published in 1892 and 1896) or now might have quoted the captain of the ship in *The Shadow-Line* and judged Hope's novels as exercising 'the privilege of early youth' which is 'to live in advance of its days in all the beautiful continuity of hope which knows no pauses and no introspection'. It is a reasonable thing to say of *The Shadow-Line*, for instance, that it would be too old for this or that reader. One could hardly see its point until a man had some inkling that ahead lies 'a shadow-line warning one that the regions of early youth, too, must be left behind'. Hope's novel speaks to that simpler, unintrospective earlier youth, and speaks to it out of a social structure which encouraged novelists to sentimentalize the facts of life in order to make them bearable.

Ruritania was the only place where the manly virtues could thrive without malodorous compromise. You remember the story of *The Prisoner of Zenda*: Rudolf Rassendyll, a perfect English gentleman, is the exact double of the weak, vacillating drunkard of a King (both parts played by Stewart Granger in the coy remake of 1955). When the King is kidnapped by Black Michael and Rupert Hentzau on the eve of his coronation, Rassendyll stands in for him with such courageous charm, panache, wit and modesty, that the Princess falls in love with the transfiguration of a man she had always hitherto despised. The day is saved, the King brilliantly rescued after midnight swimmings in the moat, swordplay on the stairs, and the cutting of the drawbridge rope. Rudolf and the Princess renounce one another in a mist of tears. The *coup de théâtre* perfectly combines the renunciations of passionate and illicit love with the call of duty, and withdraws the hero from the dreary obligations of a footling political despotism as soon as the occasion for boyish and reckless courage is past. In this novel and its shamelessly repetitive sequel, Hope endorses the nobility of renounced love, the primacy of caste and class, of duty and loyalty. To do this, as I have said elsewhere,[7] he has to discard Edwardian capitalism, and reinvent the idyll and courtly love. He then inserts into this anachronism the code of an English gentleman of leisure, whose income is safely at a distance from his ideals, and whose honour and suppressed sexuality will naturally respond to the feudal chords of Ruritanian ritual without his having to relinquish his life as an adventurer and irresponsible gentleman-dandy. In the sequel Hope mixes the same recipe except for the much more gamey flavour provided by the apparent death of the King and the Queen's unconsummated adultery with Rudolf.

Such novels consoled the young man then, as now, for the impending loss of manly opportunity. Their images of the honour and loyalty for which it is *worth* showing such courage are only possible in a society where one's membership of an

[7] In my *Ideology and the Imagination* (1975), p. 149.

institution is more important than one's standing as an individual. Rassendyll can have it both ways, which is the pleasure
of a fantasy incapable of reflecting back on action. Hope gives
the hero temporary status as a member of the royal house
opposing the straightforward wickedness of Black Michael,
and Rudolf need therefore ask no questions about loyalty and
duty; at the same time he can comfortably return to his life as a
gentleman of leisure without having to see what happens in the
exercise of power by the regime he has saved from overthrow.
The reader can return to the binding loyalties of a feudal society
without having to renounce the joys of the free uncommitted
self.

The attractiveness of such a moral life recurs constantly in the
novels of a period in which manliness was so uncomplicatedly
attached to courage, honour, physical accomplishments, and
the comradeship of other men. Women figure in it largely as the
space into which men may pour their very generalized feelings
of self-sacrifice and the yearning for self-display. Anthony
Hope's women, like Rider Haggard's, and those of the lesser
historical romancers like D. K. Broster – like Conrad's for that
matter – are the prizes for and the spectators of the action of
their men. They sit apart and more than a little above the action;
they sit in the place allotted them by Victorian England: beautiful, passionate, passive, the necessary antithesis to the dominant versions of manliness.

That picture of manliness suffered terribly, particularly on
the Somme, not because men were unable to embody it in those
dreadful circumstances, but because they did so pointlessly.
The courage was available in awful plenty, but it was betrayed
by the institutions which demanded it as a duty. Consequently,
that manliness has played an increasingly ambiguous part in
growing up in Britain and the USA since 1917. Appeals to its
most visible version – courage in battle – made sense after
Dunkirk and Pearl Harbor, but always in such a distinctly
ironic and equivocal way that no boy could connect such action
with life in a world not officially at war. The American experience in Vietnam served, half a century after the first American
troops went into action at Château-Thierry, to clinch the
lessons begun in the poems of Wilfred Owen.

Perhaps this is why bestsellers of this kind have been reallocated as boys' reading. We tend to feel (don't we?) that the

primitive simplicity of these novels 'can do no harm', while at the same time they keep alive this necessary and noble picture of acting courageously because it is your duty to do so. The comparable images of courage in contemporary box-office movies accompany such explicitly blood-boltered evidence of the cost of courage that any parent might recoil from them. They are in any case largely of a piece with the ethics of *The Deer Hunter* (with its uneasily explicit savagery and the strong implication of a coarse power worship) in their admiration of power and revenge as seen in terms of the sweaty, stubbly Western.

The difficulty of datedness comes out with special force in *King Solomon's Mines*. Now I realize that I may seem to be writing of novels as though they were practical guides to action; and no novel is. But the argument is not entirely simple-minded. A novel may well be about exploration and adventure in an unvisited land, but no less embody a scheme of values – in Lucien Goldmann's phrase, a 'non-conscious structure'[8] – which connects with and criticizes the real world. This critical strength, as the earlier examples of *Alice* or *The Railway Children* make clear, is what marks off the good novel for children from the reallocated bestseller. The relation of what looks like the 'pure fantasy' of the rabbits' story in *Watership Down* or of the boy Jim in *Treasure Island* or of Mowgli in *The Jungle Book* or of the best *Dr Who* stories or of *Right Ho, Jeeves* to their own world and to ours is that of metaphor to reality. In other words, they permit us to carry their scheme of interpretation back to the real world and to use it to see that world as potentially different. A metaphor (which is what a story is) is a sort of concept; it gives a way of seeing what is really there without which the world is an undifferentiated blur. If you tried in 1885, its year of publication, to see the world as *King Solomon's Mines* does, you could do it, but only by some rather brutal exclusions and annihilation. If you were to try to do so now, you simply couldn't: the concepts have changed too much. This bestseller has therefore become genuinely of the category 'pure fantasy'. It cannot be pinned onto the world. There may be good reasons for reading such a 'rattling good yarn', and many more for not being such a poker-faced, humourless bully as to *stop* a child reading it; but its ballooning fantasy has no

---

[8] As he summarizes its use in *The Human Sciences and Philosophy* (1969).

solid ballast, and only the thinnest of ropes to anchor it to the world.

Thus, its three heroes echo the power-structure of Victorian enterprise: Sir Henry and Commander Good are respectively the aristocrat–entrepreneur–soldier and his subordinate manager (Good's skills as a doctor being emblem for the pro-- fessional services needed by the ruling and imperializing Sir Henry Curtis). Quartermain is their experienced soldier– technocrat (imperialism naturally requiring the close collusion of military and capital) and Umbopa their NCO, whose pos- ition as a high-status African indicates the alleged coincidence of interests between native and colonizer, especially since Umbopa knows enough English and enough weapon tech- nology to qualify him for assimilation into the party.

It's easy to stand on the shoulders of the Left some hundred years later and call the book imperialist hyena and capitalist running dog. The predatory purposes of the party come out with a certain disgusting innocence as they casually slaughter their way across Ethiopia leaving a trail of elephants', giraffes', antelopes', and black Africans' bones behind them on the way to the prize of the diamonds as big as the Ritz which are their plunder. At every turn, European technology and the splendid arrogance of the English and the South African confound the blacks until in the not unmoving brotherhood of Sir Henry and Ignosi, courage in a battle fought only with primitive weapons (and therefore fair) is celebrated (as in Homer) as the highest value; the tyrant is slain, and the white men re-establish a just black king upon his rightful throne. As a picture of British Imperial benignity, it is far from empty, including as it does a real mutual respect, a decent rule imposed with foreign help, and the withdrawal of raw resources without interest or re- investment. The tale is grandly told, the pace terrific, the de- scriptions of both landscape and action bold and memorable. Put the book beside such masterpieces as *Kim, Puck of Pook's Hill, Rewards and Fairies,* and *The Jungle Book,* and its puffed- up, lurid, and yet threadbare canopy collapses at once.

In saying that, I do not wish to join in too headlong a way the present rush to push Kipling back among the great. Given his historical context, the gifts which mark him out as such a won- derful writer for children are just those which, when he seeks to address himself to major historical themes in a fully adult and artistic way, so completely let him down. Appointing himself, a short-sighted, small, bookish journalist, as spokesman for an administrative class in a huge empire meant that he had to speak to and for his seniors in a deferential voice and from the far corner of their rooms. The ugliness and cruelty often noted in Kipling was a way of winning favour with the manly men whose recognition he sought; the complement to that cruelty is the strange nursery–psychological sentimentality of stories like *The Brushwood Boy*. What come out, however, when Kipling speaks to children are his very best attributes, and they find their mode of expression in a faultlessly sustained style. He strikes exactly the right tone in which to describe initiation into the world of men and women, and he does so in such a way as to suggest the limits of that world. Moreover, he offers to the two representative children in *Puck* and *Rewards and Fairies*, as he does to Kim and Mowgli, the strongly self-conscious sense of history seen, so to speak, from the side, which the stolidly un-imaginative worthies who ran India entirely lacked. In *The Jungle Book* he gives Mowgli grip upon a whole society and its structure: the boy is first of all a member of a wolf pack, and then outgrows it.[9] He outgrows it with the help of a sequence of admirable fathers – Bagheera, Baloo, Hathi, Kaa – each one of them a comment on their living versions in the Victorian family. So with *Kim*, which is a magnificent book. Kipling gives the young reader (at what age? 12? 13?) what he can at his best give any reader: an intense, fierce, muffled love of a country, a love to which the grey, drab vastnesses of Indian plains give life quite as much as does its rich, smelly, mysterious and shocking picturesqueness. At the same time, Kim is also graced with a sequence of fathers – the Lama, Ali, and Colonel Strickland – who between them represent pretty well the casts of mind needed to tolerate, understand, and govern India.

But I think it is the *Puck* stories which are the least damaged by Kipling's ugly callousness towards nameless, ordinary people caught in murderous events, by his lack of interest in *ideas* – though too great an interest in ideas can kill your wits just as surely as mindlessness. This lack means that he substitutes

---

[9] I take some valuable points here from Lionel Trilling in *The Liberal Imagination* (1951), but very little from Edmund Wilson's essay on Kipling in *The Wound and the Bow*.

the deep throb of atavism for any worked-out picture of history. The history of England in *Puck* and in *Rewards and Fairies* doesn't go anywhere; all we sense with the children is the darkness and mystery of power, the irresistible darkness of the call to duty, the thrilling intrigue the other side of allusion – the intrigue and allusions of the usurper Maximus, of Talleyrand's stool-pigeon, of William the Conqueror's general, of Gloriana herself. These are political pragmatists, the doers and the executioners; *what* they do is unnameable and irrelevant. They deepen the timeless atavism of an old England which predates history – for example in *The Knife and the Naked Chalk* – and it is to this atavism that both the Centurion and the Norman really join themselves. The idea of England transcends the real history of empire, devastation, invasion, and re-colonization.

The Puck stories are gently and affectionately told, and told moreover in a powerful, sun-stilled evocation of Sussex in hottest July during one of the first and best of the ideal summers which dominate the children's novel:

They were not, of course, allowed to act on Midsummer Night itself, but they went down after tea on Midsummer Eve, when the shadows were growing, and they took their supper – hard-boiled eggs, Bath Oliver biscuits, and salt in an envelope – with them. Three Cows had been milked and were grazing steadily with a tearing noise that one could hear all down the meadow; and the noise of the Mill at work sounded like bare feet running on hard ground. A cuckoo sat on a gate-post singing his broken June tune, 'cuckoo-cuk', while a busy kingfisher crossed from the mill-stream to the brook which ran on the other side of the meadow. Everything else was a sort of thick, sleepy stillness smelling of meadow-sweet and dry grass. (*Puck of Pook's Hill*, p. 6)

At the same time, Kipling devises the syllabus of the historical events which were to be described by the writers of historical novels who followed him: the Iron Age, the decline and fall of the Roman Empire, 1066 and All That, Queen Bess, Trafalgar. The mixture of companionability and awfulness set in the easy-going summer draws a child into the book's rather coarse, spicy, very rich-tasting prose. Kipling is clean opposite to the good historian-novelist Tolstoy would have wanted him to be:

Nowhere is the commandment not to taste of the fruit of the tree of knowledge so clearly written as in the course of history. Only unconscious activity bears fruit, and the individual who plays a part in historical events never understands their significance. If he attempts to understand them, he is struck with sterility . . . History, that is the unconscious, general swarm-life of Mankind, uses every moment of the life of kings as a tool for its own purposes.[10]

Kipling makes his characters intensely aware of their own significance in history-making, but he does so in music infinitely seductive to children:

'And then there's the verse about the Rings,' said Dan. 'When I was little it always made me feel unhappy in my inside.'
    'Witness those rings and roundelays, do you mean?' boomed Puck, with a voice like a great church organ.

> 'Of theirs which yet remain,
> Were footed in Queen Mary's days
> On many a grassy plain.
> But since of late Elizabeth,
> And, later, James came in,
> Are never seen on any heath
> As when the time hath been.

    It's some time since I heard that sung, but there's no good beating about the bush: it's true. The People of the Hills have all left. I saw them come into Old England and I saw them go. Giants, trolls, kelpies, brownies, goblins, imps; wood, tree, mound, and water-spirits; heath-people, hill-watchers, treasure-guards, good people, little people, pishogues, leprechauns, nightriders, and the rest – gone, all gone! I came into England with Oak, Ash and Thorn, and when Oak, Ash, and Thorn are gone I shall go too.'
    Dan looked round the meadows – at Una's oak by the lower-gate; at the line of ash trees that overhang Otter Pool where the mill-stream spills over, when the Mill does not need it, and at the old Whitethorn where Three Cows scratched their necks.
    'It's all right,' he said; and added, 'I'm planting a lot of acorns this autumn too.' (*Puck of Pook's Hill*, p. 10)

There is so much to charm children into the tale, if their stomachs are strong enough for Kipling's curried brew. He can touch so lightly the quick fondnesses of a child ('unhappy in my inside'), and their deep want to keep the world wonderful ('I'm

[10] *War and Peace*, trans. L. and A. Maude (London: Macmillan 1942), p. 666.

planting a lot of acorns'), and he can hint at horrors and violences which out of a proper respect for the children's sensibilities can be taken no further (which would *have* to go further
with an adult). Thus Sir Richard Dalyngridge in *Young Men at
the Manor* speaks of the casualness with which De Aquila would
have killed his Saxon molesters, and Parnesius in *A Centurion of
the Thirtieth* spends long days in slaughter of the Winged Hats.
But Kipling's imagination shies away from the detail, and we
can only be glad. (Rosemary Sutcliff, who owes as much to
Kipling, is much more honest about pain and wounds and dead
bodies – with a proper tact also.) Instead he notes the exquisite
details which stud the book with life – De Aquila hopping
about on one foot, his other toe poking in his horse's girth,
Hobden 'eating his potato with the curious neatness of men
who make most of their meals in the blowy open', or the stirring moment at the end of *The Conversion of St. Wilfrid* when the
organist sings the *Dies Irae*:

It rang out suddenly from a dark arch of lonely noises – every word
spoken to the very end:

> 'Dies Irae, dies illa,
> Solvet saeculum in favilla,
> Teste David cum Sibylla.'

The Archbishop caught his breath and moved forward. The music
carried on by itself a while.
   'Now it's calling all the light out of the windows,' Una whispered
to Dan.
   'I think it's more like a horse neighing in battle,' he whispered back.
The voice cried:

> 'Tuba mirum spargens sonum
> Per sepulchra regionum.'

Deeper and deeper the organ dived down, but far below its deepest
note they heard Puck's voice joining in the last line:

> 'Coget omnes ante thronum.'

As they looked in wonder, for it sounded like the dull jar of one of the
very pillars shifting, the little fellow turned and went out through the
south door.
   'Now's the sorrowful part, but it's very beautiful.' Una found
herself speaking to the empty chair in front of her.

'What are you doing that for?' Dan said behind her. 'You spoke so politely too.'

'I don't know . . . I thought . . .' said Una. 'Funny!'

' 'Tisn't. It's the part you like best,' Dan grunted.

The music had turned soft – full of little sounds that chased each other on wings across the broad gentle flood of the main tune. But the voice was ten times lovelier than the music.

> 'Recordare Jesu pie,
> Quod sum causa Tuae viae,
> Ne me perdas illa die!'

There was no more. They moved out into the centre aisle.
(*Rewards and Fairies*, pp. 196–7)

There's a lot of Kipling in that paragraph: the vulgarity inseparable from really rousing and tolling music (even in Gregorian chant), the nice mixture of pagan and Christian, the gentleness towards children, the brief condescension to *any* adults, even the saint, lest they face Kipling with something greater than he could encompass.

For he knows very certainly, if inarticulately, what he wants boys to become as men. Indeed it mustn't be too explicit, or the secrecy of membership, the air heavy with withheld meanings, the unquestioning stoic duty, the warm, immediate, unspoken friendships, are all lost. These are the circumstances of manhood, and manhood thrives in them especially when it has the luck to hit on one of the crowded upheavals of English history – the fall of the Romans (as I have mentioned), the dissolution of the monasteries in *Dymchurch Flit*, the plague in *Doctor of Medicine*, King John's pogrom of the Jews in the extraordinary tale *The Treasure and the Law*. The two books are densely populated with the figures of a boldly drawn cartoon history of England according to the syllabus of Westward Ho School, a minor and progressive public school for the training of poets (Kipling – Beatle in *Stalky and Co.*), of administrators (McTurk), and of soldiers (Stalky himself).

At its heart, as I have been at pains to emphasize, the manliness which Kipling admires is hollow. The young subalterns of the Wall 'give of one's best once, to one only. That given, there remains no second worth giving or taking.' They love their autocratic master, whose putsch has failed, for his calm decisiveness, his knowing, shrewd eye for men, his laughing, ironic commitment to power, his absolute efficiency in discharging debts of honour, his good losing right up to the sweep of the executioner's sword. Beyond love for their master, they have nothing to do but their duty. It's a bleak vision, its bleakness no doubt a consequence of Kipling's being a much more intelligent writer than Rider Haggard. You get things done by nods and winks and tricks and craftiness, and you laugh till the tears run down brown cheeks and great shoulders shake, but all you can do is your job, and your job is your duty.

Not much to build on there. *Treasure Island* will do by contrast to suggest the whole range of feeling and valuing which ideologizing for the Empire cut out. For although Stevenson unforgettably re-writes the old knight-errantry and quest in terms of the new piracy, Jim Hawkins is normally and naturally terrified as well as brave, and at the end is simply relieved to be home and settled for good in his domestic life. The excitement of the adventure is enough reason for enjoying the book, the colour of the characters matches its pace; but what keeps the heroes to their purpose is a determination not to be beaten and an eagerness to get to the treasure first for its own sake. The crossplay of character means that there's no room for sanctimony either about imperial duty or about the realm of Kukuanaland. Long John Silver catches in a single character all that Stevenson did for children's novels: he made something deeply ambiguous out of Silver's enormous vitality, his combination of callous and murderous greed with great likeability.

Much has been written of *Treasure Island*.[11] I use it here to note that it belongs with the very best early novels for children, and that it does have a tremendous dash and pace which makes Dickens a valid comparison. Furthermore, its triumph of 'luck rather than righteousness',[12] its clear sense that ruthlessness and resolution attached to an adventurous acquisitiveness deserve better and will probably do better than disorderly and cowardly acquisitiveness are far truer to the facts of late nineteenth-century fortune-making than any other children's book. What is best about it is its ringing end:

The bar silver and the arms still lie, for all that I know, where Flint

---

[11] Especially in an excellent essay by Douglas Brown, 'R. L. S. Inspiration and Industry', in *Young Writers, Young Readers*, ed. R. B. Ford (1963).

[12] Harvey Darton, quoted by John Rowe Townsend, *Written for Children* (1976), p. 64.

buried them; and certainly they shall lie there for me. Oxen and wain-ropes would not bring me back to that accursed island; and the worst dreams that ever I have are when I hear the surf booming about its coasts, or start upright in bed, with the sharp voice of Captain Flint still ringing in my ears: 'Pieces of Eight! Pieces of eight!' (p. 281)

Jim Hawkins, with a fuller diction than he really would have employed, has always been clear about what the treasure has cost – 'what blood and sorrow, what good ships scuttled on the deep, what brave men walking the plank blindfold, what shot of cannon, what shame and lies and cruelty' (p. 273). He passes a proper judgement on treasure-hunting, and at the end is re-lieved to be clear of it with his health and safety.

Part of Jim's acquitting himself manfully is his homecoming and his sane judgement on the frantic adventure. Home is what men return to when they have been away. It is both the actual and the moral journey which the history of family defines. Women, however, make the journey in one direction only, or they do not make it at all. The bestselling lessons for women among the contemporaries of Haggard and Kipling were those of Marie Corelli, who is now forgotten. Her tougher success-ors Daphne du Maurier and Georgette Heyer suggest what I mean by speaking of a one-way journey. Daphne du Maurier's heroines – in *Jamaica Inn*, in *Frenchman's Creek*, in *Rebecca* and *Anne Marie* – register in prose the conscious, passive passion to be loved if possible, but to be wanted and possessed at all costs, including the cost of freedom. It is this same passive passion which John Berger finds in the tradition of the nude in Western art:

To be naked is to be oneself.

To be nude is to be seen naked by others and yet not recognised for oneself. (The sight of it as an object stimulates the use of it as an object.) Nakedness reveals itself. Nudity is placed on display.

To be naked is to be without disguise.

To be on display is to have the surface of one's own skin, the hairs of one's own body, turned into a disguise which, in the situation, can never be discarded. The nude is condemned to never being naked. Nudity is a form of dress.

In the average European oil painting of the nude the principal pro-tagonist is never painted. He is the spectator in front of the picture and he is presumed to be a man. Everything is addressed to him. Every-

thing must appear to be the result of his being there. But he, by definition, is a stranger – with his clothes still on.[13]

Daphne du Maurier's nameless heroine is the complement to
the ghost of Rebecca which dominates the famous novel: the
one brilliant, beautiful, attractive, the other mute, docile, and
mousey. Both women seek their vision of sexual power by
making themselves the women Max de Winter will want.
Rebecca, however, seeks to make herself that woman
overwhelmingly, and in order to prevent his manly possession
of her being overwhelmed (and his self-possession being lost)
Max kills her. The nameless new wife, as Mrs Danvers tells her,
is the shadow and the ghost. 'It's you that's forgotten and not
wanted and pushed aside . . . It's you who ought to be dead not
Mrs de Winter' (*Rebecca*, p. 257). The core of the book is its
intense sexuality. The book permits the girl reader both to be
jealous of Rebecca and to have supplanted her, both to fear and
to envy her. She has been glamorously murdered. She can be
the bored mousy wife *and* imagine herself the *femme fatale*.
Either way she seeks to be possessed by the man. She seeks for
him because to be in love – the phrase which within the
bestselling women's and girls' novels focusses and justifies
sexual desire – ensures that her world assumes place and order.
When everything else is fluid and unsure, sexuality is certain,
hard and accurate. When, as it usually does, sexuality
disappoints, she tells herself that it is because she cannot meet
his and the world's expectations. She whirls about this spiral of
infinite expectation and certain disappointment. Spinning in
the opposite direction, the spiral twists her into tight knots of
self-pity. Either way, she must suspect, and be resigned to, the
likelihood that he has another mistress.

Rebecca brightly illuminates this diagram of desire in so
many post-Victorian women. The novel perfects the picture
by making the rival woman a ghost, and therefore beyond
confirmation. The ghost cannot be laid even by the fire which
ends the tale. The sweet inescapable corruption is the magnet in
the book which pulls girls so strongly towards it. Georgette
Heyer makes a much less steamy read because, working within
the same frame of mind, she is loath to get her hands quite so
sticky. Moreover, she takes her lead, some 130 years after the

[13] John Berger, *Ways of Seeing* (1972), p. 54.

event, from Jane Austen's Elizabeth Bennet, whose example of intelligence and independence had long been learned by Mrs Hodgson Burnett and Edith Nesbit, but who had been largely excluded from bestsellers either by dewy-eyed yielders with clouds of raven-black hair, or by passionate-mouthed, tumbling-locked eyefuls, collapsing into rows of asterisks. Georgette Heyer's heroines cultivate a rather more modern pose of slangy pertness, but of course they know nothing of the reality of Elizabeth Bennet's vigour and fieriness, nor of her keen sensitiveness to Darcy's arrogance of caste. The Heyer heroine melts just as languishingly as Daphne du Maurier's onto the broad shoulders of lazy-eyed nephews of the Scarlet Pimpernel. Both novelists console women for their helplessness by showing them how to maintain the inner tension which keeps them upright in the regard of men. Daphne du Maurier in particular speaks with a considerable plangent force against the freedom and self-criticism, the truth-telling goodness which we have set out as the epistemes (that is, the absolutely *given* grounds of being) of human action and the essences of meaning.

This is not to endorse a narrow polemic on behalf of the left wing of Women's Liberation. Taking part in its more strident and sectarian version deprives women of what the culture at large most lacks in its public places: tenderness, peacefulness, care and love, sweetness, long-suffering. If women do not look after these things, no men will.

The truth-telling which is missing from the bestsellers for girls and big girls is present in the books of Laura Ingalls Wilder. These are the true record of the Ingalls family as they strove to establish their farms on the frontiers of the New World at the turn of the century. Laura Ingalls Wilder is writing her family's true story, but that family being where it was, she is also in a position to join personal biographies with the march of a larger history as it was made into the new countries of Canada and the USA. She stood at the point at which career and politics cross, and she has a true and momentous story to tell.

That momentum is felt in private lives; but they are not (for once) swept and broken by it. The economic conditions of the Frontier in 1900 were those of what Macpherson calls 'a simple market society'[14] in which the division of labour is still at a suf-

---

[14] C. B. Macpherson, *The Political Theory of Possessive Individualism* (1962), pp. 51–3.

ficiently early stage for individuals to make pretty free choices as to occupation. There is a noticeable loosening of the close or one-to-one relations of production to consumption, while at the same time the individual retains a measure of control over his means of production. Although the little township is very dependent on the big centres of capital for supplies and communication, its self-sufficiency and the dignities and democracies which depend on its economy are real, and shape the economy as it shapes them.

I take *The Long Winter* because I think it is the best of an excellent series, not because it fits a thesis. Its prose is, in Rowe Townsend's memorable words, 'clear, plain, and as good as bread'[15] *because* its political origins – that family, that township, those shops and schools and ways of husbandry – were as they were. Its strength in showing daughters how to become women is so much greater than that of the bestsellers, not only because the story is moved by the absoluteness of historical fact. *The Long Winter* has its force because the story and the prose in which it is told lie so close to the author's morality. There is no strain upon the writer in her seeking to commend what is beautiful and rational and good. The way the little family acts is the way it ought to act, and this congruence of culture and nature, of economics and action, means that Laura Ingalls Wilder can tell her tale quite purely. The sanctions and piety of the Ingalls are open and lovely, although they are so because they do not have to encompass the greater moral contortions of life in a more complex social structure. It is to the point to note that within the Ingalls family and their little community, we find a perfect expression of the just society, ordered on the principles of liberal theory. It is the theme I most wish to tackle in this book, and it runs as a ground bass through the discussion of each novelist and his relation to his readers. We return to it explicitly in the last chapter; here I only stress that the novelist's preoccupation with an ideal social order and the materials to hand for its creation must, as it is communicated to children, provide a picture either of an imaginable future or of a real past. *The Long Winter* and its companion books hold past and future together. Life at the Frontier really was like that, but life ought also to be like that again. The community's life is

---

[15] *Written for Children*, p. 181.

ordered by the two principles of justice: that each person is to have equal rights to the most extensive basic liberty compatible with a similar liberty for others; and that inequalities work in such an arrangement that they are to everyone's advantage and attached to offices open to all.[16]

These principles penetrate the government of the township, and order it when the unprecedentedly long winter breaks down the usual economy. The fundamental liberalism comes out in the fine scenes in which the two very young men, Cap Garland and Almanzo Wilder (whom Laura later marries), go out of town in a brief lull between the appalling blizzards and just get back safely with a wagon-load of life-saving wheat. They sell it at a fair price to the store-holder and he, faced by starving townsfolk, tries to charge an extortionate one.

Mr Ingalls told him they thought he was charging too much for the wheat.

'That's my business,' said Loftus. 'It's my wheat, isn't it? I paid good hard money for it.'

'A dollar and a quarter a bushel, we understand,' Mr Ingalls said.

'That's my business,' Mr Loftus repeated.

'We'll show you whose business it is,' the angry man shouted.

'You fellows so much as touch my property and I'll have the law on you', Mr Loftus answered. Some of them laughed snarlingly. But Loftus was not going to back down. He banged his fist on the counter and told them, 'That wheat's mine and I've got a right to charge any price I want for it.'

'That's so, Loftus, you have', Mr Ingalls agreed with him. 'This is a free country and every man's got a right to do as he pleases with his own property.' He said to the crowd, 'You know it's a fact, boys,' and he went on, 'don't forget every one of us is free and independent, Loftus. This winter won't last forever and maybe you want to go on doing business after it's over.'

'Threatening me, are you?' Mr Loftus demanded.

'We don't need to,' Mr Ingalls replied. 'It's a plain fact. If you've got a right to do as you please, we've got a right to do as we please. It works both ways. You've got us down now. That's your business, as you say. But your business depends on our good will. You maybe don't notice that now, but along next summer you'll likely notice it.'

'That's so, Loftus,' Gerald Fuller said. 'You got to treat folks right or you don't last long in business, not in this country.'

[16] I take these from John Rawls, *A Theory of Justice* (1972), p. 60.

The angry man said, 'We're not here to palaver. Where's that wheat?'

'Don't be a fool, Loftus,' Mr Harthorn said.

'The money wasn't out of your till more than a day,' Mr Ingalls said. 'And the boys didn't charge you a cent for hauling it. Charge a fair profit and you'll have the cash back inside of an hour.'

'What do you call a fair profit?' Mr Loftus asked. 'I buy as low as I can and sell as high as I can; that's good business.'

'That's not my idea,' said Gerald Fuller. 'I say it's good business to treat people right.'

'We wouldn't object to your price, if Wilder and Garland here had charged you what it was worth to go after that wheat,' Mr Ingalls told Loftus.

'Well, why didn't you?' Mr Loftus asked them. 'I stood ready to pay any reasonable charge for hauling.'

Cap Garland spoke up. He was not grinning. He had the look that had made the railroader back down. 'Don't offer us any of your filthy cash. Wilder and I didn't make that trip to skin a profit off folks that are hungry.'

Almanzo was angry, too. 'Get it through your head if you can, there's not money enough in the mint to pay for that trip. We didn't make it for you and you can't pay us for it.'

Mr Loftus looked from Cap to Almanzo and then around at the other faces. They all despised him. He opened his mouth and shut it. He looked beaten. Then he said, 'I'll tell you what I'll do, boys. You can buy the wheat for just what it cost me, a dollar twenty-five cents a bushel.'

'We don't object to your making a fair profit, Loftus,' Mr Ingalls said, but Loftus shook his head.

'No, I'll let it go for what it cost me.'

This was so unexpected that for a moment no one knew exactly how to take it. Then Mr Ingalls suggested, 'What do you say if we all get together and kind of ration it out, on a basis of how much our families need to last through till spring?'

They did this. (pp. 227–9)

The telling of the incident and of the whole tale is more than a moral homily. The way of telling it could only have come from the way of seeing the events. That way of seeing, growing in the social and moral structures of Frontier life, pumped the blood through the great principles of liberalism. If the book still leaves us puzzled as to how the intricate and topheavy moral economies of the 'advanced' nations can learn from *The Long Winter*, this puzzlement does nothing to impair the force

of the book for children, who all rightly see fairness as the first
social principle.

What isn't 'fair' in the book is the length and severity of the
winter. The seven months' savage weather is the family's bitter
enemy. But Mrs Wilder is too admirable and pious an artist not
to acknowledge the bounty of nature first, and the first fifth of
the book describes a rich, glowing and splendid autumn, a
heavy harvest, and the joys of the hot sun on the prairie. The
pleasure of reading these pages sharpens because we know
what is coming. In everyday life children find it particularly
pleasurable to anticipate a storm rolling in from the sea in
purple dark clouds and grumbling thunder, especially when
they are still in bright sun. The opening chapters of *The Long
Winter* give you that feeling. When the blizzard breaks, the
sensation is like that of hearing from a warm bed the rain driven
onto the window pane in spatters, while the wind howls. The
child's eyes shine to hear Mrs Wilder describe the weather, but
she shivers in sympathy with Laura:

That blizzard never seemed to end. It paused sometimes, only to roar
again quickly and more furiously out of the north-west. Three days
and nights of yelling shrill winds and roaring fury beat at the dark,
cold house and ceaselessly scoured it with ice-sand. Then the sun
shone out, from morning till noon perhaps, and the dark anger of
winds and icy snow came again.

Sometimes in the night, half-awake and cold, Laura half-dreamed
that the roof was scoured thin. Horribly the great blizzard, large as the
sky, bent over it and scoured with an enormous invisible cloth, round
and round on the paper-thin roof, till a hole wore through and
squealing, chuckling, laughing a deep Ha! Ha! the blizzard whirled in.
Barely in time to save herself, Laura jumped awake.

Then she did not dare to sleep again. She lay still and small in the
dark, and all around her the black darkness of night, that had always
been restful and kind to her, was now a horror. She had never been
afraid of the dark. 'I am not afraid of the dark,' she said to herself over
and over, but she felt that the dark would catch her with claws and
teeth if it could hear her move or breathe. Inside the walls, under the
roof where the nails were clumps of frost, even under the covers
where she huddled, the dark was crouched and listening. (p. 170)

The pacing of the book is unimprovable. Each chapter is
quite short, nicely adjusted to a young reader's stamina, but
each shifts the story a little way on in to the long, rhythmless

tedium of the winter. The family very nearly starve. They kindle for themselves a thin edge of warmth in temperatures 40° below zero, burning light sticks of tightly twisted hay. They bend a serene patience against the killing cold and their boredom. The girls' dependence on their parents is absolute, of course, but their work is essential to survival (the hay Laura brings in sees them through the last month). Father, being the only man of the family, and with a man's strength, has to face the storm most directly. His courage is of an utterly different and superior order to that of Allan Quartermain. And for all that his strength is essential to protect the weaker women, he could not live without their help, both practical and affectionate.

The love that holds the family upright against the winter is amazing; it gives endurance its meaning as experience, and as we see at the Ingalls's Christmas, it always makes happiness possible. When relief comes, the joy of the moment expresses itself in the delighted suddenness with which the rhythm and diction of the prose change:

Laura and Pa were holding their stiff, swollen red hands over the stove, Ma was cutting the coarse brown bread for supper. The blizzard was loud and furious.

'It can't beat us!' Pa said.

'Can't it, Pa?' Laura asked stupidly.

'No', said Pa. 'It's got to quit sometime and we don't. It can't lick us. We won't give up.'

Then Laura felt a warmth inside her. It was very small but it was strong. It was steady, like a tiny light in the dark, and it burned very low but no winds could make it flicker because it would not give up.

They ate the coarse brown bread and went through the dark and cold upstairs to bed. Shivering in the cold bed Laura and Mary silently said their prayers and slowly grew warm enough to sleep.

Sometime in the night Laura heard the wind. It was still blowing furiously but there were no voices, no howls or shrieks in it. And with it there was another sound, a tiny, uncertain, liquid sound that she couldn't understand.

She listened as hard as she could. She uncovered her ear to listen and the cold did not bite her cheek. The dark was warmer. She put out her hand and only felt a coolness. The little sound that she heard was the trickling of waterdrops. The eaves were dripping. Then she knew.

She sprang up in bed and called aloud, 'Pa! Pa! The Chinook is blowing!'

'I hear it, Laura,' Pa answered from the other room. 'Spring has come. Go back to sleep.'

The Chinook was blowing. Spring had come. The blizzard had given up; it was driven back to the north. Blissfully Laura stretched out in bed; she put both arms on top of the quilts and they were not very cold. She listened to the blowing wind and dripping eaves and she knew that in the other room Pa was lying awake, too, listening and glad. The Chinook, the wind of the spring was blowing. Winter was ended. (pp. 232–3)

Even then the book paces evenly to an end which insists on the continuity of life and the worthwhileness of the struggle against that dreadful winter. Supplies are delayed, and it is mid-May before town and family open the Christmas barrel.

The tale is not a lesson. It is a piece of folk-history – though perfectly accurate. Folk-history is just as scientific and ideological as academic history. The ceremonious mode of narration is necessary to give order to a dangerous and uncertain life. That life image is the best part of America, especially its womenfolk.

7

Let's be friends

I spoke earlier (on p. 29) of the main dimensions of personal and critical meaning, which I am taking as home, friendship, nation, history, intelligence, love, independence. The books I have written about so far are so impressive in my judgement because they take in so many of these dimensions. But they are none of them 'about' history or home in some thematically limited way. The essential distinction between the two halves of Chapter 6 – between Kipling and Laura Ingalls Wilder – is that the dimensions, as I have called them, take actuality from a very much stronger institutional form in Kipling than in Mrs Wilder. In the technical-military group for whom Kipling wrote, honour remained a central value.[1] The honour of a regiment or of a family, a caste or a wolf pack, is an implicit appeal in judging action in Kipling. Mr Ingalls would not make that appeal. Like his pioneer forebear in Arthur Miller's *The Crucible*, his appeal would be to his own good name. His ultimate commitment is to himself as an individual; not in an egotistical way, but such as to affirm the universal dignity of individuals, and himself as literally embodying that dignity on behalf of all men, and equally beside them. So too his daughters would defend him and one another in the name of their freedom. By contrast, the white and the black men and women in Rider Haggard are intricately related through the etiquette which ritualizes the notion of honour. Equals like Sir Henry and Commander Good (but of course not *quite* equal) maintain their bonds with each other by marking themselves off from their inferiors; honour confirms status. At the same time, as the great regal tragedies like *Oedipus Rex* and *Macbeth* make clear, status and honour confer responsibility for a people upon their

[1] Honour is the crux for examining value change in the chapter 'Excursus: On the Obsolescence of the Concept of Honour', in Peter and Brigitte Berger, *The Homeless Mind* (1974). I come to some different conclusions, however, here.

holders. The three worthies in *King Solomon's Mines* deal in kingdoms, and with a due sense of what they are doing. Mr Ingalls would do no such thing, even if he could.

It follows that the enormous shift away from tribal, conservative, institutional values towards personal, radical, and domestic values which marks the near limit of the history in this book, emphasizes the dimensions of home and friendship at the expense of history and nation. In a well-known essay called 'What I Believe' in *Two Cheers for Democracy*, E. M. Forster mused that while he hoped never to be tested in a choice between betraying his friends and betraying his country, if it came to it he would wish to have the courage to betray his country. The decision would not only have gone the other way in Kipling or Rider Haggard, it would also have done so for the Resistance fighters in Sartre's play *Men Without Shadows*. Forster represents the decent Bloomsbury liberal whose stomach has been turned by the extremes of chauvinism for which Kipling is often, if unjustly, blamed. As I have already noted, when the necessity for patriotism came round again in 1940, it had to find a very post-1916 language in which to speak. But this is a way of saying more than that styles of rhetoric have changed. The confident manliness of 1914 disappeared because it had been betrayed. Men felt like that in 1914 because, at least in part, they *trusted* the structures of authority – the generals and staff officers – which deployed that courage. They continued to show that courage when it clearly had no point to it, as all the books and poems, diaries and letters show that men knew, because there was no shared system of belief and metaphysic which could be invoked in order to dominate and put down the call to arms.

In the face of this collapse, E. M. Forster, and many writers with him, advertised the morality whose long historical roots in the Romantic movement gave it a tried respectability but whose immediate appeal lay in its counting upon the extremities neither of Fascism nor of Communism – upon neither the dark tide of the blood nor the future of the masses – but in the sanction it gave to the individual himself. The preferred moral terms of liberalism are integrity and dignity, honesty and sincerity; its scale of moral measurement is the individual and personal relationship; it is local, contextual and insistently relativist.

The paradox is that, in the strong suspicion it feels for all the threatening size and impersonality of institutions, its aversion to everything rational and bureaucratic and for what it sees as the counter-intuitive and disenchanting modes of modern life, the liberal ethic tends to cut itself off from moral values essential to the maintenance of the personal life; from fidelity, loyalty, trust, friendship itself. Friendship is surely a value central to the doctrines of liberal individualism. It is an oddity worth remarking that the ludicrous language of the encounter groups and their preposterous prophets very rarely invokes 'friendship' at all. They speak instead of 'getting in touch with their feelings', 'exploring abilities to make sustained human contact', 'awareness of oneself in the here-and-now'.[2] The absence of friendship as a point of appeal turns out, however oddly, to be a structural feature of the doctrine. For, as a consequence of loosening the hold of institutions, the ideas of loyalty and fidelity must themselves suffer sharp attenuation. This is visible in a whole range of social memberships from marriage to political parties. (In the latter case, it is almost invariably seen to be admirable to prefer the claims of individual conscience, say in the case of a mass vote, to the claims of loyalty to the membership.) If loyalty and fidelity lose weight, it is that much harder to know not only how to value but how to *experience* friendship at all. A whole family of values, including not only loyalty and fidelity, but such powerful ideas as trust, allegiance, hospitality, devotion, forgiveness, go out of focus once it is not clear which institutions are felt to be worth a man's oath, and when, in the confusion of such a hesitant and exiguous reality, the individual is held to be paramount over *all* institutional claims, obligations, and duties.

It is easy to fall into a commination of the modern world which, starting from the obvious facts of far greater institutional porousness, the loosening of the bonds of family and community, the necessary anonymities of modern bureaucracy, the substitution of contract for oath, of subscription for fealty, ends with letters to the *Reader's Digest* bemoaning the dissolution of human kindness and the breakdown of neighbourhood and family by the welfare state. Well, there would be truth in such letters, although the same kind of letters could be

---

[2] Phrases taken from R. W. Libby and R. N. Whitehurst (eds.), *Renovating Marriage: Towards New Sexual Life-styles* (1973).

written blaming different instruments of the demons of capitalism: the enforced mobility of labour, the killing opiates of
the mass media, the alienations of Taylorized work. Either
way, mass society is also atomized society. Cronyhood
replaces friendship. Does it matter?

It looks a silly question. Simply to start from our intuitions
and our long experience is enough of an answer at first. Friendship as a value is given its concrete life by the actuality of our
friends. If our friends betray us we feel wronged and badly hurt;
if we lack friends we feel lonely and afraid. Our friends guarantee our worth to ourselves, the existence of human warmth;
they answer the need for company. But what of the ruthlessly
sceptical individualist, the loner who protests suspicion of the
self-seekingness of *all* human closeness? The low-key reply
might be to concede the self-seekingness, but pay it as a cost of
satisfying the need for the company of others, however predatory or cringing they may be.

There is a larger claim.[3] The ruthless sceptic has a way, when
cruelty or wrong is done to him, of suddenly invoking
principles opposed to a self-seeking or solipsistic picture of the
world. He needs objective reasons to express his resentment. In
these circumstances the primary form of moral argument is to
ask the sceptic to imagine himself in the situation of another
person. For even the sceptic cannot renounce, as though it were
a sentimentalism of the moralist, the grip upon all human
beings of certain fundamental forms of practical reasoning and
the view of oneself which they entail, notably the imaginative
ability to see oneself and others from a detached position.
Consequently, the possibility of acting selflessly rests upon the
fact that we all recognize the reality of other persons, even
though we don't always act on the recognition.

The reality of this recognition begins from friendship. I do
not mean that once we recognize the reality of others we will act
well. It is all too clear that men are not basically impelled
towards goodness. My point is that the reality of others is the
objective ground of morality; friendship marks out such
ground very visibly, but friendship can occur only when the
conditions are right.

The conditions are not natural, they are historical. When

---

[3] The arguments for which I partly quote, partly adapt, from Thomas Nagel, *The Possibility of Altruism* (1970), pp. 143 ff.

William Golding sets up the conditions for the action of *Lord of the Flies* – a book which now stands well across the margins of children's and adults' novels – he wants to show that Ralph, weeping at the end 'for the end of innocence, the darkness of man's heart, and the fall through the air of the true, wise friend called Piggy' (p. 192), laments the timeless, predestined wickedness of men. The friendship quickened at the start of the book by 'the strange glamour that had once invested the beaches' was, on such a view, bound to break down into the wolfish atavism of slaughter and sacrifice. But the conditions for friendship, like those of community and altruism, are social and historical. Friendship exists naturally amongst children and grown-ups when there are close likenesses and complementary world-pictures and beliefs, temperaments and feelings, when there is the strong chance of great happiness and fulfilment. By contrast, friendships are *made* when all action is heightened by drama and danger, when there are great works to be done and a common enemy. Ratty, Mole, and Badger are friends in outlook, pastimes, class. The depth of that friendship is implicit in the calm and level sunlight of Edwardian society. Mary and Colin grow into the deep friendship of the secret garden as they come to recognize the reality of one another, to forget their bilious self-absorption, and to experience the joy of natural beauty. The nursery friendships in the Hundred Acre Wood of Winnie-the-Pooh, Piglet, Tigger, Kanga and all are woven from the ample spaces of the Wood, its paradisal calm and equality, its freedom from production, its splendid safety. In Arthur Ransome, sailing expands in its meanings until it not only represents all economic systems, its structures are also moral and political. It is a way of ordering lives. Friendship therefore, can grow quite easily and naturally within a stability as unquestionable as that of Kenneth Grahame's Thames, Just William's 1930s Croydon, or Little Grey Rabbit's Derbyshire.

Mention of *Just William* must do to remind us that the most settled social system children experience is that of school. William's exploits with his gang occupy the spaces left by home and school. The school story, in all its extraordinary variety and vitality, is one of the biggest monuments in popular culture to the institution of friendship. Emerging from the dark of history, groups of laughing, noisy, back-slapping, japing and swaggering fourth-formers come up the staircase into the light and walk past us: Tom Brown and Harry East; Stalky and Co.; Bob Cherry, Harry Wharton, Frank Nugent, Hurree Jamset Ram Singh, and some paces behind, Billy Bunter – 'I say, you chaps'; Joey Bettany, Grizel Cochrane, and the girls of Chalet School; the prefects of Malory Towers and St Clare's. Even at their most routine, the school stories retain their power. The fact that so many of them are set in boarding schools has nothing much to do with class and the alleged wistfulness of the poor to go to posh schools, but has much more to do with removing parents from the story, and providing a structure which promises safety while making resistance attractive and understandable. The stunning snobberies of these tales, awful though they are, are unimportant to their readers beside the celebrations of friendship. The shape and meaning of the friendship is peculiar to the total nature of the little world the children inhabit. The school provides, as I said, stability and a clear demarcation of private and ethical space: you know where you are. It also provides a common work-situation, a common authority to be acknowledged and sometimes flouted, common rites of passage and membership. In these stories, this completeness of structure is shared with, for instance, regiments, ships, airforce squadrons, POW camps, coal miners, groups isolated by danger and adventure in solitary parts of the world (or the solar system), and, more recently, hospitals (hence the success of the TV series like *Angels*). Schools and their like provide the old order within which the new can begin to take shape.

It takes a writer of Mark Twain's genius to remove society to the banks of the Mississippi so that the quite unprecedented friendship of white boy Huck Finn and black runaway slave Jim can convincingly create the image of the new order. Twain changed the picture of what was possible in friendships, and he did so in the new name of human rights and individual dignity for which the USA at its best stood, for which indeed it had made its Declaration of Independence and fought its revolution. Twain was a great enough writer to break the conventional structures right open, and leave Huck and Jim to build their own new order on the river. It is a disappointment felt by everybody (whatever may be said about a necessary return to everyday life) when Tom Sawyer reasserts the grip of his tedious fantasies at the end.

Huckleberry Finn suggests the creative strength which is needed if a writer is to grasp and realize the entirely new possibilities of a change in values and feelings in the world about him. The friendship of Huck and Jim is more than just a friendship; it is also a picture of the best American life in the dreamed-of future.

E. B. White's delicate little fable, *Charlotte's Web*, provides a measure of the daring and difficulty of Twain's achievement. White tells the story of a portly little pig called Wilbur who is saved from the slaughterer and the Sunday roast by the efforts of a spider called Charlotte who lives in the corner of his sty. Charlotte weaves the words 'Some Pig' over Wilbur, who thereby becomes the most visited pig in the locality and is kept on permanent show by his owner. Charlotte sustains her triumph by spelling 'radiant', 'terrific' and most touchingly, 'humble' over Wilbur. At the end, she weaves her sac, fills it to bulging with the eggs of her 514 children, and dies.

The action is accompanied by the population of the little barn: a truculent, gluttonous rat called Templeton, the stammering, stupid geese, and the little girl, Fern, who isn't believed when she passes on the tales she has heard in the barn to her mother. The tale is both poignant and boisterous, and it takes place on a quiet farm in a Midwestern state, with its ordered sequence of seasonal tasks, its tranquil affirmation of the cycles of life and death: Fern grows up to prefer the big wheel at the fair to the gentle, absorbing barn society; Charlotte dies and her children take her place. Its main interest, however, centres in the suddenness and good fortune, together with the strangeness of the idea, with which the spider and the pig befriend each other. White's dream, like so many stories for children, is of a new garden of Eden in which unalike creatures of all kinds lie down together. But he has good plain sense as well, so he makes Templeton surly and the goose effortfully dim, like one's aunt. The beauty of the book lies in such an exchange as this, when the bereaved Wilbur befriends three of Charlotte's children who have stayed in the barn:

When he woke it was late afternoon. He looked at the egg sac. It was empty. He looked into the air. The balloonists were gone. Then he walked drearily to the doorway, where Charlotte's web used to be. He was standing there, thinking of her, when he heard a small voice.

'Salutations!' it said. 'I'm up here.'

'So am I,' said another tiny voice.

'So am I,' said a third voice. 'Three of us are staying. We like this place, and we like you.'

Wilbur looked up. At the top of the doorway three small webs were being constructed. On each web, working busily, was one of Charlotte's daughters.

'Can I take this to mean,' asked Wilbur, 'that you have definitely decided to live here in the barn cellar, and that I am going to have three friends?'

'You can indeed,' said the spiders.

'What are your names, please?' asked Wilbur, trembling with joy.

'I'll tell you my name,' replied the first little spider, 'if you'll tell me why you are trembling.'

'I'm trembling with joy,' said Wilbur.

'Then my name is Joy,' said the first spider.

'What was my mother's middle initial?' asked the second spider.

'A,' said Wilbur.

'Then my name is Aranea,' said the spider.

'How about me?' asked the third spider. 'Will you just pick out a nice sensible name for me – something not too long, not too fancy, and not too dumb?'

Wilbur thought hard.

'Nellie?' he suggested.

'Fine, I like that very much,' said the third spider. 'You may call me Nellie.' She daintily fastened her orb-line to the next spoke of the web.

Wilbur's heart brimmed with happiness. He felt that he should make a short speech on this very important occasion. (pp. 172–3)

Just how good the little parable is comes out in this gentle, touching prose. If we compare it with the cartoon film,[4] however, we can see the limitations of both. For that film, a faithful version of the book, follows the main style of Walt Disney in devising images of perfectly unselfconscious and therefore non-reflexive characters. In doing so, Walt Disney caught a dominant feeling in the popular culture of mass society: the feeling that consciousness is overrated, that people live and act in terms of broad humours and passions, that reflexive thought changes nothing and is conceited and pointless. The cartoon styles which were picked up by the pop artists of the sixties accurately reflect this resignation: they

[4] Made by Sagittarius and Hanna–Barbera films, 1962.

come out with the same self-confidence in the smartest
spaghetti Western.

In spite of their perkiness and mindless resilience, the
American cartoon heroes – Tom and Jerry, Dumbo and Jiminy
Cricket, the Disney Mowgli and Baloo, the Rescuer mice, and
Charlotte the Spider and Wilbur Pig are, when the adult
watches them, the myth heroes of the resigned and hopeless.
This is particularly visible in the great Peanuts cult. Schulz's
Peanuts characters endear themselves by turning instinctive,
unconscious, amoral action into cuteness. Charlie Brown,
Lucy, and company are entirely natural (and therefore
admirable to their readers) and entirely unethical.

E. B. White has something of the same ear and eye as Schulz,
though the attractiveness of his characters is not quite so
remorselessly cute. The actions of Charlotte are as random and
blind as the rat's – hers just happen to be affectionate. The story
therefore fits its cartoon version quite perfectly, in a way that,
say, *Snow White* doesn't – Disney's witch is purposelessly
wicked, but in the fairy story she knows exactly what she is
doing.

The point is developmental. *Charlotte's Web* is limited in its
force to small children; friendship is to them an arbitrary
bestowal. It comes as a perfectly uncaused gift. In Meindert
DeJong's *The Wheel on the School*, the meaning of friendship is
returned to the solid moral strengths of domestic work in a
Dutch village half a century or more ago. I am sure it is a fine
novel, and it is symptomatic in that Meindert DeJong was a
Dutch migrant to the United States who told his story in the
new country, of the settled community he and his fellows had
left behind. He tells the story quite without wistfulness, and
tells it, one assumes, as so many European migrants – Sicilians,
Norwegians, Jews of the Hasidim, Bosnians, Lithuanians –
told their tales, to suggest to his audience a vision of the future
made from the best of the life they had left behind.

The story is pretty well known. The local village
schoolchildren have seen a picture of storks nesting on roofs,
and, helped on by their teacher and a legless, irascible recluse
named Janus, find an old wheel buried in the hard, flat sand.
After a thrilling storm, they recover two almost drowned
storks to nest on their wheel, perched on the school roof. The
storks, the wheel, and the work are living and real; they are also

an image of renewal created by and for the children. The hard and difficult labour required to complete the task binds the children together in work whose purpose is to reaffirm the identity of the community. In so doing, they draw the whole community closer together and the effort and companionship restore Janus to his place as a respected member of the village. The memories of the old grandmother re-consecrate the present in terms of ancient pieties. The novel confirms the great strengths of the old world, while making them imaginable in the new. The little community is not unlike that of Laura Ingalls Wilder's; but with the beauty and security of long standing. Its order and hierarchy are just, its labour does not alienate, its scale is small enough to be human; and the relation of old and young, senior and junior, beautifully pictured in the talk of little Lina and old Grandmother Sibble III, is such as to permit a discreet and courteous distance as well as the quickness of personal spontaneity. The balance of ritual and freedom, the community of values embedded in the education of the children, provide the intelligible space in which friendship may flower. Such friendship may well run across the generations, and a society whose structures forbid such bonds can mark neither beginnings nor ends, and lives in oblivion.

8

Cult and culture:
a political–psychological excursus

Some such failure typifies the present spirit of popular culture. It has done so, in one form or another, ever since mass-industrialization gave a more or less single outline and direction to the drift of civilization. That is, while the divisions and structures of modern labour and its moral economy have broken the community of values, separated old from young, men from women, class from class, so the forms of popular culture have run into escape rather than into a critical response. Popular culture has not so much reflected upon the costs of industrial living as it has sought, in its fictions and its imagined alternatives, to deny the realities of that life.

If the term 'culture' is to include, as it plausibly may, all the shaped and handled forms of experience which either individuals or classes may use to express and contain their spirit, their minds and feelings, the system of their social relations, then it is hard to know what to exclude. If all this is culture, what is 'not-culture'?[1]

For our purposes, let us shrink the domain of culture to the modes, purposes and uses conventionally expected of the arts. This does not mean that only art is culture; it is too late in the democratic day to revive Matthew Arnold's terminology; we shall return in a moment to necessary distinctions *not* between 'high' and 'low' in culture, but between good and bad, genuine and fake. But in normal usage, an art is a form of expression which, in Auden's phrase, 'makes nothing happen'. That is, it renders ordinary, everyday experience comprehensible by presenting it in terms of actions and objects which have had their practical consequences removed;[2] they become, so to

---

[1] Cf. E. P. Thompson's review-article 'The Long Revolution', *New Left Review*, 9–10 (July–August 1961).

[2] I take this way of putting the point from Clifford Geertz, *The Interpretation of Cultures* (1975), p. 443.

speak, sheer appearance, and therefore we can see and understand the power of their meaning with some detachment. We
don't have to worry about what will happen next, because we
can ourselves control the gap between appearance and reality.
(That is why it is so intensely disconcerting when a fiction gets
out of control, and seems temporarily to close the gap – the film
is 'too real' we say; or our children get frightened and watch
television from behind the sofa, where the monster can't get at
them.) What the appearance does in its capacity as metaphor
and metonymy is place the flux of experience within an encompassing form whose arbitrary order (pentameter or adagio)
throws into sharp relief a view of what the unstoppable process
of experience means.

This definition of art pulls it away from its trivial and careless
position simply as the bucket into which, if we are artists, we
pour our feelings, or out of which, if we are audience, we pour
other people's feelings over ourselves. It makes possible a view
of art, and many other forms of culture, which ratifies their
strong *cognitive* grip upon the world. In other words,[3] art takes
its place among cultural activities which have devised ways of
thinking about society, and while the experience of beauty
importantly typifies the experience of art, it is just as much a
cognitive as an emotional experience. Its constituents –
elegance, strength, order, chastity – give shape to thought as
much as to feeling. They characterize science as much as art.

Culture, on this account, is a congeries of social activities
which provide ways of ordering and distancing experience.
Cultural forms are different ways of organizing symbol
systems. Some systems are more abstract than others:
mathematics and music probably the most abstract. Some
cultural activities are only secondarily cognitive – most sports,
for example; but they are still intensely thoughtful activities for
all that they are so busy. A painter takes his body with him: we
cannot imagine how a mind could paint.[4] But the painter's
paintings, like the chess-player's move, the tennis-player's
smash, are modes of ordering the world to one's intentions.
This is the deep affinity of forms of cultural expression. They
are concrete pleasures in themselves; they are ways of thinking
about and representing the world; they are useful theories.

[3] Some of them taken from Nelson Goodman, *Languages of Art* (1976), pp. 262 ff.
[4] See Maurice Merleau-Ponty, 'Eye and Mind', in *The Primacy of Perception* (1964).

Popular culture is weakly escapist when its theories are unusable. 'Escapist' is itself a slippery term. People generally use it in a disapproving way, especially when they refer to popular fiction. They mean by 'escapist' a tendency in a story which sorts with a tendency in most people to want to escape from the real world into one of fantasy, to escape from harshness and ugliness (which are real) to softness and beauty (which on this argument are *not*). Walter Mitty, whom we have met already, is the arch-escapist.

Escape, on the contrary, can take many forms. Its non-metaphoric use always designates escape from imprisonment into freedom, and the use admirably reminds us that, whatever it does with itself, the imagination is *free*. It may die, certainly; it may imagine no less creatively for imagining horribly. But as long as the imagination is still freely at work, a man is still a man. Furthermore, if a schoolchild, in reading or watching a fiction, escapes out of a world which is brutal, callous, or unfeeling – or indeed simply out of a classroom whose lessons are entirely boring – the pejorative overtones of 'escape' come to sound merely insulting. A reader may escape from a real world in which experience is reduced to a dead minimum into one in which the author deepens and intensifies life in such a way as to constitute its permanent criticism. In any case, the uses of literacy are many. Not only may a reader escape from our world into a much darker and more horrifying one – from watering the geraniums to a novel by Dostoievsky; but even the same novel may mean very different things to different people, or different things to the same people at different times. If we may say that it is going backwards for a child to read a novel which constricts and doesn't liberate, stifles rather than prompts self-awareness, consoles and chloroforms rather than fulfils and deepens meaning, we may say that at the same time, the same novel might mark the outer limits of another child's reach (let alone grasp), and we would press the book upon him. It is the fact of obvious differences between different children and their development, sensibility, intelligence, and gifts which make it such a difficult and sometimes unhelpful business allotting school readers to particular years and ages.[5] Equally well, any person may decide to read a book which is

[5] Michael Jones's *Penguinways* (1978) is one provisionally useful aid.

decidedly within his or her reach, just because that's how he or she happens to feel today. In much the same spirit, you settle comfortably down with a can of beer and a plate of biriani to watch *The Sweeney* or *All Creatures Great and Small*. These serials, packed tidily into their fifty minutes of pleasurably predictable and familiar routine, may be just what your rather ragged-edged psyche needs for its repair-time tonight. By some trivial homoeopathy of the imagination, the banal decencies of English cop or vet will invisibly stitch up the ravelled sleeve of a day pulled all to pieces by small accidents. And yet the same programmes may do far more for your small son or daughter sitting beside you.

What the novel or the TV programme does for and to its audience is doubtless immeasurable, because both too tiny and too immense. But the effect is due partly to the fiction and partly to the audience. Literary students and teachers at all levels have for so long made such confident play with very different models of the psychology of reading that there needs to be an explicit challenge made. Conventional teaching accounts of reading behaviour deploy as their essential concepts 'vicarious experience', 'identification', 'escape', 'light entertainment', 'wish-fulfilment', 'fantasy'. But a novel is not vicarious experience, it is reported and (perhaps) imaginary experience; we do not 'identify' with the characters, we respond in complex ways with, to, and for them out of the framework of all our prior experience, literary or not. No reader imagines that his alleged desires are gaining actual satisfaction. Rather, what is happening is that his desire for affection or romantic love, for adventure, prestige, or cheerfulness, defines itself in a new context. The reader discusses with the novelist the possibilities of giving his desires statement in a social setting.

As a function of our humanity, we constantly imagine entry into other people's lives and derive from these excursions an extension of what we imagine to be possible in life.

The institutional fantasies of television and the novel are dead or alive according as they permit this reflexive thought. When I spoke earlier of popular culture as largely discouraging such reflexivity,[6] as running strongly into escape rather than

---

[6] Cf. Andrew Harrison, *Making and Thinking* (1979), especially chapter x.

criticism, I classed together not only form and content in popular fictions, but also their superordinate and nonconscious frames of reference. The novels of Ian Fleming and Enid Blyton are alike in their closed circularity, the entire unconsciousness of the robot heroes and heroines who need strive neither to *do* anything nor to become anything, because they are defined as adequate to whatever may happen. They are radically unreflexive, and therefore exempt from history.

The criticism of dead fiction is that it ignores history. It cannot interrogate its experience in terms of what has happened in a past from which the present comes. It is this that is missing in Walt Disney cartoons. The past is present in the timeless fairy story where magic and goodness are the only instruments of action available to the powerless. But the powerless are children and members of the poor; their condition begins from history. The worst aspect of modern industrial fantasy – to be found in *The Omen*, in *Star Wars*, in the latest brutal thriller, or in Enid Blyton – is that it permits no interplay, no exchange between metaphor and reality, theory and practice. It is closed. This is its deadness.

The same is true of many less than popular novels. (By 'popular' I mean just that: read by large numbers, as are Enid Blyton, *Watership Down, Lord of the Rings*, and the Bible.) For the deadliness of such closure may be found in allegedly intellectual novels such as Mervyn Peake's or Hermann Hesse's. These exhibit that lack of life which is due to their having no historical meaning. They are dead because they are merely fantastic.

Death, however, appears in many guises. It is not only decadent and sweetly corrupt; it may be inorganic and fossilized. It may just be inert matter.

Much turns on the metaphor. For no book which aims to deal ambitiously with children's reading can simply condemn the novels of Enid Blyton, and have done with her. She raises in a specially piercing way questions as to what popularity really is, how it is won and whether it matters. She is the world's bestselling English author (though for all that, her books are translated into 128 languages); she comes below Lenin's sales, massively subsidized by the Communists' Foreign Languages Publishing Houses in Moscow, Peking, Bombay and elsewhere; but she comfortably outstrips Shakespeare, who is hardly less supported by those well-known agencies of imperialism, the English and international examination systems. She stands as a supreme example of the twistpoint between manipulation and expression upon which much of the speculation in this book turns. As her very interesting biography[7] makes clear, Enid Blyton lived her life as a writer very committedly. It's hardly the word which sounds at first sight applicable, but she was *engagée*. She wrote at a staggering rate – over 200 narratives of varied lengths, another 200 school-books – a daily output in long-hand of anything up to 10,000 words. Nor was she in any usual sense a hack – she wrote because she wanted to and, no doubt, needed to. She was intensely concerned about her popularity, rapt in the preservation of a numberless audience and readership, anxious up to the moment of her death to maintain her imaginary contact with these children and to keep them in ignorance of her illness.

She is ostentatiously 'a case'. For the details of her life make clear that she stood at no remove at all from the moral and emotional world of which she wrote; at the end, as Barbara Stoney delicately tells us, her control over both mind and body was distressingly intermittent, and she sought to hide herself from the reality of her illness and approaching end by living in the world she had created in 200-odd children's novels. Brian Jackson, in a striking article on Enid Blyton,[8] wrote that

Enid Blyton reads like one of her own children: in her twenties she embarrasses her friends by calling herself 'Richard' or 'Cabin Boy', and whistling hands-in-pockets like a young jack tar from some Victorian boys' yarn. In her forties, she is playing conkers with her husband and confiding to her diary that she's 'got an eighter'.

And he goes on, 'The fantasies she focuses into childish fiction protect her from the emotional realities', and this is no doubt a substantial part of her own psychological story. Indeed when she is obviously living in the real world, she does so with a disagreeable selfishness – offhand, cruel indifference and vengefulness towards her mother, her first husband, her friends and her servants – which emphasizes the rightness of Jackson's

[7] *Enid Blyton: A Biography*, by Barbara Stoney (1974).
[8] A review of Barbara Stoney's biography in *Use of English*, 26, 3 (1975).

judgement. But the self-protectiveness of her psychology is the high degree of her involvement in the fantasies, together with her keen, energetic sense of how to make a fortune out of them.

The components which Jackson mentions as typifying her successful recipe, 'the grafting of the saccharine remains of old Bavarian toyland culture onto the world-wide hunger for miniature Disneyland', are certainly part of the instant mixture of her stories; just as solid and regular are the doses of high Beaconsfield snobbery, the picture-postcard nursery ruralism of Mistletoe Farm, the childish frame of legalism and retribution which shapes all the stories and gives the policemen such prominence.

Any success in popular culture will draw out a mixture of ready-to-hand substitute foods, brightly coloured, fatty, sweet; and bad for you. But it is not enough to rest on the solidarity of the educated, and to wait for laughs. It is clear that Enid Blyton calculated her successes shrewdly, and became with increasing experience a very able businesswoman – able, according to the best tenets of marketing, to manipulate her customers, to catch and feed that strange but surprisingly stable monster, popular taste. She sensed with 'an instinctive creativity [which is] simultaneously naive and masterful' (Jackson's words) the conservatism of children, and built for it an enclave whose geography was drawn from the rich residues of a popular culture where the scenery is always and by definition behind the times. To say this, however, is to do no more than describe her recipe book. As we shall see, both J. R. R. Tolkien and Richard Adams turn to some of the same shelves in the kitchen, but the result is much richer and deeper. Enid Blyton's unique achievement is to have made of her mixture an entirely flat geography, but to have written so much and so repetitively that this one-dimensional world becomes to its tourists as familiar and as easily traversed as the world of the *Beano, Krazy* and *Whizzer and Chips*.

Its lack, when compared with the comics, is to have none of their lurid cheerfulness, their noisy irreverence and barmy characters. The similarity is the entire safety of both worlds. Enid Blyton invites children to hold her hand on a walk through an adventure recounted with such flatness both of diction and of representation that any reader could be sure that no threat either to experience or to technique lurked in any sentence. Jackson mentions the safety which she offers to children whose grip on reading is perhaps premature and often uncertain:

Possibly the explanation lies nearer sociology than either personal psychology or literature. I suspect it begins with the determination of advanced economies that children should be taught to read at seven. Few of us ever master so difficult an intellectual art as literacy ever again in life; and perhaps millions of us, during those titanic years, need to enjoy our new-found gains not tautly, as in school, but in regressive comfort. The bright and beautiful and private world of Enid Blyton met that desire.

Reading by its very nature rebuts the separation between skilfulness and cognition. You can't just learn to read without taking in what you are reading. Reading Enid Blyton is technically easy, but it is also emotionally and cognitively easy. In a useful note which Barbara Stoney reprints in the biography, Michael Woods guesses that Enid Blyton can never have been troubled by the tension felt by the adult writer for children between the world as it is and the vision he presents to children of the better place he would wish them to make it. 'She was a child, she thought as a child, and she wrote as a child . . . the basic feeling is essentially pre-adolescent . . . Enid Blyton has no moral dilemmas . . . Inevitably Enid Blyton was labelled by rumour a child-hater. If true, such a fact should come as no surprise to us, for as a child herself all other children can be nothing but rivals to her.'[9]

That last remark compresses psychological explanation into a *very* narrow morality. Children do not merely hate their rivals, and both the life and writing of Enid Blyton evidences the extent to which she cherished the devotion and admiration of children. But like all of a certain class of really gigantic bestsellers – like Edgar Rice Burroughs,[10] creator of Tarzan, like Luke Short and Ian Fleming, like Jean Plaidy and Mary Stewart – Enid Blyton gives all her enormous energy for work and her powerful belief in what she creates to representing the crude moral diagrams and garish fantasies of a readership which needs its authors far less than they, the authors, need the

[9] Stoney, *Enid Blyton*, Appendix 10, p. 220.
[10] See his apologia for himself in Q. D. Leavis, *Fiction and the Reading Public* (1932), pp. 40ff.

readers. Enid Blyton, like, so far as one can tell, Ian Fleming,[11] precisely occupied the frame of moral reference of her own books. The lack of reality in both authors – what I have called 'flatness' – is in some sense quite intentional. To push the prose into the depths of experience is to put yourself in danger. The point is rather to present a one-dimensional reflection in which a few, very simple, flat cues are enough to release a fantasy which never gets out of hand. An analogy with violence in certain TV serials is helpful. For it seems[12] that in watching television, children are made anxious and distressed – or, indeed prompted to imitative action – only insofar as the violence breaks the convention of harmlessness. The conventional death by clutch-and-crumple in cowboy movies is, as we would all guess, entirely untroubling. There are hazards in saying so, because it's hard to tell what children are really watching for: plenty of girls, apparently, remain unmoved by the simple bullet holes in shoulder or chest, but become most anxious for the welfare of the cowboys' horses as they are tumbled over in a cloud of prairie dust.

But the general and familiar point stands. A high degree of conventionality permits reader and watcher to organize and manipulate their own fantasy. So with Enid Blyton, the one-dimensionality of the reflection guarantees a happily and safely unimaginative world where there is neither thought nor action but only the representation of an image with which you can do what you like. It is a paradoxical way to put the point, but I would say that children read Enid Blyton in order to *avoid* 'using their imaginations', and that this would be true even for the most backward and reluctant reader. Hence the great happiness she undoubtedly brings. This happiness is completely of a piece with Enid Blyton's urgent need to pretend that the world is the world of 'Green Hedges' and 'Elfin Cottage' and 'Old Thatch'. Her particular 'promise of happiness' *cannot* be kept. That is perhaps why so many teachers and parents of earnest persuasion (and who would not think it important to be earnest for his or her children?) become so angry with Enid Blyton. She promises that the falsehoods in

[11] See his biography, by John Pearson, *The Life of Ian Fleming: Creator of James Bond* (1966).

[12] See, first, Hilde Himmelweit, P. Oppenheim, A. N. Vance, *Children and Television* (1958); subsequently, in a long bibliography, see W. Belson, *Television Violence and the Adolescent Boy* (1978).

which she herself strenuously wished to believe will come true. And her falsehoods are in no way related to the ordinary, necessary fictions of the imagination, precisely because although they can't be taken back to the world, they can only make it uninhabitable. If a child were to try to live Enid Blyton's narrow snobberies and vengefulness, her pitiful fancies of secret seven and famous five, in the real world, he or she would only come to disaster. But no normal child does. The imaginative charge simply isn't strong enough. So the pleasure of reading her on such a scale is like that of tirelessly bouncing a ball against a wall. It is contented and tranquil. In the strict sense, it is marginal; the pleasure of such privacy is only possible in its own little enclave. The novels transform time into a safe anaesthetic.

The pharmaceutical metaphor is only slightly helpful. Children seem to have no difficulty in resisting Enid Blyton when it suits them. Even for those children who are saturated in her books, it hardly makes sense according to the definition of the word to talk about an Enid Blyton cult. But cultishness does figure largely in the bestseller world. We may define a cult as a set of preoccupations and activities whose significances bind together into a membership any substantial group of people. Enid Blyton had perhaps a temporarily cultish status when children became members of the *Sunny Stories* club, and formed their own Secret Sevens and Find-Outers. J. R. R. Tolkien's novels are interesting for our purposes in this chapter on cult and culture, because their fabulous cult success not only began with a child readership, but was entirely innocent of direct market manipulation. The Tolkien cult is therefore a genuine expression of something very strong in popular culture on both sides of the Atlantic. What Tolkien does is to take much of the furniture and wardrobe of Dingley Dell and carry it further into experience than Enid Blyton ever dared.

For all that Tolkien is incomparably the better writer, his name sits easily next to hers in a chapter with our title. His cult status is diminishing now (in 1980) but until very recently was signalled not only by the apparatus of quasi-marketing which followed his books in the form of calendars, lapel-buttons, posters, records, musical settings of the songs (by Donald Swann), even dictionaries, but also by Middle-Earth societies on a hundred Midwest campuses, and by bony, bearded thirty-five-year-olds careening along on Esalen and Meditation, and calling themselves Gandalf. The lengthy fake-scholarship of the Appendices to *The Lord of the Rings* testifies to the degree of Tolkien's commitment to his fantasy. Tolkien, as his biographer[13] tells us Auden said, lived in a 'ghastly house'. The Branksome Chine suburban lived in a house with switch-on logs and fubsy fittings. While you can hardly judge a man by pelmets and lampshades alone, the remorseless picturesquerie of faery life in Tolkien – the home-brewed beer, the great flagged halls and wide, sweeping stone stairs, testify to Tolkien's closeness to Enid Blyton's 'dear old place', in the eternal English Home Counties of fact and fiction:

They stepped out of the beech-grove in which they had lain, and passed on to a long green lawn, glowing in sunshine, bordered by stately dark-leaved trees laden with scarlet blossom. Behind them they could hear the sound of falling water, and a stream ran down before them between flowering banks, until it came to a greenwood at the lawn's foot and passed then on under an archway of trees, through which they saw the shimmer of water far away.

As they came to the opening in the wood, they were surprised to see knights in bright mail and tall guards in silver and black standing there, who greeted them with honour and bowed before them. And then one blew a long trumpet, and they went on through the aisle of trees beside the singing stream. So they came to a wide green land, and beyond it was a broad river in a silver haze, out of which rose a long wooded isle, and many ships lay by its shores. But on the field where they now stood a great host was drawn up, in ranks and companies glittering in the sun. And as the Hobbits approached swords were unsheathed, and spears were shaken, and horns and trumpets sang, and men cried with many voices and in many tongues. (*The Return of the King*, p. 231)

This is not flat writing; it is round and full. But the roundness and fullness are so often, in these long volumes, the product of hot air. I have spoken earlier of the provenance of such prose in writing of Bunyan and Buchan. Tolkien's prose lends itself all too easily to the Church Voice. It *is* moving, there is no doubt, but it moves a reader away from and never towards real life. It stands directly in the line of *Idylls of the King* and William Morris's narrative poems, and while these poems have their hypnotic quality, Tolkien's insistent heroic uplift, the

[13] H. Carpenter, *J. R. R. Tolkien: A Biography* (1976).

knightly high-mindedness, the vulgar simplicity of his ethics, share with his predecessors a thinness of moral and physical substance, a lack of experienced content, which complement much of the insubstantiality of modern life.

This is the source of his appeal. It really doesn't matter very much that the conversations in his novels sound such a mixture of flatness and fustian:

He looked round at the windows and walls, as if he was afraid they would suddenly give way. The others looked at him in silence, and exchanged meaning glances among themselves.

'It's coming out in a minute,' whispered Pippin to Merry. Merry nodded.

'Well!' said Frodo at last, sitting up and straightening his back, as if he had made a decision. 'I can't keep it dark any longer. I have got something to tell you all. But I don't know quite how to begin.'

'I think I could help you,' said Merry quietly, 'by telling you some of it myself.'

'What do you mean?' said Frodo, looking at him anxiously.

'Just this, my dear old Frodo: you are miserable, because you don't know how to say good-bye. You meant to leave the Shire, of course. But danger has come on you sooner than you expected, and now you are making up your mind to go at once. And you don't want to. We are very sorry for you.'

Frodo opened his mouth and shut it again. His look of surprise was so comical that they laughed. 'Dear old Frodo!' said Pippin. 'Did you really think you had thrown dust in all our eyes? You have not been nearly careful or clever enough for that! You have obviously been planning to go and saying farewell to all your haunts all this year since April. We have constantly heard you muttering: "Shall I ever look down into that valley again, I wonder,"and things like that. And pretending that you had come to the end of your money, and actually selling your beloved Bag End to those Sackville-Bagginses! And all those close talks with Gandalf.'

'Good heavens!' said Frodo. 'I thought I had been both careful and clever. I don't know what Gandalf would say. Is all the Shire discussing my departure then?'

'Oh no!' said Merry. 'Don't worry about that! The secret won't keep for long, of course; but at present it is, I think, only known to us conspirators. After all, you must remember that we know you well, and are often with you. We can usually guess what you are thinking.'
(*The Fellowship of the Ring*, p. 113)

The diction is literary, bookish, and stilted; this is speech written by a man who is trying to concoct modes of speech unlike those of the contemporary world, but who cannot really *hear* living speech at all. Any writer must, by definition, make his characters utter a diction unlike the stops and starts, the repetitions and clumsiness of ordinary speech; he must make them speak a literary tongue. This is the difficulty for the artist, to weld and balance living irregularities and artistic form. Tolkien sets himself the problem of all authors of mythical history, one to which the solution comes harder in prose than in verse. I mentioned Tennyson and Morris as his poetic antecedents, and as his great admirer C. S. Lewis pointed out, Tolkien had Malory and Ariosto always at his elbow when writing his trilogy. But a novel is not a poem; it is written in prose and in the kind of detail about everyday banalities and routine which simply make for bathos if you write of them in iambic pentameters. But there is no longer an audience for long narrative poems, although there is an audience – an enormous, worldwide audience as Tolkien found to his surprise – for mystic-historical romances written partly in a prose taken from the Authorized Version, or at least from Deuteronomy, Ecclesiastes, and some of the later prophets, and partly from a Celtic Twilight prose of the kind Yeats wrote in *The Trembling of the Veil*. Most of all, such prose moves in the cadences of the late-night, off-syllabus reading of a cultivated Oxonian littérateur of the thirties, a prose which, even when it included writing as good as Walter Pater's in *Marius the Epicurean* (for striking an attitude) or Richard Jefferies' *Amaryllis at the Fair* (for local colour), was well written at a long distance from the common speech and almost unable to move without round resonant gestures, even when these came off.

Such a prose is evidence of the deep divisions of academic labour. Its gentlemanly mixture of folklore, etymology, literary palaeography and Pre-Raphaelite poetry cuts it off from the toughness of more strenuously intellectual discourse, such as a critical philosophy; and the genteel extremity of class barriers in ancient universities cuts it off also from the rhythmic speech in which the folklore carries its life. Consequently, Tolkien's prose, as I said, lacks the weight and suddenness of real speech, just as it lacks the substantiality of physical presence and solid experience. It is complementary to much modern life in this thinness and lack of experience just because so much of what should be decisive action for individuals can find no responsible resistance, cannot discover a real enemy or a visible, conclusive form of expression. High ideals are then forced into a disembodied realm which, if we feel generous, we call myth or allegory, but in which the actors have only ritual or legendary tasks to perform – the long ride, the last swordfight, the climb to the crack of doom, all told in the generalized, unactual liturgy of a long-since-unrealizable heroic.

'Ride forward! Ride!' cried Glorfindel to Frodo.

He did not obey at once, for a strange reluctance seized him. Checking the horse to a walk, he turned and looked back. The Riders seemed to sit upon their great steeds like threatening statues upon a hill, dark and solid, while all the woods and land about them receded as if into a mist. Suddenly he knew in his heart that they were silently commanding him to wait. Then at once fear and hatred awoke in him. His hand left the bridle and gripped the hilt of his sword, and with a red flash he drew it.

'Ride on! Ride on!' cried Glorfindel, and then loud and clear he called to the horse in the elf-tongue: *noro lim, noro lim, Asfaloth!*

At once the white horse sprang away and sped like the wind along the last lap of the Road. At the same moment the black horses leaped down the hill in pursuit, and from the Riders came a terrible cry, such as Frodo had heard filling the woods with horror in the East-farthing far away. It was answered; and to the dismay of Frodo and his friends out from the trees and rocks away on the left four other Riders came flying. Two rode towards Frodo: two galloped madly towards the Ford to cut off his escape. They seemed to him to run like the wind and to grow swiftly larger and darker, as their courses converged with his.

Frodo looked back for a moment over his shoulder. He could no longer see his friends. The Riders behind were falling back: even their great steeds were no match in speed for the white elf-horse of Glorfindel. He looked forward again, and hope faded. There seemed no chance of reaching the Ford before he was cut off by the others that had lain in ambush. He could see them clearly now: they appeared to have cast aside their hoods and black cloaks, and they were robed in white and grey. Swords were naked in their pale hands; helms were on their heads. Their cold eyes glittered, and they called to him with fell voices.

Fear now filled all Frodo's mind. He thought no longer of his sword. No cry came from him. He shut his eyes and clung to the horse's mane. The wind whistled in his ears, and the bells upon the harness rang wild and shrill. A breath of deadly cold pierced him like a spear, as with a last spurt, like a flash of white fire, the elf-horse speeding as if on wings, passed right before the face of the foremost Rider. (*The Fellowship of the Ring*, p. 225)

There is something genuinely stirring about the tableau of this first curtain. Tolkien's high, crude diction and rhythm cannot accommodate the real life, the sweat and cramp, the fury and terror of T. H. White's *The Sword in the Stone*; Tolkien's popularity lies in just that. He offers to his ardent audience a desperate glory without either physical or moral effort. Precisely because his ideals can find no body – the lothely lady Goldberry is sexlessly beautiful – he can rouse his readers to a dazed intensity of feeling without issue or complexity. Frodo and his fellows are appropriately enough in much the same position as the heroes of the old *Wizard*: the self, the role, and its duties are all of a kind. The ethics are those of the cowboy picture aligned with those of the knight errant: a man must do what a man must do, but a man in this story is not so much a Greek or Trojan or even a Franklin's knight; Frodo is an impossible version of Julian Grenfell, the beautiful subaltern and the flower of his year at Balliol.

At first sight it is weird that the order of chivalry of *The Lord of the Rings* should appeal so strongly to the counter-culture. But pulling together Blake, Tolkien, the early Marx, Che Guevara, Bob Dylan, Jeremiah Johnson, Ken Kesey, Luther King, the counter-culturalist voiced the same ideological critique signified by his brown rice cuisine, his fringed and shaggy clothes, his genially non-committal pantisocracy. That life resisted by example the notorious anonymity, the aseptic blankness and technological explicitness of industrial society. Tolkien joins the other worthies as the spokesman of the tournament, the lonely hero, the big land and sky. Frodo and Sam Gangee follow not only the heroes of Malory and Ariosto, but the Lone Ranger and Tonto, Leatherstocking and Chingachook as well.[14]

This is not to dismiss *The Lord of the Rings* as rubbish. It is rather to place the cult in the culture. Tolkien himself was puzzled perhaps by some of his allies and admirers, but I think he would have signed the alliance against the modern world – the technology and the working class he scarcely saw and did

[14] I am adding them to Leslie Fiedler's short, fanciful dynasty in *The Return of the Vanishing American* (1972).

not understand, the dispersal of moral responsibility, the confusion of friend and enemy, the bureaucratization of language, all of which he sought to dispel by the magical invocation of a spacious, unmistakable moral world and a ceremonious archaeology.

Reading Tolkien is sometimes like listening to a schmaltz-*Götterdämmerung*. It makes you drunk. Just as, genius though no doubt Wagner was, it is no surprise that the teetotal Hitler admired him so much, so for once it makes sense to use that much-abused adjective, and call Tolkien a Fascist. Can the word be used, just momentarily, in a quite non-hostile sense? Fascism, as I noted after John Fraser earlier, appeals to genuine human needs. It speaks up for 'the individual against the machine', and, for all that Tolkien says nothing to or for the body, and that his is an extraordinarily *dis*embodied book, his tribal structures (elves, hobbits, orcs, goblins, men, etc.), his yeoman hero and freeman servant, his rituals and ceremonies and fealties, all belong to the hornbooks of a non-historical, romantic Fascism. He is ambivalent about this, as one would expect. The book abounds in battles, but pre-technological battles. In spite of this, the hills of Mordor and Mount Doom look very like the headquarters of the dirty, rough-spoken, brutal proletariat, just as Gandalf whisked away from one corner of the battle by the great eagle, Gwaihir the Windlord, reminds us irresistibly of a US marine general in his Cobra helicopter. Sometimes the rotund prose and heady chivalry look as though they are called to put down modern Socialism rather than the Last Enemy.

The Lord of the Rings is a heady book. It attempts, in one enormous incantation, to crush together the many disjunctions, the alien formations, of modern political and personal life. The child who reads it will be puzzled and stirred, and that is right. The adult who turns it into cult has shut himself in a rather grander version of Mistletoe Farm, and is trapped accordingly. Tolkien offers no key to the way out.

The Hobbit is another matter, and much more relevant. It is, for one thing, much more straightforwardly a children's book, attractive and genial as it is. Tolkien strikes a far less upstage attitude and as a result his tone is, when it needs to be, more vivid and more moving. The eloquent style of *Lord of the Rings* is an astonishing achievement in its way, of course; its anachronism is its political point. 'Listen', he says, or rather, 'harken', and goes on to tell us of heroes such as we can no longer have, by perilous seas, in faery lands forlorn. The cult of Tolkien includes the earlier novel perhaps only because it has the same scenery. In the writing and the reading of it, we find a much less intoxicating but much more tasty and satisfying plateful.

It is, in the most visible way, a rattling good yarn for children. It contains a quest across a fearsome landscape, a splendid wizard, monster spiders in an enchanted forest, goblins, Smaug the dragon, and beneath his dreadful length, the fabulous treasure. Tolkien finds exactly the right voices in which to mix these traditional allsorts; *The Hobbit* does not depend on the heroic style of the later work – a heroic which, so to speak, pretends that the Romantic movement brought only medievalism back to life, and didn't bring with it the intensely lived moral sensibility of the individual. Tolkien's heroes have no psychology, which is exactly why his effortless prose can carry them across the waste land to the crack of doom. He writes as though the agonized individuality with which the Romantic moralists wrote – men like Kierkegaard, Nietzsche, Lawrence – had never changed the lives of modern men. Or perhaps he writes as if he wished modern life hadn't happened.

The more domestic music of *The Hobbit* does not reach out into those desert spaces. It's never clear why Bilbo Baggins ever goes on a journey he so dislikes, but the unclarity doesn't matter. His psychology is sketchy in the extreme; it is small and sufficiently a mixture of Ratty and Mole, of the brave and the timid, to accommodate a gentle reader of about ten and to introduce him or her to the pageantry and geography of an incomparable folklore. The death-dealing is lightly done – Bilbo's sword Sting puts paid only to a giant spider or two, he is an honourable legate of peace upon the mountain, and even the mighty Battle of the Five Armies is merely a grand and general procession to Thorin's dignified end and Bilbo's journey home, after which Tolkien returns us to the comedy of the interrupted house auction.

I do not praise the novel as being an aperitif for a budding folklorist. To do so, as the devout project-builder is so apt to do, is to fall once more into bibliotherapy, and to use novels as propaedeutics to the real business of birdwatching, researching the social history of witches, or launching into astrophysics. *The Hobbit* is an intrinsic part of English folklore and fairy-tale, and not to have read it is to be that much less familiar with the wealth of the culture. Perhaps this is what is meant by the much professed and sound argument that a nation's culture is its heritage, and to be educated is to enter into that heritage. What can this mean? Why do I feel my children, and anyone else's children, to be ill-educated if they're not familiar with fairy-stories?

Partly it is a matter of the pleasure they will have lost by their ignorance, partly it is that the universe will be a less enchanted place. But setting aside enchantment for a later chapter, the heritage of fairy-tale remains like an enormous, forgotten treasure-house where a child may wander, picking up and fingering the abandoned relics which once were matters of life and death to their owners. Fairy-tales are a sort of Xanadu. In Joyce Wood's and Frank Francis' delicious little illustrated story called *Grandmother Lucy and Her Hats*, the small, remembering narrator tells how her Grandmother took her upstairs past the fearsome longcase clock in which Grandfather lived to the attic, where she showed the little girl her beautiful collection of hats – fur hats, feather hats, veiled hats, and her silk hat which 'was shiny, and full of colours like a rainbow, and it was all folded. It was beautiful like my Grandmother and soft like my Grandmother. It made her eyes sparkle.' Wandering round the enormous, vaulted and Gothic attic of fairy-tales is like looking at Grandmother Lucy's hats. These are the lovely treasures of the past, and the visiting child wonders at them, lets them catch the light and run through her fingers, plays with them and dresses up in them, and then comes back downstairs for tea, when the attic door is once more locked up.

The Hobbit is the best link I know between a present-day child and the world which made these stories up in order to describe the early colonizing of England. Its pace and fullness, its good temper, the scale of its protagonists, its manageable horrors and disasters, its simple triumphs and morals, all fit it to the child's-eye view. Reading it, I remember the heroine of *Cold Comfort Farm*, Flora Poste, who liked certain novels because 'they were the only sort you could read while eating an apple'.

· But Tolkien is so much more than the author of *The Hobbit*. The amazing cult surrounding his books glints at the leading edge of the cultural formation I have sketched out. He devised a prose, a landscape, and a pre-Romantic, motiveless heroism which consoled a large section of the bookish classes for their powerlessness in the modern world. Or perhaps it is not so much the bookish class which reads Tolkien as those to whom a long read does not come altogether easily. Many of this social formation now have the official care of children in and out of schools. After Tolkien, a whole new galaxy of writers has emerged to write for children out of a deep, swelling sense that the world has been stripped of its magic, the throat of poetry cut, the cherished individual severed both from his own significance and the chance of action which will make a difference to things. Their sense of crisis is accurate, and their response has been to re-invent medievalism and the historical romance, and to seek to recover in prose the cadences of incantation and magic. Writing ostensibly to and for children, these writers are gratefully caught up by a readership scattered through the cherry-blossom suburbs, concentrated in libraries and primary schools and bookshops, as well as sprinkled through amateur antique, home-baking, and cottage weaving shops along the tourist highways.

The Hobbit fits easily enough into the shelves of children's novels as they are ordered in the traditional catalogue. *Lord of the Rings* moves between the grown-ups and the children for reasons which Mrs Leavis most succinctly proposed fifty years ago in her classic, *Fiction and the Reading Public*. Its colossal success rests in the appeal it makes to the entirely unrealizable fantasies of the Western world, especially when it has bolted its gates and raised its drawbridge against the monsters of its own political and technological economy. But 'bestseller' does not only designate rubbish, as it is the point of this chapter to insist. Mrs Leavis's model for the advent of the bestseller is that unhappy coincidence of mass production with mass audiences which broke up the self-explanatory coherence and rhythm of values and production in devout, largely rural communities. Left to itself, unrestrained by older pieties, the new market pounced rapaciously upon the defenceless, untutored sensibility of urban man, and caught him in the solar plexus for its own greater profit.

This picture, as we have seen, pretty well stands for Enid Blyton, although, faced now with far worse in the 'undergrowth of literature' where the horrible quarries really need hunting down,[15] we may be left undismayed by Enid Blyton's success. But bestsellers may also be novels for children and adults with enormously more serious and realizable intentions. Indeed, as the example of Dickens again emphasizes, the greatest novelists have a strongly bestselling appeal in them. That is, they not only master a rich range of dictions, a wide rhetoric, they are also able to make themselves listened to. Of course, Dickens's majestic achievement is in part a happy accident: he was the genius he was *and* he had to hand an extraordinary range of language – the language of salon, street, factory, church, workhouse, law-court. The unprecedented conditions of the new industrial capital had not yet forced these languages apart into impermeable divisions: Dickens held them together in a rich, dense poetry which commanded an enormous audience.

A novelist today wins popularity much more hardly. Whatever his genius, he cannot make so much of it. The novel is still full of life and vigour, but it would be an even more astonishing novelist than Dickens who could force into a single book the technical languages of our time, the gathering and dwindling tide of social affairs, and the historical subject. To bring off a bestselling achievement like *Watership Down* seems to me to meet a sufficiently tall order. Richard Adams's book satisfies both cult and culture much more impressively than *The Lord of the Rings*, and in a way to rebut the worst forecasts of *Fiction and the Reading Public*.

Watership Down is so strong because it brims over the flow-charted stratification of cultural life. It is far more than the bestselling novel which in one month alone (October 1974) sold 145,000 copies in the thirteen languages into which it is translated, and went past the million mark before it had been in the Puffin list for three years.[16] Adams's strength is that he draws upon the materials of popular culture but in such a way as to break critically with the conventions of the liberal novel for children. He draws together in a new synthesis old heroics and new psychology. That is, he seeks to render certain drastically

---

[15] See Gillian Freeman, *The Undergrowth of Literature* (1968).
[16] *Guardian*, 6 August 1976.

changed features of the intellectual landscape, the contours of
the mind, in such a way as to make children experience these
changes for themselves.

One cannot doubt that Richard Adams intends to strike this
pedagogic note. Indeed, he strikes it often clumsily – he can be
clumsy in many ways, both when trying too hard and when not
trying enough:

When Marco Polo came at last to Cathay, seven hundred years ago,
did he not feel – and did his heart not falter as he realised – that this
great and splendid capital of an empire had had its being all the years of
his life and far longer, and that he had been ignorant of it? That it was
in need of nothing from him, from Venice, from Europe? That it was
full of wonders beyond his understanding? That his arrival was a
matter of no importance whatever? We know that he felt these things,
and so has many a traveller in foreign parts who did not know what he
was going to find. There is nothing that cuts you down to size like
coming to some strange and marvellous place where no one even
stops to notice that you stare about you. (*Watership Down*, p. 299)

That is a lapse into avuncularity which occurs a number of
times in the novel. Indeed it is not unendearing; it has the ring of
someone who has come to teaching during middle-age, benign
but often awkward. He has a teacherly point. Adams aims to
create enough disorientation in children's minds to enable
them to see the world in a new way. This new way becomes
clearer when Adams begins the tricky business of making his
rabbits both alien and familiar, non-human and sympathetic,
to his readers:

Rabbits, of course, have no idea of precise time or of punctuality. In
this respect they are much the same as primitive people, who often
take several days over assembling for some purpose and then several
more to get started. Before such people can act together, a kind of tele-
pathic feeling has to flow through them and ripen to the point when all
know that they are ready to begin. (p. 28)

There is more than a touch here, as elsewhere in Richard
Adams, of a Victorian explorer's bluff patronage which sorts
perfectly well with the glimpses we get of the red-bereted
officer elsewhere, with his Sergeant-major Bigwig, his
Captain Holly, his 'Thus it fell to one of the rank-and-file to
make a lucky find' (p. 136). But the same pages give us a different cue as well; they make the connection, certainly, with the

anthropologists, but not merely the anthropologists hired by the nineteenth-century Empire to report on the peculiarities of colonial peoples. Adams's novel has moved with the times which have dispersed that Empire, and it seeks to give a moral account of the change, an account which will explain some of the varieties of human experience, its openness and closures. To do this, it enters alien minds and experiences the world with the concepts and values of those minds.

Adams works to bring together two post-Romantic modes of thought in a common, though necessarily blurred focus. For he is a novelist and as such, he is committed to the understanding and inhabitation of other frames of mind. Because novels are the product of one tributary from the Enlightenment, he is engaged upon the traditional Romantic enterprise of examining subjectivities. But there is a different anthropology astir as well, and insofar as Adams seeks systematically to render an alien perception of the world, he is very much engaged in the new science, which, as Isaiah Berlin says, seeks for

yet another type of awareness, unlike a priori knowledge in that it is empirical, unlike deduction in that it yields new knowledge of facts, and unlike perception of the external world, in that it informs us not merely of what exists or occurs, and in what spatial or temporal order, but also why what is, or occurs, is as it is, i.e. in some sense *per causas*. This species is self-knowledge: knowledge of activities of which we, the knowing subjects, are ourselves the authors, endowed with motives, purposes, and a continuous social life, which we understand, as it were, from the inside. . . [17]

What Berlin goes on to show is not so much 'self-knowledge' as the phrase is conventionally understood, as knowledge of others, and it is this technique of empathic interpretation which he commends to us as the life- and truth-giving tendency of a new hermeneutic,[18] or system of understanding and explanation. The bearing of this on Richard Adams's work is brought out in this famous passage by Ernest Hemingway, who like Adams is seeking 'empathic knowledge' not even of other humans, but of animals, in this case a lion:

The lion still stood looking majestically and coolly towards this

[17] Isaiah Berlin, *Vico and Herder: Two Studies in the History of Ideas* (1975), pp. 21–2.
[18] A newly fashionable word with a long provenance, starting from Biblical scholars in the seventeenth century. It means 'the science of interpretations'.

object that his eyes only showed in silhouette, bulking like some super-rhino. There was no man smell carried toward him and he watched the object, moving his great head a little from side to side. Then watching the object, not afraid, but hesitating before going down the bank to drink with such a thing opposite him, he saw a man figure detach itself from it and he turned his heavy head and swung away toward the cover of the trees as he heard a cracking crash and felt the slam of a .30–06 220-grain solid bullet that bit his flank and ripped in sudden hot scalding nausea through his stomach. He trotted, heavy, big-footed, swinging wounded full-bellied, through the trees toward the tall grass and cover, and the crash came again to go past him ripping the air apart. Then it crashed again and he felt the blow as it hit his lower ribs and ripped on through, blood sudden hot and frothy in his mouth, and he galloped toward the high grass where he could crouch and not be seen and make them bring the crashing thing close enough so he could make a rush and get the man that held it. (*The Short Happy Life of Francis Macomber* in *The First 49*, p. 21)

Adams is hardly less effective in the suddenness and truthfulness with which he presents the familiarly human to a pair of eyes which finds the object not just unfamiliar, but unintelligible:

They ran on and crept through the hedge. Hazel looked down at the road in astonishment. For a moment he thought that he was looking at another river – black, smooth and straight between its banks. Then he saw the gravel embedded in the tar and watched a spider running over the surface. (*Watership Down*, p. 164)

This is a small example of what Adams does so consistently and powerfully throughout his novel. In the very striking scene in which the last survivors of the gassed-out warren catch up with a group of refugees who left before the disaster, Captain Holly describes a bulldozer (the lapine for any noisy machine is 'hrududu'):

'a great hrududu came into the field from the lane. It wasn't the one the man came in. It was very noisy and it was yellow – as yellow as charlock: and in front there was a great silver, shining thing that it held in its huge front paws. I don't know how to describe it to you. It looked like Inle, but it was broad and not so bright. And this thing – how can I tell you? It tore the field to bits. It destroyed the field.'

. He stopped again.
'Captain,' said Silver, 'we all know you've seen things bad beyond telling. But surely that's not quite what you mean?'

'Upon my life (said Holly, trembling), it buried itself in the ground and pushed great masses of earth in front of it until the field was destroyed. The whole place became like a cattle-wade in winter and you could no longer tell where any part of the field had been, between the wood and the brook. Earth and roots and grass and bushes it pushed before it – and other things as well, from underground.' (p. 164)

This unusual capacity for presenting the familiar as terrifyingly unprecedented is what – to return to the question of values – I would most want children to experience in the book. For the ten-year-old reading Captain Holly's description knows what a bulldozer is; he is in the traditional relationship of child to pet or doll or Peter Rabbit; for once, in a world otherwise full of giant grown-ups, abrupt and arbitrary eventualities, fixed authorities, wide open and hostile spaces, the child knows better than the hero. He can experience the rabbits' bewilderment while understanding what is going on. (The same thing is brilliantly and sickeningly done for adults by Golding in *The Inheritors*, the tale which follows the slaughter of a group of defenceless Neanderthalers by men with a bow-and-arrow technology. With Golding, however, Darwin and St Paul are called silently to witness that all this destructive evil was inevitable.) More impressively yet, Adams takes us through the incomprehension of the rabbits into the moment at which they think themselves beyond what was hitherto thinkable. The first such moment arrives when the escaping rabbits come across a little stream called the Enborne, and their group intellectual, a rabbit called Blackberry, works out how to use a loose plank as a boat. Similarly, when, with the foresight which we share with the heroes, we know that the punt is ready for their escape with the captured doe rabbits, and we see Hazel and company drawn away into the current of the river Test under the nose of the pursuing tyrant General Woundwort, we experience at once the familiar satisfaction of relief at the last-minute safety of our side and at the same time the pleasure of understanding the incomprehension of the enemy as in his eyes solid ground moves magically away out of his reach.

It is this knot between *how* we see and the intellectual and verbal mechanisms we have for telling us *what* we see which Adams so vividly unties and ties again; to put it more technically, the central structure of the book builds and rebuilds the intricate, intercellular relations of perception and cognition, of image and idea. It gives us – and 'us' includes children – a strong, clear picture of how culture develops, and it does this broadly and simply in a dozen different ways. At one moment Adams notes in an aside that rabbits cannot count beyond four; after that numbers blur into 'lots'. The seagull Kehaar classifies 'all insects as beetles' (p. 199) – only their edibility is significant. At another moment, Fiver the seer struggles with the idea of shaking sounds and meaning out of 'the black sticks [which] flickered on the white surface' of a noticeboard as 'they raised their sharp, wedge-shaped little heads and chattered together like a nestful of young weasels' (p. 235); a little before, we experience with the rabbits the stupefying glare of a car's headlights, the 'awful brightness [of which] seemed to cut into the brain' (p. 228). In all these and many other instances we are made to know the strangeness and omnipotence of an alien human technology, or else we are made to recognize the singularity and, as one might say, *interestedness*, of our systems of concepts and the percepts which are a consequence of the concepts. Adams unfixes and refixes,[19] in the way only a novelist can, the fluidity of experience, the facts of an intelligent eye and a brain which has to shape the world for the eye to see. This movement from dissolution to coagulation of ideas is sustained with the slow growth in the hero-rabbits' community of a dynamic culture. Hazel and company leave a static society, adroit and intelligent enough in its own way – its leader gives all the eerily familiar political reasons for not seeing crisis as crisis – and gradually construct a frame of thought capable of extension and adjustment, and of resistance and rejection too. Even from the doomed warren, which acts as the farmer's leader, they learn to carry and store food (p. 97). They learn, against all their nature and their instincts, to travel long distances, to fight when they have to and not to run away from cats and dogs and foxes. They learn achitectonics or how to build piered and vaulted underground halls (p. 151). They learn friendship and dependence when their instinct is to scatter in a rout. These are the strengths of the book, that it insists upon the protracted difficulty of making a home out of exile, a society out of a gang of scared, forlorn, hungry bits and pieces, order and ceremony out of a sandy hill-top, a ride of sweet turf, and the cover of the

[19] Compare Richard Gregory's two classics on perception, *Eye and Brain* (1966) and *The Intelligent Eye* (1970).

tall pine trees. Culture is made out of the hard years, out of the permanence of fear, the threat of desert places:

Rabbits above ground, unless they are in proved, familiar surroundings close to their holes, live in continual fear. If it grows intense enough they can become glazed and paralysed by it – *tharn*, to use their own word. Hazel and his companions had been on the jump for nearly two days. (p. 133)

This is the broad moral of his task, and when it issues in generalization, then for all Dr Adams's slight pomposity of manner, it rings true enough. In the long paragraph which opens chapter 22, he reconnects the analogy between rabbits and communitarian (i.e. non-individualist) primitive peoples:

Rabbits (says Mr Lockley) are like human beings in many ways. One of these is certainly their staunch ability to withstand disaster and to let the stream of their life carry them along, past reaches of terror and loss. They have a certain quality which it would not be accurate to describe as callousness or indifference. It is, rather, a blessedly circumscribed imagination and an intuitive feeling that Life is Now . . .
. . . Hazel and his companions had suffered extremes of grief and horror during the telling of Holly's tale. Pipkin had cried and trembled piteously at the death of Scabious, and Acorn and Speedwell had been seized with convulsive choking as Bluebell told of the poisonous gas that murdered underground. Yet, as with primitive humans, the very strength and vividness of their sympathy brought with it a true release. Their feelings were not false or assumed. While the story was being told, they heard it without any of the reserve or detachment that the kindest of civilized humans retains as he reads his newspaper. To themselves, they seemed to struggle in the poisoned runs and to blaze with rage for poor Pimpernel in the ditch. This was their way of honouring the dead. The story over, the demands of their own hard, rough lives began to reassert themselves in their hearts, in their nerves, their blood and appetites.

And he goes on to modulate into bolder and, we may feel, justifiably strong moral assertion:

Would that the dead were not dead! But there is grass that must be eaten, pellets that must be chewed, hraka that must be passed, holes that must be dug, sleep that must be slept. Odysseus brings not one man to shore with him. Yet he sleeps sound beside Calypso and when he wakes thinks only of Penelope. (pp. 169–70)

The Homeric reference is typical of the man who so loads even the rifts between chapters with epigraphs from Congreve, Xenophon, Sidney Keyes, folksong, Clausewitz, Robinson Jeffers. Adams is a manly man, and none the worse for it. But to say so brings me to the point at which his special limitations must be named. For the strong, rich, savoury presence in this novel which comes from its cultural ancestry in Western literature seems to run, however strongly, into some very stereotypical forms.

In the first place, Adams is up against the structural difficulty of any anthropomorphic storyteller. He gives rabbits consciousness, which they do not have, but keeps them as rabbits. It won't do simply to say, with Richard Boston,[20] that Germaine Greer would hate the book because the female rabbits are simply there to bear children and to dig burrows while all the real friendships and human qualities are shown by the men. Adams's creation of an alien set of values and ideas out of which to see the world resists our making the novel into an animal fable; it is not the *Nonne's Preeste's Tale*, nor is it *Animal Farm*.

The kind of ideas that have become natural to many male human beings in thinking of females – ideas of protection, fidelity, romantic love and so on – are, of course, unknown to rabbits, although rabbits certainly do form exclusive attachments much more frequently than most people realise. However, they are not romantic and it came naturally to Hazel and Holly to consider the two Nuthanger does simply as breeding stock for the warren. This was what they had risked their lives for. (p. 256)

To do this he must give rabbits language and consciousness, and he must make these both inhuman and intelligible. The trouble with this sprawling, immoderate, unreflective book is that Adams has such an uneven touch in making such a language. He is by turns clumsy, portentous, long-winded, and magnificent. What makes the book into an unprecedented bestseller is this adventitious mixture.[21]

There is, as they say, something for everyone. For the intel-

[20] *Guardian*, 6 August 1976.
[21] But see Graham Hammond's excellent and very critical essay in *Children's Literature in Education*, 12 (1973).

lectual child or adult there is the rabbit lore, the creatively non-positivist animal behaviourism, and there are the makings of other cultures. Crossing into this territory, there is the ecology and the heady stuff of the conservation polemic, lapsing at times (p. 298) into an involuntary parody of *The Observer's Book of Wild Flowers*. Woven into this thick technicolour, with all its living detail and the samples pasted in from the author's commonplace book, is the war thriller. Richard Boston has very amusingly ripped out this structure, and mocked the 'onion-seller French and organ-grinder Italian' of Kehaar and 'maquis mouse'.[22] Certainly the main group of rabbits are portioned out with a haversack of iron moral rations which would look best in a commando sortie: 'Leadership for you, Hazel'; 'Brainbox for you, Blackberry'; 'Bulldog Drummond kit for you, Bigwig'; 'Nervous loyalty for raw recruits, Pipkin'; 'Mad poet's outfit to Fiver' – 'Now, who's for a futile gesture?' But the success of any book for children in part depends on a simple moral structure and a rattling good yarn; its strength and its weakness and, because of both, its sales, depend on having hit the right moment with this cultural recipe. It is a depressing consequence of such success that as Adams becomes a more accomplished writer, if *Shardik* is anything to go by, the limitations of his mind and his imagination, once his ambitions draw him away from that simple, honest morality, leave him with nothing but the fashionable camp of Aztec cruelty, of a slow, ceremonious, picturesque, and brocaded dose of the horrors.

With *Shardik* we enter the world of *She*-in-the-seventies, a world in which *Equus, Rollerball*, and the wardrobe epics of regal serials on television combine to make their special, irresistible appeal to prurience, crass psychologism, cruelty and sentimentality. It is not a surprising direction for an imagination with Adams's colour and eventfulness to take. *Shardik* exposes the absence of a critical community of values for the support of a novelist these days; *The Plague Dogs*, another book to stand across the limits of adults' and children's reading, must be left here only as a warning of what happens to genuine gifts when success, however late, arrives in overwhelming quantities.

Watership Down is vital to my thesis, as it is to children's

[22] *Guardian*, 6 August 1976.

novels in general, because it truthfully and livingly imagines a
frame of mind, both human and lapine, which makes new
values rational and intelligent.[23] It is not a way of doing social
science (a dreadful thought – 'Here, have a dose of Marx with
your *Tale of Ginger and Pickles*'). It *is* a way of learning to understand other cultures and the modes of living things as they make
up culture and society. If these claims are fair, its status as cult
novel can only be a matter for rejoicing. Its novelty and its
strong traditionalism make it one of the best examples we shall
find of a brave effort to maintain continuity across deep historical chasms.

---

[23] It is worth saying that the brave attempt at a box-office film of the novel (1978),
though much better than the film of *Charlotte's Web* mentioned in the last chapter, can
only give us the structure and never the process of the novel. Much of it is very striking
to look at, but always external.

Part III

Paradise Lost and Paradise Regained

The New Work

9

History absolves nobody –
ritual and romance

Tolkien's popular success and his achievement light up the formation of a group of people central to this inquiry. Such a formation rapidly becomes more than a membership; it becomes a social process which declares itself in the outlines of ideas, in the substance of writing, in the forms of social practice, as well as in the nature of its individual contributors. I cite Tolkien as both representing and energizing one such formation, one which then finds its forms and narratives in two distinguishable but related strands of fiction-making.

The Tolkien formation – it might be the name of some latter-day radical commando – is typified by two kinds of fiction. Both are deeply influenced by the medievalism, the gorgeous colours and stylization of the Pre-Raphaelites and their still uncalculated and immense presence in British culture. The first kind transpires in historical novels, simply so called; they are the subject of this chapter. The second, which is the subject of the next chapter, pulls away from more or less straight history (inevitably selective as to moments and events) towards legend, myth, fairy-tales, and the great underworld of magic and the occult. Tolkien himself stands in the subject-matter and the prose style of the second line, but for all that, he is the figure amongst recent writers who is most responsible for re-animating the thick, rich, but oddly insubstantial brew of the Pre-Raphaelites and the historical hero-worshippers who were their contemporaries in the 1890s.

I have criticized Tolkien for the intoxicating fumes of his writing as blurring over in gorgeous colour the knotty, corrugated actualities of myth and history. His success, I suggest, is in direct proportion to his misty enlargements and simplifications. But he does not exhaust the genre. Indeed, the rooms kept in the house of fiction for the historical romance in English are exceptionally large and although Tolkien has, in style and tone and structure, proved such a spectacular custodian, they would have remained in busy occupation, especially by novelists for children. The historical romances take up the great themes of a nation, its history and its heroes, and commend them to its children. They are a means of ensuring a continuity of memory and therefore of national identity, and the way in which they compress values into historical events tells us what we want to know about the popular view of history.

'Popular', however, is not quite the right word. For the Tolkien formation draws its leading membership from that broad section of the lower-middle classes which justifies itself as cherishing the best symbols and ideals of a society. 'Petty bourgeois' is far too loose a category in which to place these men and women. They are the modest machine-minders of the meaning industry; as I remarked, they include HMIs, school teachers, librarians, local television producers and presenters, vicars, radio announcers, journalists on evening newspapers, as well as a whole range of services to tourism. They shade out into the private lives of many in the other professional occupations, especially those at several removes from the centres of power – country GPs, local solicitors, crammer-accountants, probation officers, provincial advertisers, wine-merchants. Historical romances by the best children's novelists are the political myths of the powerlessly genteel in modern industrial states. They represent versions of history which these decent, earnest, non-specialist men and women want to read for themselves at the same time as they give them to their children. Their own grip on history is confined to the big, obtrusive jugholds on a climb marked out by the dedicated tradition-builders I mentioned at the beginning: Walter Scott, Kipling, then Rider Haggard, and the best worthies of the British adventure stories – Ballantyne, Henty, Marryat, and the *Boys' Own Paper*. And for all the Empire-bound and public-school frame of this strong line, it found its siblings across the Atlantic readily enough, not as historical romance but as declaration of independence and as frontier tale: Shaeffer's *Shane*, Forbes's *Johnny Tremain* and London's *White Fang*. The small, still air, the tiny range of permitted political and historical action, the diffusion and porousness of personal life in a modern suburban garden launch the owner-occupier's imagination into the endless blue

air above the great historical peaks: Roman Britain, the Crusades, the defeat of the Spanish Armada and the execution of
Mary Queen of Scots, the Civil War, 1745 and the defeat at Culloden, Nelson and Wellington in the Napoleonic Wars,
Dickens's London – the dark, deep chambers, the strong,
brown river, Christmas snow, wills, bequests, wealth, all
bound together by the thrilling fog. The last two such dates on
this range of history are 1914 and 1940: the most recent chance
which individuals have had to act convincingly, in concert, and
on behalf of private lives.

Running together such a variety of fictional possibilities
means running together a very varied collection of writers,
some good, some bad, in an effort to characterize this critical
formation of imaginative myth-makers. Geoffrey Trease in his
Robin Hood tale *Bows Against the Barons* is making very different political points from D. K. Broster's tale of the post-
Culloden Highlands in *The Dark Mile*. Trease aims to speak
from a simple, generous communism for the poor against the
rich; Broster's is an old-style, royalist romance, hero and
heroine alike shining-eyed and burnished with a nameless
desire (finely remembered by Patricia Beer in *Mrs. Beer's
House*). Both, however, stand easily within the always impossible heroics, the yearned-for individual significance of the
social formation I have described. Hester Burton's tale of Trafalgar, *Castors Away!*, Ronald Welch's tale of the Crusades,
Knight Crusader, Alison Uttley's ingenuously ardent champion
of the doomed Queen Mary in *A Traveller in Time*, even as
good a novel as Jill Paton Walsh's *The Dolphin Crossing*, all
align themselves comfortably within the poetics of a pre-
multinational, pre-nuclear, dramatic novel. That is, all present
a hero who is still capable of acting heroically and not simply
enduring as a victim; all take a historical moment – the old tales
of King John's tyranny, the threat of Philip II, of Napoleon, of
Hitler – from which the Whig interpretations of history have
drawn enthusiastic encouragement. That interpretation is still
part of the residual culture of the primary- and middle-school
project in history, of the public schools' common-entrance
examination, and of the historical curriculum of children's television. It sees British – largely English – history as progressive
and as given shape and movement by certain important concentrations of energy, followed by their explosion across the

globe in the form of empire: of capital, production, culture, beliefs, social organization.

These concentrations become the battle honours of liberal democracy, free enterprise, and individual creativity. Thus Robin Hood is the champion less of the poor than of the patriotic self: not a Bakunin so much as a de Gaulle; so the hero of *Knight Crusader*, Philip d'Aubigny, swinging his sword cheerfully along swathes of routine corpses, fights against Saracen tyranny and domestic dispossession; so, too, the unkillable attractions of Mary Queen of Scots (in *A Traveller in Time*) and Bonnie Prince Charlie (in D. K. Broster's trilogy) are that both, in their flashing, gallant, incompetent way, are presented as unjustly dispossessed. In these and in a dozen other novels from Captain Marryat's *The Children of the New Forest* in 1847 via C. S. Forester's *Hornblower* to recent prizewinners like John Christopher's science-fiction novel *Beyond the Burning Lands*, the story goes out that the movement of history is impelled by the voluntary decisions of individuals, rationally chosen and endorsed by victory and the greater settlement of a morally excellent and commonly assented-to political order: the merry men support King Richard just as the clans support Prince Charlie and the children support the Royalists. Indeed, it is a prominent mark of the historical romance that it fights by its Whiggish lights for the freedom of the individual who gives his support to a popular and traditional regime with a strong hierarchy and a dashing leader. The admirably pithy account of the English Civil War in *1066 and All That* is, as is well known, that the Roundheads were right but repulsive, and the Cavaliers wrong but romantic. That view of history deeply stains the historical romance for children.

The curriculum of such romances derives in a very long historical account from the assiduous effort of the victorious rulers after 1688 to justify the new regime. With William secured on the throne and the battle of the Boyne behind them, the new conservatives set out to make the regime legitimate, and they did so through the invention of tradition[1] and dynasty. They wrote a version of the rhetoric by which most regimes when they first arrive try to explain how they come to be here. They claim that they have not usurped but simply

[1] See J. H. Plumb, *The Growth of Political Stability in England 1688–1789* (1967); also *Past and Present* conference papers, 'The Invention of Tradition', 1977.

sustained and extended the real line of continuity, the real spirit of the laws.

But it is itself slightly spurious to go back to the glorious revolution in order to find the origins of the Whig interpretation of history, as conceived in these romances. The momentous upheavals in Europe from 1848 onwards meant that the new social classes in England who were stage-managing the industrialization and its veering, uncontrollable cycles of boom and slump had to explain their part in things and hand on honour and prosperity to their children. This is the genesis of children's novels, as Chapter 3 describes it, and Rudyard Kipling is its most influential curriculum developer. The class he represented and gave energy to believed that the identity of nations is the motor of history, and that these are shaped by sudden concentrations of social energy in key segments of the community, an energy naturally expressing itself in deliberate, vigorous action. Such action is focussed by intelligent and attractive leaders, and is largely defensive of the great liberal virtues, particularly the maintenance of the social order and the protection of domestic lives. The surge of nationalism in all this accounts for the continued attractions of the Scottish secessionists, especially as Mary and Charlie, along with Richard Lionheart, Nelson, Churchill, and the other cheerful captains whose failures have been winnowed from them by popular culture, stand for the tribal thrills and the leader's hard and glowing energy which readily magnetize childish imaginations.

This historiography lies as a thick, potent residue in the social imagination. Its potency is easy to feel, less easy to account for. Faced with the savage ruptures of the century, some recent children's novelists have tried to design an image of historical continuity which keeps faith with the best and strongest elements of this thick residue, so important in their own lives and in the formation whose morality, psychology, and politics they share. Thus, Rosemary Sutcliff[2] reconstructs from Rudyard Kipling's Roman Britain – the tales of Parnesius in *Puck of Pook's Hill* and *Rewards and Fairies* – a parallel structure of regimental loyalty, strong nationalism, honour and duty as the bonds which hold individuals upright in institutions, mili-

---

[2] I have written at some length on her novels, which I greatly enjoy, in *Ideology and the Imagination* (1975).

tary courage and colour. Over all she sings a sweet lament for a
sun-soaked and lovely landscape, especially on its most Words-
worthian moors, downs, dales and fells:

The snows were melting on the high southern face of Yr Widdfa, and
the sound of running water was everywhere, mingling with the wild,
sweet, bubbling call of curlews from the high heather slopes above the
valley; and the hazel scrub along the skirts of the fortress hill was
dappled mealy gold with catkins. The strangeness was gone from the
fortress hill, no mist hung above it now save the faint blue haze of
cooking-fires, as Aquila looked up at it. It was just a place that he
knew, as he knew other places, with people that he knew in it: old
Finnen the Harper, and Valarius with his pouchy red face and watery
blue eyes, who had been of Constantine's body-guard in his better
days; fat Eugenus, and the lean and fiery little priest Eliphias, with his
prophet's eye; Brychan with his two great hounds – the men, mostly
young, who formed a kind of inner circle, a brotherhood, round
Ambrosius, and whom he called his Companions.
  He headed for the winding cleft in the hillside where the trickle
from the fortress spring in its little hollow came down. It was a climb
for goats, but it saved going round to pick up the track on the north
side of the hill. There was a thin warmth from the sun on the back of
his neck as he climbed, and a flittering of tits among the still-bare
blackthorn bushes that arched over the little thread of water, and the
small purple flowers of the butterwort cushioned the wet, starling-
coloured rocks. More than half-way up, where the cleft widened and
the freshet had worn a tiny pool for itself among rocks and tree-roots,
he found a small boy and a hound puppy very intent on a hole under a
brown tumble of last year's fern. He would have passed by without
speaking, and left them to it, but the small boy sat up and grinned at
him, thrusting back a shock of hair the warm, silvery-mouse colour
of a hayfield in June, and the puppy thumped its tail. (*The Lantern
Bearers*, pp. 119–20)

It is at such moments that her touch becomes stickier by far than
Kipling's. The fine evocation of Sussex in *Puck* can remain
unforced because it is directly experienced. Rosemary Sutcliff
has to recreate a landscape which, except for odd corners of the
National Parks (hence her reliance on heather), is now irretriev-
ably altered, busy with people, and often horrible to look at.
Her very deep feeling for the English landscape is given its
shape and meaning by Gerard Manley Hopkins and the Scholar
Gypsy.
  The trouble is that it takes exceptional finesse to prevent such

reconstruction becoming vulgar. The appearance in innumerable homes of the farmhouse kitchen as reproduced by Habitat and Guild shops testifies to the longing Rosemary Sutcliff expresses with such plangency. For what are her novels seeking to do? They seek to create in children their author's love for a landscape no longer there. But not just a landscape; natural beauty in her novels is presented as a frame whose order, tranquillity, cultivation, and culture are metaphors for an analogous order in social and personal life. It is a metaphor with a long pedigree. Landscapes, however, can be deceptive. Sometimes a landscape seems to be less a setting for the life of its inhabitants than a curtain behind which their struggles, achievements, and accidents take place. The tricky part of Rosemary Sutcliff's ambition, as it is of the other children's writers who work to create a picture of history as reasonably continuous with the present, is to avoid her landscape-as-setting becoming another tourist attraction. To move through the curtain is to make the landmarks personal and biographical, as well as picturesque.

She is much too intelligent not to know this. But she writes on the swell of a tide of feeling larger than any one writer; the tide carries her away from writing real history, into the unreal tempests and enchanted islands of romance. Much, of course, may happen on those seas, shores, and grey rocks, which is every bit as real as history – as Prospero, Caliban and Miranda show us. The strong, regressive pull of some, at least, of Rosemary Sutcliff's novels is towards stable institutions and memberships which command a loyalty fixed by ceremony and fealty, deepened by a sweeping iambic prose. The weakness is not that she writes of these things at all, for one duty of a writer is to count the costs of change, to criticize the present values by their own best standard *and* by the standard of those they have displaced. Thus, the gains won this century for human freedom, individual dignity and sincerity, must be judged by the writer against the loss of dread, awe, mystery, which gave gravity and meaning to the grimness of old authority. Too often, Rosemary Sutcliff sounds as though she speaks for the Tolkien formation by simply lamenting the age of chivalry and its demise. In Kipling, and much more in Conrad, the gains to life provided by the immovable structures of Mercantile Marine, Roman Legion, and Indian Army regiment, are clear:

they enforce the idea of a job well done, they create the central concept of duty, they permit friendship. By the time Rosemary Sutcliff wrote her Roman sequence, *The Eagle of the Ninth* (1954), *The Silver Branch* (1956), *The Lantern Bearers* (1959), *Dawn Wind* (1963), and *The Mark of the Horse Lord* (1965), the work of maintaining nuclear tankers and political regimes in the bauxite islands of the West Indies and aboriginal Queensland[3] was too boring and too destructive to justify the lives of good men. As a result, her novels, insofar as they commend Kipling's and Conrad's morality, are just romancing. As such, they are fetching, often touching; a child might become rapt and bewitched by them. But if so, it would be a spell bound by an irrevocable past.

This is not all there is to say of these novels, by any means. I have paid a longer tribute elsewhere. Miss Sutcliff, however, embodies another, more active moral strain in the genteel politics of her genesis. As she works away at the historical experience which absorbs her – the colonizing of Britain during and after the fall of Rome – she outlines a new and shadowy figure in the wide spaces of the heath. This figure – Owain in *Dawn Wind*, or the freed gladiator–guerrilla leader in *The Mark of the Horse Lord* – breaks clear of the institutions which lie in ruins about him and endures shocking hardship in his own name. In her stately, slightly rigid prose, the novelist sets her heroes and heroines stubbornly to resist the cruelties of empires and ideologies. They will live through, if only just, the advent of both the Saxons and St Augustine.

The hero of these novels is much more of a victim than the hero described in Chapter 6; Owain is a slave for most of the book, the dawn wind is barely stirring. So her message is – to speak crudely – that the individual spirit will survive the loss of nation, family, tribe, or regiment. She seems to say with Ben Jonson:

> Not for my peace will I go far
> As wanderers do, that still do roam,
> But make my strengths, such as they are,
> Here in my bosom, and at home. (*A Farewell to the World*)

Rosemary Sutcliff sets herself a large task: to catch some-

---

[3] See, for an example from fiction, V. S. Naipaul's *Guerillas* (London, André Deutsch 1975; Harmondsworth, Penguin 1977).

thing of the movements of empire and history in the thick, unbending prose of the bestseller romance, with its black and white conventions, Maydays and waste lands, perilous chapels, cups and quests, lothely ladies and grene men.[4] As things are, she is more likely to catch teacher-readers than children.

This is less true of another noteworthy contributor to the same formation, Katherine Peyton. Her trilogy, *Flambards, The Edge of the Cloud,* and *Flambards in Summer,* poises itself at another of the critical hinges of English history, and tries to situate change of epoch and establish the meaning of continuity. Once more, if we compare the prose of the trilogy – which is perfectly unlike the prose of K. M. Peyton's better book *A Pattern of Roses* – we find the heavy iambic cadences, the Elgarian chords, the savoury, filling hotpot which is the suppertime dish of an adult readership denied such nourishment in the Tiresias voices of upmarket novelists like (say) Nadine Gordimer, Margaret Drabble, Günter Grass, and Dan Jacobson.

> But, watching him, Christina could feel Sweetbriar's long stride, see the hedge as Mark saw it: a trifling obstacle between him and that galloping pack whose wild music was filling the valley. Seeing the hedge in cold blood, from up the hill, Christina shivered, and said, 'Oh, Dick, the mare!'
>
> Even as Sweetbriar rose at it, Christina knew that she was watching disaster. She saw the gallant attempt at a take-off from a ditch lip of brimming mud, heard the crack of the rails as the mare hit them with her forelegs, then the cartwheel arc of her iron shoes as she catapulted out of sight through the crackling brushwood. Christina looked at Dick. Even then, it was the mare's plight she was thinking of, not Mark's. Her own excitement was quenched; hounds were already out of sight in the woodlands along the bottom of the valley, and she felt cold at the sight of the accident.
>
> 'I reckon the mare'll be no better for that,' Dick said shortly.
>
> He mounted Treasure, and pulled the lame Woodpigeon up beside him. 'We'd best go and see.' (*Flambards*, p. 80)

The past is surpassed, but mythologized. Its carnal brutalities (Uncle Russell's beastly drunkenness); its arrogance of caste (Mark's getting Dick's sister Violet pregnant); its squalid,

---

[4] Whose historical origins lie with King Arthur just the other side of real history. The most famous inventory of the story is Jessie Weston's *From Ritual to Romance* (1920).

overgrown picturesqueries of house and stable; all these are
balanced against the great joy of hunting and horsemanship.
The trilogy gives shape and meaning to the historical transition
which has seized the imagination of English writers since
Shakespeare. Like Rosemary Sutcliff, Katherine Peyton is
trying to make accessible to the children she hopes are listening
the momentous idea that social orders change hugely, that
people are swept along in such changes but that they aren't
merely the object of the change, they are also its subjects and
may bend it, however slightly, if they have the luck and the
courage, to their own will. Uncle Russell and Mark together
stand for the remnants of the old feudal order. Their
horsemanship and their drinking testify both to their social
irresponsibility and to their assumption of their own mastery.
To ride is to rule. It is to connect the master on the horse with
the traditions of knight errantry and chivalry. These traditions
live in the elaborateness of ritual, in the insistence that the rider
does everything correctly, but also that the precision of this
correctness and, in the revealing phrase, its 'good form' make
ample room for the correctness of recklessly brave and
thrusting riding. Hunting permits a spontaneity absent from
all other social intercourse.

Will, the younger brother, hates the Russell life with an
intensity and daring which are completely of a piece with his
brother's and father's blazingly passionate natures. He is
utterly brave, and so afraid of riding that after breaking his leg
in an accident, he deliberately and agonizingly prevents the
break from knitting properly and thereby disqualifies himself
from riding for ever. His passion is for aeronautics; his guide
and teacher Mr Dermot is a master of the new sciences, and
lives in a house whose coolness and tidiness are placed in firm
contrast to the colour and squalor of Flambards. His is the
future, as the last paragraphs, in which Will elopes with
Christina, make clear. The borrowed Rolls Royce slides
effortlessly away from Mark, crazily pursuing the car on
horseback.

The *Flambards* trilogy should have become established as a
classic introduction to adolescence. It is so clearly and firmly
organized; the tale moves along with such pace and colour; and
the heroine has that warm, quick, generous sensibility, rich
with the feelings of both tenderness and rage which must be

deeply lived as well as merely controlled if a young woman is to become distinctive and exciting, to herself as well as to the world. Christina's sensibility is capacious and interesting, always larger than her likely reader's, and therefore enlarging; but not overwhelmingly so. She lives through the meaning of historical change, an experience which Katherine Peyton and the larger formation of which she is part would wish above all to urge upon children. In *The Edge of the Cloud* Christina's new husband Will is killed flying in the war. His death also is nicely adjusted to the adolescent reader. What fourteen-year-old worth anything has not imagined herself, bravely holding back her tears, in the becoming black, the puff sleeves and heavy stuff of Edwardian mourning? But the point is made in that novel, and in the third one, that progress is not just the supersession of the horse by the internal combustion engine. The feudal world goes down in the mud of 1916, but the reckless young airmen – spiritedly recreated in anticipation of the recent cult of early-aircraft movies like *Aces High* – go down also. It is then up to Christina, one of the new women, to take the best of the old history and lead it into a freer future. She marries Dick, the stableboy, safely has the child Will gave her just before his death, and adopts the illegitimate baby her arrogant, infuriating and attractive cousin Mark fathered upon the housemaid, Dick's sister. Finally, she takes in a German prisoner and makes him part of the newly profitable farm.

It is the best picture the honest liberal could wish upon the world as it might become, not so much in 1919 as in 1945. A manageable peace settlement which allowed West Germany to make good; the new class compromise set on its way; the economy put to rights by hard work, by culture and industry combined.

Mrs Peyton writes well, and firmly. If the trilogy is too briskly diagrammatic, the diagram is both admirable and believable enough; it provides a picture of what to do next, and what has been done with the past. The history is continuous and progressive. The present is more prosperous if less romantic than the past; decency, equality, cooperation, a gentled technology, have outrun poverty, beatings, and the servants.

It makes a cheerful historiography. While it may be none the worse for cheerfulness, the demands of real life and real history, with its sudden breaks, its pointlessness, its deep contradictions, must have their say. Perhaps Mrs Peyton hasn't *thought* hard enough. The narrative itself is terrific – full of passion and event, and as it ought to be, larger than life. One would surely want children to have read these books. And yet, if we are speaking of what the past means and how we come to discover and interpret that meaning, the boldness and confidence of their scheme can seem at times ingenuous, at times even offensive. I do not mean by this that repossessing the past must be made difficult and ramified, and that novels should impress on children all kinds of awful lessons about the bloodiness of the struggle and the inconsequence of its end. Neither Rosemary Sutcliff nor Katherine Peyton is reticent about the bloodshed (though they are admirably tactful about it), and only the dim or the crass would want children to get too heavy a dose of what such elders call realism. My point is more personal. Schemes of history emerge from the variety of experiences gained and the process of putting these experiences together. The unsolved problem of the children's novelist is how to avoid either casting characters as implausibly prominent on the stage of history, or placing them not very interestingly in the wings. The liberal tradition I have referred to has largely placed its actors in the middle of the action, and made the action so well known and spectacular – the Crusades, the Civil War, Trafalgar, the Somme – that there is no need to insist on its significance.

There is a harder way, off the main road with its bestseller signposts, and therefore without their striking simplifications, bold narrative lines, bright and vivid plots. Three writers occur to me as having tried to follow it, and there are no doubt more. The first is Gillian Avery, and her novel *The Warden's Niece*, now (surprisingly) over twenty years old, is all the more exemplary for rendering its unusual purpose in so lively and straightforward a way. For I take its subject-matter to be the inevitably personal interpretation of history, a process which is no less personal for being set in a particular time and place, and given meaning and dimension by far more than personal quality. The tale begins with the heroine moving from the conventional and deadening life of her school and her orphan status in order, timorously and solitarily, to rediscover an unconventional independence, both of mind and of society, as the niece and ward of her elderly bachelor uncle, Warden of what is called Canterbury College, Oxford (which seems to be somewhere near and like Magdalen). It is instructive that all the children in these exemplary novels do their history out of school, but Gillian Avery's lessons are the nearest to the classroom. Her heroine is resilient and determined, but she is also very quiet, withdrawn, and shy. She becomes caught up with the three cheerful brothers next door and their gawky, comic, dignified but ungainly tutor Mr Copplestone, in whose creation Gillian Avery has learned with profit from Dickens.

The brothers, Mr Copplestone, and Maria all visit, in the name of cultivation, education, and a day out, a stately home called Jerusalem House, which is open to the public, where they see a fine Lely drawing of an unknown seventeenth-century son of the family. The unknown boy, it turns out, has cut the mysterious inscription 'Begone, ye foul traitors' on some stone garden steps, and signed and dated his message 'S.St.G.F. 20 July 1654'. The novel is then carried along by Maria's intent resolution to find out what the words mean and whether the boy in the picture really wrote them. Her search and research take her to the Bodleian, and Duke Humphrey's library where women are hindered but allowed, to the cartoon scholar in his paper-crammed attic, up river by punt and back again by cab to steal into the house on a dare and without permission, until she has made the connection between portrait and inscription and discovered that the boy scratched in the letters as his only redress when Cromwell's men commandeered the house and he was about to follow his family into exile.

The point is beautifully and lightly pressed home. In less sensitive hands, the subject-matter could far too easily have become a pale ontological project – how to do a spot of local history, using local resources. But the characters are too varied for a reader ever to lose sight of the livingness and contingent quality of full-blooded historical inquiry. Maria's lively commitment to her search, her excitement when she clinches it, are nicely placed beside Thomas's amiable interest and his wanting his muffins much more than he wants to listen to Maria.

Gillian Avery is speaking up for much more than scholarship. Maria is a determined scholar; she learns, as they say, by discovery. And we learn with her the complex connections which bring together the portrait, the inscription, a country churchyard in Kent, and the regicides of 1649, all as a living image of a single moment reconstructed and understood by the Warden's niece about 230 years later. It is a modest enough book, but its theme is large. It suggests another, no less decently liberal and educational way of making world-pictures of history in a world which the old syllabus no longer explains.[5]

The other authors I take as breaking the ranks of the Tolkien formation are Penelope Lively in *The Driftway, Going Back* and *The House in Norham Gardens*, and one of the masters of children's writing, William Mayne, in his *The Battlefield* and *The Jersey Shore*, to say nothing of *Earthfasts* and *A Grass Rope*. Mention of these novels brings me close to the subject-matter of the next chapter, in which we cross the line between history and myth. Penelope Lively in *The House in Norham Gardens* picks up the old device of a magic totem which charges the house in Oxford with the rituals and mysteries of its origins. As a consequence, she is stuck with a certain straightforward spookiness of effect which obstructs rather than brings out her real theme. And if that sounds impertinent – the claim on the part of the critic to know better than the novelist – I excuse myself by quoting the end of *The House in Norham Gardens*:

'I wonder,' said Clare, 'if this house will be here when I'm old. If I'll live in it.'

'I don't imagine so for a moment. The whole place will have been razed to the ground to make way for a housing estate.'

'Maybe not,' said Aunt Anne. 'You never know. The road may be considered highly desirable. Preserved for posterity.'

'Either way, you won't need it. You will have furnished your own life, with other places and other things.'

'I shall keep the photographs from the drawing-room,' said Clare, 'and the clothes in the trunks in the attic, and the portraits in the dining-room and . . .'

'My dear child,' said Aunt Susan, 'you can't carry a museum round with you. Neither will you need to. What you need, you will find you already have to hand – of that I've not the slightest doubt. You are a listener. It is only those who have never listened who find themselves in trouble eventually.'

'Why?'

'Because it is extremely dull,' said Aunt Susan tartly, 'to grow old

[5] I have in mind R. G. Collingwood's *The Idea of History* (1946).

with nothing inside your head but your own voice. Tedious, to put it mildly.'

The fire heaved, flared up for a moment and settled itself again. The logs hissed. Outside, a car went past. How odd, Clare thought, to sit here talking about me as though I were another person. Someone quite different. She tried to project herself forwards in time to meet her, this unknown woman with her name and her face, and failed. She walked away, the woman, a stranger, familiar and unreachable. The only thing you could know about her for certain was that all this would be part of her: this room, this conversation, the aunts.

The aunts. Aunt Anne, seventy-eight: Aunt Susan, eighty-one. I can't make it stop at now, Clare thought, and you shouldn't want to, not really.

She looked at them, intently, at their faces and their hands and the shape of them. I'm learning them by heart, she thought, that's what I'm doing, that's all I can do, only that.

I choose Penelope Lively as an example to follow because I would judge – I have only the novels to go on – that she takes some more or less active interest in the remaking of academic history.[6] This is my cue for placing her alongside Gillian Avery. *The Driftway*, a fairly early novel in her prodigal output, suggests that she is consciously if clumsily seeking a way out of historical romancing *and* the familiar idea of revenants on the landing. The subject of *The Driftway* is the old road itself. The ghosts whom the little boy sees and hears telling him their tales of past events on the road are not presented or thought of as blood-boltered Banquos; they have no glare and they do not terrify, only impress. They are images produced by little local concentrations of intense electro-emotional life left clotted on the road for somebody's transistor to pick up when his private emotional radio is sufficiently charged to reactivate the flow. What he then hears, in the words of the wise old tinker in the tale, are 'messages':

'How do you know all that?' said Paul.

'Ah, I've read books in my time. I told you it don't suit me not knowing about things. Know nothing, and you are nothing. Though it's not all in books, mind. Now that's history, what I've just been saying. But to my way of thinking history's just another word for messages. You can dress it up in fancy language, but in the end it's

---

[6] Although Peter Abbs, in an interesting essay in *Children's Literature in Education*, 18 (1975), makes rather differently speculative points.

people sending each other messages, isn't it? Trying to find out about each other: tell each other how it is. Eh?'

'I s'pose so,' said Paul. (*The Driftway*, p. 33)

The novel, as I say, doesn't really find a form in which to render this complex, truthful idea of history. *Going Back* is another try at the same intransigent stuff, this time a straight and sunlit reminiscence of another grand, parentless, and unending summer sequence – the summers of the Second War, lived on a farm in the Quantocks. As such the book stands amongst its peers in Chapter 11: it seeks to do what the two masterpieces (as it isn't too much to call them) *Tom's Midnight Garden* and *Carrie's War* so triumphantly bring off: the intelligible ordering of a personal identity in an impersonal past – T. S. Eliot's majestic project in *Four Quartets*. But *Going Back* is another essay on Penelope Lively's historical theme. Her view of history and her place of honourable mention in this chapter connect with what I wrote about gossip in the first part of the book. Gossip, as I used the term, is the shared reconstruction of a small community's picture of itself. It isn't – or not significantly – the maliciously motivated passing-on of information you can use to establish power over someone else. It is the texture of sharp observation and the daily recounting of commonplace events and encounters woven in with lifelong mutual familiarities. The moral tone of such narrative has to be tolerant and conducive to tolerance, because it involves all those who are listening and who have to go on living together. For children's novels try to tell children how to live together better, in both present and future. They seek to portray as many people as they can, and to make as many people as possible recognize themselves as being portrayed. That is the best common purpose which holds all children's writers in a single community. The new formations come into being to extend the portraits, and include the excluded.

William Mayne is the last hero of this trio. He is an extraordinarily prolific writer whose writing addresses itself time and again to the point at which past and present, individual biography and historical movement may be caught in intersection. I spoke earlier of the exceptional purity of his prose, and the fidelity of his attention to children's lives. These are the really indispensable attributes of the rare children's writer who is also, at times, a great writer. To adapt a famous formulation,

Mayne seems to be making major fiction out of a minor mode –
'as if, that is, the genius of a major poet were working in the
material of minor poetry'.[7] The point about Mayne here is not
so much his major or minor status, however, as the strength
and breadth of a man whose writing about and for children
gives him a subject-matter and diction in which to make a series
of structures capable of encompassing some of the main
experiences of the present time. His gifts make him an excep-
tion to Yvor Winters's stricture on most of the adult novelists
now around, and turn our cheerful and our generous optimism
about children's novelists into something rather more quali-
fied:

The most damnable fact about most novelists, I suppose, is their
simple lack of intelligence: the fact that they seem to consider themselves professional writers and hence justified in being amateur intellectuals. They do not find it necessary, so far as one can judge, to study
the other forms of literature, or even forms of the novel other than
those they practice; they do not find it necessary to think like mature
men and women or to study the history of thought; they do not find it
necessary to master the art of prose. And these remarks are equally
true, so far as my experience goes, of those novelists who write pri-
marily for profit, and who boast of being able 'to tell a good story',
and of those who are fiddling with outmoded experimental proce-
dures in the interests of originality and who are sometimes praised in
the quarterlies. In fact the history of the novel is littered with the
remains of genius sacrificed to ignorance and haste.[8]

Once more, the point is not merely to draw up a list of who's
in and who's out. I shall go at greater length into the claims I
make for Mayne in the next chapter but one, when talking of
Earthfasts. Mayne's rarity and relevance for the time being are
that he has found new, simple, and piercingly familiar
metaphors with which to render and understand the presence
of the past. In the brief, beautiful tale *The Battlefield*, the two
children find an old cannon in a field turned to glutinous black
mud by the torrents of rain. Later, when they are sleeping out
(without permission) in the old tower, half-martello half-
medieval, their sense of displacement into a magic, historical
loop tangled up in the old cannon receives dramatic

<hr/>

[7] F. R. Leavis on Keats in *Revaluation: Tradition and Development in English Poetry*
(1936), p. 25.
[8] Yvor Winters, *The Function of Criticism* (1962), p. 39.

confirmation when the tower itself slides on a long moraine of mud into the very centre of the village. One's credulity is not stretched too far by the tale: mountains of mud slid half a mile at Aberfan in Wales in 1966 and at Hazard, Kentucky, in 1963. So you can call the miracle (the children are unhurt) a coincidence, or you can call it magic.

The same magic holds together Mayne's incomparable *The Jersey Shore*. But no, not incomparable: it sits beside Philippa Pearce's *The Children of the House* as another of the kind which makes the distinction between adults' and children's classics temporarily needless. In *The Jersey Shore*, the little boy Arthur, sitting beside his grandfather on the New Jersey seaboard flats some years before the outbreak of the Second World War, hears him speak aloud the narrative of his family history in Norfolk up to the point of his departure for the States in 1886. Piece by piece the story is told, but the old cliché 'jigsaw' does not apply; for Arthur – Art as he is known – does not assemble it according to a pattern. He relives the history – he, a little boy on an old, creaking, unpainted wooden step. The history is in any case his, but he has to hear it in order to reconstruct its meaning.

It may be – the point is very fine – that the novel is *too* opaque for children to understand. Yet children will listen, raptly uncomprehending, as an ancient relative talks unseeingly over their heads. If they refuse to listen – 'Gran's so boring, Miss' – they join the hordes of the amnesiacs. Arthur listens, and is chivvied by his widowed mother, and leaves the stories to settle in his mind. At the serene, elegiac end, he returns to England – or rather, comes home for the first time – as a USAF bomber crew member and, making his way laboriously across the Fens, finds his village, his family, and his history. Finding it out like this – learning by discovery – breaks the grip of the chains which hold men in invisible slavery.

The last, lovely paragraphs are their own commentary, and close my chapter. Perhaps their mode illustrates what I mean by saying that this is major writing within a minor subject-matter. But the moral of *that* is that historical novelists must know how to turn Eliot's *Little Gidding* to such magnificent account as William Mayne does here:

He was about to knock, but he heard people inside and waited a moment in case they had seen him and were coming to the door. They did not come. Above him hung the chain, the chain that had bound the man from the sea, that was to hang there until it broke and freed the family of that man.

He put up a hand and lifted the last link from the nail that held it. The weight fell down the steel loops and rested in his hand. He looped some of the flexible heaviness over his wrist and lifted down the centre of the chain, and then the far end, where the iron collar was that had been round the man's neck when he landed.

The chain swung and rapped on the door for him. He gathered it in to himself, understanding every part of it. He remembered things his father had told him, things that his grandfather had perhaps not clearly known. His grandmother, Florence, the mother of his father, had been born a slave, in captivity. In the first years of her life she had known what chains like this, collars like this, were. Art was descended from slaves. The Lovings were descended from a slave. His grandmother had been freed by a war; the man from the sea by escape and shipwreck.

The door of the house opened. A girl held it open. She drew in her breath when she saw him. She was beautiful. But he had not come to find that out, in particular. He had come to see what it was that had formed his grandfather, and to find the graves he loved and lay some earth from his own grave in them, and raise a headstone. He would have to write home for the names of the children.

But now he understood completely why Benjamin Thatcher had married someone born a slave. He saw that this beautiful girl had the same skin as himself, the same skin as his grandmother; that it was part of her beauty. He was himself captured by it, too. He tried to put the chain down, but dropped one end of it. Somehow he pulled it in two, and a broken link fell separate to the floor.

It was love at first sight; slow, quiet love. He put up his hand to that dark face, as Benjamin had put his to her grandmother, and she pushed her lips against it, almost in a kiss. Then she kissed it, and the rust from the chain marked her lips and cheek, and his hand, light markings against their dark skins. He had come back to Osney, and now between them they had enough years of freedom to be truly free.

IO

Rumours of angels and spells
in the suburbs

History is an intellectually more respectable practice than mythologizing and legend-making. The one shades into the other, as even some recent children's serials on television and the box-office film (which includes Sean Connery's ageing Robin Hood) are earnest to emphasize. No doubt there really was a ragged and raucous British cavalry leader who led a guerrilla group from the Welsh mountains against other chieftains and the new colonizers from Jutland and north-west Europe. The tales of King Arthur then became the consolations of the colonized, and the support of the few who kept up some kind of fight against incomprehensible invasions in the lowlands. To conclude that there is real history concealed in ancient myth is not to say that there is a straight line from the historical novelists to the mythmakers divided only by the boundary between the truths of fact and those of the imagination. Nor does the plain, blunt teacher want to commend the realities of history at the expense of superstition and the supernatural. Rather, I want to establish the deep affinity of two wings of the Tolkien formation, and ask what it is about modern life which has made the rediscovery of the supernatural so intense and familiar a personal experience.

Obviously enough, *The Lord of the Rings* did not *create* this tendency; but it may be taken to stand for it, and it is certainly taken by members of the formation as their emblem. The passage I quoted on p. 195 resounded both with the echoes of high, heroic, and individual action, and with the plangent music of fairyland. That call to action is answered by the historical novelists in their different ways – guarded, or reckless. The music of fairyland is played by its instrumentalists just over the hill of history and buried deep in the next valley glade.

The subject of this chapter is the meaning of that music. It is important to ask, in a general way, why such a mixed bag of students, teachers, parents, symbol minders, and self-sufficient producers, ever emerged under the banners of the counter-culture.[1] We may reply, also in a general way, that they came to see the dominant modes of public thought, the official models of reason, as stunted and pitiful. In judging this way, they joined a long, honourable line of post-Romantic critics of industrial society who have been voicing for many years a proper human distaste for the over-productivity, the waste and headlong destructiveness of an economic and political system which is also capable of freeing men and women from pestilence and famine.

If 'counter-culture' signifies very broadly the student generations of 1968 and after, it makes sense to think of its carrying a strong political charge. The international movements of 1968 drew together the radical student critics of industrialism and gave them a single, striking silhouette. What concerns me here are the theories they proposed that certain important chambers of experience are kept closed by our public thought forms, that it is essential for psychic and for social health that these rooms are aired, and that it is largely in fictions that we may find forms of life capable of using these chambers and restoring them to purpose and humanity. It is no disqualification of the validity of this experience that it is confined to the personal and private world of the novel. An important, necessary aspect of the world-view of the counter-culture is that, although it is itself a sizeable and also socially significant group, it can't really get very much purchase on the levers of power. Consequently, it seeks to imagine values, ways of life, and forms of thinking and imagining – all that may be intended by the term 'ideology' – which are capable of keeping alive a resistance to all in the polity which it condemns, and of nurturing the privacies which make it mean what it does to itself.

These are the political ethics of the back garden. Such ethics may of course lead to inconsistency: the strident damnation of consumerism delivered from the seat of a hatchback sports car. But the seriousness of enclave politics and its imaginary ideal

[1] I first found this term in Theodore Roszak's book, *The Making of a Counter-Culture* (1970), and continue to find that book provides the readiest inventory of the phenomenon.

order is that it seeks to measure its moral action on the scale of its children's lives. It is this practical truth which perhaps accounts for the present degree of interest in children's fiction; certainly it is the truth whose meaning this study most seeks to disclose. The modest, loose-knit family formation which seeks to make its children feel the force of the supernatural, the power of magic, the reality of fairyland, does not on the whole expect to touch the wider fabric of social life, and has no political ambition. It is a voluntary association of a genteelly experimental kind,[2] which does not possess any large theory (though it may seek one) by which to situate itself in the polity and with which to give its moral critique of that polity purchase and plausibility. Rather, it intends no grander consequence for its beliefs than that the lives of its children be given the sense of mystery, magic, faery, and supernatural dread, without which those lives will be ungentle and dried up, coarsened by the vulgar calculus of market-place utilitarianism.

Consequently, teachers and their novelists – the leading architects of this frame of mind – have consciously sought to re-enchant the universe. To make the point vividly, which of us would not be entirely taken aback by the parent who, as I heard one do, breezily insisted to his five-year-old that there was no Father Christmas, that he and his wife filled the child's stocking?

What is it that takes us aback in the anecdote? It is partly the open declaration of the candid rationalism which has won the day for modern science and enlightened social policy. It is partly the secularization of theology which the same victory has brought about, a victory marked by the attempt even on the part of the theologians[3] to accommodate their claims to the dominant styles of thought, definitions of evidence, and admissions of authority. It is partly the denial of what is felt to be part of a child's natural heritage, a heritage which he must grow out of, but which is irreplaceably precious to the process whereby childhood experience becomes treasurable memory. Lastly, what is deadly about such a parent is the clear implication that he will never connive at the deception of his chil-

[2] I take the point here from Stuart Hampshire, 'Russell, Radicalism, and Reason', in *Philosophy and Political Action*, ed. Virginia Held *et al.* (1972).
[3] See Peter Berger's book, which I quote in the chapter heading, *A Rumour of Angels: Modern Society and the Rediscovery of the Supernatural* (1970).

dren, even in the name of the child's greater and harmless pleasure.

The tale of the rationalist parent throws into relief the strong negation of the other side. The rationalist will reappear in Chapter 12 with the vulgar naturalists of the Topliner school of children's fiction. For the moment, he is put down by the army of re-enchanters, whose deep conviction that the world is poorer for being explained by natural science sends it to novels whose purpose is to recreate the reality of magic. Their conviction can, of course, feed on deep, fertile currents in the residues of popular culture. Ghosts and fairies, astrology and palmistry have long worked as the entirely credible political science of the powerless. If the choices open to an individual are finite and very limited, the imagination, if it is to stay alive, thus guaranteeing the freedom of the individual, must provide alternatives whose only hope of realization is by way of chance, spell-weaving or miracle. Any change in such an experience is extraordinary. Hence the importance of fairy godmothers, unicorns, severed heads, Rumpelstiltskins. Magic change is arbitrary and unlooked for. Superstition is its science. In a fixed life without choices, goodness is the only rational virtue, and while such virtue is its own reward, a fairy godmother disguised as an old beggarwoman may still transform the life of the good girl. This is the appeal of the Cinderella story.

The experience of children, even in the rich nations, remains in touch with the pre-industrial peasants who developed the fairy story. Children's experience of the world is hugely contingent: if you transgress what seem to be quite arbitrary rules, noisy and gigantic men will chase and eat you; the dark world is entirely lethal, busy with wolves and demons, and all you can oppose to it is your courage, your docility, and your virtue; the obsession of your elders with love and money turns those mysteries into treasures which may be discovered with the help of magic – you will weave straw into gold, and the glass slipper will fit your tiny, pink foot.

It is fair to say that the structure of these stories has been weakened for those who now seek to guarantee magic a central place in education precisely because their children *have* greater independence, freedom of choice, and some picture not so much of destiny as of private interests. Modern individualism has, for better and worse, diffused the model of a dark and sudden authority which dominates fairy stories with its inevitably Freudian shadow.

In the immense new literature which has sought to work out on behalf of the modern, happy primary-school child a balance between personal autonomy and the many hearts of darkness, little attention seems to have been paid to just how hard it is, what finesse is needed, to match the claims of traditional magicality, usable theory, degrees of personal freedom, and a proper story. A brief example will do to suggest what is involved in the tricky business of bringing magic up to date. Doing so is not a matter of secularizing the magic so that we can see how science really is doing the job. The instinct to re-enchant the universe is a right one: accident, apocalypse, miracle, coincidence, are too everyday for us to dispense with a world-picture which seeks to accommodate and to preserve a proper respect for them.

In her brief, brilliant fairy-tales, *A Necklace of Raindrops*, Joan Aiken understands this. The beautiful title story touches us at our tenderest: the gift of the necklace from the North Wind ensures the safety of the baby from the natural dangers the wind brings – lightning, flood, drowning. The baby can control the rain. But she cannot control human envy and meanness; as she grows up, the necklace is stolen by her jealous friend, recovered by the tiny, gentle creatures (fish, birds, mice) the little girl has befriended, and used by the child at last to bring water to the desert. The tale is, indeed, enchanting. The fantastic power to control the rain is delightful, the moral 'be gentle' is excellent (only harridans would not have children be gentle), the aesthetic truth that the North Wind is strong and necessary is accurate, and the retribution dealt to the thief is fair. A contrast may be made with Roald Dahl's successful *Charlie and the Chocolate Factory* and its sequels. Dahl has a vigorous feel for the raucous, crude vengefulness of children: he catches and endorses this nicely. But his book is stuck for ever in the second and third stages – the legalistic, retributive stages – of Piaget's and Kohlberg's moral development. There is no way with him, as there is so finely in Joan Aiken, of balancing the claims of one's childishness, one's morality, and the mysteries of the natural world.

Joan Aiken's book serves to suggest the artistry needed by the spellbinder. But her artistry *is* artistry because in the end she takes us beyond the magic. To take a point from R. G. Collingwood: 'A magical art is an art which is representative and there-fore evocative of emotion and evokes of set purpose some emotions rather than others in order to discharge them into the affairs of practical life.'[4]

As he goes on to note, it doesn't matter whether such art is good or bad by aesthetic or moral standards, so long as it creates and concentrates strong feeling. My point about Joan Aiken and, later, about Ursula Le Guin's trilogy *Earthsea* and Ted Hughes's tale *The Iron Man* is that their purpose is not only to provoke strong feelings of dread, awe, and mystery which would otherwise be left dormant or unexperienced in children's lives. These writers do undoubtedly create the feelings of dread, but they do not in Collingwood's words narrowly 'discharge them into the affairs of practical life'. What Ursula Le Guin and Ted Hughes do is create a narrative image to which our and our children's right response is 'woe and wonder'.[5] The power of this image to compress real meaning is such that we can carry the image over to the every-day world as a contrast to and measure of its beauty or its blank-ness, its happiness or misery. What, by contrast, the 'magical artists' do, to greater or lesser effect, according to their gifts, is try to raise in children feelings of dread, awe – fear of Dionysus – and panic fear – fear of the great god Pan.

These intentions are prompted, one may say, by the mixture of circumstances and feelings towards them with which we began: science's disenchantment of the universe, the seculariza-tion of religious language and argument, the rationality by computation of the public realm. What it seems some novelists seek to do is arouse these strong feelings via magical art, but en-tirely without any picture of where such feelings can go. Unlike the primitive magical art which Collingwood describes, unlike the example of Kipling (which Collingwood takes) whose arousal of powerfully atavistic feeling could be given up to 1914 a perfectly *practical* context, the undoubtedly strong feelings which these novelists and their admirers wish children to have cannot turn into practical action, nor go any-where in particular. The hoped-for experience is simply the

---

[4] 'Art as Magic', in *The Principles of Art* (1938), chap. IV, p. 69.
[5] Donatus's version of Aristotle's 'Pity and Fear'. Its relevance here is that the terms are not attached to the idea of 'catharsis' or purging of emotion. See J. V. Cunningham, *Tradition and Poetic Structure* (1960).

feelings themselves. Such a novel is then, insofar as it is success-ful, rightly called escapist. It heightens and intensifies emo-tional life, without giving either these emotions or the images which provoke them a way back into experience.

We can see the temptations and the difficulty being worked through with great and stylish enthusiasm in Alan Garner's *Elidor*. Garner's first two novels, *The Weirdstone of Brisingamen* and *The Moon of Gomrath*, are ready examples of the Tolkien formation. As Garner has said with endearing candour, the books are 'the usual condescending pap' but – and much to our point – 'there had to be a start somewhere'.[6] If condescension implies a knowingness about its own peculiar quality, I would say the books are not condescending enough. The novelist seems all too ready with the embarrassing paraphernalia of a phoney magic language, ubiquitous spookiness and totems, two worlds, and all the rest of it. Whether or not it is true for Garner, it is true that the cumbrous, iambic prose of the elo-quent style in these books is uncritically favoured by his fol-lowers, both readers and novelists. Susan Cooper, in her ambitious five-decker *The Dark is Rising*, and Judy Allen both wheel on the same scenery and wardrobe with a readiness and familiarity which underline the availability of the conventions in the genre. Their novels, and those of half a dozen other writers such as Rosemary Harris in *The Bright and Morning Star*, Dennis Hamley in *Pageants of Despair*, Diana Wynne Jones in *Cart and Cwidder* testify to the strong membership and deep feeling evinced in allegiance to these structures and conven-tions.

It is no accident that so many of the tales are set in Wales, or invoke echoes of Arthurian legend and *Idylls of the King*. Judy Allen, at the end of *The Spring on the Mountain*, refers to the book of which Garner first and most tellingly saw the poetic meaning – Alfred Watkins's *The Old Straight Track*. Watkins was an honest antiquarian in the Edwardian mould; his splen-did book records his own patient efforts to reconstruct the ancient system of 'leys' – the intricate grid of 'mounds, beacons, moats, sites, and mark stones', the certain existence of which his single epiphany convinced him:

In his Preface (page v) to *The Old Straight Track* Watkins wrote, 'some

---

[6] In Meek *et al.*, *The Cool Web* (1977), p. 197.

four years ago there stood revealed the original sighting pegs used by the earliest track makers in marking out their travel ways.' The revelation took place when Watkins was 65 years old. Riding across the hills near Bredwardine in his native county, he pulled up his horse to look out over the landscape below. At that moment he became aware of a network of lines, standing out like glowing wires all over the surface of the country, intersecting at the sites of churches, old stones and other spots of traditional sanctity. The vision is not recorded in *The Old Straight Track*, but throughout his life Watkins privately maintained that he had perceived the existence of the ley system in a single flash and, for all his subsequent study, he added nothing to his conviction, save only the realization of the particular significance of beacon hills as terminal points in the alignments.[7]

Garner discovered this book for himself. The moon of Gomrath, rising rarely at the set time and place, reveals the path to the child hero and heroine in a stirring moment. The plot and prose are clumsy; what is so fine is the way Garner captures the prehistoric reality that Watkins patiently documents, and makes it glow again in his imagination.

It is this restoration of electrical tension to old England which these writers seek to achieve. They join, on the shelves, the new guides to megalithic sites, new speculations about the hidden algebra of Stonehenge, walks along Hadrian's wall, herbal remedies, Yoga, meditation, studies in Tarot arts, the novels of John Cowper Powys, the mysteries of Udolpho. The one brilliant image of an otherwise stagey novel, *The Moon of Gomrath*, is the shimmering path caught and lit by the moonbeams, cutting sharp and straight across the countryside to the next Tor. The thrill of that moment is the simplest, essential response to these novels. They intend to press and impress children with the force of time – not, that is to say, with its lessons: they suggest no interrogation of the past, like some of the novelists previously mentioned. They present Time as immense, awful, and as heavy as the atmosphere.

Their devices are largely conventional in the mediocre sense; however decently they do it, they serve merely pedagogic ends. Thus Dennis Hamley in his *Pageants of Despair* is interested to persuade his readers, to the point (surely) of extreme exaggeration, that the Wakefield Mystery plays were both ritual and reality to their medieval audience, being the one

---

[7] Introduction by John Michell, p. xv.

because of the other. It is the sort of point which a good teacher
has to stick rather bluntly into children if they are not to dismiss
all the literature of the past as being less important than *Cross-
roads* simply *because* it is of the past. But such novels smell
perhaps fatally of the project-folder. The converse convention
works only in the holidays. In the novels of Susan Cooper and
Judy Allen, the children are placed in King Arthur's geography
– in Wales, or Cornwall, or Glastonbury – and are set to save the
world from the forces of darkness, before the end of the holidays and without their parents. When all is said and done about
the suspension of disbelief, they remain not just richly improbable – *The Rime of the Ancient Mariner* is that – but either weird
or plain silly. There is no doubt that told by the right teller they
have their power. They exert that power over the harmless,
limited imaginations of the medievalists' commando. Its
members stand staring, caught by the dream of Dartmoor or
the Brecon beacons.

Many of these novelists can touch stirring chords in their
prose. They are the same old druid rhythms as ever, cadenced,
plangent; but for want of their music in the workaday prose of
modern politics and modern novels, or in the dreadful banality
of the Series III prayer book, the prose of these writers, stilted
on ancient place-names and archaic stones, has to do to keep
alive the rhythms of old litanies and incantations.

The implicit form of the mythic novels dramatizes the ne-
gations of liberal individualism. Where the historical novels
threw into relief the meanings and purposes of personal action,
these foreshortened myths cancel the individual in the play of
vast, superhuman forces meeting and swirling on Cader Idris.
The structure is dictated by quite external conditions – the
intersection of place, time, rhymes, and chance, all brought
about by a talisman. The mighty coincidence is set off by
extremes of weather – tempest, flood, balmy maytime, soft,
deep, drifted snows. These are the stage props of the Romantic
agony; the novelists put together the bits and pieces of Yeats's
Celtic twilight and T. S. Eliot's Madame Sosostris in a late,
brave, but largely Georgian and cherryblossom set of minia-
tures. These novels, which some children and more adults read
until they are glassy-eyed and stupefied, take the measure of a
deep longing to hear these decadent rhythms again, and to re-
enchant a world in which magic not only confutes science but

returns the individual to a grander, sacred, but non-political destiny. The danger of the dark is only bookish.

It is, you might say, the Absolute Ideal. That is, in some grisly mixture of Descartes and Hegel and spellbinding thrown up in this corner of popular culture, these novels all rest upon the power of the mind to create and occupy the material world. The hero of Susan Cooper's pentalogy, Will Stanton, seventh son of a seventh son, plays his part in an action dominating the material world but occupying an ideal one. Peter Dickinson's Merlin, in *The Weathermonger*, turns back the clock a thousand years because he hates the industrial revolution, and prefers to bend the national consciousness back into a frame of mind which will outlaw the machine. The wizard of Earthsea, in Ursula Le Guin's trilogy *Earthsea*, fights *his* last battle to the death with his own mind on an islet imagined for the purpose, in a swelling sea. Dr Who fights an entire sequence of Dick Barton duels, ending with upper-cuts in a swamp, while lying unconscious in his evil enemy's laboratory.

Idealism, we recall, is the philosophic doctrine which teaches that the world we know is the product of our ideas about it. At its most extreme, Idealism wonders whether, if we do not think it there, the floor will actually *be* there when we step out of bed. In its commonplace forms it is the doctrine which most people in Britain and the United States learn naturally as they grow up; its limitation is of course that by definition it tends to overvalue the place of ideas in life, and to underplay the significance of material forces, from physical to economic ones. What it obviously permits is the possibility of an ideal world at some remove from the real one. Such a movement of the imagination is presumably possible in any culture, but the habits of Idealist thought enable us to move very much more freely into an imagined world, and having got there, to give it greater significance than the real one.

A radical tradition has long accused Western society of doing this to art. The bourgeoisie, the case goes, has used art as an ideal refuge from an awful reality, and abused it to *justify* that reality. Its critical, reflexive power has been switched off insofar as it has been made merely an escape. Such a charge sticks fairly and squarely to many of the mythic or crypto-Arthurian novels. Dickinson in *The Weathermonger* tries ingeniously to get round it by making the science-fiction into a

critical comparison of industrial and pre-industrial society: he
does this in a necessarily coarse and caricatured picture of
medieval life, bonded by bigotry and cruelty as well as by the
slow, wholesome rhythms of rural work deepened and
enriched by the return of pre-pesticide butterflies and wild
flowers. At the same time he notes not only the convenience of
machinery and medicine, but the tolerance and reasonableness
of the way of life it brings. Furthermore, he devises an attractive way of giving his two children something to do. They are
not the ciphers of so many similar novels; they seek out Merlin
in his latter-day castle, and find that he has been discovered in
his age-old sleep by a well-meaning, small-minded chemist
who sought to bind the magician's power by addicting him in
his sleep to morphine. Merlin's terrible and magnificent spirit
is distorted by the drug but rules the chemist; he causes England
to revert to an Arthurian society, and only when the children
explain his plight to him (in Cambridge Project Latin) does he
renounce the drug voluntarily, 'Perdurabo, deo volente', and
after a hideous withdrawal, unclenches his grip on the country.

It is a rather roughed-out, racy tale, strong and crude.
According to the conventions, it presents to children a picture
of the power of magic and the beauty and honour of the ancient
order. Its narrative fairly strides along. What Dickinson does
not give his novel is a means of mitigating the crude Idealism
whereby Merlin creates a material forest and castle by imagining it, and Geoffrey, the 16-year-old hero, changes the weather
by thinking hard in poetic-meteorological diction. By the
same token, he gives his reader (and the novelist's own intelligence) nowhere to live. For all the agreeable detailing of road
numbers – the A35, the M5 – and place names, the regression of
the country to the old order is as placeless as any monastery or
castle in Hermann Hesse or Mervyn Peake. The strength of the
book lies in its brisk invitation to compare the present outside
the novel with the new machineless age inside it. But the
writer's cheerful, breezy way with his excellent tale only makes
the comparison a casual idea; it is not worked out in any subjective intensity.

Alan Garner, in *Elidor, does* do the working-out. This novel
may be taken to stand for the most forceful version of the re-
statements of magic, and of the complex balance between a felt,
sensational world and an idealized, imaginary one, the first

ugly and workaday, the second picturesque and mysterious. Garner has perhaps the surest ear among these novelists for the strains of a music which, if the analogy will hold, is further from Wagner and closer to the thinner, more plaintive mode of Delius. Moreover, he knows some science, and has thought hard about the question of realizing old magic in the imagery of new electronics. The idea of materializing the visitors from Elidor like television images works excellently:

A white spot had appeared in the middle of each shadow, quivering like a focused beam of light. The spots grew, lessened their intensity, changed, congealed, and became the expanding forms of two men, rigid as dolls, hurtling towards the children. They matched the out-lines of the shadows, and were rising like bubbles to their surface. As they came nearer their speed increased: they rushed upon the children, and filled the shadows, and eclipsed them – and at that instant they lost their woodenness and stepped, two men of Elidor, into the garden.

They were dressed in tunics and cloaks and carried spears. Shields hung on their backs. They were bewildered, and stood as if they had woken in the middle of a dream. Then they both looked at the soil between them where the Treasures were buried.

There was no static electricity in the air, and the hold on the children disappeared. (p. 127)

Garner's achievement is to have given magic a credibility in the terms of modern science. He has brought off on the modest scale of a children's novel what Peter Berger criticizes modern theology for failing in.[8] The theologians, trying to match the supernatural to modern physics, give all the ground away to the enemy. They accept his vocabulary as the only one in which to speak. Garner, sticking to the charter of his formation, and therefore confining his influence to the progressive-primary school, brings together old legend and the inner city. Thus, the three traditional treasures of cross, chalice, and golden stone; thus, too, the electrical overloading which sets unplugged appliances humming, makes all the ammeters peak in the house, sears the TV screen, and crackles on the end of a comb; and thus the transformation of a building site into the Waste Land, a demolished Nonconformist church into the Chapel Perilous, and the sacred objects into an old railing, bits of wood, and a heavy stone.

---

[8] *The Homeless Mind* (1974).

But, alas, Garner wins his success only by archaizing his characters to nothing. His form, his ideas, perhaps his talents, are too clumsy to allow living subjectivity any room. The parents are mere parodies of domestic incomprehension, the children are blanks. Garner's powers of writing an intermittently noble, chaste and silvery prose give his story its genuineness:

David and Nicholas closed round the unicorn, but there was nothing they could do.

'Sing!' cried Roland. 'Before it's too late! You'll be killed!'

Findhorn strove almost as if to speak, but he could not, and he could not.

The man paused: balanced himself to throw.

'Sing: oh, sing.'

Helen cradled his head, and stroked the curls of light.

'Up!' shouted Roland. 'Up! Findhorn! Run! Oh, Findhorn! Findhorn! No!'

The spear hissed down, and sank between the unicorn's ribs to the heart. The white neck arched, and the head lifted to the stars and gave tongue of fire that rang beyond the streets, the city, the cold hills and the sky. The worlds shook at the song.

A brightness grew on the windows of the terrace, and in the brightness was Elidor, and the four golden castles. Behind Gorias a sun-burst swept the land with colour. Streams danced, and rivers were set free, and all the shining air was new. But a mist was covering Findhorn's eyes.

'Now!' said Nicholas. 'Now's our chance! Give them back now!'

He broke the straps on the rucksack to pull at the stone.

The song went on, a note of beauty and terror.

Roland looked through the windows out over Elidor. He saw the tall figure on the battlements of Gorias, with the golden cloak about him. He saw the life spring in the land from Mondrum to the mountains of the north. He saw the morning. It was not enough.

'Yes! Take them!'

He cried his pain, and snatching the cup from Helen, he threw it and the railing at the windows. Nicholas and David threw their Treasures. They struck together, and the windows blazed outwards, and for an instant the glories of stone, sword, spear, and cauldron hung in their true shapes, almost a trick of the splintering glass, the golden light.

The song faded.

The children were alone with the broken window of a slum.

(p. 158)

It is lovely, but it is not true. The old falsehood that poetry
creates a beautiful world of images which can redeem the ugly
world of fact is not strong enough to hold up a novel in
experience. The illusion fades as we put down the book; this
book, and many like it, can only live on as a curious glow in our
memories and imaginations, which lights nothing in our
experience, and only brightens when we hurry back to the
book which charges it. Garner can't write himself out of his
atavism even when he tries to push his characters into the
struggles of class and the geometry of sex. *The Owl Service*
remains fixed in the forcefield of the myth, and the characters
distinct in the stereotypes of upper and working class and the
eternal triangle.

Ursula Le Guin's way out of the arbitrary parallelism of
Now and Then is to make up a new world.[9] It is the device of the
science-fiction writer she is also, and *Earthsea*, though archaic
and picturesque in a Yeatsian sort of way – 'cold Clare rock and
Galway rock and thorn' – is a science-fiction archipelago, a
bleak, vivid reminiscence of Seattle and the Orkneys. But
because her subject matter is larger and more critical than
others in this chapter, her book both meets C. S. Lewis's test –
adults may enjoy it as well as children – and convincingly holds
together the ideal and the real world. That subject-matter
includes far more than the fixed fight between the ideal and the
real. Indeed, she gives children a way of acknowledging the
uncertainty of both categories, and of understanding that the
most universal of human gifts, language, is also the most
wonderful.

She does so, at times, in a dauntingly high-minded tone:

He looked for a spell of self-transformation, but being slow to read the
runes yet and understanding little of what he read, he could not find
what he sought. These books were very ancient, Ogion having them
from his own master Heleth Farseer, and Heleth from his master the
Mage of Perregal, and so back into the times of myth. Small and
strange was the writing, overwritten and interlined by many hands,
and all those hands were dust now. (*A Wizard of Earthsea*, p. 61)

The hand is the hand of Mrs Le Guin, but the voice is her
master's voice, the familiar compound ghost who speaks

9 *A Wizard of Earthsea, The Tombs of Atuan, The Farthest Shore.*

through and for Alan Garner, Susan Cooper, Judy Allen, Rosemary Harris, and all. Ursula Le Guin speaks to a wide audience – her Puffin trilogy has sold over 20,000 copies a year since 1971, and in 1978 was in its eighth printing. She speaks to her audience, I think, on behalf of intelligence, and its struggle to command, however precariously, the surging and unquenchable magic of language itself. She is, after all, an anthropologist and the daughter of anthropologists, concerned with the human science above all. She makes language, as it always was and is for Magi, the special preoccupation of her hero-intellectual. She sends him to university – the island of Roke – and she makes his access to learning the slow, difficult initiation by rite and discipline which for an intellectual it must be. She makes thought a rare vocation, which it is, although she fails to add that those so called to the vocation take the thought in trust for others (the phrase tells); a proper wizard is a man of the people who look up to him, *and* he serves the human mind and its unique responsibility towards the 'living principle' which is given form and regulation in language.

Her books are spare and stark, consciously wrought and shaped. They smell, sometimes intolerably (as Garner's books do), of the study and the library stack; like their fellows they lack not only colour and eventfulness, but also a depth of characterization in which the author is hardly interested, but which it is simply unimaginative and therefore morally unsympathetic to suppose her audience does not count on. With Yeats, she wants to make a 'great magic book of the people', to simplify landscape to cold stone and thorn, character to hawk-like and sinewy purpose, eschatology to the self, pitching in the huge swell of empty seas. Time and again, her brief, rapid, striking tale gets onto the stilts of the epic movie – 'the great oars shot out ... the rowers bent their strong backs' (p. 39) – and a Goodies pastiche – 'I do not understand.' 'That is because my lord Benderesk has not been wholly frank with you. I will be frank. Come sit by me here' (p. 132). Never mind. The best events in these books – the first and last splits Ged causes in the universe, the last defeat of the dragons, the two passages through the valley of the shadow of death, the rescue of the mistress of Atuan – these are set pieces of grand storytelling.

The larger moral climate they move in is abstract and austere. Ursula Le Guin rescues Idealism and its magic grammar from its role in children's novels as a measure of the dreariness of the present day, and restores it to its importance at the heart of intellectual life. She leaves children out of it, gives the action back to the Shaman-Magus, and simply assumes that the children will follow such a man – he starts out a boy – wherever he goes. Her ideal world of Earthsea is, for all its archaism, a recognizable and real world – it has its Cities of the Plain, its plague, treason, and debauchery, as well as the lean, brown, long-striding wizard.

Some remarks of Walter Benjamin's, though difficult, may help to suggest the evanescence, however haunting, of so much children's myth-literature:

The image becomes a rune in the sphere of allegorical intuition. When touched by the light of theology, its symbolic beauty is gone. The false appearance of totality vanishes. The image dies; the parable no longer holds true; the world it once contained disappears.[10]

It is an opaque passage. I use it to claim that *Elidor* and company separate the inner from the outer worlds, the subjective from the objective. When these novels do this, as it is the distinction of *Elidor* to show so clearly, objective reality becomes fixed and harsh, the subjective, inner world transforms itself into something unintelligible, glimmering, substanceless, something beautiful and sinister. Both are static. Mrs Le Guin, however, keeps her hero busy, and even though her only moral lesson is the strong moral of the liberal tradition, 'know thyself', it is good enough to keep someone as important as a Magus upright, and to lend him both concrete life and moral typicality.

For magic to matter, it must give rise to more than unfocussed feelings of dread. For children this latter is at best a pleasant thrill in a firelit evening room, a nice dose of the horrors. In a magnificently clear, strong essay Ted Hughes analyses the meaning of myths in a modern child's education:

In the last decade or two, the imprisonment of the camera lens has begun to crack. The demonized state of our inner world has made itself felt in a million ways. How is it that children are so attracted

---

[10] *The Origin of German Tragic Drama* (1977), p. 166.

towards it? Every new child is nature's chance to correct culture's error. Children are most sensitive to it, because they are the least conditioned by scientific objectivity to life in the camera lens. They have a double motive, in attempting to break from the lens. They want to escape the ugliness of the despiritualized world in which they see their parents imprisoned. And they are aware that this inner world we have rejected is not merely an inferno of depraved impulses and crazy explosions of embittered energy. Our real selves lie down there. Down there, mixed up among all the madness, is everything that once made life worth living. All the lost awareness and powers and allegiances of our biological and spiritual being. The attempt to re-enter that lost inheritance takes many forms, but it is the chief business of the swarming cults . . .

Objective imagination, then, important as it is, is not enough. What about a 'subjective' imagination? It is only logical to suppose that a faculty developed specially for peering into the inner world might end up as specialized and destructive as the faculty for peering into the outer one. Besides, the real problem comes from the fact that outer world and inner world are interdependent at every moment. We are simply the locus of their collision. Two worlds, with mutually contradictory laws, or laws that seem to be so, colliding afresh every second, struggling for peaceful coexistence. And whether we like it or not our life is what we are able to make of that collision and struggle.

So what we need, evidently, is a faculty that embraces both worlds simultaneously. A large, flexible grasp, an inner vision which holds wide open, like a great theatre, the arena of contention, and which pays equal respects to both sides, which keeps faith, as Goethe says, with the world of things and the world of spirits equally. [11]

He exemplifies his own homily in his tale, *The Iron Man*, *A Story in Five Nights*. It is only 59 pages long, and intended, I suppose, for quite little children; but it is indisputably a great modern myth.

Hughes's energy and his humour are enormous, and his prose is up to both. When the Iron Man lies smashed at the foot of the cliff, only this astonishing imagination could perform its reassembly for us:

Then the other gull flew up, wheeled around, and landed and picked something up. Some awkward, heavy thing. The gull flew low and slowly, dragging the heavy thing. Finally, the gull dropped it beside the eye. This new thing had five legs. It moved. The gulls thought it was a strange kind of crab. They thought they had found a strange

---

[11] 'Myth and Education', in Fox *et al.*, *Writers, Critics and Children* (1976), pp. 91–2.

crab and a strange clam. They did not know they had found the Iron Man's eye and the Iron Man's right hand.

But as soon as the eye and the hand got together the eye looked at the hand. Its light glowed blue. The hand stood up on three fingers and its thumb, and craned its forefinger like a long nose. It felt around. It touched the eye. Gleefully it picked up the eye, and tucked it under its middle finger. The eye peered out, between the forefinger and thumb. Now the hand could see.

It looked around. Then it darted and jabbed one of the gulls with its stiffly held finger, then darted at the other and jabbed him. The two gulls flew up into the wind with a frightened cry. (pp. 15–16)

Hughes's brief tale resists with a poet's power any plonking attempt to tuck it into sociology. The concrete life is unquenchable; the muscular prose gets up off the page. Hughes creates from nothing a new myth of industrial society. The monster of technology is at first motivelessly auto-destructive, and gradually gains its own mysterious autonomy in collaboration with human kindness. The unforgettable picture of the Iron Man's feast in the scrapyard catches in the ancient myth of Gargantua the idea of an ordered, self-replenishing, benign, and *tidy* industrial machine, such as is prohibited by the squalid wastefulness of modern productivity. But the machine saves the world, once the world understands it. When the fearful space–bat–angel–dragon flattens Australia and comes to eat the world up, the small giant of technology challenges and defeats the vast threat of the cosmos. Culture defeats nature. But only just.

The Iron Man nodded. But his answer was to signal to the engineers. Once more they poured oil into the trough under the grid. Once more they lit up. Once more the flames roared up and the black smoke billowed up into the clear blue. And once more the Iron Man stretched himself out on the grid of the raging furnace.

The space-bat–angel–dragon watched in horror. He knew what this meant for him. He would have to go once more into the sun's flames.

And now the Iron Man's hair and toes and elbows were red-hot. He lay back in the flames, smiling up at the dragon. And his whole body was becoming red-hot, then orange, and finally white, like the blazing wire inside an electric bulb.

At this point, the Iron Man was terribly afraid. For what would happen if the flames went on getting fiercer and fiercer? He would melt. He would melt and drip into the flames like so much treacle and that would be the end of him. So even though he grinned up at the dragon as though he were enjoying the flames, he was not enjoying them at all, and he was very very frightened. (p. 53)

I cannot give the close reading this richly good-humoured tale deserves. When I read it, I think of George Orwell's sympathetic impression when reading any 'strongly individual piece of writing' of 'a face somewhere behind the page that the writer *ought* to have'.[12] Hughes's face is that of a big, enormously powerful man, a man in his forties with a deeply lined and rugged face, a deep kindly voice, a clapping, generous laugh and wide, grim smile. It is the face of a capacious and contained man. His story *The Iron Man*, like his poems *Season Songs*, restores real magic to the material world by force of a new ideal language. That force splits the hairline between ideal and material pictures of the world. It is the energy of myth, and proper magic.

[12] 'Charles Dickens', in *Collected Essays* (1961).

I I

Experiments with time
and notes on nostalgia

Hughes sets his brief, bold tale in an everyday geography. I
have criticized the other myth-makers for having removed
themselves too exclusively to more remote lands – either to the
galaxies of inner space, within individual minds, or to a world
in which inhuman forces push the not very convincing characters around the chequer-board of a doom-laden determinism.
In the novels, though it is always a very near thing, apocalypse
never comes, nor do these writers even imagine what it would
look like. As I have suggested, their static, timeless territory is
made exempt from history and state; that is why the prose
sounds such an archaic harmony. The novelists generalize their
perfectly justifiable fear of the modern world into unspecific
and stateless menace. It is too crude to say that because they are
members of a powerless elite, their stories symbolize their
helpless incomprehension before the tides of politics. That
would deny the strength of an individual intelligence to reach
out and seize the meanings of what is going on apparently
without meaning round about him. The greatest novelists –
Tolstoy, Dickens, George Eliot – *are* great because they can do
this. They have, as we say, the grasp. The three greatest children's novelists of the present – William Mayne, Philippa
Pearce, and Joan Aiken – bring off, in a smaller compass, the
same triumph.

Thus, the forms and conventions of imaginative expression
in a particular genre – the novel, in this case – show us the truths
and fictions, the *meanings*, possible to a social formation at a
given time. The myth-makers try to bring out the mystery of
the universe, and the uncontrollable nature of some of the
forces in life. But in taking the expression they do, they tend in
their very different ways to omit the value dimensions they
most cherish. They rightly sense a crisis of definition in time
and the self. But in the structure of their stories they deny the

movement of the first and cut out the intensity of the second.

It is presumably a consequence of the fact that, as Marx announced in 1848, 'all history has become world history',[1] that our models of time have become various and contradictory. Rates of change speed up and slow down in wholly unpredictable ways; they vary according to the knowledge you have, and where you live, according to whether you are inside or outside a particular society. Science-fiction is both a symptom of and a response to this state of affairs. By and large, science-fiction written for children is a pretty crude affair. There are exceptions, as we have seen, in *The Weathermonger* and, if we call it science-fiction, in *Earthsea*. According to staffroom folklore, science-fiction appeals to boys, and insofar as it is supposed to be boyish to enjoy a dose of the horrors and a taste for violence, then a brief tale like Nicholas Fisk's *Grinny* illustrates the genre. Grinny is some sort of extra-stellar android who arrives with sudden, muffled but malignant purpose, who is thwarted in this purpose, and ends by being nastily disembowelled. The novel reveals no interest in either science or its fiction: it turns on the horrid fascination *Grand Guignol* has always had with being eaten alive by rats, but makes this less awful by transforming both rat and body into machines. Which is all very well, or rather nasty, depending how it takes you, but is nothing to do with the serious business of placing yourself in a manageable chronology.

The preferable way is not necessarily to write deliberately political novels. John Christopher was well acknowledged in winning the *Guardian*'s award for a children's novel in 1971 with the novel *The Guardians*. His scheme derives from *The First Men on the Moon*, with its simply divided play-creatures and proletariat, and *1984*, with its extreme notions of super-efficient mind-control. Christopher asserts, against the menaces of mindlessness (a result of lobotomy or of idle over-cultivation, or of popular vulgarity), the good radical virtues of free thought and speech, and direct subversion. Well and good enough for a short political lesson, but a lesson all too easily read at any modern matins. We all hate the prospect of *1984*; the strong-jawed defence of personal freedom is by now no more than a decent banality.

[1] In *The German Ideology*, with Friedrich Engels, trans. and ed. T. J. Arthur (1970), p. 69.

What makes a novel, for adults and children alike, so unique an instrument of moral and metaphysical inquiry is, in the hands of an artist, its insistent, searching movement along the line between the ideal and the real, the inner and the outer, the subjective and the objective. Because their business is language, the best writers know that they live in the 'third realm', the domain which is neither subjective nor objective, but the locus of symbols which control our versions of both. William Mayne's novel *Earthfasts* is, in its way, an example of science-fiction, but what is so strong and vivid in it is the way he presses the strong personalities of his two heroes up against their possible understanding of time. Their effort to understand their experience of time is never merely self-absorbed – they want most urgently to understand the things which are happening *out there*. Nonetheless, the understanding lives necessarily in terms of the boys' friendships, their schooling, the little Northern market town, the present day.

The book is not therefore an experiment in time. Time is just the strongest dimension, the concept in terms of which friendship, intelligence, and independence find their embodiment. To say so makes the novel sound as though it is merely experimental. But its opening pages are sharp and immediate, and extremely frightening. They end with the reappearance of the solid, actual, eighteenth-century drummer boy who had disappeared into a tunnel 200 years ago, trying to discover where it came out. The first section of the book becomes an object lesson in the first principle of placing yourself in time: that you measure yourself against someone differently placed. The shock of both difference and recognition in the encounter between the drummer boy and Keith and David brings home not only the ghostliness of the moment (although Nellie Jack John is steadfastly *not* a ghost) but also its humanity.

Keith took the map and looked at it. 'He's been by Heseltine's farm,' he said. 'The two Miss Heseltines still wear black clothes like a hundred years ago, so they won't look very different.'

'But their brother has a tractor,' said David. 'That'd make him think. And young turkeys. There might not have been turkeys in his day.'

'Nor Northern Dairy Shorthorns,' said Keith. 'I wonder what he'd think to that, with them all dehorned. He won't have seen that.'

'The trouble is,' said David, 'you're like everybody else will be. You're thinking that it'll be interesting to see what he'll do when he sees unusual things. Everybody's a blooming scientist.'

'Well,' said Keith.

'Well,' said David. 'That isn't the point. He isn't a sort of rat to do experiments on. We haven't got to see what he does about things. We've got to see what they do to him. He's a person, isn't he? He's a human. He's got his own private life and his thoughts, and his feelings; and he never meant to come here. He isn't a flying saucer, exploring. He shouldn't be here at all. I don't think he can ever get back to where he came from, or find anybody he ever knew. So what we've got to do is help him to be happy now he's got here. It would be cruel to experiment with him, and wrong. When he's got used to this world, then we can ask him what it felt like at first. He isn't a rat.'

'You've said that,' said Keith.

'I know,' said David. 'It's the most important thing after saying he *is* human. He isn't a rat, so there's no excuse for observing him. He can tell us with his own mouth all the rest of his life. So stop being a scientist, and start being a person yourself, and let's try to help him.'

'I agree with you, really,' said Keith. 'Only it's easy to see the other way. That's all. It's the quickest thought.'

'It's a hire-purchase thought,' said David. 'You think of it and buy it, and pay for it all the rest of your life. Now let's find another place to watch from. We're not observing, we're a lifeboat.'

'Haul away,' said Keith. (pp. 40–1)

Mayne stresses a central moral point, and makes it tellingly simple to experience (and therefore to believe) a moral lesson which is as powerful as it is traditionally liberal. It underlies the theory of literature and its relation to life which this book expresses. I paraphrase from the writings of Peter Strawson.[2] Exceptionally, we can have direct dealings with human beings without any degree of personal involvement, treating them simply as creatures to be handled in some special way suitable to their own or society's interests (idiots are an example). In a parallel but not identical way, we may do the same with ordinary people to 'see how they work' (the anthropologist or the educational researcher, perhaps, in his participant observation). But in either case we are clearly abandoning the normal attitudes of interpersonal relations for different and local reasons; we are, as David says in *Earthfasts*, treating the subject as a sort of rat. To that extent, we are denying not so

[2] In the title essay of his collection of papers, *Freedom and Resentment* (1975).

much the freedom or otherwise of human action, but the rationality of interpersonal life. That rationality, in turn, rests upon our living within the facts, such as they are, of human nature, and understanding that our moral attitudes *express* (as well as distort) that nature. Any effort to over-objectify or analyse that nature, or to over-homilize it, leads to a loss of human balance and too much intellectualism.

Earthfasts is so good because it dramatizes these facts, in the lives of its characters. In the second section of the book, after the drummer boy goes back into the ground, David pursues the meaning of the dislocations in time round about him which have produced medieval boars and antediluvian giants. Mayne picks up and weaves together old legend and new science in a way which shows up the legends as useful hypotheses and the new science as methodically powerful and personally dangerous. The giants have decongealed from the massive stones they have been for many millennia. A boggart, which is a slightly touchy house spirit, with a taste for milk and other little gifts, which doesn't 'greatly care for cats and dogs', moves in on a harmless, cheerful farmer and his wife, turns their milk, and teases the pets. The details of the timeslip go along with the loving care with which Mayne creates the life of Arkengarthdale – as witness the escaped foxhounds who look in at church, 'sneeze very loudly, and go into the public bar of the Rose & Crown, behind the counter, and lap up a great deal of beer and a tin of crisps' (p. 90). When David is inexplicably removed from the open, empty fell, Mayne is well able to show us the human terms of the shock, the dreadful loss both to Keith and to David's widower father.

The range of feeling in the novel is wide: from the great good humour with which the attractively maddening boggart is described, to the grief which overcomes the initial shock when Keith goes back to the place where David disappeared:

'You shouldn't be up here,' said the policeman, with no touch of authority in his voice, only sympathy.

'This is the place,' said Keith, and his voice lost itself on the hillside.

'Aye, but not the place for you, lad,' said the policeman. 'Don't you think I'd better take you home?'

Keith looked at the ground. There was no sign of anything strange there at all. There was only the level sheep pasture, and the Trod dinting it. There was no mark to indicate that here David had died in a way that Keith himself had only just begun to realize. To him it had been a black line, to Frank Watson it had been lightning. Whatever it had been, it had taken David; and never again would he walk here with him, never again talk to him or see him, or hold any traffic of conversation with him. He had gone, as the drummer boy had gone, and unless some future time brought him out again, he was gone for ever.

'I will go,' he said, and turned. He saw the whole world empty before him, the town smoke showing beyond the next ridge, and nothing left in it for him, now that David had been pulled out from it. All at once he knew what it had felt like to be a lost being in a strange world, what it had felt like to be Nellie Jack John, and why David had been so careful with him and for him. He understood, now that his face was put against it, what David had known by instinct, that the lost places are in this world and belong to the people in it and are all that they have to call home.

A wave of physical sorrow came to him, and he went on his knees and covered his face, though that would not hide it. It did not hide the sobs that came now; and the tears that sprang against his will from his tissues, out from his body like earthquakes. The policeman stood by making a comforting noise, and urging him to stand up with a hand under his arm. Keith stood, at last, and the policeman led him down the hill, and to his house, empty of everything, and new. (pp. 136–7)

The third section of the book recounts how Keith, always more warmly earthbound and less physically and metaphysically speculative than David, follows his friend to the source of the timeslip and replaces in its rightful socket the cold flame of the candle the drummer boy carried. The candle is a sort of rivet of time; out of place, the cogs of time slip, wrong points on their rims come together. We may say that the wheels turn momentously towards each other, crossing the space-time which they regulate; once more King Arthur is the dynamo of enormous temporal disturbance. (His story is an extraordinary power-line to the imagination of many writers.) Keith just escapes from Arthur's sword, returns the King and his knights to limestone, and finds David and Nellie Jack John braced against the gravity of the time-loop.

'He's pushing against time,' said Keith. 'Try going back.'

David took a step back the way they had come. At once he found what Nellie Jack John was pushing against. He had once been on the back of a motor bike coming down Vendale. At a twisty humpy railway bridge the driver had put the brakes on firmly, and had slowed from eighty-five to twenty-five in the shortest possible space of time. David, hidden behind the driver, had felt the deceleration right through himself, as if the world were slowing down with him and becoming heavier with him.

'It's the weight,' he said. 'What shall we do with him?'

'He's been going a long time,' said Keith. 'There's hardly any light left in the torch.'

'It's been thinned out by time,' said David. 'That would be a natural effect. Shall we turn him round?'

So they turned him slowly round. One moment he was a dead weight in their hands, and the next he was running as fast as they could go, drumming violently, and sniffing at the same time.

'He's been all this time,' said David. 'Gosh.'

'We shouldn't have done it,' said Keith. 'It was wrong. He should have gone back the way he was going.'

'He never got there,' said David. 'You know he didn't. It would be better if he came with us, wouldn't it? It isn't an experiment any more. It's an actual event.' (pp. 179–80)

Nor, as I said, is the novel an experiment; it is an actual event. In an affectionately relieving end, all three boys go safely home (in 1966), and the excellent coroner

came in, twisted his yellow jaws, looked at David, put the jaw back in place, and said it was the first time he had spoken to a client after the event. (p. 186)

If the pleasure of science-fiction is to amaze its reader with the improbability of its future, the point of real fiction is to return us to the real world with a larger sense of what it may become. *Earthfasts* has its slips, no doubt – the cold flame itself is a bit weak – but it breaks any too compact account of genres, form, social classes and the like. It is a mark of our times to be anxious about time; Mayne turns anxiety into experience, both joyous and fearful, and does so by filling to the brim the terms of human reference available to him, in the very tip of a North Yorkshire town in 1966, with its first-rate grammar school, stability and continuity with its past, its gifted doctor, sane and steady policeman, farmers, and housewives.

I judge *Earthfasts* to be a classic, as I hope I have explained and justified the term. *Tom's Midnight Garden* is its peer. It is, if you like, a less intellectual novel, although there can be no doubt at all about the strength and stamina of Philippa Pearce's intelligence. It has a less explicit purpose and, in spite of Tom's desperate curiosity and speculation about the location of himself and Hatty, and of both in relation to the garden, it is less directly theoretical about the ways we can understand time. I suppose the novel acknowledges the truth of Lukács's insight into modernism that 'subjective idealism has already separated time, abstractly conceived, from historical change and particularity of place'. 'Experienced time', he goes on, 'now [i.e. with the advent of Kafka and Musil, the philosophy of Bergson] became identical with real time; [and] the rift between this time and that of the objective world was complete. [Those] who took up and varied this theme claimed that their concept of time alone afforded insight into authentic reality.'[3] William Mayne, faced with these disjunctures and, like Philippa Pearce, far too intelligent not to see how centrally important they are to all that his novels embody – the definitions of personal identity made possible by inter-personal and *impersonal* values – comes up with a brisker answer than Mrs Pearce's. Brisker, but not necessarily more truthful. His continued attention to the meanings of time, its amenability to science and metaphor, from *A Grass Rope* (1957) via *Earthfasts* and *Ravensgill* (1970) to *The Jersey Shore* (1973), is a token of the importance of the matter to this most intelligent man.

Philippa Pearce's attention is of a different order. She acknowledges, as I say, that time is a deep problem in the structure of modern experience. She is however less directly interested in the contradiction of personal with objective time; what she wants to do is to use the break as the space in which to place her graceful reminiscence. It sounds too tricky a point to make in connection with what is, on the face of it, a simple and diagrammatic plot. Tom, holidaying in quarantine with his dull, childless uncle and aunt who live in a flat converted from an old house notices an exceptionally fine longcase clock in the hall. Though so distinguished, it is idiosyncratic; it is also masterful of time itself. When it strikes thirteen each night, Tom can go downstairs, unfasten the heavy, latticed and beamed back door, and go out into the most perfect of great Victorian gardens, where by day there are only the dustbins, a hard lean-to, and the divided suburban gardens beyond. In the garden he finds Hatty, an orphan taken in for cold, deadly charity by her aunt, mistress of the house. Hatty is tolerated by her three boy-cousins, and loved by Tom. Only she, the

[3] Georg Lukács, *The Meaning of Contemporary Realism* (1963), p. 37.

benign gardener Abel, and the fauna of garden and meadow can see Tom.

Mrs Pearce writes, in contrast to William Mayne's plain and beautiful observation, the poetry of reminiscence. As Walter Benjamin writes:

For an experienced event is finite – at any rate, confined to one sphere of experience; a remembered event is infinite, because it is only a key to everything that happened before it and after it. There is yet another sense in which memory issues strict weaving regulations. Only the actus purus of recollection itself, not the author or the plot, constitutes the unity of the text. One may even say that the intermittence of author and plot is only the reverse of the continuum of memory, the pattern on the back side of the tapestry. [4]

Philippa Pearce removes Tom from his well-loved family and the brother Peter who earnestly tries to dream himself into his beloved brother's new world. Once with the dreary Kitsons, Tom can find a past which in its splendour *and* its miseries – Hatty's relatives are cold and cruel to her – gives the reminisced past its intolerably attractive richness and meaning. The novel once more turns to the remembered golden summers and white winters of its oldest inhabitants. (The winter of 1895 when Tom and Hatty skate from Castleford to Ely is the one which Arthur Ransome was recalling when he transposed it to *Winter Holiday*.) Philippa Pearce's writing belongs to a later period. I take *Tom's Midnight Garden* to inaugurate the present 'golden age of children's literature';[5] her self-awareness is such that she can both understand clearly that she is celebrating an idealized past, and make that reminiscence (not a literal reminiscence, but Walter Benjamin's 'fiction, autobiography, and commentary in one') into her own real subject. For the garden is the garden of old Mrs Bartholomew the landlady's dream, and the landlady is Hatty.

Tom nodded. He understood so much now: why the weather in the garden had always been perfect; why Time in the garden had sometimes jumped far ahead, and sometimes gone backwards. It had all depended upon what old Mrs Bartholomew had chosen to remember in her dreams.

Yet perhaps Mrs Bartholomew was not solely responsible for the garden's being there, night after night, these last weeks. For she

[4] *Illuminations* (1970), pp. 204–5.
[5] John Rowe Townsend, *Written for Children* (1976), p. 332.

remarked to Tom now that never before this summer had she
dreamed of the garden so often, and never before this summer had she
been able to remember so vividly what it had felt like to be the little
Hatty – to be longing for someone to play with and for somewhere to
play.

'But those were the things I wanted here, this summer,' said Tom,
suddenly recognizing himself exactly in Mrs Bartholomew's description. He had longed for someone to play with and for somewhere to
play; and that great longing, beating about unhappily in the big
house, must have made its entry into Mrs Bartholomew's dreaming
mind and had brought back to her the little Hatty of long ago. Mrs
Bartholomew had gone back in Time to when she was a girl, wanting
to play in the garden; and Tom had been able to go back with her, to
that same garden. (p. 224)

This, it must be admitted, is in its triteness something of a dis-
appointing solution to the miraculous displacement in time
which has been the heart of Tom's being for the length of the
book. And it doesn't explain everything: Hatty really did
know Tom when she was a girl; she kept her promise to leave
her skates for him to find sixty-odd years later in a secret hiding
place and for him to take back in 1895 and skate on, beside and
distinct from her, while she skated on the same boots.
So there is a fudging at the very heart of the novel. It will
bother every reader, adult or child, who wishes to follow the
author to the deep truths of which her eloquent, plain prose is
capable. It is not enough to say, with the aestheticians of the
romantic image, that time is a mystery and that it does not do to
poke and pry too much into the meaning of a symbol. A poet is
an image-maker, certainly; and an image is worshipful; but it is
not ineffable – a crucifix or a madonna *mean* much, but mean
them precisely. So the picture of time in this novel is muddled.
The noble quotation from Revelation doesn't help us to see
what is so important to Tom and to us. What he seeks is his
place in the factual world of the late nineteenth century, as well
as the meaning of his friendship with Hatty, both for him and
for her. If these matters are to be left not so much unanswered as
unanswerable, then the book begins to look like a spoof, and all
we can salvage from it are the lovely evocations of the English
garden at the most perfect point of its historical development.
But of course, 'salvaging' a whole novel is hardly a useful metaphor. The midnight garden *is* the novel, and the pure joy and

happiness it brings to Tom necessarily engage with the time problem at the twistpoint of the book.

At the end of chapter IV, Tom has sufficiently understood the strangeness of the conundrum to know that when he goes outside at the thirteenth hour, the garden will be there:

And the grandfather clock still went on striking, as if it had lost all count of time; and, while it struck, Tom, with joy in his heart, drew the bolt, turned the door-handle, opened the door and walked out into his garden, that he knew was waiting for him. (p. 35)

At the wonderful beginning of chapter V, so it is:

This grey, still hour before morning was the time in which Tom walked into his garden. He had come down the stairs and along the hall to the garden door at midnight; but when he opened that door and stepped out into the garden, the time was much later. All night – moonlit or swathed in darkness – the garden had stayed awake; now, after that night-long vigil, it had dozed off.

The green of the garden was greyed over with dew; indeed, all its colours were gone until the touch of sunrise. The air was still, and the tree-shapes crouched down upon themselves. One bird spoke; and there was a movement when an awkward parcel of feathers dislodged itself from the tall fir-tree at the corner of the lawn, seemed for a second to fall and then at once was swept up and along, outspread, on a wind that never blew, to another, farther tree: an owl. It wore the ruffled, dazed appearance of one who has been up all night.

Tom began to walk round the garden, on tiptoe. At first he took the outermost paths, gravelled and box-edged, intending to map for himself their farthest extent. Then he broke away impatiently on a cross-path. It tunnelled through the gloom of yew-trees arching overhead from one side, and hazel nut stubs from the other: ahead was a grey-green triangle of light where the path must come out into the open again. Underfoot the earth was soft with the humus of last year's rotted leaves. (pp. 35–6)

The suddenly glad quickening of rhythm in the sentences from the end of chapter IV realize, make real, the excited anticipation with which we all step out of the door. Thereafter, with slow, careful, absorbing detail, the author educates her reader into the rich, dense culture (in all senses) of the classical English garden. It is amazingly well done. But there is a parallel narrative. The magnificent freedoms of the garden are dearly bought at the expense of systematic cruelty and repression from Aunt

Melbourne and at the expense, too, of the anguished premature experience of the orphan we meet on page 96:

Even her hair was black, and had been tied with a black hair-ribbon. Now the ribbon had come undone and her loose hair fell forward over her face, and her hands were up to her face too, hiding it; she was sobbing into her hands.

Tom had never seen a grief like this. He was going to tiptoe away, but there was something in the child's loneliness and littleness that made him change his mind. This morning especially, for some reason, he could not say this was none of his business. He came up close to the child, and – it seemed silly, for no one but Hatty in all that garden had ever heard his voice – he spoke. 'Don't cry,' he said.

To his surprise, she did hear him: she turned slightly towards him, as if for comfort; but she did not cease her weeping, nor take her hands from her face.

'What are you crying for?' asked Tom gently.

'For home!' she wept. 'For my mother – for my father!'

Then Tom understood the meaning of the funeral black she was wearing and of that desolate, ceaseless crying.

Philippa Pearce intends that her boy shall be neither an implausible young adventurer nor a passive observer. His ordinary, irresistible human sympathy forces him into human contact across and through the peculiar dislocation of time and space which joins him to and separates him from the garden. He learns again what he knows of the great joy of gardens, and all they provide by way of freedom and order, nature and culture. He learns also that such freedom and beauty not only coincided with but were a consequence of the hateful Aunt Melbourne and the way of life of which she was a significant stay. He learns, as the children of the house learn, that the oppressed befriend the oppressed: Abel the gardener watches over and protects Hatty to the limits of his powers, both social and religious. This learning is made open to him by the author's faultless tact. She pushes past the mistiness and plangency, which are always apt to hang over reminiscence, into the plenitude of facts her transparent, solid prose is well able to carry:

They advanced slowly – Hatty slightly in the rear; the goslings steered far ahead, squeaking and making for the river, and the two geese went with them, and then, last of all, came the gander. He lurched along, his voice calling angrily, the feathers of his long neck rutted with anger, his head turning now to one side, now to the other, so that one eye was always backward-looking on his enemies. Every so often, he would slew round altogether, and raise himself high to front them, and then suddenly drop his head and neck forward and down, almost level with the ground, and begin a snake-like run at Tom, hissing. It was always Tom he ran at, because by then Hatty would be well behind Tom and concealed by him as far as was possible.

The gander's run stopped short of Tom. He sheered off at the last instant, and went back to his waddling; he caught up with the geese and goslings and followed them, on the look-out, as before.

By this progress, the whole gaggle in time reached the river and launched themselves upon it. Then they swam up and down in the water – the elders squawking protests, the goslings rather forgetting the danger they were supposed to have been in. Tom and Hatty sat down on the river-bank, or wandered by it. (p. 86)

At such a moment, the fidelity of detail takes us far beyond accurate observation: the hard realization of the scene gives us its value. There is no strain on the prose imposed by the disloca-ton in time – the children are themselves, braving the geese for the sake of the adventure.

And yet, of course, the source of the novel's energy is the time-slip, the contrast between the past and present which it permits. And having done all she does, having rendered the garden and the unforgettable beauty of the skating expedition which evidences the great extension of the maturing Hatty's geography, Philippa Pearce still can't quite crack the complex atomic totality of the whole problem. Tom is never really at risk. His stable self remains what it always has been, in spite of the breaking of the constant of time. Similarly, Hatty simply grows up and away from her solitary playmate into a natural womanhood. She is, in both senses, only touched by Tom's love.

A defender of the novel may rejoin that children could hardly cope with a novel which really loosened the structures of self into time, and sought to see what friendship could then mean. He might justly say that she has done so much – within itself the book is so beautifully plotted and every detail, such as the fallen fir-tree or Abel's Bible, safely gathered in – that to ask for more is to muddle things. I think not. She has not thought herself far enough into the metaphors of time; she pulls back into the inad-equate dream-explanation, which only leaves her with the moving, small moral that a boy may see in an old lady not only her achieved old age, but her girlhood also:

Afterwards, Aunt Gwen tried to describe to her husband that second parting between them. 'He ran up to her, and they hugged each other as if they had known each other for years and years, instead of only having met for the first time this morning. There was something else, too, Alan, although I know you'll say it sounds even more absurd . . . Of course, Mrs Bartholomew's such a shrunken little old woman, she's hardly bigger than Tom, anyway: but, you know, he put his arms right round her and he hugged her good-bye as if she were a little girl.' (p. 229)

It is a time for tears. The tears would signify, in Yeats's phrase, 'the melting of the dykes which separate men from men'. Such tears are the proper end of such a tale for children and their parents; they soften the heart. They are warmly sympathetic and all the better for that. The two novels with which I end this chapter, however, provoke tears in a different way. In *The Children of the House*, Philippa Pearce partly puts aside the time questions, partly holds them at the distance of another person's memoir, and therefore resolves her difficulties of form. In any case, she produces – with her co-author – another classic. In *Carrie's War*, Nina Bawden uses the same form – a mother's tale (presumably autobiographical, at least in its germination) told to her children, thirty years on. In both novels, we can hear clearly the tone of an adult (a parent perhaps, or even a stranger) whose tact with children is unfailing telling children about his or her own childhood, simply because children love such tales. 'Tell us about when you were a little boy, Daddy.' Both writers hit with absolute unselfconsciousness the note with which to oblige such a demand.

The Children of the House resumes the same themes and experience as *Tom's Midnight Garden*. The present day is taken for granted as the experience and knowledge with which the reader arrives; we are placed in the present by the first and last pages, which open with the same sentences:

No children live at Stanford Hall now.
No one lives here except the old caretaker and his wife.

On the opening page, she touches with the lightest of fingers the poignant note which sounds somewhere behind the whole novel and makes it the memoir for children the authors intend:

Every day in summer the caretaker throws open the great gates to coachloads of sightseers that come down the long avenue to the Hall. They are shown round the state rooms: the drawing-room with cushions plumped upon chairs and sofas, with the gilt harp standing ready and the spinet open, as if for some musical evening that never begins; the dining-room with its long table covered to the floor with double damask, with branched candelabra down the middle, and twenty places laid with silver, glass and china – but nobody ever eats and drinks here; the library with a thousand calf-bound volumes that nobody ever opens. (p. 5)

I used Denys Harding's definition of nostalgia[6] earlier when I spoke of it as expressing and defining a strong sense of incomplete membership of a social group. Philippa Pearce's novel speaks from a present in which *any* lived, committed, and deeply believed-in membership is exceptionally difficult to find. The children in her novel are staunchly members one of another, and make their lives out of a way of life shaped in strong social structures and sequences. The authority of parents, the meaning of social class, the orders and seasons of the year, are the absolutely *given* forms within which they create a new life. Thus, the cycle of punting, riding, birdnesting, detention, tutelage, which is bounded by the chilling, rigorously stupid parents, the servants, the gamekeeper, the schoolmaster's son whose inferior status disqualifies him from friendship, these all are the necessary and special conditions for the boredom, the horror and the glory of the childhood we see in the novel. The glory of the marvellous scene in which the children go hunting for burglars and find Hugh's friend Victor's last gift of a heron's egg, blown and perfect, is only so radiant because of the grim, mean terms on which the parents keep them.

But their world is on the move. In a dozen ways, fearsome to the timorous Margaret, bracing to the robust Laura, the novel takes the measure of the decline of the Hattons. The tremendous break comes when the children openly defy Lady Hatton. It is most stirringly done. No child reading it is likely to be troubled for more than a moment by the diction; no child could fail to stand beside the children, nor fail to be moved by the

---

[6] In his paper, 'Raids on the Inarticulate', *Use of English*, 19, 2 (1971). Also 'A Note on Nostalgia', *Scrutiny*, I, 3 (1932).

complex loyalties and hypocrisies which cause their mother not to punish them:

So Lady Hatton appeared among them, awe-inspiring in her long black lace dress, arms bare and jewels sparkling in the fading light. A chill silence fell upon her four children.

'Why are you not dressed, Laura?' their mother said in a harsh voice. 'Or you, Hugh? Get ready immediately, or I shall send for Papa.'

Laura stood her ground in her underclothes, her legs apart, her arms folded: 'I'm not going to wear that horrible frock. I'm not going to be made a laughing-stock!'

'You ungrateful child! When I got Papa to buy that lovely material, and Hortense has taken so much trouble to make it up for you!' She turned to Tom as to the eldest, the heir to Stanford, her hope. 'Tom, you must tell Laura to get ready.'

Tom was very pale. He knew the other three were watching him, waiting for him to speak. In the past they had always relied upon him, but often – although they would never admit it – he had let them down. Laura was remembering those occasions as she watched him: he could see it in her eyes . . .

'Tom, tell Laura to get ready.'

'No, Mama, I am not going to. Laura looks silly in the dress, as she says; and Hugh can't get his trousers on because they've grown too small.'

Lady Hatton was staggered. 'Such impudence! I shall tell Papa.' She tried to regain control of the situation. 'Your dress is very suitable, Laura; and you must put it on at once.' Laura did not stir, and Lady Hatton turned to Hugh: 'You never told me your trousers were too small. They were perfectly all right last term.'

'No, they were not,' said Hugh. 'Matron wrote to you about them and said I must have a new suit, and I had a letter from Papa saying you had decided it was quite unnecessary.'

Their mother did not deny this; she only said, 'Well, then, Hugh, you must wear Tom's last sailor suit; you will not have grown too big for that.'

Hugh was about to say, 'I'm not going to,' when Tom began steadily to speak: 'You bring this kind of misery on us, Mama, because Papa is too mean – and you seem to agree with him – to buy us any new clothes. That's not all. We don't get enough to eat. And that's not all. We are kept short of all kinds of things, just so that Papa can keep all the horses he wants and you can live at Stanford Park like Grandfather.'

'It's wicked – wicked of you to speak so of your father and mother, Tom, who have brought you up in this lovely place, with special governesses, and schools, and wholesome food! It's very bad for children to eat rich food; and Papa says you must learn not to waste money. And, anyway, Papa keeps the ponies for you to ride.'

'I don't want a pony,' Hugh said. 'I'd rather have clothes that fit and boots that don't let in the water.' (*The Children of the House*, pp. 116–17)

In some ways, the moral politics of this noble novel compare with those of K. M. Peyton's *Flambards* books. What pushes Philippa Pearce to the keenest edge of liberalism, and that sensitive, responsible intelligentsia (these latter-day Fabians) for whom she speaks, is her greater emotional range and delicacy. She brings the children to the great fracture of 1914. The old order is kissed goodbye when Tom, the son of the house, kisses Elsie the between-maid, and after a painfully vivid farewell, Elsie shares the abandoned bedroom with Margaret. Mrs Peyton, bravely but unconvincingly, tries to gather up the future into *Flambards in Summer*. But the children of Philippa Pearce's title are scattered abroad by the war, and three of them are killed.

Carrie's War depicts the future their children might have had. It tells the same tale thirty years on.

Nina Bawden's book can stand the comparison with *The Children of the House*, and that is to say everything for her. *Carrie's War* also begins with a prologue from the present, but one less bleak. Carrie comes with her children to see the place where she had spent her years as an evacuee with her stout, hungry, young brother. A war has already pulled them clean out of any safe social location. The children are on their own and have to develop their strengths, as best they can. The Welsh Baptist shopkeeper and his timid sister Lou give them, in their grim, narrow, bleakly provincial way, an ordered home; by contrast Hepzibah, Mister Johnny, the natural, and the clever bookworm-evacuee Albert Sandwich, provide the love, the warmth, the freedom, *and* the fearfulness of a finer, more splendid and aspiring life. Hepzibah's kitchen is the companion to many beautiful kitchens of children's fiction, and a complement to the many ideal gardens:

A warm, safe, lighted place.

Hepzibah's kitchen was always like that, and not only that evening. Coming into it was like coming home on a bitter cold day to a bright, leaping fire. It was like the smell of bacon when you were hungry;

loving arms when you were lonely; safety when you were scared . . .

Not that they stopped being scared at once, that first, frightened time. They were indoors, it was true, but the door was still open. And the woman seemed in no hurry to close it and shut out the dangerous night; she simply stood, looking down at the children and smiling. She was tall with shining hair the colour of copper. She wore a white apron, the sleeves of her dress were rolled up, showing big, fair, freckled arms, and there was flour on her hands.

Carrie saw her, then the room. A big, stone-flagged kitchen, shadowy in the corners but bright near the fire. A dresser with blue and white plates; a scrubbed, wooden table; a hanging oil lamp. And Albert Sandwich, sitting at the table with an open book where the light fell upon it.

He opened his mouth to speak but Carrie had turned. She said, 'Shut the door!' The woman looked puzzled – people were always so slow, Carrie thought. She said desperately, 'Miss Evans sent us for the goose. But something chased us. We ran and ran but it chased us. Sort of gobbling.'

The woman peered where she pointed, out into the night.

'Oh shut the door,' Carrie cried. 'It'll come in.'

The woman smiled broadly. She had lovely, white teeth with a gap in the middle. 'Bless you, love, it's only Master Johnny. I didn't know he was out.'

'He went to shut up the chickens,' Albert Sandwich said. 'I expect he went for a walk after.'

'But it wasn't a person,' Carrie said, speaking slowly to make them understand. She wasn't so frightened now. Albert had spoken so calmly that it made her calm too. She said, 'It didn't talk, it went gobble-gobble.'

'That's Mister Johnny's way of talking,' Albert Sandwich said. 'You must admit, Hepzibah, it could frighten someone.' He looked at Carrie, quite sternly. 'Though I expect you frightened him just as much. How would you feel if people ran away from you when you didn't mean to hurt them?' (pp. 52–3)

Nina Bawden's fault, if I must name one, is perhaps a faint worthiness of purpose not far enough away from the strenuous progressivism of teachers' journals. Maybe both she and Philippa Pearce lack something a bit vulgar, something I can only call *fight*. Nothing in all these books is quite arbitrary enough, or uncaused, until, that is, we come to Aunt Lou's elopement, Carrie's quite unexpected reversal of feeling for the broken, listless, abruptly gentle Mr Evans, and the burning of Druid's Bottom.

In the climax of the novel, Mrs Bawden makes something which takes the children who read her well beyond the decent range of values which might be read back from a summary of the plot. A summary would tell us only of the contrast between the Evans household and the paradise at the end of the Druid's Grove. It would tell us also of the strengths as well as the drearinesses of Welsh shopkeeping and chapel culture, and of the upheaval brought to the stability of mid-Wales or Norfolk or North Yorkshire or Eastern Scotland by the arrival of American soldiers.

But the end of the book has far more to it than these excellent lessons; it creates, in its straight, workmanlike prose, the reality of what most threatens our children – that they will lose those they most love, uncomprehendingly destroy what they most cherish, and for years weep out their hearts at night – 'on and on, like a waterfall' – for the sake of lost happiness and home, and something else more precious still and beyond naming.

Carrie herself is the focus of this experience, and she is painfully lifelike. She seeks so *anxiously* to please, not to be noticed, to do her duty, to be loved. In her dark hour, and for years after, Carrie forgets old Mrs Gotobed's very slightly too sententious admonition:

She said, 'Things are seldom as bad as you think they're going to be. Not when you come to them. So it's a waste of time, being afraid. You remember that!' She laughed softly, leaning on Hepzibah's arm. (p. 106)

Nina Bawden is too compassionate to leave Carrie at the end of the novel in desolation. Not only that. She has the future, the future of the children who read her, to think of. So Carrie comes back with her children to what she is convinced will be a derelict ruin. And the children find Hepzibah safe and sound, still living in the old house.

He said, speaking fast to get it over with, but politely, 'Are you Miss Hepzibah Green? If you are, my mother remembers you.'

She stared at him. Stared and stared – and her grey eyes seemed to grow larger and brighter. At last she said, 'Carrie? Carrie's boy?'

He nodded, and her eyes shone brilliant as diamonds. Her face cracked in a thousand lines when she smiled. 'And the others?'

'Yes.'

'Gracious Heavens!' (p. 157)

Hepzibah knows that Carrie will follow the children down to Druid's Bottom nicely in time to find her egg boiled:

Her voice had a clear command in it and the children stood up and went meekly out of the kitchen, past the old, ruined house, past the horse pond . . .

As they crossed the yard the oldest boy stopped being indignant with Hepzibah and felt sorry instead because [s]he was so foolishly sure and was going to be disappointed. She thought she knew their mother was coming, and she couldn't possibly know! She wasn't a witch; just an old woman who was quite good at guessing, but had guessed wrong, this time.

'There's no point in hanging about,' he said. 'We'll wait a minute to please Hepzibah and then we'll go back and finish our breakfast. I daresay one of us can eat an extra egg!'

But the others were younger than he was and so still believing, still trusting. They looked at him, then at each other, and laughed.

And ran ahead to meet their mother, coming through the Druid's Grove. (p. 158)

By this point (the clumsiness of 'she couldn't possibly know' set aside) a reader's tears flow naturally for the sake of restoration. These pages heal the deep wound in Carrie's life; she has been wounded because there is so much more to her, especially of love, than there is to her portly brother. The novel's end teaches what you must do to time, and what luck must do for you, if in the present time you are to keep your life whole.[7]

---

[7] The luck is confirmed in Nina Bawden's sequel, *Rebel on a Rock* (1978), in which Carrie has married Albert Sandwich.

12

Love and death in children's novels

In Eliot's lovely poem *Marina*, he catches up the great themes which in coarser tones Sweeney lists as 'birth and copulation and death', and places each with piercing beauty against the remembered images of childhood and the impending clouds of the death which comes to all men. Marina was daughter to Pericles in Shakespeare's tragedy, and Eliot rewrites for his own purposes the moment of the King's reawakening.

> What seas what shores what grey rocks and what islands
> What water lapping the bow
> And scent of pine and the woodthrush singing through the
>   fog
> What images return
> O my daughter.

And having considered the insubstantiality of all those who, insisting upon a graceless and degraded actuality and the complacent self-indulgence with which they live in it, tend only to deathliness, he turns to greet and bid farewell to the next generation, and its spirit in his daughter:

> This form, this face, this life
> Living to live in a world of time beyond me; let me
> Resign my life for this life, my speech for that unspoken,
> The awakened, lips parted, the hope, the new ships.

> What seas what shores what granite islands towards my
>   timbers
> And woodthrush calling through the fog
> My daughter.

Philippa Pearce, William Mayne, and (in a slightly smaller compass) Nina Bawden are three examples of the very best modern writers for children who transpose the meaning of Eliot's noble valediction into a diction and movement which the daughters themselves, and the sons, can accommodate. None of the novels I treated in the last chapter came explicitly to the deathbed, although the bell is distantly tolling both for Mrs Bartholomew and for Hepzibah, and the children of the house are now, alas, dead. Each novel, however, spoke of the arbitrariness of an ending, and won its success from the grace and beauty with which it ended matters *and* made continuity possible.

It is a tricky business to define what I want to speak of in this chapter. As always, not only in literary criticism but also (it may be) in the inevitably personal ethics of our time, definition comes best from examples. I have quoted several which could well stand for what I mean; it is no accident that William Mayne wrote two of them – the endings of *No More School* and *The Jersey Shore*. For it is also not in the least accidental that this book itself quotes so many endings, and Tom's farewell to Hatty, Hepzibah's boiled egg for Carrie, are two more of the best. The Mayne, the Pearce, and the Bawden each exemplify (as does *Marina*) the greeting and the farewell necessary to the generations, necessary also to individuals amongst themselves and even, perhaps most of all, *to* themselves, as a man or woman takes leave of his or her past, of all that has been lost and will not be recovered, of people, of hopes, of youth.

The child who lives the loss as she reads the novels cries a little into her pillow, or so it is very much to be hoped. And then, comforted by a parent, by her own good sense, but most of all by the comfort in the strength of love which, if they are good enough, the novelists make their prose (their *voice*) carry, the child goes cheerfully and unquenchably on. The loss and the ending are done with; on now to a new beginning:

> The awakened, lips parted, the hope, the new ships.

This is, I suppose, the language of natural continuity. The novels mentioned in Chapter 11 are fine, strong books, and they make loss, death, and continuity features of a natural and comprehensible order. Their authors devise – at the level of intelligibility proper to their audience – a litany, that is, a pure and profound language capable in its rhythms and vocabulary of talking of matters of life and death. We have seen examples of this at work. In each case, the writer has held all but one part of the syntax of experience steady. Mayne and Pearce have hugely dislocated time, while Nina Bawden dislocates personal history – Carrie and Nick are evacuated to Wales. After this single, momentous disturbance, the order and naturalness of the Melbournes' house and garden, of Arkengarthdale, of the Welsh village, remain in their reassuring place. One thing at a time, and in these novels that thing *is* time. As I remarked, un-certainty about time, about what constitutes a beginning and an end[1] in life and lives, characterizes modern history and, very visibly, modern poetics. My chosen novels treat it carefully, even gingerly, and keep their world steady around one centre of confusion.

There are however many different voices in the camps calling children to their red, white, or blue colours, which seek to insist on a more drastically discontinuous history and a disintegrated poetics, especially as this deals with poetic justice. It doesn't take much literary-critical acumen to be able to hear, in the shift from the novels of Part II to those of Part III, a loss of gentility in the tones of voice, an increase of candour, and a consequent and large-scale redefinition of decorum in the conventions which control what may be said to children, which define what are the awkward ages, and what will or will not bring a blush to a young person's cheek. Remember Mrs General, brought in as governess by Mr Dorrit after his family had adventitiously returned to fortune and gentility:

Mrs General had no opinions. Her way of forming a mind was to prevent it from forming opinions. She had a little circular set of mental grooves or rails on which she started little trains of other people's opinions, which never overtook one another, and never got anywhere. Even her propriety could not dispute that there was impropriety in the world; but Mrs General's way of getting rid of it was to put it out of sight, and make believe that there was no such thing. This was another of her ways of forming a mind – to cram all articles of difficulty into cupboards, lock them up, and say they had no existence. It was the easiest way, and, beyond all comparison, the properest.

Mrs General was not to be told of anything shocking. Accidents, miseries, and offences, were never to be mentioned before her. Passion was to go to sleep in the presence of Mrs General, and blood

[1] See Frank Kermode's *The Sense of an Ending: Studies in the Theory of Fiction* (1967).

was to change to milk and water. The little that was left in the world, when all these deductions were made, it was Mrs General's province to varnish. In that formation process of hers, she dipped the smallest of brushes into the largest of pots, and varnished the surface of every object that came under consideration. The more cracked it was, the more Mrs General varnished it. (Charles Dickens, *Little Dorrit*, p. 503)

There is a famous remark of Marx's in his early essay called 'The Jewish Question', written in 1844: 'Every emancipation is a restoration of the human world and of human relationships to man himself.' Something of this view underlies what I wrote of the great Victorian and Edwardian children's books. The victories won by Alice, by the railway children, and by the secret gardeners were victories won for freedom, for a larger, richer space in which to live. Similarly, the freedom Tom brings to Hatty, the freedom of invisible movement he enjoys in the garden, is in part a measure of the future emancipation which his life and times can show to those of the Melbournes, an emancipation accompanied by an equitable parcelling out of the garden, for the greatest good of the greatest number, into small suburban lots. The audible difference between Tom and Hatty and the children of the earlier tales is in the greater range of their passions, the depth and maturity of their sensibilities. It is easiest to make the point by saying that the railway children were and are much more innocent than Philippa Pearce's, William Mayne's, and Nina Bawden's children.

Innocence is partly grounded in ignorance; expulsion from the Garden of Eden followed eating the fruit of the Tree of Knowledge. But ignorance is merely a condition of the right working of innocence; the simple expectation that good and not evil will be done to us, of which Simone Weil writes so movingly, is a continuing characteristic of the innocent. To have lost the expectation absolutely is to have lapsed into the extreme opposite of innocence – cynicism – and it is also to have lost the dynamic possibility of innocence itself. As we saw, for instance, in *We Didn't Mean to Go to Sea*, the innocence which causes children to act right up to the level of the best standards set for them by adults qualifies the behaviour of the adults themselves. They are rebuked by the children's excellence, and although that rebuke may itself anger them by pressing home their own shortcomings (as happens in, say, Paula Fox's novel

Blowfish Live in the Sea), it may also conduce to virtue, to the adults' trying to live up to their own best standards as seen through their children's eyes.

I do not mean to imply that morality is simply a name for our consciousness of other people watching us. And it is also clear that the family of moral cognates amongst which innocence lives – such concepts as 'ingenuousness', 'naïvety', 'simplicity', 'guilelessness', 'nescience', 'inexperience' – are not necessarily those we would want to cherish in children or adults. But the innocent child and the saint embody a version of selfhood which is necessary for right judgement. Unless a part of you keeps its innocence, old corruption will have you for its own. You will be unable to act uprightly, cleanly, selflessly, fiercely. Inasmuch as the more famous examples of innocent men must include Socrates and Christ, and among our heroes we find such innocents as Huckleberry Finn, Alice, Jim Hawkins, and Laura Wilder, it is certain that innocence does not seek to *deny* experience.

The word stands for an insistent purity of heart and of attention. It may miss, for very ignorance, both danger and evil; it cannot be insincere. To be innocent is not to be virtuous, but innocence is a ground of virtue.

Perhaps it is this ambiguity which has brought the term such demotion in the moral scale. If innocence *is* to be worth anything, and not merely to be a sort of transparent self-assertion, it must express a moral view which is larger than the individual. Inasmuch as moral structures have been notoriously eaten into by the corrosive acids of individualism this past century and a half, innocence becomes harder to live in any significant way. Deprived of moral structures and driven back into the individual's all-relative gaze, innocence becomes indistinguishable from mere inexperience. With the best will in the world, the progressives have, on another wing from that on which they seek to bind the back-garden in the spells of Arthur, set themselves to the revision of innocence.

The crudest form of this movement is not revision at all, but destruction. The complex forces which have repoliticized some of the more private areas of experience amongst the bourgeoisie in the last twenty years have also led the most politically progressive vanguard to reduce the moral-political world to the mere antinomy: power–exploitation. Its spokesmen seek to place all social relations in terms of that tiny segment on the arc of human exchange. Not surprisingly, they suffer from a drunken vertigo directly attendant upon so foreshortening the theory of interpretation. Vertigo, however, has its excitements, and the excitement felt by a group like the Children's Rights Workshop generates itself from the slightly delirious self-righteousness which a sense that blowing the gaff to children about their exploitation by adults brings to its secret agents. Their annual prize, The Other Award, is given to those novels which set out to make children see the structures of power and oppression which prevent equality, tip the scales of justice, and keep the poor, the coloured, the weak, helplessly under the thumb of their governors.

Now this book has been at pains to make clear that the fixed points of the human sciences and what is given as the grounds of their operation include the always immanent movement of the human spirit towards greater freedom, fulfilment, and critical self-awareness.[2] So this criticism of the Children's Rights Workshop and the novels it prefers is not seeking to put down the noble and excellent ends of justice and equality. It is saying that these qualities can thrive only in a moral vocabulary and a social life with a wide range of reference capable of seeing that moral goods may conflict, tragically and comically, that individuals must live in social structures of some kind in order to be individuals at all, and that the Grand Inquisitor's terrible trio, miracle, mystery, and authority, must have their due place in public rituals, lest they be compelled upon us by men in uniform, over whom we have no control at all.

Out of a long, varied list of contenders, including many of the black-and-white school of social realism in the Windmill, Topliner, and Knockout series, let us take as a not unimpressive example Robert Cormier's *The Chocolate War*. The action is set in a private school of Catholic foundation in the States, and it is its American flavour which first strikes an English reader.

[2] I acknowledge in Chapter 1 some of the provenance of these three terms, which I take directly from Charles Taylor. More historically, they derive, doubtless, from the Romantic world-picture codified by Kant and Hegel, especially in (respectively) *Fundamental Principles of the Metaphysic of Ethics* and *The Phenomenology of Mind*. But I want to underline the Englishness with which I use the Germans here, and to take my version of Idealism by way of Wordsworth and the Victorians, T. H. Green and William Morris.

This is partly its literary convention and diction – a grating, staccato mixture of Salinger's *The Catcher in the Rye* and its much less accomplished, more deliberately gruesome and unreflective successors in the graduate schools of creative writing for teenagers. But also, and more pervasively, its American quality comes out in the conventional determination to tear away all the conventions of writing for children. The hero is not victorious, he is broken and humiliated; the repressive Mafiosi who run the school have clenched their fists even more tightly upon their power; the story is remorselessly tense, and only loosens the tension momentarily in order to tighten it more frighteningly in a new corner – a sort of *Marathon Man* for children. The hero is entirely a victim,[3] but the more entirely a latter-day victim in that his victimization stands for nothing redemptive or succouring to others in his community. He is entirely solitary, and his defeat is only debilitating.

But to judge in this way is to invite misunderstandings. My criticism is not simply a consequence of disliking and fearing the author's world-picture; it is obviously possible that the heroic resistance of individuals to evil and cruelty may be futile, and the fiction of the twentieth century furnishes many convincing examples: Conrad's *Nostromo* and Gabriel Marquez's *One Hundred Years of Solitude* are only two of the classics in the literature of oppression. What is deeply wrong with *The Chocolate War*, which is why I am considering it here, is its grossness and indelicacy in telling its child-readers that heroism is, strictly, such a dead end. Trapped by prose and convention within the hero's skull, the author can find no way to qualify the helpless narrowness of his vision, and give the reader some detachment from and purchase on the hero's plight. This wouldn't matter if the only moral were to advise children not to let their parents send them to such a school. But Cormier sounds like yet another dispirited radical of the 1968 generation, of Miami and the siege of Chicago. The radical moral taken to heart after a term and a half on the steps of Nixon's Pentagon was that *all* structures of authority and institutions were deadly, and all would, in their super-ruthless and efficient way, break the spirit of the individual.

Jerry Renault, the hero in *The Chocolate War*, is first detailed by the bullies to refuse his school duty to sell chocolates for

[3] A distinction taken from Raymond Williams, *Modern Tragedy* (1964).

school funds, so that the gang may assert their grip on all pupils by humiliating the deputy principal who has tried to double sales. When the ban is lifted, on his own brave decision he keeps up his refusal to sell the chocolates. The gang, with the connivance of the priests – the collusion of formal and informal Old Corruptions – then beat him up horribly and break his spirit as well as his body. It is at such moments, as is always the case with this familiar genre, that the prose moves with the greatest conviction. It runs its fingernail along the line of the nerve, and the reader wriggles with the routine sympathetic thrill of at once feeling and inflicting pain:[4]

His stomach caved in as Janza's fist sank into the flesh. He clutched at his stomach protectively and his face absorbed two stunning blows – his left eye felt smashed, the pupil crushed. His body sang with pain. (p. 182)

Hero-victim and reader are left with the pain, and the clichés of concussion. The crude lesson is threefold: that all institutions systematize violence; that violence upholds power without reason; that individuals cannot hope to change these facts. These are the sentimentalities of disenchantment, understandable enough when you are faced with the 'realism' of Kissinger's and Nixon's blockade of Vietnam. But they are constantly rebutted in history and they leave no room for the necessary violence without which decency and civilization will not survive.[5]

The Chocolate War is a children's novel. Inasmuch as this is so, the thrill and relish with which it plays on the raw edge of its readers' nerves seem not to spring from the old having-it-both-ways of the realistic thriller as Hoggart analyses it. The sex-and-violence thriller – to accept that association – notoriously gained a spurious moral credit by being on the side of right while permitting the reader to enjoy all the sadistic satisfactions of inflicting pain and enjoying cruel power. There may be a touch of this in Cormier's novel, but if the argument I have put about innocence is at all adequate, the more likely responses on

---

[4] A response classically analysed by Richard Hoggart in The Uses of Literacy (1958), pp. 215–24.
[5] A point very forcefully made in Fraser, Violence in the Arts (1974), especially his chapter 'Thought', and Orwell's remark (made apropos Kipling) that 'men can only be highly civilized while other men, inevitably less civilized, are there to guard them'.

the part of a child aged, say, twelve are horror and incomprehension. Even the toughest egg of the second year expects more justice from life than this, and insofar as the prose is effective in creating the thrill of pain, the novel has something of the realism of a movie like *Marathon Man* with its torture scenes in a dentist's chair, or Boorman's *Deliverance* with its discomfortingly immediate wounding and dreadful deaths. The writing is never far from the clichés of echo-chamber and beating-up by sound waves, of course, but its vividness makes its strongest effects very hard to negotiate, to know what to do with. The difference in moral climate could be best brought out if one were to compare in tone, reticence, and decorum the description in *War and Peace* of Pierre's narrow escape from execution after capture at Borodino, and the shockingly unfeeling explicitness with which a crude war novel like Mailer's *The Naked and the Dead* details arbitrary murder, mutilation, and callousness.

This is more than fixing a fight between the giant Tolstoy and the modern pygmy. It is also a matter of social convention and literary decorum, particularly since the audience at hand are children. The *intention* of *The Chocolate War* seems to be to force the child directly up against the pain of pain, the facts of cruelty and oppression, by way of showing him that the adults have always told lies about the world's being a fine and benign place, the guardians of the social order being friendly and just, the nature of action being unambiguous and generous. 'Here, kid, this is how it really is.' Time they lost their innocence.

Now adults have often lied, as it is the point of *Huckleberry Finn* to show us. It has already been suggested that some idealizing of what really happens is necessary, not in order to fool children, but in order to show them an image of finer forms of life. We tell children of a more nearly excellent world (Chigley, Trumpton, or Camberwick Green) not in order to anaesthetize them but as a prompt to the future. Or so the best novelists do. Their business, as it has been the business of this book to urge upon them, is to come to the life they write about with a keen, reciprocal, and animating sense of the finest life they can imagine.

The Chocolate War, and many lesser novels, fails that test. Luxuriating in their radical realism, the authors make an evil of necessity, and leave no means of criticizing on behalf of a better life the oppressions, power systems, and their violences, which the novelists seek to expose. The group of writers in question intend to pull the mask of benignity from society's cruel face, or to show that experience is bitter and painful. This eddy of our social formation is often American, and its national quality comes out clearly in Robert Cormier's novels, Hamilton's *M. C. Higgins the Great*, Paula Fox's novels, William Armstrong's *Sounder*, and the Australian Ivan Southall's *Josh*. These authors insist on the cowardliness, infidelity, drunkenness, and childishness of all power systems from home and parents via schools to state and states. These writers stand in the line so many critics and historians of ideas have picked out in the American tradition; the line of those who would sign the declaration of 'radical personalization',[6] and the freeing of the self from *all* social structures, all being seen as uniformly oppressive. Their great originals, after all, made their declaration against the intolerable stuffinesses and imprisonments of Europe in the name of the self-evident equality of all men. The latter-day radical, turning to his children, has lost sight of the necessary structures of Laura Ingalls Wilder's frontier, and tells a tale of the corruption and deadliness of all social life, which leaves children nowhere to live at all. Truth-telling is replaced by lie-seeking, and the radical-without-a-history is become just a terrorist.

Children, of course, like a dose of the terrors at times – well-controlled times, with a warm fire and all the lights on all the way upstairs to bed. But as we have already noted, the choice to take a deliberate dose probably needs to be nicely balanced against the incredibility of the tale. If ghost or horror stories and films press too hard against the limits of the conventions, then the imaginative experience begins to get out of hand and 'become too real'.

It is not however such studied risk-taking which we are talking about; the author–teachers in hand seek to break the convention, precisely because it doesn't permit them to tell children about the many political menaces and atrocities of the real world, and allows children far too much well-lit room to escape into, on the way to bed or into adolescent life. My objection to *The Chocolate War* and some of its peers is that this determination leads the author–teacher into three related errors all

[6] Basil Bernstein's phrase, as noted earlier, in *Class, Codes, Control*, vol. III (1977).

evident in their prose and structure: first, a grossness and inde-
corum which forces brutal events too abruptly on the reader;
second, a raw thrillingness about the prose which makes the
authors' attitudes to power very ambiguous – the ambiguity of
many modern films like *A Clockwork Orange*, as we noted;
third, the narrative convention which traps us inside the hero's
skull and denies us the means of freeing ourselves from and criticizing his plight. The strictures stand; so does the charge that
children must know political wrong for what it is. What would
it be like to take seriously the claim that the soft evasions of political convention in children's novels have entailed hypocrisies
about history and society? How shall we produce a novel which
brings off the artful balance of tact and plain-speaking, of
making imaginable the intolerable, of keeping innocence while
teaching dire knowledge?

We are once more on the edge of 'bibliotherapy'. One blunt
answer to the question as I have put it is to say, 'Read very great
novels.' The best novels tell the truth about the dreadfulness of
men to men, and in such a way, as Keats noted, as to make

all disagreeables evaporate, from their being in close relationship
with Beauty and Truth. [otherwise] We have unpleasantness without
any momentous depth of speculation excited, in which to bury its
repulsiveness.[7]

By the same token, a great many novels discussed in this book
embody a view of and a living in the pain, want, cruelty, and
loss of all history. But the muck-rakers may still plausibly insist
that these examples are not direct enough. Parts of history must
be plainly rewritten, or written for the first time for children.
The claim comes most audibly from the United States; the
history of black slavery is a test case, Paula Fox's *The Slave
Dancer* a gallant effort to provide the absent novel.

Her novel tells the tale of an émigré boy of Spanish origin
pressed into service on a slaver because of his skill on a penny
whistle. His ghastly task is to play his little melodies to the
slaves brought back from Africa, in an effort to force them into
a hideous semblance of a dance, and to keep them in barely sufficient health to make them saleable on the return to the
southern States. Paula Fox's novel follows at a fairly short
interval after the remarkable efforts of a group of American

[7] Letter to his brothers, December 1817, in *Selected Letters*, ed. Page (1954), p. 52.

historians, whose boldest and most striking writer is Eugene Genovese,[8] to write anew the history of the blacks and of slavery in the USA, and – the harder task – to find the roots and development of modern racism.

Ideas, you may say, are death to the novelist. With Keats's remarks in mind about the poet's equal delight in creating either Imogen or Iago, or Lawrence's remarks about hammering the nail of an idea through the novel until it is dead, it may seem that to set out with Paula Fox to write a novel-against-racism can have only plonking results. The novel has, indeed, its *lourdeurs*. She isn't quite enough of a novelist – that is, of an intellectual and an artist – to create a structure which will carry her theme. Her hero is *not* a victim, but being a child, is left only as an observer. It may seem unfair to contrast the book with Twain's classic, but Huck Finn is a hero because he is an actor in his own story, and his energy as well as Jim's make their tale about very much more than the evils of slavery. Paula Fox is more simply concerned to tell to children the pretty well unknown and disgraceful tale of slavery, but the simplicity of her intention works, as one might expect, against largeness of life. She does have the tact not to press too hard with her typewriter at the really shocking moments – when, for instance, the body of a little African girl killed by the rigours of the journey and the inhuman conditions in the hold is carried by the bland, inhuman Benjamin Stout,

upside down, his fingers gripping one thin brown ankle. Her eyes were open, staring at nothing. Foam had dried about her mouth. With one gesture, Stout flung her into the water. I cried out. Ned smacked me across the face with such force I fell to the deck. (*The Slave Dancer*, p. 66)

Nonetheless, the difficulties of writing such a tale successfully are those of anyone who seeks to give an account of disapproved-of practices from a subsequent intellectual and objective standpoint. The casual cruelties she describes, such as the stinking, jammed hold, the ritual of the slow, clanking dance, the fact of the sale of human beings for cash, the demotion of black men and women from the rank of human being, are all naturally horrible to the boy, to us, and to any person not inured to misery by practice and practices. But this is the problem. It requires the astonishing re-creative powers of

[8] See his *The Political Economy of Slavery* (1965) and *Roll, Jordan, Roll* (1975).

the 'chameleon–poet' (or anthropologist–historian, if you like) to novelize (that is, theorize) the practices of a man like the master, Captain Cawthorne, the first mate, Nicholas Spark, or the slave dancer's only human contact in the crew, Clay Purvis.

The result of such a novelistic theory would then be more than a novel about black slavery, and of course not a novel readily identifiable as being written for children. Social biblio-therapy, or the repair of social ignorance by novels, is a wrongly conceived enterprise not because the sacred domain of art must not be contaminated by the impurity of real political and moral convictions, but because conviction is only adequate when it is completed by both judgement *and* understanding. That is to say, a satisfactory narrative carries us through the subjective understanding of the characters to an account of the practices and structures which make the characters what they are, and leaves us in a position to judge the whole by placing it in a present context. Paula Fox seeks gamely to move the novel on to this level by the hero's rescue of the boy his own age during the shipwreck, and their subsequent brief sojourn in an Eden of equality, tenderly and restoratively nursed and fed back to freedom. But this, according to her ambitions, is merely a pla-titude. The return of the hero to normal life with his widowed mother in New Orleans gives us no enlarged grip on our own future, and the novel, useful as it is, remains at the level of the humanities project resource.

This judgement perhaps comes home if we contrast *The Slave Dancer* with a novel which seeks to explain not the always corrigible wickedness of men to men, but the necessities which stand the other side of social action. The socially conscientious novels exemplify a good side of modern progressive doctrines: they teach that pain, cruelty, and want are not facts of life, and that the four ghastly Horsemen of the Apocalypse may on some occasions be driven out of the citadels they have laid waste, and the citadels themselves be rebuilt.

I began with Sweeney's trio, 'birth and copulation and death'.

> Doris: I'd be bored.
> Sweeney: You'd be bored.
>   Birth and copulation and death
>   That's all the facts when you come to brass tacks.[9]

[9] T. S. Eliot, 'Fragment of an Agon', *Complete Poems and Plays* (1969), p. 124.

These are indeed the facts, if not *all* of them. Sometimes in a similar spirit to the black-and-white social realists, a writer for children starts out to show children the fact of death (or of copulation) but because he is dealing with facts, however socially mediated and shaped, his intention and its creative realization stand in an easier relation than when we speak, in abstract terms, of 'practices and structures'. The most familiar device is for the novelist to take hero or heroine through the experience of loving and caring for a pet, and having it die. Steinbeck's *The Red Pony*, Marjorie Rawlings's *The Yearling*, the lovely Australian tale *Storm-Boy* by Colin Thiele which tells of a boy's friendship with a pelican pointlessly shot at the end by a hunter, are all examples of such a framework. Each book maintains the simple, two-way movement of child and creature, and restores their relationship to a paradise in which the inevitable innocence of both creates a mutual trust which has no need of speech nor of society. Adults only break into the charmed circle of loving, speechless understanding when death and danger threaten. Before then, the child returns to a natural state which has no need of grace, and to which he is not so much tutored as *recalled* by the animal: the pony, the deer, the pelican. (*Charlotte's Web* has something of the same quality.) The beauty of these tales is their paradisal quality – and it is important to say that paradises may come true in any life. The boy in *Kes*[10] frees himself of the grim constrictions of his poor world by discovering with the kestrel the perfect freedom of an always provisional friendship. The sacred bird comes to home by virtue of temporary trust; its savage nature may at any point release it from those uncertain bonds. Each novel celebrates the beauty of natural loyalty and unpossessive love. Death threatens, and then appears as loss. Loss cuts both ways. It is experienced partly as bitter, intolerable anguish for oneself ('How shall I manage without him?') and partly as some larger groping into the dark unknown sea for an explanation, a yearning outwards to know what has happened to the lost being, how he fares in the lost world, what can be made *im*personally of this broken connection, this for the moment inescapable feeling of incompleteness.

[10] Barry Hines, *Kes*, first published as *A Kestrel for a Knave* (1968), then brilliantly filmed in 1970 by Kenneth Loach. The film, to my mind, brings out the beauty of which I write more than the novel does.

Loss is, we say, like something being cut off. It is an amputation. This is not true for children (and for the essential childishness of all good men and women) who relish fiercely present joy because they know it will soon be lost: this afternoon on a summery beach, this birthday picnic, this Christmas Day. The loss by death in these novels is abrupt and arbitrary. In our times, perhaps this is the best a novelist can do. In a novel which addresses itself directly to a now-rare experience, the death of a child, the novelist can do little, though she does it beautifully, but write of the loss as a sudden severance.

The novel in question is Constance Greene's *Beat the Turtle Drum*, which tells of two sisters through the voice of the elder, thirteen years old, and of the sudden death of the enchanting eleven-year-old Joss who breaks her neck as she falls while tree-climbing. The shock hits suddenly and solidly, as it would in life. The plainness of the prose, having established Joss and her sister as the merry, alert, exquisite little girls they are (not knowing or smart like Annabel in *Freaky Friday*), is well up to recording the plain facts, the simple pain, of seeing Joss in her coffin, and thereafter the flat, unrumpled sheets and pillows of her still-made-up bed. The reading is as painful as the living would be. The loss is terrible. And, these secular days, that is probably what it would be for a child. Deaths in Dickens, by contrast, evoke the dread and mystery of the fact, even with Mrs Gradgrind in *Hard Times*:

'But there is something – not an Ology at all – that your father has missed, or forgotten, Louisa. I don't know what it is. I have often sat with Sissy near me, and thought about it. I shall never get its name now. But your father may. It makes me restless. I want to write to him, to find out, for God's sake, what it is. Give me a pen, give me a pen.'

Even the power of restlessness was gone, except for the poor head, which could just turn from side to side.

She fancied, however, that her request had been complied with, and that the pen she could not have held was in her hand. It matters little what figures of wonderful no-meaning she began to trace upon her wrappers. The hand soon stopped in the midst of them; the light that had always been feeble and dim behind the weak transparency, went out; and even Mrs Gradgrind, emerged from the shadow in which man walketh and disquieteth himself in vain, took upon her the dread solemnity of the sages and patriarchs. (pp. 225–6)

Individual pain and general loss are the nearest qualities we can find with which to value death for children in the novels we give them. It is hardly enough; it has to do.

In that case, how do we value for children the other mystery, sexuality, which is such a source of dread in all cultures? A first difficulty in seeking answers to that question is that the power of sexuality as a source of piety, dread, and guilt has ebbed away into some unknown recess these past twenty years. In adolescent groups, as in industrial culture at large, sex in all its strange guises has become more interesting than grave, more a matter of exploration than ritual, more permeable than fixed, more consequential than moral. In which case, all a novel for a child on the edge of puberty can do is frame the gateway into an uncertain excitement. In a lovely poem, J. V. Cunningham sets the scene for a love affair, and it suggests the threshold at which the modern novelist for children stops:

> The night is still. The unfailing surf
> In passion and subsidence moves
> As at a distance. The glass walls,
> And redwood, are my utmost being.
> And is there in the last shadow,
> There in the final privacies
> Of unaccosted grace, – is there,
> Gracing the tedium to death,
> An intimation? Something much
> Like love, like loneliness adrowse
> In states more primitive than peace,
> In the warm wonder of winter sun.[11]

Going further, we may say, is impious, and impiety is becoming nowadays only a cliché. In *Red Shift*, Alan Garner attempts to set the formlessness of modern love affairs against the cruelty and brutality of times in which love affairs were more binding by virtue of the power of belief, the mystery of copulation, the dread and acceptance of conception. It comes over clumsily, and Garner's always strong, bookish atavism leads him to the melodrama and clichés of teenage tantrums.

---

[11] From 'To What Strangers, What Welcome', in *Collected Poems* (1972).

His attempt to place the lurid silhouette of the lovers on the tower against the metaphor of the red shift which betokens the hurtling, spectral lines of the infinitely exploding galaxies is just fancy. Going all out for sex-and-violence as a necessary ritual, his music sounds flat and shrill. His novel is all theory. The honourable alternative, short of writing manuals for coping like Josephine Kamm's *Young Mother*, is to put your trust in both innocence and the intense self-consciousness of adolescence, and to invoke the old, unkillable magic of falling in love with the stranger who knows immediately who you are in your truest self without taking away from you all that you may become. He is Don Giovanni and she is Aphrodite.

The powerful tradition of the Victorian novel, of *Jane Eyre, Tess of the D'Urbervilles,* and *Anna Karenina,* is there to help the children's novelists; and so, just as worthily to the point, is the present-day women's magazine. Catherine Storr's *Thursday,* K. M. Peyton's *The Beethoven Medal,* Jill Paton Walsh's *Fireweed* (and, more obliquely, *Goldengrove*), Nina Bawden's *Rebel on a Rock,* all the work of mother–novelists, echo the exquisite form of Turgenev's classic, *First Love.* Jane Gardam's *A Long Way from Verona,* a modest, affecting tale, will do as our example.

Begin where one must, with the prose. Jane Gardam steps straight through the conventions of fine writing for the young teenager, a convention which betrays Mrs Paton Walsh in *Goldengrove* into occasional lapses into picturesquerie, and into the literary references with which, rightly enough, she seeks to entice a thirteen-year-old schoolgirl reader into English literature. Such writing is good enough in its way, but even with so sound a writer as Jill Paton Walsh, it smells a little of the library stack, the busy typewriter in a crowded, cluttered, handsomely decorated living-room in Holland Park or North Oxford or Martha's Vineyard; it tastes of a well-taken degree in English.

Well, why not? A central, unifying feature of the many women novelists for children is that they studied English literature at ancient, oldish, or Ivy League universities at a time when that activity was natural, rational and self-justifying to a generation of middle-class women about to become the first legion of women in the symbol and knowledge industries: journalism, television, publishing, schoolteaching, and, after marriage, novel-writing for children. English literature in the university was then a dynamic subject; it gave to its students a liveable picture of the relations between forms of the educated and forms of the customary life, and it drew a strong line between biography and history, personal life and the tides of politics.

This was the social and intellectual genesis of so many of the novelists this book treats of. It is clear enough that Jane Gardam occupies the same world. Her heroine, Jessica Vye, at school by the sea in Saltburn in 1941, wants only to be a writer, has a clergyman father who writes for the *New Statesman*, falls in and out of love a very long way from Verona, and is (temporarily) convinced by *Jude the Obscure* that good fortune never happens.

But a punchcard summary can tell us little about Mrs Gardam's strictly literary capacity to push her imagination well beyond the limits of university English – further, for instance, than the interesting theorist and storyteller Penelope Lively, with whom she has a strong affinity, based on similar experiences. In *A Long Way from Verona* Jessica and three friends meet a dotty old lady in a dreadful tea-room:

'I know them all,' said the woman across the room, staring ahead of her through the archway at the quiet, drizzly road. She stubbed out her cigarette in the éclair and pushed her plate away. 'Now I don't suppose you girls even know who Henry James was?'

'The Old Pretender,' I said. It was polite to have a go.

'That's her,' said Florence. Cissie collapsed. So did I as a matter of fact, but Mrs Hopkins didn't appear to notice.

'He was a Man. He was more than a Man, he was a Mind. He was a great and civilized Mind. He loved England. He understood England. He even lived in England.'

'Well we all live in England,' I said.

'Shrup,' said Florence, 'I think he must have been an American.'

'The Old Pretender was a Scotsman.'

'The Old Pretender was *not* the same as Henry James,' said Florence.

'Why wasn't he?' I said, getting angry.

'He was Henry James to all the world,' said Mrs Hopkins. 'But he was Harry to me.'

'Oh, Henry Fifth,' I said. 'God for Harry.' It was something my father was always saying.

'WHAT did you say?' For the first time Mrs Hopkins seemed to see us. 'You, child, what did you say?'

'I said "God for Harry",' I said uncomfortably, and then I added, 'England and St George.' I shouldn't have.

'My dear child!' she cried, 'my dear child! That's what I thought you said. My *dear* child!' and she came tweedle-deeing over the room and kissed me! There was a terrible old smell about her like chests of drawers, and I shuddered and pressed back and nearly sent the busy-lizzie going for the second time. 'Well, would you believe it!' she said.

'"God for Harry, England and St George". My dear children, might I just shake you by the hand? I'm going to write this down. Every word. I'm going to send it to the papers. I'm going to send it to Winston. Now would you mind if I were just to ask you your ages?'

'Around twelve,' said Florence, watchfully.

'And thirteen,' said Helen.

'My dears! Oh, my dears, how lovely. On the threshold. Four little Juliets. Younger than she are married mothers made! My dears, I want to repay you. Repay you just for being what you are. Little English Juliets. Lovers of dear old England. Now, I'm going to tell Winston about all this.' She spotted Helen's roll of music under the table. 'And what's this, you play music, too – what's this? Chopin? No! This has been a wonderful afternoon. Oh I do wish I could thank you *dear* children for it in some way.'

She shook hands all round and went off. We heard her saying 'Chopin, Grace,' to the counter lady, 'Chopin! He may have been Chopin to all the world but he was . . .'

'Quick,' said Florence, 'get her tea.'

We divided sandwiches, éclair, bread, butter, jam, sugar lumps. In less than two minutes there were none of them to be seen. (pp. 28–9)

There is great love and a strong smell of death in the book. This passage is entirely typical of what Jane Gardam can do. She can recreate the rambling, directionless lines of such conversation with the fidelity of Harold Pinter and the much more satisfactory humour of Alan Galton, and at the same time give the scene its historical location, in a beleaguered, incoherently patriotic England in which healthy schoolgirls living out of ration-books are inevitably hungry. Since Jessica is a striking and exceptional girl, though believable and natural for all that, we are not trapped but freed by living in her consciousness. She is spontaneously funny – 'a terrible old smell about her like chests of drawers' – and the novelist creates brief spaces in the narrative for her own contribution to a novel with a strong sense of the interdependence of comedy and tragedy, and a style capable of insisting that both may include laughter.

Jessica's adenoidal brother; her only just overdrawn clergyman-father, exuberant, generous, huge, funny; the crushingly upper-class trio Claire, Sophie, and Magdalene whom naturally Jessica loathes on the spot: all sort perfectly in their admirably comic way with the scene in which a random bomb blows up the street in downtown Middlesbrough, and almost kills the heroine and her newfound social-conscience-stricken Romeo:

When I opened my eyes I was right down the street by myself lying on the pavement and looking at a broken china alsatian. There was glass everywhere. I felt about and found I was near the doorstep of one of the houses. The door had blown inwards and there was someone lying still in the passage just inside. 'Where's Christian?' I thought – I think I said it. 'Oh goodness! Where's Christian?' The dark bundle in the passage got up and began crawling towards me. It wasn't Christian but the man who had been coughing. We looked at each other on our hands and knees about a foot from the ground for what seemed a very long time. Then the man turned his head away and began to cough again, very horribly, until he was tired of it. He sat back on his haunches and leaned back against the wall just inside the door. 'Aye-oop!' he said.

I blinked. 'Aye-oop now. We'd best go inside and see what's tooken moother.'

'What?'

'Aye-oop now. That's a daisy. 'Ere we are. Now then.' He was heaving me up and pushing me along the passage as he spoke and into a front room where a man was cowering in a corner with his back to the room like a shell and the most enormous woman I had ever seen was bulging back in a battered arm-chair. She had no legs and she was roaring with laughter.

I began to shake. For the first time since I had opened my eyes after the bomb – it must have been a bomb. That terrible avalanche, that dreadful wind – for the first time I began to be afraid. 'She has no legs. She has no legs,' I heard myself saying. I saw the little old man shaking his head back across the room, and back on to his chair. 'No legs. No legs.'

They must have been blown off. I found myself looking round the room for the legs.

'Eh, Ernie lad, bring 'er. Bring 'er 'ere,' said the woman. 'Now then! Now then! Thast all right. Hush then. Hush lass, thast all right.'

(No legs. No legs.)

'I cannot come to thee,' said the great woman. 'I cannot come. I's no legs. Never for years. Not sin a bairn. There lass, there. Git kettle on now, Ern lad. Hush lass, hush. She's afeared . . .' (pp. 137–8)

The terrific life of people, of *the* people, goes on, but there is a death, as Jessica's father shrewdly and sympathetically sees. Jessica sees its shadow in some inconsequential and unstated way, when her stunning new Rupert Brookeish boyfriend goes vaguely home to mother after the air-raid and abandons her, and she emerges from colossal concussion and its aftermath of despair into an unforeseen and surging renewal of her love for life. The book returns great moral force to that grand cliché. Its wartime setting is without nostalgia, but provides a way of speaking of love and death which subordinates both to the necessity of life.

Jane Gardam's example serves to underline the thrust of this chapter. The programmatic writers throw their enterprise out of focus by envisaging neither prose nor structure capable of placing their simple intention – to tell children about death or sex or power – in a sufficiently real, practical and practicable world. A novel must *be* a world, not a lesson, although some lessons, like that of *The Slave Dancer*, are more interesting than others. The ungainliness of the socially conscientious writers repeats for us a morality which has lost richness. Political morality, being helplessly divided into left and right by the lines of 1789 and 1917 and today's reductions in its vocabulary, leaves these novelists with far too crude a picture of action. Where the novelists in question seek to open the practices of sexuality and the fact of death, and are too intelligent to adopt the slogans, they can only frame an opening – raise the lid, so to speak, with a proper reverence. A novelist must speak of life and death; it is his job; but not by way of making these matters either his subject or his object.

My last chapter takes as its themes Joan Aiken's *Midnight is a Place* and Russell Hoban's *The Mouse and His Child*, and it will be my contention that these fine books join *A Long Way from Verona* in doing all that the social realists want, and doing it better, and that their exemplary success is won because they attend not to social realism as a matter of conscience, but to the real world as a matter of their responsibility, and to its life as lived in their language.

13

Resolution and independence

For the reasons which I set out in the first two chapters, Dickens stands as exemplary of the best that we may look for in children's novelists. He does so in those of his novels that deal, as so many do, at any length with childhood: *Oliver Twist*, the first parts of *Nicholas Nickleby* and *Dombey and Son*, *Great Expectations*, *David Copperfield*, *Bleak House*, *Little Dorrit*, *Our Mutual Friend*. He is such a great novelist because he was so capacious and extraordinary in his understanding of all that was happening in Victorian life, and so able to give that understanding immediate image and embodiment. At the same time, writing in and about London, the mighty centre of the age's great energies, capital and production, he was able to express the movement of an epoch by living the right life at the right moment. More than this, his moral sympathy and attention are characterized, as the quotation on p. 37 from *David Copperfield* suggests, by their 'quite wonderful ... closeness and accuracy', their 'freshness, and gentleness, and capacity of being pleased', and it is these qualities which, for whatever complex historical reasons, we may expect to find amongst contemporary novelists for children rather than for adults. To have such qualities and to make them live in your prose is to cross from being a good man or woman to being a great novelist.

Dickens, as anyone would say, is a giant, and naturally enough none of the novelists considered in this book is anything more than tiny in his shadow. But comparison of stature is not my point. Dickens spoke both a popular and an intellectual rhetoric, and made that rhetoric out of a rich, dense, astonishingly expressive seriality of street and drawing-room languages, of parliament and chapel, fairground and four-ale bar, old school and new bureaucracy, dosshouse and waterfront, police station and lawyers' small-talk. In all this Shakespearean range and depth of realization, he was – in Leavis's memorable words – intent upon seeing 'how the diverse inter-playing currents of life flowed strongly and gathered force here, dwindled there from importance to relative unimport-ance, settled there into something oppressively stagnant, reass-erted themselves elsewhere as strong new promise'.[1]

Quoting those remarks at once suggests the impossibility of getting such a vision clear and comprehensive in a novel for children. Dickens was a popular entertainer of unrivalled mag-netism and following – this was the great supporting and killing fact about his biography. He had travelled with facility up and down the many floors of Victorian society; by defi-nition, a present-day novel for children cuts itself off from the power centres of a society. That is to say, the inevitable limi-tations of scope, in language, in moral and emotional refer-ence, in the nature of the experiences rendered and the way in which they draw in the essential energy-lines of society, make it hard for the children's novelist to get a grip on a large enough model of the world to suggest the interconnectedness and con-tradictions of all its parts.

I do not, however, mean that a novelist must include the White House and the House of Commons, or the board rooms of the finance houses and the floor of the Stock Exchange, or wherever else power is supposed to conceal itself in the rich West, if he or she is to speak commandingly on the state of the nation. To stay with Dickens as our example, *Little Dorrit* is as marvellous as it is because the image of the prison gives Dickens a bold and brilliant silhouette to place around the outline of society, and within which to locate the rich particu-larity, either of William or Frederick Dorrit and the turnkeys in the prison, or of Merdle and his household, or of the deadlier prison in which Mrs Clennam is locked and Arthur Clennam brought up. Merdle's crash and suicide, for all that they are perhaps the weakest stroke in the novel, certainly echo throughout large portions of metropolitan society and bank-rupt some of the main characters. But *Little Dorrit* does not take its great energy and realism from the fact that part of the machinery of the plot is driven by an entrepreneur's cheque book and the financial confidence it commands. *Little Dorrit* embodies the structures of power and oppression in the sense

[1] F. R. and Q. D. Leavis, *Lectures in America* (1969), p. 8.

connoted by Leavis – it renders the sources of life and death in the society where Victorian life runs strongly and freshly, as it does in Fanny Dorrit's strong, naïve, self-assertive snobberies, as it does in the smaller, contradictory spirit of young John the turnkey; *and* where it dwindles to something feeble, as it does behind the large façade of Mr Dorrit's pretensions, or even as it does in Arthur Clennam, after what he takes to be his disgrace. These are the force-lines of distortion and renewal which the mighty press of Victorian life, both ideal and material, gave to these particular and representative lives. The interplay of practice and structure, the 'habitus' of Victorian England, is caught and held in the novel. It is also important to grasp that although each of his characters cannot, any more than their author, be mistaken for anything other than an English Victorian, there is nothing determinist in such a statement. However conditional and conditioned, Little Dorrit herself emerges from the Marshalsea untainted, and a free woman. She has *not* been enclosed in the simple, predetermined nullities of some versions of history and social structure.

This is why, for a teenage reader, Dickens may lead the way to serious thought about society and serious living in it. His novels are, if you like, a general theory of social practices and their structures: or so a political scientist might put it. We might say instead that the novels, by way of the universally respected practice of storytelling, make sense of the vast and endless inanity of everyday experience. They take the ingenuous and fugitive reasons and motives of individual lives and bind them to a much larger, more inclusive historical wheel. Dickens's great wheel trundles over the broken ground, marking its own road as it goes.

Implied in that last paragraph is the theory of a liberal education – and of education in the liberal art of the novel – which this book argues for and commends. I take my final texts by way of trying to confirm and expound that argument. Dickens is my object-lesson not only because of the majesty of his achievement, but precisely because he was so popular, and handled with such facility the stuff of popular culture.[2] That is to say, he could not have done what he did without the materials of popular fiction, and these include not only the

[2] The point of Raymond Williams's view of Dickens, in *The English Novel from Dickens to Lawrence* (1970).

language he stitched together from the many linguistic fabrics he found about him, but also the rhetorical effects: the sharp silhouettes, the tableaux, the melodramatic rescues and reversals, the stunning boldness of feature and gesture – Magwitch in the graveyard, the unmasking of Uriah Heep, the murderous quest of Rogue Riderhood up the Thames – the grisly array of unforgettable rogues and hypocrites – Chadband, Grandfather Smallweed, Mr Carker, Fagin, Mrs Gamp, Silas Wegg, Pecksniff, Podsnap. 'When people say Dickens exaggerates, it seems to me they can have no eyes and no ears. They probably only have *notions* of what things and people are; they accept them conventionally, at their diplomatic value. Their minds run on in the region of discourse, where there are masks only and no faces, ideas and no facts . . .'[3] Santayana imagines the polite world saying to itself, '*I* was never so sentimental as that; *I* never say anything so dreadful; *I* don't believe there were ever such people like Quilp, or Squeers, or Serjeant Buzfuz'; then he retorts, 'But the polite world is lying; there *are* such people; we are such people ourselves . . .'

Dickens's force as object-lesson to children's novelists is his popularity and those things which made him popular: the boldness, colour, and intensification of both effect and structure; all those things and, above all, his laughter. *Laughter* is the great, the crucial word. It underlines Dickens's other force as object-lesson: that straightness of seeing which picks out Chadband or Podsnap as the disgusting, but disgustingly *funny*, hypocrites they are. Children have not lost ears and eyes, substituted ideas for facts. Whether little innocents or limbs of Satan, they can see straight, see 'closely and accurately', and except perhaps for the really hard nuts of the comprehensive-school fourth year, retain that 'freshness, and gentleness, and capacity of being pleased' without which there will be no virtue and no good novelists either.

So I take Joan Aiken's classic *Midnight is a Place* to exemplify the dependence of an exceptional and intelligent novelist for children upon Dickens's achievement. To say so is not to lay claim to a piece of successful influence-spotting. Joan Aiken might never have read a word of Dickens, but *Midnight is a Place* shows the presence of Dickens in the forms and contents which

---

[3] George Santayana, 'Dickens', in *Selected Critical Writings*, ed. Norman Henfrey (1968), vol. I, p. 195.

are to hand for a children's novelist to work with. I spoke in Part I of the closeness (though not the identity) of morality and feeling, and of the way novels may teach us both. A novelist who wishes to speak of 'freshness, and gentleness, and the capacity of being pleased', and who wishes to combine generosity and the anger which is the natural expression of thwarted generosity, works from a comic vision, in which laughter is not only a response, it is a *value*.

These are strong lessons to teach children. But they are neither heady nor intoxicating. Joan Aiken, I suggest, seeks to carry such messages to children, not so much in the hope that they will become entranced by their own exuberant and colourful individuality, as in the hope that they will learn to swell in the spaciousness of a hearty and durable altruism. And if altruism as a word has a slightly cold-fingered look about it, I assume that it connotes the richer moral vocabulary suggested by such underused terms as love, joy, peace, long-suffering, gentleness, truth.

Midnight is a Place shows how a novelist may work within the tradition – the forms of thought and imagining – made possible by Dickens. The book is one of the author's most recent full-length novels, but she is a varied and prodigal writer, and her virtues are consistent. In all her writing, one finds high spirits, indomitable children, the *coups de théâtre* and lurid stage effects which I have often mentioned as the tasty, typifying flavour of the line of poetic fiction which runs from the great Victorians by way of the bestsellers - become - junior - fiction to the best present-day children's novels. She turns therefore to the materials of a popular tradition. A novelist of the present day looking for a recent voice to follow in that tradition is likely to have to go back as far as D. H. Lawrence. Lawrence was the last great all-popular novelist, but the oddities of his twentieth-century reputation make him hardly comparable to Dickens. He wrote of himself that 'I am English, and my Englishness is my vision', but his version of English individualism took him far from the busy city life in which Dickens sat so easily at home. His version of English Romanticism stopped in an intense state of personal feeling but without a social world in which to live it through. He wrote himself, we might say, into a cul-de-sac, and his exile and the solitudes of his last novels are its dead end.

A children's novelist is writing for a comparatively unintrospective and physically active audience. The importance of Dickens for Joan Aiken is that his novels, and beside them the novels once handed to adolescents as a suitable introduction to the classics, works such as *Jane Eyre, Pride and Prejudice, The Mill on the Floss, Far from the Madding Crowd, Youth* and *Typhoon,* can express their intensity of feeling in an active public world. Now I have argued throughout this book that to take seriously the business of writing novels for children is to show the way the world goes, and how they should act in it. A great deal of contemporary literature emphasizes a world in which it is very hard to act at all, partly because its agents or characters are so very much men and women without qualities, partly because it is so obviously hard to know where to act so that what you do has responsible and effectual consequences. The withdrawal of present-day adult literature into tiny placeless rooms – bedsitters, flats, prison cells, motor cars, seminar rooms, hospital wards, telephone kiosks – leaves children's novelists without the contemporary support they need, and everything to do for themselves. The metonymy of helplessness – the small room with its mean emotions from whose windows you may if you are lucky catch a glimpse of what will happen to you[4] – is a dismal place for the children's novelist.

Looking for larger premises and fresher air with which to regale children, Joan Aiken and her peers have to rejoice in anachronism; they choose their sources and construct their traditions more singlemindedly than writers for adults. For it has been my argument that as men and women speaking to children they are obliged to forswear the readymix literary glutamate of self-accusation, moral guilt, black comedy, and the rather insubstantial despair which characterizes so much modern literature, even that written by adult novelists as obviously talented as those I listed. If it is not a duty, it is surely a necessary virtue in children's novelists to offer their readers confidence and hope in the future. And therefore, whatever the arbitrariness and naïvety of the materials out of which to make form and content, structure and substance, convention and value, they all are forced by their situation out of the margin, in

---

[4] E.g. David Storey's *Pasmore,* Nadine Gordimer's *The Conservationist,* Doris Lessing's *Memoirs of a Survivor,* Bellow's *Mr. Sammler's Planet,* Dan Jacobson's *Confessions of Joseph Baisz.*

which so many of their adult counterparts have struck their attitudes, into the broad centre of the unwritten page. Writing for children commits the novelists to one ideal centre of modern life, and commits them to a child's-eye view of that centre. From such a position they cannot, as we noted, gain much purchase on the levers of power, but they can, supremely, pick up the best images for positive action, which nowadays we give to children. (The stories are our guarantee that there will *be* a future.) Most children begin from a family, however awful it may be; it is that strictly material fact from which the novelists begin, and it is my cue for taking *Midnight is a Place* as a generally admirable example, and one that falls very neatly to hand in its smaller, broadly simplified pastiche of the earlier Dickens.

Joan Aiken is no innocent, though she creates a memorable innocence. Her children have to piece their ideal family together, gradually and painfully. Lucas begins as the orphan ward of the drunken, vindictive ex-blade, Sir Randolph, prowling around the empty shell of Midnight Place under the intermittent eye of Mr Oakapple his distant but decent tutor. He acquires as a putative sister the French-speaking waif, Anna-Marie Murgatroyd, when Sir Randolph's terrifying self-immolation in the sensational blaze of the old pile[5] leaves the two children destitute. In the face of daunting humiliation and squalor, in which they scrape a living from trawling for valuables in the sewers and making new cigars from waste ends, as well as paying a convincingly fearsome protection gang of bullies, they seek out a refuge and a new mother:

She was an old lady. The word lady immediately came into Lucas's mind, although her dress was extremely rough, made of woollen material, and covered with a sacking apron. She wore battered old boots as well, and her snowy hair was skewered up on top of her head in a large untidy knot by what looked like a twig of yew. She was tall – rather taller than Lucas – and thin as a scarecrow. In the dim light it was hard to make out the colour of her cheeks, but they looked wrinkled and weather-beaten, like the skin of an old apple that has been left in the grass all winter. Her hands were thin as gulls' claws. But her face! Lucas thought he had never seen a face combining such authority and such goodness. The nose was so straight, and the

---

[5] The whole novel, particularly the tableaux, was brilliantly dramatized by Granada TV in 1977 and 1979.

sockets of the eyes so deep, that the old lady's face reminded Lucas of a yoke – the kind of yoke used for carrying two milk-pails, with a bar across the top. It had that firmness and strength. And her eyes, deepset in triangular caverns, were bright – bright – but what colour, in that hazy light, neither Lucas nor Anna-Marie could determine. (*Midnight is a Place*, pp. 180–1)

Joan Aiken knows that she can trust children to understand her use of the word 'lady'. Lady Murgatroyd brings no fairy-godmaternal rescue. She too has to build with the children and with Mr Oakapple, invalided by burns from the fire, a new moral and political economy. They must all of them work within the beastliness, cruelty, and injustices which characterize the life of Blastburn, and the terms of their economy are taken straight from *Hard Times*'s Coketown and the Thames of *Our Mutual Friend*.

Those two novels stand respectively for the history and geography of industrialization. Blastburn incorporates the killing oppressions of a nineteenth-century carpet factory and the vast effluent which runs in the sewer rivers below. There is no need for symbolization: the carpet press which kills the poor children who are too slow to get away is real and terrible (satisfyingly smashed in a grand scene by Lucas); the treasure which Lucas recovers from the revolting swill and the hogs which scavenge in it is the papers which defeat the crooked lawyer and ensure a rather more just future for the factory.

The determination of the odd little family, with its mixture of histories from a now superannuated ruling class, creates the new possibilities of the future – that and their direct experience of the pain, want, cruelty, and injustice of the lives they are forced to lead. But those lives are portrayed quite without over-earnestness. The institutionalization of self-pity, and its obverse, self-disgust, is always to be expected in a culture that maintains its stability as ours does by balancing the claims and the disparities in power and longevity of various interest groups. Politics is defined as the negotiation of those who are invited to come to the table. In such circumstances, the best way to get your claims listened to, short of overturning the stability upon which they rest, is to say how sorry you are for yourself, and therefore how sorry other people ought to be for you as well. By such arguments, adjusted against a distributive grid of status and reward which has little more validity than that of having been as it is for a long time, the modern social calculus computes its system of wages, welfare, representation, say in its affairs, and so on.

The intensifications of Joan Aiken's Blastburn, placed in a slightly more lurid and compressed image of nineteenth-century industrialization than Joseph Wright ever painted or Friedrich Engels ever described, show a modern child not so much the historical world we have lost as the better world we might have gained. The two children, Anna-Marie and Lucas, and the grand old lady are resourceful in entirely present-day terms – they have learned to make their living and to keep up their fight from the labour and guerrilla experiences of the past forty years. They hold together, alongside the wounded tutor, an image of a perfectly *déclassé* cultivation – Lady Murgatroyd's thrifty, savoury cuisine, her ladylike way, Mr Oakapple's music, relearned for his unmutilated left hand, Lucas's novel-writing, Anna's technological inventiveness and her leadership of industrial resistance. Conventional divisions of labour by both sex and age are here reversed and reinvented for a new economy, confirmed in the happiness of the home they make out of the abandoned hovel, a home completed by the baby left in their care and the timeless reassurance of a big, safe dog.

Joan Aiken's realistic world lacks, we may say, the alleged realism which creates cowardly or drunken parents, bullying brothers or incontinent relatives. Her home is a real haven. Well, what else may a child cherish? The quartet in the novel *build* their home; they do not buy it ready-made, nor do they keep it as a redoubt against the world. They carry its values out into the world and seek the connections which will extend their power. Thus, when Lucas is rescued almost drowned from the sewers and the crazed evangelist for whom he works amongst the filth, the house he is taken to belongs to the Scatcherds, a vigorous and independent dynasty of working-class leaders, whose oldest member connived at the fraud which disinherited Lucas, who have lost children in the inhuman conditions at the carpet factory, and whose boldest young man, Davey, is now leader of the real union of the men just emerging to fight both the brutal managers and the even more brutal Friendly Society led by the ice-cold cripple, Bludward. In a set-piece duel fought with blunt, solid little hammerguns loaded with bolts taken from the factory machines, Davey is mortally wounded, having refused to kill Bludward when he could. To crown a very traditional tableau, Bludward breaks honour, steers his wheelchair out of the line of fire, and goes through the ice of the lake, to be drowned by poetic justice.

The measure of the book may be taken in a very brief comparison with another novel whose author shows a marked admiration for Dickens. In Leon Garfield's *Smith*, the vigour, pace, and tearing high spirits of the prose suggest an instrument of strikingly inclusive powers. The description of Smith's first bath shows the bite and movement of which Garfield is capable:

At last he crouched, naked as a charred twig, quivering and twitching as if the air was full of tickling feathers.

'Ready,' he said, in a low, uneasy voice, and the four footmen set to work.

Two men held him in the tub; one scrubbed, and one acted as ladle-man. This last task was on account of the water having been dosed with sulphur, and it consisted in spooning off Smith's livestock as it rushed to the surface in a speckled throng.

From beginning to end, the washing of Smith took close upon three hours, with the scullery so filled with sulphurous steam that the footmen's misted faces grew red as the copper saucepans that hung like midnight suns on the scullery's streaming walls. (pp. 52–3)

The trouble is that Garfield rests at the strictly external level of this example; it makes his novel a marvellous read, but he can only sustain the simple line and momentum of thrilling suspense. In spite of the strikingness of the image of Smith rescuing a blind Justice of the Peace, the allegory becomes a simple, necessary platitude purporting to justify a traditional treasure hunt for a Will, a Prodigal Son, and a casket of coins. Garfield is very good, there is no doubt: his imagining of Newgate is intensely picturesque, with the sentimentality of heartiness without which no child ever discovered a proper moral sympathy. What he takes from Victorian melodrama however is just the colour, and such novel-writing lends itself to the colour-charting which passes for academic criticism of the tourist office kind – 'colour' and 'movement' are what Dickens was and is most praised for.

What Joan Aiken's novel gives us through these qualities – energy, pace, vividness, and so on – is a way of responding to and living through real social lives and their connections. That is why I cast her as the last heroine of this book.

> We were the last romantics, chose for theme
> Traditional sanctity and loveliness . . .[6]

Not a bit of it; Joan Aiken is a romantic, and there is no reason why the great battle cries of Romanticism – freedom, sincerity, love, independence, courage (the Kantian virtues) – which have all had their say in the children's novels commended here, should not still ring true for their readers.

Those readers are, admittedly, members of the novel-buying classes in the English-speaking world. Liberal education has pushed the boundaries of those classes back a little way, but that is not immediately the point. The point is whether the social formations who produce the novels and who dominate the manufacture of symbolism – art, public communications, education – in the English-speaking nations are capable of imagining stories which will keep faith with the old meanings parents and children can give allegiance to and understand, as well as convert those master-symbols into the currency of a new world. The modest object-lesson Joan Aiken provides is how to make the conversion. She takes the traditional forms of popular Victorian drama and throws them into a new configuration, keeping as much of the old as she needs – the moral concept of a lady, the necessity of music, change of heart in people as more important than ideology (Anna-Marie is made to say so rather stiffly at the end) – and goes on to sketch the moral and material benefits of a rewritten nineteenth-century industrial history. She sustains our educational custom of seeing the past, as I put it earlier, as surpassed but mythologized – that is, present happiness as built on the heroic self-sacrifice of our fathers and mothers, who for all their undoubted suffering enjoyed greater closeness and comradeship than we do, because of their great purpose. She goes on, as we have seen, to tie the traditional virtues to a new economy, and by dissolving the existing structure of power and money, releases her characters at the end to try and make it work on new terms. Ned Bludward is dead; Lucas will become a novelist and factory adviser; Anna-Marie will still lead the little fluff-pickers; Lady Murgatroyd continues as classless

[6] W. B. Yeats, 'Coole Park and Ballylee, 1931', *Collected Poems* (1961), p. 276.

doyenne of the town.

At the same time, Joan Aiken has found the right language in which to tell the tale, a more than merely linguistic point. The orchestration of details as small as the *names* of the characters and the places in *Midnight is a Place* is of a piece with the lessons being taught. For the briskness and livingness of the writing carry the reader *on*; the prose is not surrendered, like the writing of books as different in theme as *Red Shift* or *Sounder*.

Something of the same judgement could be made about Russell Hoban's *The Mouse and His Child*. It is not necessary to quote at length to make this point, but it is enough to mention Hoban's little masterpiece to remind us that contemporary realism in children's novels need not mean dealing grimly with the facts of industrial life. Hoban's prose, like Joan Aiken's, moves you on. Addressed directly to its readers (who may or may not be children), its sane, affirmative speech has no recourse to the desperations of interior monologue (such as we find in the thriller) nor to the exiguous resonances which the Tolkien commando continues to beat out of its antique drum. Both writers find a prose and a plot which frees them from the spirals of subjective inner space, but these are not as strictly superficial as, say, the busy surface life of Leon Garfield's *Smith*.

The line of Hoban's characters is more serpentine than Joan Aiken's, and his plot more deliberately a sequence of episodes. Hoban is a formal writer, at times diagrammatically so, but the form of *The Mouse and His Child* is traced along their wandering through the waste land of American literature – from the trash heap of Gatsby's West Egg and back again, so to say. His formality and its tendency to clumsiness[7] come out in the way the long pilgrimage home by the little mouse and his father, and its deadly pursuit by the magnificently raffish Manny Rat, is portioned out to the different masters of slavery and exploitation. The father mouse and his son are the patient, determined slaves of crooks and then of mountebanks, of phoney art (the Caws of Art) and pseudo-science (the Muskrat), and the tolerant, amiable audience of the massively pointless philosopher-turtle, C. Serpentina. Throughout the tale, Hoban's genially creative energy grates slightly upon his no

[7] Commented on by Ian MacKillop in *Good Writers for Young Readers*, ed. Dennis Butts (1977), pp. 57–67.

less serious but awkward and effortful reaching for significance in his novel. The effort appears in the rather studied sequence of emblems and allegory in the story – the gold coin, the image of the 'last visible dog' on the label of the dogfood, the fortune-telling Frog, the forced joke of the Muskrat's techno-babble. Each of these items from the creative writer's course manual (Symbols and structures: Advanced) *has* a real life of its own as well, no doubt; the tin of dog food with a picture on the label of a dog carrying a tin of dog food with a picture of a dog carrying a tin ... and so on, is an example of a puzzle which has delighted children perennially. But it is a heavy-handed as well as an obscure little message if you try to unpack its meaning. Hoban is much better in the unforced, easy strength with which he brings together comicality and nonchalant cruelty, the dim, fierce perseverance of his heroes and their friends and the supple, attractive malignity of Manny Rat. Better still is his carnal and vigorous eye for incongruity – the eye which appoints the grand and dowdy elephant wife to the mouse, which dresses the raucous frog in a tatty old mitten, which sweeps up two loving, deadly weasels with the even deadlier talons of the owl through either brain.

Hoban is a strong, exuberant writer, with something of Ted Hughes and Mark Twain in him (plus far too much of, let us say, Oliver Wendell Holmes). I put him briefly with Joan Aiken as another example of the way of thinking, imagining, and moralizing which we may call Dickensian, and which writers for children – and writers for adults as well – so much need to draw on. It is a way of moralizing which deals straightly with pains and want without making them the trivial or banal object of social medicine.

The strength of each writer is a comic strength. If I feel I must stress as my conclusion the necessity of comedy or its rebirth, I do not intend any vague homily on 'joy in life' or 'comic vision'. The particular embodiments that life or comedy may take on in a culture and its history depend on the sort of chance they get. It isn't enough to look to a riotous art to put right the deadly order and dullness of everyday life. Dickens's 'energy' and 'vitality', his 'naturalness' and his rich array of characters, are not artistic compensations for a dull world, nor overflowing caricatures of a life-force which cannot be confined to ideological, political, or historical categories. The greater the novelist, the more largely and intelligently he or she seeks to render by imitation *and* to overcome in resolution the deep, painful fractures, woundings, contradictions and tragedies of the times.[8]

Tragedy, in present-day terms, is the living-through of the waste, pain, and cruelty caused by the killing divisions and contradictions of historical motion. This post–Hegelian definition will perhaps do for the time being. It does not issue in a 'tragic vision' (or only in the pages of examination papers) nor does it imply determinist beliefs. Tragedy is both process and experience; it depends first on life in earnest, and then upon an understanding of it. Comedy, by the same token, is the binding concept which gives meaning to forms and outlines in the life lived around and through us. To see the comedy is to live through some of the same disorders as before, but with a more serene and tranquil eye for their misrule and subversion: the restoration of stability succeeds inevitably, the essential kinship of politics and politeness reaffirms itself.

Any serious person must, with enough luck, find the experience of his life both comic and tragic. But in suggesting, with a proper tact, that children learn to see the shapes of comedy and tragedy as connecting and giving meaning to the ceaseless motion of experience, we might refer again to the title-phrase and look to the novels which are such an essential part of a liberal education as to hold out in Stendhal's words 'la promesse de bonheur', for which 'the promise of happiness' will only just do as a translation.[9] Novels, like paintings or music or sport, should hold out to children the promise of happiness, and the certainty of laughter.

Laughter, like love, is one of those things which disappear if you talk about them too much. The great love poems rarely talk about what love *is*; they describe what it is like to feel it, to answer its imperious demands, whether divine or human, to regret its elusiveness, to insist on it as a duty. Now while there is no doubt what laughter *is*, as a physical, psychological, tropistic behaviour, it is much harder to say what *causes* it. Yet com-

[8] This paragraph repeats something of the critical and political positions of this book. It is perhaps useful to note that it represents an effort to bring together F. R. Leavis's kind of criticism of the novel with that of some European neo-Marxist aestheticians of his lifetime, especially George Lukács, Lucien Goldmann, and Walter Benjamin.

[9] 'Bonheur', after all, resists Kant's separation of goodness and happiness; it means both qualities at once.

edians at least since Aristophanes have sought to cause it, and for the purposes of these last observations about novels and the brave new world which children will make from them, laughter and a love of life may be said to be necessarily connected. There is indeed a family of moral cognates which any parent or teacher would want children to make their own, as personal qualities and as experiences: happiness, love, joy, delight, renewal, glee, and all these as lived in laughter. A laughing man is a free man. He laughs because the displacements, the disorderly analogies, the turning of the world upside down, all serve to confirm a sense of how the world really will be, when it reverts to, or achieves, its propriety. When it does, in some ideal, always unrealized social order, politeness will be its own politics. Until then, a laughter-maintaining language holds back the forces of darkness and depression, and keeps a large space open for the play of those great names – joy, freedom, happiness, and so forth.

So a reader might go from Joan Aiken to Charles Dickens by way of P. G. Wodehouse. I promised in Chapter 2 that we would return to Wodehouse, and enough has been said in these pages by now to make the stupid use of class-bias irrelevant as a criticism, and to put aside any notion that Wodehouse's tremendous joyfulness is artless and placeless. The incomparably funny sequence in *Right Ho, Jeeves* in which the helpless goof Gussie Fink-Nottle is enticed by Bertie Wooster and Jeeves to address the local grammar-school speech-day only after 'inserting a liberal dose of mixed spirits in this normally abstemious man' is so rich because of Wodehouse's mastery of a language perfectly combining fastidious hyperbole, intense parody of upper-class formality, natural and eloquent gracefulness, and music hall bathos. The result is a brilliant and endlessly inventive play of surfaces. What is more, for all that his comic world is kept safely within the entirely untroubling conventions of temporarily divided lovers, absconding masterchefs, and overpowering aunts, Wodehouse's language as a way of describing the world is as *usable* as Dickens's. Apply Santayana's words to Wodehouse: 'When people say that [Wodehouse] exaggerates, it seems to me they can have no eyes and no ears.' Thus, as preliminary to the Market Snodsbury speech-day platform:

I had only just time to shove the jug behind the photograph of Uncle Tom on the mantelpiece before the door opened and in came Gussie, curveting like a circus horse.

'What-ho, Bertie,' he said. 'What-ho, what-ho, what-ho, and again what-ho. What a beautiful world this is, Bertie. One of the nicest I ever met.'

I stared at him, speechless. We Woosters are as quick as lightning, and I saw at once that something had happened.

I mean to say, I told you about him walking round in circles. I recorded what passed between us on the lawn. And if I portrayed the scene with anything like adequate skill, the picture you will have retained of this Fink-Nottle will have been that of a nervous wreck, sagging at the knees, green about the gills, and picking feverishly at the lapels of his coat in an ecstasy of craven fear. In a word, defeatist. Gussie, during that interview, had, in fine, exhibited all the earmarks of one licked to a custard.

Vastly different was the Gussie who stood before me now. Self-confidence seemed to ooze from the fellow's every pore. His face was flushed, there was a jovial light in his eyes, the lips were parted in a swashbuckling smile. And when with a genial hand he sloshed me on the back before I could sidestep, it was as if I had been kicked by a mule.

'Well, Bertie,' he proceeded, as blithely as a linnet without a thing on his mind, 'you will be glad to hear that you were right. Your theory has been tested and proved correct. I feel like a fighting cock.'

My brain ceased to reel. I saw all.

'Have you been having a drink?'

'I have. As you advised. Unpleasant stuff. Like medicine. Burns your throat, too, and makes one as thirsty as the dickens. How anyone can mop it up, as you do, for pleasure beats me. Still, I would be the last to deny that it tunes up the system. I could bite a tiger.'

It would be gratuitous once more to unpack the local effects, and indeed it's hard to sample Wodehouse in small extracts without missing the multitudes of verbal displacements and incongruous juxtapositions by which he wins his effects. Of course, his range cannot take in everything; of course, it is strongly marked by certain class origins – it is meant to be; but it is wrong to suppose that such speech cannot, as they say, nego-tiate the world. The headlong interplay of its constituents – the young-man-about-town-slang, Jeeves's verbose formality, Wodehouse's Eliotic and piquant use of literary reference, Aunt Dahlia's genteel but racy invective – holds together by virtue of its charm, as we might say; it is spellbound. That is the heart of comedy, that we acquiesce in the idea of order, and can therefore tolerate disorder, indeed look out for it with a grateful and brimming eye. (The great thing about Bertie is that he stands exactly on the moral division between saintliness and fatheadedness, so one never knows how much admiration for his excellence tempers one's laughter.) The passage continues:

He moved buoyantly from the wash-stand, and endeavoured to slosh me on the back again. Foiled by my nimble footwork, he staggered to the bed and sat down upon it.

'Braced? Did I say I could bite a tiger?'

'You did.'

'Make it two tigers. I could chew holes in a steel door. What an ass you must have thought me out there in the garden. I see now you were laughing in your sleeve.'

'No, no.'

'Yes,' insisted Gussie. 'That very sleeve,' he said, pointing. 'And I don't blame you. I can't imagine why I made all that fuss about a potty job like distributing prizes at a rotten little country grammar school. Can you imagine, Bertie?'

'No.'

'Exactly. Nor can I imagine. There's simply nothing to it. I just shin up on the platform, drop a few gracious words, hand the little blighters their prizes, and hop down again, admired by all. Not a suggestion of split trousers from start to finish. I mean, why should anybody split his trousers? I can't imagine. Can you imagine?'

'No.'

'Nor can I imagine. I shall be a riot. I know just the sort of stuff that's needed – simple, manly, optimistic stuff straight from the shoulder. This shoulder,' said Gussie, tapping. 'Why I was so nervous this morning I can't imagine. For anything simpler than distributing a few footling books to a bunch of grimy-faced kids I can't imagine. Still, for some reason I can't imagine, I was feeling a little nervous, but now I feel fine, Bertie – fine, fine, fine – and I say this to you as an old friend. Because that's what you are, old man, when all the smoke has cleared away – an old friend. I don't think I've ever met an older friend. How long have you been an old friend of mine, Bertie?'

'Oh, years and years.'

'Imagine? Though, of course, there must have been a time when you were a new friend . . . Hullo, the luncheon gong. Come on, old friend.'

And, rising from the bed like a performing flea, he made for the door. (pp. 159–61)

The high spirits are so bracing; the detail so hilariously small ('that very sleeve ... pointing ... This shoulder ... tapping'). There are some funny drunks in European literature but none funnier than Gussie, caught rising in the purity of Wodehouse's diction, 'like a performing flea'.

Laughter puts a meaning on the world. It is self-confident. A funny story is a way of turning things upside down in order to understand them better. In Clifford Geertz's useful phrase, 'it is the use of emotion for cognitive ends'.[10] And so is any story; so are gossip and literature. Storytelling is, after all, an entirely universal human activity. A story, as John Berger puts it, is not a wheel; we may say it goes for a walk like a child. It does not touch the ground at every point, but walks, runs, bounds, stops to inspect something closely, hurries on again, according to the pace of reader and narrator. The homely metaphors of 'keeping up', 'making strides', 'skipping', 'getting lost', 'feeling out of one's depth', 'being at home with' fit the experience of storytelling and novel-reading perfectly. These are the ways all men and women have of making sense of their world;[11] it is how, if they are lucky, they learn to make sense when mother and father talk to them in long, uncomprehended commentaries during infancy, as mother tours the supermarket or father shows them his vegetable patch. Stories shape a child's day until, as it was the point of The Tale of Peter Rabbit to press home earlier, aesthetic shape and moral understanding share a common structure. Making sense of a child's day is then a matter of giving it a proper shape. So we put a child's distress right by insisting on the rituals of bedtime which confirm shape: a hot drink in bed, a story, a good-night kiss, a coming-back-in-a-minute-to-put-the-light-out. So too we try to give our life and lives a proper shape, and criticize the mess we've made of them in the name of a greater coherence and a perfected, rational order.

These processes indicate the essential hermeneutic of reason and epistemology. That is to make my conclusion grandly. Say simply, that making sense of the world is both critical and creative. We criticize its nonsense in the name of the greater sense we can create in our stories. Improvement, both personal and

---

[10] In The Interpretation of Cultures (1975), p. 449.
[11] I am most grateful here to Hugo McCann for ideas he gave me during a long conversation in Hobart in 1978.

political, is then a matter of creating more adequate and satisfying stories – better novels, in fact. They then become instruments with which to criticize the gap between vision and
actuality.

In the course of this book I have spoken of this process as continuous with that of imagining anything at all, as long as such
imagining has the structure of a narrative. That is to say, our
psychology works to connect what we see and how we think
about it, the intricate reciprocity of percept and concept, by
constructing a narrative capable of leading us along some sort
of pathway through the inane eventualities of everyday life.
When the path leads somewhere and follows an intelligible
line, we call it experience. I have laboured this argument in the
first part of the book. Narratives, stories, or fictions, give us a
way of connecting arbitrary eventualities; the author is our self,
who insists on trying to make sense of life, to find or to give it
meaning and significance. The difficulty is to make the narrative stick to the facts.

The narrative is not, of course, in any way an unchanging
structure. The narrative of a person's life and its larger echo,
Edwin Muir's fable (that is, the ideal but impossible life each
person lives unnoticingly in her imagination), has to incorpo-
rate breaks and divisions, stops and retreats, changes of heart
and mind. We discard a narrative as it no longer sticks fast to the
facts. Or more insistently and habitually, we revise it; we take
the real events of life and revise them to suit ourselves and our
picture of what our life is really like. At once, if our revision is
too much for our truthfulness, is too self-indulgent, in the
blitheness with which reality has been revised to cheer ourselves up, our sense of reality rises up to check the fantasy
against the facts, criticize it and restore it in a further revision to
some more rightful relation to truth and reality.

The process is endless and necessary. It turns along a spiral of
creation and criticism in which it is not always clear which is
which. Criticism and creation are the turns of the mind by
which reality is circumscribed, assimilated, judged and
rejudged.

Our public fictions repeat this process. Novels are the disciplined and public versions of the fictions we must have if we are
to think at all. Children's novels are proposed to children by
adults as the imaginative forms of life which they may work

with and turn into their future lives.

To take such an argument seriously is to place the study of fiction at the very heart of education, both official and informal. It is to cut back the dominance of social calculus and computational science in public thought and its schemes of reason. Literature is then no longer the consolation of your private life. Fiction-making cannot guarantee virtue, but it can freedom. And it is much better able to work for the common good than any of the alternatives which ensure the death of public thought and feeling in and out of school.

Bibliography

Primary

The following list includes all the novels which I treat in the book. In nearly all cases, I have used the paperback edition most readily available; on occasions, I have used old or first editions which I have on my own shelves. Page references in the text refer to one or other of these editions, but in the event of the reader wishing to check up, they should not be difficult to find in whatever copy he or she has to hand. This is perhaps also the place to acknowledge that, in the rich store of good children's fiction presently and cheaply available in the bookshops, the contribution made by Puffins is enormous and amazing. While doubtless remaining a strictly commercial organization, Kaye Webb and her team of editors showed a consistency of judgement, a generosity of range, and a commitment to standards for which the reward must be the maintenance of intelligent standards and the shoring up of honourable culture among their customers and readers.

Adams, R. *Watership Down*, London: Rex Collings 1972; Harmondsworth: Puffin 1973.
    Shardik, London: Allen Lane with Rex Collings 1974; Harmondsworth: Penguin 1976.
    The Plague Dogs, London: Allen Lane with Rex Collings 1977; Harmondsworth: Penguin 1978.
Aiken, J. *A Necklace of Raindrops*, London: Cape 1968; Harmondsworth: Puffin 1975.
    Midnight is a Place, London: Cape 1974; Harmondsworth: Puffin 1976.
Allen, J. *The Spring on the Mountain*, London: Cape 1973; Harmondsworth: Puffin 1977.
Avery, G. *The Warden's Niece*, London: Collins 1957, Lion 1974.
Bawden, N. *Carrie's War*, London: Gollancz 1973; Harmondsworth: Puffin 1974.
    Rebel on a Rock, London: Gollancz 1978.
Broster, D. K. *The Dark Mile*, London: Heinemann 1926; Harmondsworth: Peacock 1974.
Buchan, J. *The Thirty Nine Steps*, London: Hodder & Stoughton 1915.
    Greenmantle, London: Hodder & Stoughton 1916.

Mr Standfast, London: Nelson 1924.

The Three Hostages, London: Nelson 1926.

all collected as:

The Four Adventures of Richard Hannay, London: Nelson 1930.

John Macnab, London: Nelson 1920.

Bunyan, J. *Pilgrim's Progress* (1678), London: Oxford University Press: Oxford Standard Authors Series 1904.

Burnett, F. H. *The Secret Garden*, London: Heinemann 1911; Harmondsworth: Puffin 1951.

Burton, H. *Castors Away!*, London: Oxford University Press 1962; Harmondsworth: Puffin 1978.

Carroll, L. *Alice's Adventures in Wonderland*, London: Macmillan 1865.

Through the Looking-Glass, London: Macmillan 1872.

Christopher, J. *The Guardians*, London: Hamish Hamilton 1970; Harmondsworth: Puffin 1973.

Conrad, J. *The Shadow-Line* (1917), London: Dent 1945.

Constantine, L. *Cricketers' Carnival*, London: Hutchinson 1948.

Cooper, S. *The Dark is Rising*, London: Chatto & Windus 1972; Harmondsworth: Puffin 1976.

Over Sea, Under Stone, London: Chatto & Windus 1973; Harmondsworth: Puffin 1976.

Greenwitch, London: Chatto & Windus 1974; Harmondsworth: Puffin 1977.

The Grey King, London: Chatto & Windus 1975; Harmondsworth: Puffin 1977.

Silver on the Tree, London: Chatto & Windus 1977; Harmondsworth: Puffin 1979.

Cormier, R. *The Chocolate War*, New York: Pantheon 1974, Dell 1975; London: Gollancz and Fontana 1974.

Dahl, R. *Charlie and the Chocolate Factory*, London: Allen & Unwin 1967; Harmondsworth: Puffin 1973.

DeJong, M. *The Wheel on the School*, New York: Harper & Row 1954; Harmondsworth: Puffin 1961.

De la Mare, W. *Collected Poems,* London: Faber & Faber 1955.

Dickens, C. *David Copperfield* (1850), Harmondsworth: Penguin English Library 1967.

Hard Times (1854), Harmondsworth: Penguin English Library 1968.

Little Dorrit (1857), Harmondsworth: Penguin English Library 1967.

Dickinson, P. *The Weathermonger*, London: Gollancz 1968; Harmondsworth: Puffin 1970.

Du Maurier, D. *Rebecca*, London: Gollancz 1938, Pan 1976.

Fisk, N. *Grinny*, London: Heinemann 1973; Harmondsworth: Puffin 1975.

Fox, P. *Blowfish Live in the Sea*, New York: Macmillan 1970; Harmondsworth: Puffin 1974.

The Slave Dancer, New York: Bradbury 1974; London: Pan 1977.

Gardam, J. *A Long Way from Verona*, London: Hamish Hamilton 1971; Harmondsworth: Puffin 1973.

Garfield, L. *Smith*, London: Constable 1967; Harmondsworth: Puffin 1968.

Garner, A. *The Weirdstone of Brisingamen*, London: Collins 1962, Lion 1974.

The Moon of Gomrath, London: Collins 1965, Lion 1974.

Elidor, London: Collins 1965, Lion 1974.

Red Shift, London: Collins 1973, Lion 1975.

Golding, W. *Lord of the Flies*, London: Faber & Faber 1954; Harmondsworth: Penguin 1960.

Grahame, K. *The Wind in the Willows*, London: Methuen 1908, Methuen Paperback 1961.

Greene, C. *Beat the Turtle Drum*, New York: Viking 1976.

Hamilton, V. *M. C. Higgins the Great*, New York: Macmillan 1974; London: Hamish Hamilton 1975, Lion 1976.

Hamley, D. *Pageants of Despair*, London: André Deutsch 1974; Harmondsworth: Puffin 1977.

Harris, R. *The Bright and Morning Star*, London: Faber & Faber 1972; Harmondsworth: Puffin 1978.

Hay, I. *Pip*, London: Hodder and Stoughton 1907; Harmondsworth: Penguin 1939.

Hemingway, E. *The First 49*, London: Cape 1944.

Hines, B. *Kes (A Kestrel for a Knave)*, London: Michael Joseph 1968; Harmondsworth: Penguin 1969.

Hoban, R. *The Mouse and His Child*, New York: Harper & Row 1967; London: Faber & Faber 1969; Harmondsworth: Puffin 1976.

Hughes, T. *The Iron Man*, London: Faber & Faber 1968.

Kipling, R. *Puck of Pook's Hill*, London: Macmillan 1908, 1951, Pan 1975.

Rewards and Fairies, London: Macmillan 1910, Pan 1975.

Le Guin, U. *Earthsea*, Berkeley, Cal.: Parnassus Press 1970.

A Wizard of Earthsea, London: Gollancz 1971; Harmondsworth: Puffin 1974.

The Tombs of Atuan, London: Gollancz 1972; Harmondsworth: Puffin 1974.

The Farthest Shore, London: Gollancz 1973; Harmondsworth: Puffin 1974.

Lively, P. *The Driftway*, London: Heinemann 1972, Pan 1976.

The House in Norham Gardens, London: Heinemann 1974, Pan 1977.

Going Back, London: Heinemann 1975, Pan 1978.

Mayne, W. *A Grass Rope*, London: Oxford University Press 1957; Harmondsworth: Puffin 1972.

No More School, London: Hamish Hamilton 1965; Harmondsworth: Puffin 1970.

Earthfasts, London: Hamish Hamilton 1966; Harmondsworth: Puffin 1969.

The Battlefield, London: Hamish Hamilton 1967.

The Jersey Shore, London: Hamish Hamilton 1973; Harmondsworth: Puffin 1976.

Milne, A. A. *Winnie-the-Pooh*, London: Methuen 1926, Methuen Paperback 1965.

The House at Pooh Corner, London: Methuen 1928, Methuen Paperback 1965.

Nesbit, E. *The Railway Children*, New York: Wells Gardner Darton 1906; Harmondsworth: Puffin 1960.

Paton Walsh, J. *The Dolphin Crossing*, London: Macmillan 1967 Harmondsworth: Puffin 1970.

Goldengrove, London: Macmillan 1972; Harmondsworth: Puffin 1975.

Pearce, P. *Tom's Midnight Garden*, London: Oxford University Press 1958; Harmondsworth: Puffin 1974.

with Fairfax-Lucy, B. *The Children of the House*, Harlow: Longmans 1968; Harmondsworth: Puffin 1974.

Peyton, K. M. *Flambards*, London: Oxford University Press 1969; Harmondsworth: Puffin 1977.

The Edge of the Cloud, London: Oxford University Press 1969; Harmondsworth: Puffin 1977.

Flambards in Summer, London: Oxford University Press 1969; Harmondsworth: Puffin 1977.

The Beethoven Medal, London: Oxford University Press 1971.

Potter, B. *The Tale of Peter Rabbit*, London: Frederick Warne n.d.

Ransome, A. *Swallows and Amazons*, London: Cape 1930; Harmondsworth: Puffin 1962.

Swallowdale, London: Cape 1931; Harmondsworth: Puffin 1968.

Pigeon Post, London: Cape 1936; Harmondsworth: Puffin 1969.

We Didn't Mean to Go to Sea, London: Cape 1937; Harmondsworth: Puffin 1969.

Great Northern?, London: Cape 1947; Harmondsworth: Puffin 1971.

Winter Holiday, London: Cape 1953; Harmondsworth: Puffin 1968.

ed. Rupert Hart-Davis *Autobiography*, London: Jonathan Cape 1976.

Rawlings, M. *The Yearling*, New York: Scribner 1937; London: Heinemann 1938, Pan 1976.

'Sapper' *Bulldog Drummond: His Four Rounds with Carl Peterson*, London: Hodder & Stoughton n.d.

Stevenson, R. L. *Treasure Island*, London: Nelson 1882, World's Classics edn 1949.

Sutcliff, R. *The Lantern Bearers*, London: Oxford University Press 1959.

Dawn Wind, London: Oxford 1963.

Thiele, C. (with Ingpen, R., illustrator) *Storm-Boy*, Norwood: Rigby 1974.

Thurber, J. 'The Secret Life of Walter Mitty', in *The Thurber Carnival*, Harmondsworth: Penguin 1957.

Tolkien, J. R. R. *The Hobbit* (1937), London: Allen & Unwin, 3rd edn 1966.

The Lord of the Rings: Part I, *The Fellowship of the Ring*; Part II, *The Two Towers*; Part III, *The Return of the King*, London: Allen & Unwin 1955.

Trease, G. *Bows Against the Barons*, Hodder & Stoughton, 1934; re-issued Brockhampton Press 1966.

Uttley, A. *A Traveller in Time*, London: Faber & Faber 1939; Harmondsworth: Puffin 1977.

Welch, R. *Knight Crusader*, London: Oxford University Press 1954; Harmondsworth: Puffin 1977.

White, E. B. *Charlotte's Web*, New York: Harper & Row 1950; Harmondsworth: Puffin 1963.

Wilder, L. I. *The Long Winter*, New York: Harper & Row 1953; Harmondsworth: Puffin 1968.

Wodehouse, P. G. *Right Ho, Jeeves*, London: Herbert Jenkins 1934; Harmondsworth: Penguin 1953.

The Mating Season, London: Herbert Jenkins 1949; Harmondsworth: Penguin 1957.

Wood, J., and Francis, F. *Grandmother Lucy and Her Hats*, London: Collins 1968.

Wynne Jones, D. *Cart and Cwidder*, London: Macmillan 1975; Harmondsworth: Puffin 1978.

Secondary

This list includes all the secondary sources cited in the text, together with a number of books which if not explicitly mentioned, have been very much in my mind while writing. This kind of pervasive influence is sometimes hard to identify, of course, but I have made particular mention of certain writers in special footnotes, as well as in the acknowledgements.

This is not, however, a general bibliography of children's fiction and its critics. Such criticism is not perhaps always characterized by its distinction, and in any case I am in no way seeking to provide an inventory of the literature. These books are simply those I have worked from and referred to; the list certainly includes a particular tradition of social and cultural theory within which I would like to count my own work, if it is good enough; but it does not imply a syllabus.

Abbs, P. 'Penelope Lively, and the Failure of Adult Culture', *Children's Literature in Education*, 18, 1975.

Althusser, L. *Lenin and Philosophy*, London: New Left Books 1971.

Ariès, P. *Centuries of Childhood*, Harmondsworth: Penguin 1973.

Arnold, M. *Essays in Criticism*, 2nd series, 1887, London: Macmillan 1938.

Avery, G. *Childhood's Pattern: Heroes and Heroines in Children's Literature 1815–1939*, London: Hodder & Stoughton 1975.

Beer, P. *Mrs. Beer's House*, London: Macmillan 1968.

Belson, W. *Television Violence and the Adolescent Boy*, Farnborough: Saxon House 1978.

Benjamin, W. *Illuminations* trans. New York: Harcourt, Brace & World Inc. 1968; London: Cape 1970.

  The Origin of German Tragic Drama, trans. John Osborne, London: New Left Books 1977.

Berger, J. *Permanent Red*, London: Methuen 1960.

  Ways of Seeing, London: BBC with Penguin 1972.

Berger, P. L. *A Rumour of Angels: Modern Society and the Rediscovery of the Supernatural*, Harmondsworth: Allen Lane 1970.

  and Berger, B., *The Homeless Mind: Modernization and Consciousness*, New York: Random House 1974.

Berlin, I. *Vico and Herder: Two Studies in the History of Ideas*, London: Hogarth Press 1975.

Bernstein, B. *Class, Codes, Control*, vol. III, rev. edn London: Routledge & Kegan Paul 1977.

Black, M. *The Literature of Fidelity*, London: Chatto & Windus 1975.

Bloom, H. *A Map of Misreading*, New York: Oxford University Press 1975.

Blythe, R. *Akenfield: Portrait of an English.Village*, London: Allen Lane 1969.

Bourdieu, P. *Outline of a Theory of Practice*, trans. R. Nice, Cambridge: University Press 1977.

Braudel, F. *The Mediterranean and the Mediterranean World in the Age of*

Philip II, New York and London: Collins and Harper & Row 1973.

Butts, D. (ed.) *Good Writers for Young Readers*, St Albans: Hart-Davis 1977.

Carpenter, H. *J. R. R. Tolkien: A Biography*, London: Allen & Unwin 1976.

Collingwood, R. G. *The Principles of Art*, Oxford: Clarendon Press 1938.

The Idea of History, Oxford: Clarendon Press 1946.

Cooper, D. *Death of the Family*, London: Allen Lane 1971; Harmondsworth: Penguin 1972.

Coveney, P. *The Image of Childhood. The Individual and Society: A Study of the Theme in English Literature*, rev. edn Harmondsworth: Penguin 1967.

Cunningham, J. V. *Tradition and Poetic Structure*, Denver: Alan Swallow 1960.

Collected Poems, Chicago: Alan Swallow 1972.

Dahrendorf, R. *Class and Class Conflict in Industrial Society*, London: Routledge & Kegan Paul 1959.

Danby, J. *Shakespeare's Doctrine of Nature*, London: Faber 1956.

Davie, D. 'The Historical Novels of Janet Lewis', *Southern Review*, II, 3, 1966.

De Mause, L. (ed.) *The History of Childhood*, New York: Psycho-history Press, 1974.

Dixon, B. *Catching Them Young: Sex, Race, and Class in Children's Fiction*, London: Pluto Press 1977.

Dummett, A. 'Racism and Sexism: A False Analogy', *New Black-friars*, November 1975.

Eliot, T. S. *Complete Poems and Plays*, London: Faber & Faber 1969.

Empson, W. *Some Versions of Pastoral*, London: Chatto & Windus 1935.

Erikson, E. *Identity: Youth and Crisis*, London: Faber & Faber 1968.

Esterson, A. *The Leaves of Spring: Schizophrenia, Family and Sacrifice*, Harmondsworth: Pelican 1972.

Fielder, L. *The Return of the Vanishing American*, London: Paladin 1972.

Ford, R. B. (ed.) *Young Writers, Young Readers*, London: Hutchinson rev. edn 1963.

Foucault, M. *The Archaeology of Knowledge*, London: Tavistock 1972.

Fox, G., Hammond, G. *et al. Writers, Critics and Children*, New York and London: Agathon and Heinemann 1976.

Fraser, J. *Violence in the Arts*, Cambridge: University Press 1974.

Frayn, M. *Towards the End of the Morning*, London: Collins 1967.

Freeman, G. *The Undergrowth of Literature*, London: Nelson 1968.

Freud, S. *Civilization and Its Discontents* (1930), Library of Psycho-analysis, ed. J. Strachey, London: Hogarth Press 1963.

Geertz, C. *The Interpretation of Cultures*, New York: Basic Books 1973, London: Hutchinson 1975.

Genovese, E. *The Political Economy of Slavery*, New York: Pantheon 1965.

Roll, Jordan, Roll: The World the Slaves Made, London: Deutsch 1975.

Gerth, H. H., and Mills, C. W. *Character and Social Structure*, London: Routledge & Kegan Paul 1954.

Giddens, A. *The Class Structure of the Advanced Societies*, London: Hutchinson 1973.

New Rules of Sociological Method, London: Hutchinson 1975.

Goldmann, L. *The Human Sciences and Philosophy*, London: Cape 1969.

Goodman, N. *Languages of Art*, Indianapolis: Hackett 1976.

Gregory, R. *The Intelligent Eye*, London: Weidenfeld & Nicolson 1970.

Eye and Brain, London: Weidenfeld & Nicolson 1966, rev. edn 1977.

'Towards a Science of Fiction', in Meek *et al.* (1977).

HMSO *Social Trends*, London: Stationery Office, annually.

Habermas, J. *Legitimation Crisis*, trans. J. McCarthy, London: Heinemann 1976.

Hammond, G. '*Watership Down* and Trouble with Rabbits', *Children's Literature in Education*, 12, 1973.

Hampshire, S. 'Russell, Radicalism and Reason' in Held *et al.* (1972).

'The Future of Knowledge', *New York Review*, 31 March 1975.

Harding, D. W. 'A Note on Nostalgia', *Scrutiny*, 1, 3, 1932.

Experience Into Words, London: Chatto & Windus 1963.

'Raids on the Inarticulate', *Use of English*, 19, 2, 1971.

'The Bond with the Author', *Use of English*, 22, 4, 1971.

Hardy, T. *Complete Poems*, ed. J. Gibson, London: Macmillan 1976.

Harrison, A. *Making and Thinking*, Hassocks: Harvester Press 1979.

Harvey, J. *Character and the Novel*, London: Chatto & Windus 1963.

Hazlitt, W. 'On Gusto', *Works*, XVIII, London 1855.

Heilbroner, R. *An Inquiry into the Human Prospect*, New York: W. W. Norton 1974.

'Sentimental Education', *New York Review*, 15 April 1976.

Held, V. *et al.* (eds.) *Philosophy and Political Action*, New York and London: Oxford University Press 1972.

Herlihy, D. 'Family Solidarity in Medieval History', in *Economy, Society and Government in Medieval Italy*, Kent, Ohio: Kent State University Press 1969.

Himmelweit, H., Oppenheim, P., Vance, A. N. *Children and Television*, London: Oxford 1958.

Hirst, P. *Knowledge and the Curriculum*, London: Routledge & Kegan Paul 1974.

Hoban, R. 'Thoughts on a Shirtless Cyclist, Robin Hood and One or Two Other Things', in Fox *et al.* (1976).

Hoggart, R. *The Uses of Literacy*, London: Chatto & Windus 1957; Harmondsworth: Penguin 1958.

Houghton, W. *The Victorian Frame of Mind*, Yale: University Press 1957.

Hudson, L. 'Life as Art', *New Society*, 12 February 1976.

Hughes, T. 'Myth and Education', in Fox *et al.* (1976).

Hunt, D. *Parents and Children in History: The Psychology of Family Life in Early Modern History*, New York: Harper Torchbooks 1972.

Hunter, J. *The Flame*, London: Faber & Faber 1966.

Illick, J. E. 'Childrearing in 17C. England and America', in De Mause (1974).

Inglis, F. *Ideology and the Imagination*, Cambridge: University Press 1975.

The Name of the Game: Sport and Industrial Society, London: Heinemann 1977.

Jackson, B. 'Enid Blyton', *Use of English*, 26, 3, 1975.

Jones, M. *Penguinways*, Harmondsworth: Penguin 1978.

Kant, I. *Fundamental Principles of the Metaphysic of Ethics*, trans. T. K. Abbott, London: Longman, Green 1913.

Keats, J. *Selected Letters*, ed. F. Page, London: Oxford World's Classics 1954.

Poems, ed. H. W. Garrod, London: Oxford University Press 1956.

Kermode, F. *The Sense of an Ending: Studies in the Theory of Fiction*, London: Oxford University Press 1967.

Kohlberg, L. 'The Development of Children's Orientations towards a Moral Order', *Vita Humana*, 6, 1963.

'Continuities and Discontinuities in Childhood and Adult Moral Development', *Human Development*, 12, 1969.

Körner, S. *Experience and Conduct*, Cambridge: University Press 1976.

Laing, R. D., and Esterson, A. *Sanity, Madness and the Family*, London: Tavistock Press 1967.

Larkin, P. *The Whitsun Weddings*, London: Faber & Faber 1964.

High Windows, London: Faber 1974.

Lasch, C. *Haven in a Heartless World: The Family Besieged,* New York: Basic Books 1978.

Laslett, P. *The World We Have Lost*, London: Methuen 1965.

and Wall, R. (eds.), *Household and Family in Past Time*, Cambridge: University Press 1972.

Lawrence, D. H. *Selected Literary Criticism*, ed. Antony Beal, London: Heinemann 1955.

Leavis, F. R. *Revaluation: Tradition and Development in English Poetry*, London: Chatto & Windus 1936.

The Great Tradition, London: Chatto & Windus 1955.

The Living Principle: English as a Discipline of Thought, London: Chatto & Windus 1975.

and Q.D. *Lectures in America*, London: Chatto & Windus 1969.

Leavis, Q. D. *Fiction and the Reading Public*, London: Chatto & Windus 1932.

Lewis, J. *The Wife of Martin Guerre*, Denver, Colorado: Alan Swallow 1947; Harmondsworth: Penguin 1977.

Libby, R. W., and Whitehurst, R. N. (eds.) *Renovating Marriage: Towards New Sexual Life-styles*, Danville, Cal. 1973.

Locke, J. *Educational Writings*, ed. J. L. Axtell, Cambridge: University Press 1968.

Lukács, G. *The Meaning of Contemporary Realism*, London: Merlin 1963.

Macfarlane, A. *The Origins of English Individualism*, Oxford: Basil Blackwell 1979.

MacIntyre, A. *A Short History of Ethics*, London: Routledge & Kegan Paul 1967.

MacKillop, I. 'Tolstoy's Tales for Children', *Children's Literature in Education*, 11, 1973.

Macpherson, C. B. *The Political Theory of Possessive Individualism*, London: Oxford University Press 1962.

Marcuse, H. *Eros and Civilization*, Boston, Mass.: Beacon Press 1955.

Marx, K. *Capital,* vol. 1, Moscow: Foreign Languages Publishing House n.d.

'The Jewish Question', in *The Early Texts*, ed. D. McLellan, London: Oxford University Press 1971.

and Engels, F. *The German Ideology*, trans. and ed. T. J. Arthur, London: Lawrence & Wishart 1970.

Mayo, R. *The English Novel in the Magazines, 1740–1815,* London: Oxford University Press 1962.

Mead, G. H. *Mind, Self and Society*, Chicago: University Press 1935.

Meek, M. *et al.* (eds.) *The Cool Web: The Pattern of Children's Reading*, London: Bodley Head 1977.

Merleau-Ponty, M. *The Primacy of Perception*, Evanston, Ill.: Northwestern University Press 1964.

Moore, B. *Reflections on the Causes of Human Misery*, London: Allen Lane 1970.

Muir, E. *An Autobiography*, London: Hogarth Press rev. edn, 1954; London: Methuen 1968.

Murdoch, I. *The Sovereignty of Good*, London: Routledge & Kegan Paul 1970.

Nagel, T. *The Possibility of Altruism*, Oxford: Clarendon Press 1970.

Oakeshott, M. *Rationalism in Politics*, London: Methuen 1962.

Orwell, G. *Collected Essays*, London: Heinemann 1961.

Past and Present, 'The Invention of Tradition', Annual Conference Papers, mimeo, 1977.

Pearson, J. *The Life of Ian Fleming: Creator of James Bond*, London: Cape 1966.

Phillips, R. (ed.) *Aspects of Alice*, Harmondsworth: Penguin 1974.

Pickard, P. M. *I Could a Tale Unfold: Violence, Horror and Sensationalism in Stories for Children*, London: Tavistock 1961.

Plumb, J. H. *The Growth of Political Stability in England 1688–1789*, London: Macmillan 1967.

'The New World of Children in 18th-Century England', *Past and Present*, 67, May 1975.

'The Rise of Love', *New York Review*, 24 November 1977.

Rawls, J. *A Theory of Justice*, Cambridge, Mass.: Harvard University Press, 1972; Oxford: Clarendon Press 1972.

Robinson, I. *The Survival of English*, Cambridge: University Press 1973.

Roscoe, S. *John Newbery and His Successors 1740–1814: A Bibliography*, Wormley, Herts.: Five Owls Press 1973.

Rosen, C. and H. *The Language of Primary School Children*, Harmondsworth: Penguin 1973.

Roszak, T. *The Making of a Counter-Culture*, London: Faber & Faber 1970.

Santayana, G. *Selected Critical Writings*, ed. N. Henfrey, Cambridge: University Press 1968.

Satterly, D. 'Stages of Development', *New Universities Quarterly*, 29, 4, 1975.

Sennett, R., and Cobb, J. *The Hidden Injuries of Class*, New York: Cambridge University Press 1972.

Shelley, P. B. 'The Defence of Poetry', in Peacock, T. L. *Four Ages of Poetry*, Percy Reprints, Oxford: Blackwell 1921.

Sidney, P. *An Apologie for Poetrie* (1595), Cambridge: University Press 1891.

Stevens, W. *Collected Poems*, London: Faber & Faber 1955.

Stone, L. *The Family, Sex and Marriage in England, 1500–1800*, London: Weidenfeld & Nicolson; New York: Harper & Row 1977.

Stoney, B. *Enid Blyton: A Biography*, London: Hodder & Stoughton 1974.

Strawson, P. F. *Freedom and Resentment*, London: Chatto & Windus 1975.

Suttie, I. *The Origins of Love and Hate*, London: Kegan Paul 1935; Harmondsworth: Pelican 1960.

Taylor, C. 'Interpretation and the Sciences of Man', *Review of Metaphysics*, xxv, 1 January 1971.

'Force et sens: les deux dimensions irréductibles d'une science de l'homme', in *Sens et Existence*, Paris: Seuil 1975.

'The Politics of the Steady State', *New Universities Quarterly*, 32, 2, 1978.

Taylor, J. J. 'The Reading of Comics by Secondary Schoolchildren', *Use of English*, 24, 1, 1972.

Thompson, E. P. 'The Long Revolution', *New Left Review*, 9–10, July–August 1961.

'Happy Families', *New Society*, 8 September 1977.

Tolstoy, L. *War and Peace*, trans. L. and A. Maude, London: Macmillan 1942.

Tomlinson, C. *A Peopled Landscape*, London: Oxford University Press 1960.

Townsend, J. R. *Written for Children*, rev. edn, Harmondsworth: Penguin 1976.

Trilling, L. *The Liberal Imagination*, New York: Macmillan 1948; London: Secker & Warburg 1951.

Sincerity and Authenticity, Oxford and Harvard: The University Presses 1972.

Warnock, M. 'The need for fiction', *TLS*, 25 March 1977.

Watkins, A. *The Old Straight Track*, London: Methuen 1925, Garnstone Press 1970, Abacus Books 1974.

Weil, S. 'La Personne et le Sacré', *Ecrits de Londres*, priv. publ. 1951.

Westergaard, J., and Resler, H. *Class in a Capitalist Society: A Study of Contemporary Britain*, London: Heinemann 1975.

Weston, J. *From Ritual to Romance*, Cambridge: University Press 1920.

Williams, B. *Morality: An Introduction to Ethics*, Cambridge: University Press 1976.

'The Truth in Relativism', *Proceedings of the Aristotelian Society*, xiv, 1976.

Williams, R. *Modern Tragedy*, London: Chatto & Windus 1964.

The English Novel from Dickens to Lawrence, London: Chatto & Windus 1970.

The Country and the City, London: Chatto & Windus 1973.

Television: Technology and Cultural Form, London: Fontana and Collins 1974.

Keywords: A Vocabulary of Culture and Society, London: Fontana and Croom Helm 1976.

Marxism and Literature, London: Oxford University Press 1976.

Winch, P. *The Idea of a Social Science*, London: Routledge & Kegan Paul 1967.

Winters, Y. *The Function of Criticism*, Denver: Alan Swallow 1957; London: Routledge 1962.

Wordsworth, W. *The Prelude* (rev. edn 1850) ed. H. de Selincourt, Oxford: The Clarendon Press 1950.

Yeats, W. B. *Collected Poems*, London: Macmillan 1961.

Index

DATE DUE

GAYLORD			PRINTED IN U.S.A.